STRATEGIC THINKING

Leadership and the Management of Change

THE STRATEGIC MANAGEMENT SERIES

Series Editor
HOWARD THOMAS

STRATEGIC THINKING
Leadership and the Management of Change
Edited by
JOHN HENDRY AND GERRY JOHNSON
WITH JULIA NEWTON

Further titles in preparation

THE STRATEGIC MANAGEMENT SERIES

STRATEGIC THINKING

Leadership and the Management of Change

Edited by

JOHN HENDRY AND GERRY JOHNSON

WITH

JULIA NEWTON

JOHN WILEY & SONS

Chichester · New York · Brisbane · Toronto · Singapore

Published 1993 by John Wiley & Sons Ltd,
                    Baffins Lane, Chichester,
                    West Sussex PO19 1UD, England

Other Wiley Editorial Offices

John Wiley & Sons, Inc., 605 Third Avenue,
New York, NY 10158-0012, USA

Jacaranda Wiley Ltd, G.P.O. Box 859, Brisbane,
Queensland 4001, Australia

John Wiley & Sons (Canada) Ltd, 22 Worcester Road,
Rexdale, Ontario M9W 1L1, Canada

John Wiley & Sons (SEA) Pte Ltd, 37 Jalan Pemimpin #05-04,
Block B, Union Industrial Building, Singapore 2057

Library of Congress Cataloging-in-Publication Data

Strategic thinking : leadership, and the management of change / edited
  by John Hendry and Gerry Johnson with Julia Newton.
      p. cm. — (The strategic management series)
    Includes bibliographical references and index.
    ISBN 0-471-93990-0 (cloth)
    1. Strategic planning. 2. Organizational change. I. Hendry,
John, 1952– . II. Johnson, Gerry. III. Newton, Julia.
IV. Series.
HD30.28.S73523   1993
658.4'012—dc20   93–7087
                                                        CIP

British Library Cataloguing in Publication Data

A catalogue record for this book is available from the British Library

ISBN 0-471-93990-0

Typeset in 10.5/12 pt Palatino by
Dobbie Typesetting Limited, Tavistock, Devon
Printed and bound in Great Britain by Biddles Ltd, Guildford, Surrey

Contents

Contributors

CHRIS BENNETT
Centre for Corporate Strategy and Change, Warwick Business School, University of Warwick, Coventry CV4 7AL, UK.
Chris is a senior research fellow at the Centre for Corporate Strategy and Change, University of Warwick. She has worked extensively in the field of health service research. Her most recent work has been funded by the Department of Health and the Welsh office and has focused on the development of services for HIV/AIDS. She has published a number of articles on this subject, and was recently commissioned by the Health Education Authority to write four chapters in *HIV Prevention: A Working Guide for Professionals* (HEA, 1992).

MARY M. CROSSAN
Western Business School, University of Western Ontario, London, Ontario N6A 3K7, Canada.
Mary is assistant professor of strategic management at the Western Business School. As a member of the Western Learning Group, her research focuses on the area of organizational learning and strategic renewal. The organizational learning concept developed by the group has been applied to joint-venture learning, Canadian retailers learning to do business in the US, and learning as a meta-competence.

YVES DOZ
INSEAD, Boulevard de Constance, Fontainebleau Cedex, F-77305, France.
Yves is the John H. Loudon professor of international management, and associate dean for research and development at INSEAD. He received his doctoral degree from Harvard University and is a

graduate of the Ecole des Hautes Etudes (Jouy-en-Josas). His research on the strategy of multinational companies, examining specifically high-technology industries has led to numerous publications including three books: *Government Control and Multinational Management* (1979), *Strategic Management in Multinational Companies* (1986), and (with C. K. Prahalad) *The Multinational Mission: Balancing Local Demands and Global Vision* (1987). His research on the power systems and telecommunications equipment industries won the A. T. Kearney Academy of Management Award.

JANE E. DUTTON
University of Michigan, School of Business Administration, Ann Arbor, Michigan 48109-1234, USA.
Jane is an associate professor of organization behavior and of corporate strategy at the University of Michigan Business School. Her research and writing concerns how decision makers in organizations interpret and respond to value-laden strategic issues. She is a co-editor of *Advances in Strategic Management* (JAI Press), and a consulting editor for the *Academy of Management Journal*.

TONY ECCLES
London Business School, Sussex Place, Regents Park, London NW1 4SA, UK.
Tony is professor of strategic management at London Business School where he also directs the senior executive programme and top management programmes for a number of organisations. Originally a shop-floor fitter and then ship's engineer, he has ten years' production management experience with Unilever. Formerly senior lecturer at Manchester Business School and professor at Glasgow University. He has consulted with a wide variety of organisations and is a director of two private companies. Author of *Under New Management*; he has just completed a book on his research in strategy implementation.

COLIN EDEN
Strathclyde University, Livingstone Tower, 26 Richmond Street, Strathclyde G11 XH, UK.
Colin is head of department and professor of management science at the Strathclyde Business School. He has been influential in the movement of management science/operational research towards the development of qualitative modelling and problem-structuring methods. His original work on managerial cognition was published

as *Thinking in Organisations* (Macmillan, 1979). He subsequently published these ideas as an approach to consulting practice and *Messing About in Problems* (with Sue Jones and David Sims; Pergamon, 1983). This pioneering work in the use of 'cognitive mapping' as an aid to resolving complex problems led to his research on strategy development as a social process. This emphasis on social processes has encompassed research and development of computer based 'Group Decision Support Systems' as a vehicle for encouraging strategic thinking.

EWAN FERLIE
Centre for Corporate Strategy and Change, Warwick Business School, University of Warwick, Coventry CV4 7AL, UK.
Ewan is associate director of the Centre for Corporate Strategy and Change, Warwick Business School, University of Warwick. He has a long-standing research interest in processes of innovation and change in public sector settings. He is currently engaged in a major study of the Government's reforms to British health care.

CHARLES M. HAMPDEN-TURNER
The Judge Institute of Management Studies, University of Cambridge, Fitzwilliam House, 32 Trumpington Street, Cambridge CB2 1QY, UK.
Charles is a permanent visitor at the Cambridge University Judge Institute of Management Studies, and professor on leave from the Wright Institute of Berkeley, California. He is also a senior fellow of the Centre for International Business Studies. His twelfth book, *Seven Cultures of Capitalism*, was published by Doubleday in New York and Nihon Keizai Shimbo in Tokyo in May 1993.

KEES VAN DER HEIJDEN
Strathclyde Graduate Business School, Strathclyde University, 130 Rottenrow, Glasgow G4 0GE, UK.
Kees is professor of business administration at the Graduate Business School of Strathclyde University, Glasgow. He is an authority on scenario planning, institutional strategic management processes and business process analysis from a strategic perspective. Before joining the SGBS faculty Prof. van der Heijden was in charge of Royal Dutch/Shell's scenario planning, as head of the group's Business Environment Division, where he was responsible for monitoring and analysing the business environment and consulting on strategic implications; he was also responsible for developing the process of scenario planning, in which the group has taken a

world-wide leading role. His research interests focus on the process of institutional strategic thinking and learning. He has consulted widely in the areas of scenario planning and strategy.

BO HELLGREN
Department of Management and Economics, Linköping University, S-581 83 Linköping, Sweden.
Bo is associate professor at the Department of Management and Economics, Linköping University. His current research interests concern strategic change processes and complex decision processes in networks of organisations.

JOHN HENDRY (Editor)
The Judge Institute of Management Studies, University of Cambridge, Fitzwilliam House, 32 Trumpington Street, Cambridge CB2 1QY, UK.
John is director of the MBA course at the Judge Institute of Management Studies, and a professorial fellow of Girton College, at the University of Cambridge. Previously he was director of the Centre for Strategic Management and Organisational Change at Cranfield School of Management, and, before that, on the staff of the Business Policy Department at the London Business School. He has also held positions with Ilford, Touche Ross, the UK Atomic Energy Authority, and both Imperial and University College, London University. He is currently a non-executive director of Venture Research International Ltd (formerly BP Venture Research). He is the author of six books and numerous articles, his most recent books being *Innovating for Failure: Government Policy and the Early British Computer Industry* (MIT Press, 1989), and, with Tony Eccles, Sumantra Ghoshal, Per Jenster and Peter Williamson, *European Cases in Strategic Management* (Chapman & Hall, 1992).

TERRY HILDEBRAND
Innovation Associates, 7070 Bayview Avenue, Thornhill, Ontario L3T 2R4, Canada.
Terry is a senior consultant with Innovation Associates of Canada, a management consulting firm dedicated to building organizations that have the inspiration and ability to produce outstanding results, while fulfilling the personal aspirations of their members. Dr Hildebrand's primary interest is in working with clients who are creating flexible organizations with a high capacity for learning and change. She has worked in a variety of industries, in the design and management of major strategic change and process

improvement initiatives. Terry has also taught organizational behaviour at the University of Western Ontario in Canada.

GERRY JOHNSON (Editor)
Cranfield School of Management, Cranfield Institute of Technology, Cranfield, Bedford MK43 0AL, UK.
Gerry is professor of strategic management, and director of research at Cranfield School of Management. After graduating from University College, London, he worked for several years in management positions with Unilever and Reed International before becoming a management consultant. From 1976 he taught at Aston University Management Centre, where he was head of the strategic management group. He then joined Manchester Business School, where he was senior fellow in strategic management. He took up his appointment at Cranfield in 1988. He has written and contributed to several books: *Strategic Change and the Management Process* (Basil Blackwell), *Exploring Corporate Strategy* (Prentice Hall), *Business Strategy and Retailing* (Wiley), *Challenge of Strategic Management* (Kogan Page) and numerous papers on strategic management. He is a member of the editorial board of the *Strategic Management Journal*.

HENRY W. LANE
Western Business School, University of Western Ontario, London, Ontario N6A 3K7, Canada.
Henry is the Donald F. Hunter professor of international business at the Western Business School. His research focuses on the concept of learning systems and learning in organizations for its applicability to organizational change, strategic renewal and foreign market entry. He recently co-authored a book about Canadian retailers that entered the United States market. He received his MBA from Boston College and DBA from the Harvard Business School. He teaches courses in organizational theory, design and change, as well as cross-cultural management. He is associate editor of the *Journal of International Business Studies*.

R. THOMAS LENZ
Professor of Management, Graduate School of Business, Indiana University, 801 W. Michigan Street, Indianapolis, IN 46202-5151, USA.
Thomas is professor of strategic management and former associate dean of the Indiana University School of Business. Professor Lenz has written widely on the topics of executive leadership, strategic planning, and corporate environmental analysis systems. He is a

member of the Academy of Management and the Strategic Management Society, and has served for several years as a member of the editorial review board of the *Strategic Management Journal*.

MICHAEL LEVENHAGEN
Western Business School, University of Western Ontario, London, Ontario N6A 3K7, Canada.
Michael is an assistant professor in strategy at the Western Business School at the University of Western Ontario, Canada. He has written on high-technology entrepreneurship and the development of emergent markets. He has started two businesses of his own and helped others to start-up in the software industry and international technology transfers. He has consulted for small- to medium-sized enterprises in high-technology sectors.

MARTHA L. MAZNEVSKI
Western Business School, University of Western Ontario, London, Ontario N6A 3K7, Canada.
Martha is a PhD candidate in organizational behavior at the Western Business School, University of Western Ontario. Her research and practical interests concern how managers integrate diverse perspectives to create and build on a negotiated view of strategy and the environment. Her current research takes these interests into the field of international management.

LIEF MELIN
Department of Management and Economics, Linköping University, S-581 83 Linköping, Sweden.
Lief is professor of strategic management at the Department of Management and Economics at Linköping University. His current research interests concern strategic change processes in different types of organizations and structural change in different industrial fields. He has published widely in edited books and international journals in his field. He serves on the editorial boards for the *Strategic Management Journal*, and the *British Journal of Management*.

JULIA NEWTON (Editor)
Cranfield School of Management, Cranfield Institute of Technology, Cranfield, Bedford MK43 0AL, UK
Julia is a teaching fellow in strategic management at Cranfield School of Management. Prior to joining the Management School at Cranfield in 1992, Julia worked as a management consultant in the

financial services consultancy division of Coopers & Lybrand. Her main research interests centre on the processes and management of strategic change in organisations.

WENDY J. PENNER
Williams College, Williamstown, MASS 01267, USA.
Wendy is currently a visiting assistant professor of psychology at Williams College. Her research examines organizational responses to trends in the institutional environment, and the relationship between cognitive processes and organizational responses to social issues.

ANDREW PETTIGREW
Centre for Corporate Strategy & Change, Warwick Business School, University of Warwick, Coventry CV4 7AL, UK.
Andrew is professor of organisational behaviour and director of the Centre for Corporate Strategy and Change, University of Warwick, England. He is author or co-author of ten books, the most recent of which are: *Managing Change for Competitive Success* (with Richard Whipp), and *Shaping Strategic Change* (with Ewan Ferlie and Lorna McKee). He is president of The British Academy of Management.

JOSEPH F. PORAC
Department of Business Administration, University of Illinois at Urbana-Champaign, 350 Commerce West, 1206 South Sixth Street, Champaign IL 61820, USA.
Joseph, who has a PhD from the University of Rochester, is a social psychologist studying the structure and dynamics of industrial belief systems. He has published several papers on the socio-cognitive foundations of organizational competition. His current research concerns the evolution of product market nomenclatures in the paper industry over a 120-year time period.

JAMES C. RUSH
Western Business School, University of Western Ontario, London, Ontario N6A 3K7, Canada.
James is an associate professor of organizational behaviour (OB) at the Western Business School where he has been teaching OB and human resource management since 1977. He has just completed a four-year term as director of the MBA program at the school. Prior to joining the school, Jim working for Control Data Corporation

in Minneapolis, and Canadian Industries Limited in Montreal. Dr Rush is a member of the Western Learning Group, an interdisciplinary group within the Business School, and is interested in the phenomenon of organizational learning, skills acquisition through university and early career, and how skills match with the demands of employers. He has co-authored two books and has published in many journals.

HEINZ THANHEISER

INSEAD, Boulevard de Constance, F-77305, Fontainebleau Cedex, France. Heinz is professor of strategy and management at INSEAD, Fontainebleau. He was dean of INSEAD in the 1980s. Currently he directs and teaches work-shops for senior managers from multinational corporations, primarily on competitive revitalisation and corporate renewal. He does consultancy work in the same area, mostly with German and American companies. He also serves on the board of directors of EIEC, a holding company conducting turn-around management of smaller companies.

HOWARD THOMAS (Series Editor)

Department of Business Administration, University of Illinois at Urbana-Champaign, Room 260, 1206 South Sixth Street, Champaign IL 61820, USA. Howard is the James F. Towey professor of strategic management, professor of business administration, director of the Office of International Strategic Management, and dean of the College of Commerce and Business Administration at the University of Illinois at Urbana Champaign (UIUC). Prior to his current appointment he was foundation professor of management at the Australian Graduate School of Management (AGSM), and director of the doctoral program at the London Business School (England). He is internationally recognized as one of the leading experts in the field of strategic management theory. Currently he serves on the Editorial Boards of many journals and is vice-president for publications for the Strategic Management Society. He is author or co-author of several books.

RICHARD WHIPP

Cardiff Business School, University of Wales College of Cardiff, Colum Drive, Cardiff CF1 3EU, UK.
Richard is deputy director of Cardiff Business School and professor of human resource management. He trained as an historian at Cambridge and has taught and researched at Aston University

Management Centre, Warwick Business School and the University of Uppsala. He is the author of *Innovation in the Auto Industry* (with P. Clark, 1986). *Patterns of Labour* (1990) and *Managing Change for Competitive Success* (with A. Pettigrew, 1991). He has published widely on management and technology, strategic change, competition and the institutional analysis of sectors.

ROD E. WHITE
Western Business School, University of Western Ontario, London, Ontario N6A 3K7, Canada.
Rod is an associate professor in the business policy area at the School of Business Administration, The University of Western Ontario where, since 1979, he has taught business policy and strategic management. He has recently been appointed director of the Western Business school's doctoral program. His research interests and consulting activities include the functioning of top management teams, questions of business strategy-organization and the strategic management of foreign owned subsidiaries. He has authored or co-authored articles on many topics and serves on the editorial board of the *Strategic Management Journal*.

RICHARD WHITTINGTON
Warwick Business School, University of Warwick, Coventry CV4 7AL, UK.
Richard is senior lecturer in marketing and strategic management at Warwick Business School. He has researched widely in the area of strategic management and is author of two books, *Corporate Strategies in Recession and Recovery* (Unwin Hyman, 1989) and *What Is Strategy – And Does It Matter?* (Routledge, 1993).

Series Preface

The purpose of the Strategic Management Society is to bring together, on a world-wide basis, academics, business practitioners and consultants for the development and dissemination of information.

Recognizing that the membership of the society is a relatively small, albeit important and representative, sample of the total population of academics, business people and consultants, THE STRATEGIC MANAGEMENT SERIES of publications is intended to play a key role in bringing information and ideas on strategic issues that are being discussed in the society to the attention of the broader interested audience. To that end, the purpose of the series is to illustrate 'The Best of Strategic Management' by publishing three types of books:

1 An annual volume based on a selection of papers from the annual Strategic Management Society conference. Selection may be based either on a particular theme or on a collection of 'best' papers from the conference, whichever seems to the editors to best exemplify that particular conference.
2 Volumes based on selected papers. Each volume is selected from mini-conferences on topical issues in strategy.
3 Short monographs on current research or novel conceptual frameworks identified, chosen and periodically reviewed by an editorial committee.

This volume is the first in the series representing Strategic Management Society mini-conferences. The society's aim in holding such conferences is to select interesting, cutting-edge topics and to encourage analysis of their content in small, discussion-type conferences of around 100 interested people. This allows examination of issues, in detail, by academics, business practitioners and consultants, and encourages presenters to develop their ideas in a manner that will appeal to a broad range of participants.

The ultimate vision is to stimulate ideas, concepts, and research about new issues and areas in the field of strategic management. Although not every Society member can attend, selected writings can illustrate the flavor of the conference, from the multiple perspectives of academics, practitioners, and consultants..

The Cambridge mini-conference brought together a group of contributors, representing many different research traditions, in order to address the theme of strategic change and the processes and issues involved in managing change. Perspectives on the topics covered varied widely, from Charles Hampden-Turner's 'Dilemmas of Strategic Learning Loops' to the more longitudinal, process-oriented views of strategic change discussed by Richard Whipp and Andrew Pettigrew in their paper 'Leading Change and the Management of Competition'.

As the field of strategic management develops, it is clear that the integration of organizational cognizance with the more economic perspectives advanced by such authorities as Michael Porter becomes an increasingly important theme. In the next ten years strategy will take an increasingly general management focus as we grapple with firm-level issues such as: how to manage change; how to design organizations; how to empower individuals while utilizing culture as a source of competitive advantage; how to manage strategic alliances; and how to effectively pair team-based management with more traditional methods.

If you conceptualize firms as bundles of resources, it is folly to think they can be effectively managed without the recognition that both organizations and people are critical resources and elements in the management of strategic change.

This first volume is, I feel, an interesting and effective integration of strategic perspectives that exemplify many of the most important issues facing strategic management, both now and in the immediate future.

An eclectic ensemble of contributors, including academics, business executives, consultants, and administrators, addresses one of the Society's primary concerns – building and maintaining bridges between management theory and business practice.

Editorial commentary provides integration among the papers included, and references some of the more appropriate previous research in each subject area, for the reader's convenience, in supplementary reading. The result is not just a volume of currently relevant papers, to be read once and set aside, but a reference manual that explores currently-relevant issues and links them with previous research streams.

HOWARD THOMAS
Series Editor

Introduction

JOHN HENDRY, GERRY JOHNSON

This book is about processes of strategic management and strategic change. The emphasis is on the way people think about strategy and make sense of their organizational worlds; on organizational learning and adaptation; and on the part played in this by leadership. The book's chapters are based on some of the papers presented and discussed at a Strategic Management Society (SMS) symposium organized by Cranfield School of Management and held at the University of Cambridge in December 1990. However, this is not just another set of academic papers. First, the papers have been revised and rewritten in the light of discussion at the symposium so as to make them accessible to non-specialist readers, including strategy consultants, practitioners and academics in related fields. Secondly, the symposium itself was an unusual one. The academics came from a variety of different research traditions. Although only half the 45 participants delivered formal papers, all were invited to the symposium on the basis of what they had to give, either in terms of their current research, their critical thinking, or their ability to reflect upon their own practical experience. The symposium itself, which lasted three days, was devoted primarily to discussion rather than presentations, with workshop sessions and a lot of informal debate. The result was something all too rare in the academic world: people actually took more interest in what others had to say than in their own contributions. They listened and thought and debated, and came away challenged, with new ideas, enthusiastic and exhilarated.

Strategic Thinking: Leadership and the Management of Change.
Edited by J. Hendry and G. Johnson with J. Newton.
Copyright © 1993 the Strategic Management Society. Published 1993 John Wiley & Sons Ltd.

Underlying this exhilaration was a sense that we had come together at a crucial stage in the development of a relatively new field of research and practice. Some of those present, such as Henry Mintzberg and Andrew Pettigrew, had been investigating the process of strategic change for many years, but this was probably the first time so many of the field's leading researchers had come together for an extended period. Moreover, the workshop brought together three research traditions: the work of those engaged in strategic change research – characterized by in-depth longitudinal studies of changing organizations – was placed alongside research into leadership and top teams, and, critically, alongside work into strategic thinking, or the cognitive processes through which organizations and environments are understood and strategies developed.

It is unrealistic to suppose that this book can capture the experience of the symposium to the full; but by including some of the papers presented, it does give a flavour of the issues and range of debate that took place.

THE LEGACY

To understand the contribution of this book, and other works related to processes of strategic management, it is useful to understand where the subject of study has come from. In the 1960s, most of what was written relating to the strategies of organization was within the corporate planning literature. Books like Ansoff's (1968) *Corporate Strategy* argued that sound strategic decisions and sound implementation of strategy could result from careful setting of objectives, systematic analysis and techniques of evaluation and planning. This literature had a profound influence on businesses. The 1960s saw the setting up of complex and sophisticated corporate planning systems, quite often with specialists and dedicated functions to deal with such systems. By the 1980s, however, this approach was being questioned, as managers realized that the benefits of such systematized approaches were less than expected.

The 1970s saw the beginnings of the search for guiding principles of strategy development. It began with the development of analytic portfolio models legitimized by concepts such as the experience curve. There then developed a concern to establish, more rigorously, relationships between the strategic direction of organizations and a host of variables that might account for success or failure of strategy. This period saw the development of the Pims database and the beginnings of a whole raft of work relating organizational diversity and performance, or structure and performance (e.g. Rumelt, 1974). By the 1980s research in the strategic management field was dominated by attempts to test the relationship between different strategic, organizational and performance variables.

This research also led to consequences in the practice of strategic management in organizations. In particular, there developed a concern for 'strategic fit' – the search for *the* strategy best suited to competitive market conditions, *the* balanced portfolio, *the* match of strategy and structure, and so on.

In the 1980s, Porter (1980, 1985) took up this theme and, building on industrial organization economics, and some of the earlier research on strategy and performance, provided academics and managers alike with frameworks for conceiving of relationships between strategies and industry contexts.

The research and writing on strategy during the 1970s and 1980s has, then, informed management debate and management practice. However, in that same time there has grown up a third field of research, which has also begun to influence practice.

STRATEGY AS PROCESS

Even the thumbnail sketch provided so far shows that the dominant theme in the strategy literature since the early 1970s has essentially been concerned with the content of strategies, and the search for provable relationships that might lead to better strategies. However, by the late 1970s there had developed a separate research question. This addressed not so much the content of strategy in organizations, but how managers dealt with strategic issues – with the *processes* of strategic management. Such research drew not so much on traditions of economics and finance, as on traditions of sociology, psychology and anthropology. Researchers here were not so much concerned about the *what* of strategy, as the *how* of strategic management; a concern that informed a new research agenda in the field, and much of the content of this book.

THE LITERATURE ON
STRATEGIC MANAGEMENT RESEARCH

In the 1960s, the notion of management as the planned search for optional solutions was being challenged (e.g. Cyert and March, 1963; Lindblom, 1959). They argued that managers made decisions that were bounded by their own experience, within organizational contexts, which were characterized by their social and political complexity, to develop strategies in an uncertain environment. In the early 1970s John Child (1972) argued that too little emphasis in management research was paid to the influence that managerial choice had on the strategic direction of firms. It was a theme that was taken up throughout the 1970s. Henry Mintzberg published papers showing that strategies typically developed through unstructured processes of managerial decision-making (Mintzberg *et al.*, 1976), and that strategies needed to be understood as emergent rather than planned processes (Mintzberg, 1978). By the late 1970s and early 1980s other researchers adopting historical and ethnographic approaches were undertaking depth case study work trying to unravel the complexity of strategy development in organizations (e.g. Pettigrew, 1973, 1985; Grinyer and Spender, 1979; Quinn, 1980; Johnson, 1986). At the same time, others were conducting surveys to establish how managers themselves understood the strategy development process in organizations. They found that many of the tenets of planning approaches were not present. Clear objectives were often not set, formal and exhaustive analysis not undertaken, decision-making was based on political processes as much as on rational evaluation and so on (Fahey, 1981; Pettigrew, 1985; Hickson *et al.*, 1986).

This questioning of the traditions of strategic planning and of strategic fit gave rise to another emphasis in research: understanding more about efficient strategy implementation was at least as important as understanding more about the content of strategies. Through the 1980s, therefore, there developed a greater emphasis on aspects of implementation of strategies, which has taken many forms. For example, in the *Strategic Management Journal* itself there have been increasing numbers of papers on topics such as management consensus (Bourgeois, 1980; Dess, 1987; Wooldridge and Floyd, 1989); top team configuration and effectiveness (Bantel and Jackson, 1989; Govindarajan, 1989; Hurst *et al.*, 1989; Murray, 1989); the effects of chief executives' succession (Beatty and Zajac,

1987) and interventions (Greiner and Bhambri, 1989); and means of managing strategic change (Guth and MacMillan, 1986; Dutton and Duncan, 1987; Nutt, 1989). Moreover, the literature on strategic change has moved from the notion of directed change to modes of strategy adaptation; notions of incrementalism (Quinn, 1980; Mintzberg and Waters, 1985; Johnson, 1988), and organizational learning (Fiol and Lyles, 1985); and how managers make sense of the complexity within which they operate (Huff, 1990).

Such research and literature is still exploratory in spirit. It would be incorrect to suggest that there is any one emerging theory of strategic management that can encapsulate such work or give such direction to modes of strategic management as was given by the corporate planning literature. However, both teachers of strategy and managers themselves might say this is no bad thing. Whilst research may be valuable if it searches for provable relationships for prescription, it can also be valuable if it seeks to clarify complexity, provide understanding and offer challenges to both the academic community and the thinking manager.

IMPLICATIONS

These changes of emphasis in management research have already begun to show themselves in the way in which consultants and managers approach the management of strategy.

Renowned for its planning systems, Shell now publicly argues (Kahane, 1991) that such systems are primarily to do with sensitizing managers to the environment and the strategic responses that might be possible. Shell is not alone in this view. Strategic management is not about establishing 'right' or 'optimal' solutions, but about understanding complex relationships, and uncertain futures. The emphasis then is on challenging management understanding and the tacit knowledge of the organization.

Strategic management is, therefore, closely linked to notions of organizational learning. The idea that a few individuals, or small groups, can direct the strategy of the organization, with others simply following, has been replaced by a concern to develop across the organization a capacity to work together to question, debate, and innovate (e.g. Peters and Waterman, 1982; Kanter, 1983). The corporate planning department may be less in evidence, but strategy development workshops, top team 'away-days', task forces and so on are becoming more common. There is a recognition that strategy development needs to involve managers widely.

Notions of strategic stability have been replaced by an emphasis on strategic change and, correspondingly, the notion of the search for the optimal strategy has been overtaken by a concern for a strategy that will work and that can be implemented. The role of the top manager and the top management team is, therefore, being reappraised; notions of strategic direction are being replaced by principles such as leadership, coaching, and team building.

All of these changes are reflected in the content of this book. It brings together research on managerial cognition, strategic change, the learning organization and the role of leaders and top managers in managing the process of strategy. In the section that follows, the chapters in the book are briefly reviewed to show how this is done.

THE BOOK IN OUTLINE

The chapters in this book have been organized into sections on two main themes – strategic thinking and strategic action.

In the first section, the papers on strategic thinking cover a broad spectrum of topics, but are linked by their intent to improve understanding of the *cognitive processes* underlying strategy development and implementation. In this section Martha Maznevski and her colleagues from the University of Western Ontario, Canada, look at how change instigated to implement the vision of a new chief executive officer (CEO) in a life insurance company affected senior management's perceptions of their company and the business environment over time. Consensual maps are developed from an analysis of the manager's assumptions about their business in 1987 and 1990 and are used to explore and explain differences in terms of the CEO's vision implementation process. The paper by Bo Hellgren and Leif Melin from Linköping University, Sweden, takes a different slant and explores the role a CEO's 'way-of-thinking' plays in strategy development within a company and how the 'way-of-thinking' of a new CEO can create impetus for strategic change.

Michael Levenhagen (University of Western Ontario) and Joseph Porac and Howard Thomas (University of Illinois, USA) extend the theme of understanding underlying cognitive dimensions of strategy development. They present a four-stage life-cycle model of market domain formation that is developed from a combination of the more traditional, materialist perspectives of market transactions and a complementary cognitive view of market transactions. The model has implications for practising managers in terms of leadership and vision formation.

The paper by Jane Dutton, University of Michigan, USA, and Wendy Penner from Williams College, USA, examines the strategy development process in more depth by attempting to answer the important question of how strategic issues get included on an organization's strategic agenda. They show organizational identity to be a crucial component of organizational context, which in turn shapes the strategic agenda-building process, and propose two different ways by which organizational identity can act as a powerful influence on the agenda-building process.

The last two papers of the first section look at techniques for improving the effectiveness of the strategy development process. Colin Eden, from the University of Strathclyde, UK, discusses the role special-purpose computer software and cognitive mapping techniques can play in the strategy development process by helping management teams 'think creatively'. Kees Van Der Heijden, also from the University of Strathclyde, sets out to identify the essential components of any managerial debate on the future strategic vision for an organization if a management team is to develop, and have commitment to, a shared vision. The concept of 'economic rent' is introduced as a means for assessing and comparing competing visions to determine which has the most potential for contributing to future organizational success.

The theme for the second section of 'strategic action' can be sub-divided into two broad topics – leadership and the implementation of strategic change. Thomas Lenz from Indiana University, USA, puts forward a contingency model of executive leadership in which the appropriate leadership style or 'influence processes' in a given situation is context dependent. Richard Whittington from Warwick Business School, UK, uses a very different approach to study leadership. He examines leadership from a sociological perspective and draws on case studies to illustrate how leaders' social backgrounds and attributes such as class and ethnic origins can affect their leadership abilities. Both of these studies have implications for organizational learning and management development. Richard Whipp (Cardiff Business School, UK) and Andrew Pettigrew

(Warwick Business School) also find leadership to be context dependent or rather context 'sensitive'. They present the findings of a study that uses case studies to examine the role of leadership in managing change and competition. The findings include a set of 'primary conditioning actions' that need to be taken by leaders to create a climate and capability for change and a set of 'secondary mechanisms' which can be used to help effect change.

Mary Crossan and Henry Lane from the University of Western Ontario and Terry Hildebrand of Innovation Associates, Canada, contribute the first chapter on the implementation of strategic change. The paper presents a socio-cognitive model of strategic management that embodies concepts of organizational learning. The model is used to explain via case studies why Canadian retailers attempting to enter the US market either failed or succeeded. The case studies illustrate the role organizational learning can play in strategy development and implementation.

In their chapter, Ewan Ferlie and Chris Bennett of Warwick Business School present their findings on strategic change in the British National Health Service as a response to the HIV/AIDS epidemic. This chapter is interesting in that there are few studies to date of change within UK public sector organizations. The roles in the change process of change agents, social movements, crisis as a mobilizing force, culture and symbolism and organizational learning are all examined. Yves Doz and Heinz Thanheiser from INSEAD, France, also write on strategic change, but their emphasis is on change or 'transformation' as a means of organizational renewal. They present a model of organizational renewal that draws on both evolutionary and programmatic approaches to change, since in their experience organization transformation processes often fail if either programmatic or evolutionary change techniques are used in isolation.

The final chapter in this section is by Tony Eccles from the London Business School, UK. His contribution is to attempt to refute two 'claims' frequently made about strategic change. Namely that strategic change takes a long time, and that strategy formulation and strategy implementation are part of one process and are frequently concurrent.

The conclusion to the book is written by Charles Hampden-Turner from the Judge Institute of Management Studies, Cambridge, UK. He attempts to draw the ideas presented in the papers together and relate them to his own framework – a 'circle of strategic learning'.

REFERENCES

Ansoff, H. I. (1968). *Corporate Strategy*. Harmondsworth, Middlesex: Penguin.

Bantel, K. A. and Jackson, S. E. (1989). Top management and innovations in banking: Does the composition of the top team make a difference? *Strategic Management Journal*, **10**, Special Issue, 107–124.

Beatty, R. P. and Zajac, E. J. (1987). CEO change and firm performance in large corporations: Succession effects and manager effects. *Strategic Management Journal*, **8**, 305–317.

Bourgeois, L. J. III. (1980). Performance and consensus. *Strategic Management Journal*, **1**, 227–248.

Child, J. (1972). Organisational structure, environment and performance: The role of strategic choice. *Sociology*, **6**, 1–22.

Cyert, R. B. and March, J. G. (1963). *A Behavioural Theory of the Firm*. Englewood Cliffs, NJ: Prentice Hall.

Dess, G. G. (1987). Consensus on strategy formulation and organisational performance: Competitors in a fragmented industry. *Strategic Management Journal*, **8**, 259–277.

Dutton, J. E. and Duncan, R. B. (1987). The creation of momentum for change through the process of strategic issue diagnosis. *Strategic Management Journal*, **8**, 279–295.

Fahey, L. (1981). On strategic management decision processes. *Strategic Management Journal*, **2**, 43–60.

Fiol, C. M. and Lyles, M. A. (1985). Organisational learning. *Academy of Management Review*, **10**, 803–813.

Govindarajan, V. J. (1989). Implementing competitive strategies at the business unit level: Implications of matching managers to strategies. *Strategic Management Journal*, **10**, 251–269.

Greiner, L. E. and Bhambri, A. (1989). New CEO intervention and dynamics of deliberate strategic change. *Strategic Management Journal*, **10**, Special Issue, 67–86.

Grinyer, P. H. and Spender, J-C. (1979). Recipes, crises and adaptation in mature businesses. *International Studies of Management and Organisation*, **IX**, 113–123.

Guth, W. D. and MacMillan, D. C. (1986). Strategy implementation vs middle management self-interest. *Strategic Management Journal*, **7**, 313–327.

Hickson, D. J., Butler, R. J., Cray, D., Mallory, G. R. and Wilson, D. C. (1986). *Top Decisions: Strategic Decision Making in Organisations*. Oxford: Basil Blackwell.

Huff, A. S. (1990). *Mapping Strategic Thought*. Chichester: John Wiley.

Hurst, D. K., Rush, J. C. and White, R. E. (1989). Top management teams and organisational renewal. *Strategic Management Journal*, **10**, Special Issue, 87–105.

Johnson, G. (1986). Managing strategic change – the role of strategic formulae. In J. McGee and H. Thomas (Eds) *Strategic Management Research*. Chichester: John Wiley.

Johnson, G. (1988). Rethinking incrementalism. *Strategic Management Journal*, **9**, 75–91.

Kahane, A. (1991). Global scenarios for the energy industry: Challenge and response. *Shell Selected Paper*, Shell publication.

Kanter, M. (1983). *The Change Masters: Innovation for Productivity in the American Corporation*. New York: Simon & Schuster.

Lindblom, C. E. (1959). The science of muddling through. *Public Administration Review*, **19**, 79–88.

Mintzberg, H. (1978). Patterns in strategic formation. *Management Science*, May, 934–948.

Mintzberg, H. and Waters, J. A. (1985). Of strategies deliberate and emergent. *Strategic Management Journal*, **6**, 257–272.

Mintzberg, H., Raisinghani, O. and Theoret, A. (1976). The structure of unstructured decision processes. *Administrative Science Quarterly*, **21**, 246–275.

Murray, A. I. (1989). Top management group heterogeneity and firm performances. *Strategic Management Journal*, **10**, Special Issue, 125–141.

Nutt, P. C. (1989) Selecting tactics to implement strategic plans. *Strategic Management Journal*, **10**, 145–161.

Peters, T. J. and Waterman, R. H. (Jr) (1982). *In Search of Excellence*. New York: Harper & Row.

Pettigrew, A. M. (1973). *The Politics of Organisational Decision Making*. London: Tavistock.

Pettigrew, A. M. (1985). *The Awakening Giant*. Oxford: Basil Blackwell.

Porter, M. E. (1980). *Competitive Strategy*. New York: Free Press/Collier MacMillan.

Porter, M. E. (1985). *Competitive Advantage*. New York: Free Press/Collier MacMillan.

Quinn, J. B. (1980). *Strategies for Change: Logical Incrementalism*. Homewood, IL: Irwin.

Rumelt, R. P. (1974). *Strategy, Structure and Economic Performance*. Boston, MA: Harvard University Press.

Wooldridge, B. and Floyd, S. W. (1989). Strategic process effects on consensus. *Strategic Management Journal*, **10**, 295–302.

Section I

Strategic Thinking

1

Drawing Meaning from Vision

MARTHA L. MAZNEVSKI, JAMES C. RUSH, ROD E. WHITE

A leader's vision can be implemented successfully only if key managers can make the vision meaningful. A vision is a top manager's or top management team's concrete idea of what the organization should be at some time in the future. A vision is usually different from a straight projection of the present, and therefore its realization usually requires a change in the way the organization goes about its business. Managers must interpret the vision and translate it into action in a unified way. This study looks at the process of vision implementation as an organizational learning phenomenon, in which potential for new behavior is acquired as a result of processing information (Huber, 1991). In vision implementation, information processing (drawing meaning) results in changes in managers' perceptions, which in turn lead to new behaviors required for the vision to be realized.

The study reported here had two main purposes. The first was to develop a procedure for mapping a management group's actual (as opposed to espoused) assumptions about causal relationships in the industry. The resulting causal map can be used by the management group to evaluate the effectiveness of their assumptions. The second purpose was to gain an understanding of how a management team's perceptions of its business changed over time as they worked as a team in response to the

Strategic Thinking: Leadership and the Management of Change.
Edited by J. Hendry and G. Johnson with J. Newton.

implementation of a vision or strategic plan (Hurst *et al.*, 1989). If we understand how these changes occur, then we can use this understanding to facilitate the management of ongoing organizational learning.

The organization studied was a small life insurance company. Managers' perceptions of their company and industry were collected in 1987 and 1990. These data were used to build organizational cause maps, or maps showing assumptions of cause and effect relationships between key variables such as company success and quality of products. The resulting maps were compared on several dimensions, and the differences were related to actions and events in the intervening period.

This chapter will present a brief review of the relevant literature on organizational learning, highlighting the importance of individual and organizational schemas. The methodology for constructing the cause maps will then be described and the results will be presented. The two sets of data will be compared in the general discussion, and lastly implications of the study will be outlined.

REVIEW OF THE LITERATURE

Organizational learning is the process of aligning and realigning an organization with its environment as both the organization and the environment change. Shrivastava (1983) outlined four types of organizational learning: adaptive learning, assumption learning, developing a knowledge base, and institutionalizing experience efforts. The last type of learning is not generally discussed by organizational theorists; it refers to experience curve learning in production and process technology. The first three types of organizational learning will frame a discussion of the views of various researchers.

Adaptive learning is best described by Cyert and March (1963), who assert that '. . . organizations exhibit (as do other social institutions) adaptive behavior over time' (p. 123). Adaptation has three phases: adaptation of goals, adaptation in attention rules, and adaptation in search rules. Fiol and Lyles (1985) distinguish adaptation from learning. They define adaptation as 'the ability to make incremental adjustments as a result of environmental changes, goal structure changes, or other changes' (p. 811). Adaptive learning is action taken after learning; learning is inferred from the result of adaptation.

Argyris and Schön (1978) characterize organizational learning as a sharing of assumptions. They propose that theories-in-use (organizational norms) are constructed and modified with individual and collective inquiry. Argyris and Schön argue that most learning is 'single-loop learning', i.e. knowledge is gathered and activities are undertaken within the norms of the organization. When members of the organization question the adequacy of the organizational norms and change them to fit new information and activities, then 'double-loop learning' has occurred. Daft and Weick (1984) develop a model of shared organizational assumptions about information interpretation. Their four interpretation modes are based on two dimensions: top management's beliefs about the environment (whether or not it is analyzable), and the intrusive nature of the organization's information-gathering activities. The type of information that members of organizations will gather and the way they seek that information will depend on the organization's interpretation mode. In organizational learning as a sharing of assumptions, learning is inferred from new information gathered within organizational norms, or from changes in organizational norms themselves.

Duncan and Weiss (1979) view organizational learning as the development of a knowledge base. They define organizational learning as 'the process within the organization by which knowledge about action–outcome relationships and the effects of the environment on these relationships is developed' (p. 84). Their emphasis is on knowledge as the only outcome of organizational learning, not any particular action or change. Organizational knowledge is distinguished by three characteristics: it is communicable, consensual, and integrated. Fiol and Lyles (1985) define learning as 'the development of insights, knowledge and associations between past actions, the effectiveness of those actions, and future actions' (p. 811). The products of learning, as described earlier, are used in the process of adaptation. In this type of organizational learning, learning is inferred from a change in knowledge.

Although authors' details vary, there is general consensus that organizational learning has both knowledge and behavioral components. Furthermore, organizational learning involves some *change* in this knowledge and/or behavior. Because good learning allows managers to increase the organization's alignment with its environment, organizations that can learn well are more effective (Fiol and Lyles, 1985).

ORGANIZATIONAL LEARNING AS A PROCESS

Organizational learning has been defined in terms of its product: adaptation, changes in norms, or knowledge. But researchers who investigate instances of organizational learning implicitly assume that the process whose outcome they are measuring transpires somehow. The nature of the process of 'organizational learning', as performed by managers, has not been emphasized. As a result, the concept of organizational learning has been useful for describing organizations that adapt successfully, but its main value has ended there. Managers who want to learn how to make their organizations more adaptable are faced with a vague set of broad prescriptions distilled from organizations who have 'learned', with very little insight into the process of learning. Research is beginning to explore the subprocesses of organizational learning. It is clear that only individuals learn, and what we call organizational learning is the result of the integration of individual managers' learning. Research has focused on individual's knowledge structures and their effects on action and interpretation of information, organizational knowledge and its effects on managers' action and interpretation of information, and changes in individual and organizational knowledge. These subprocesses will be examined in turn here.

Individual Level of Learning

The result of an individual's learning is knowledge that is stored in the form of schemas. Schemas are hypothetical structures that organize knowledge in the mind in an abstract form. Individuals' schemas affect how they interact with the environment, what they notice, how they interpret data, and how they retain information (Lord and Foti, 1986). Different types of schemas include categories and prototypes (e.g. Walton, 1986; Porac and Thomas, 1988), scripts for behavioral sequences (e.g. Gioia and Manz, 1985; Gioia, 1986a), and causal relationships (e.g. Bougon *et al.*, 1977; Stubbart and Ramaprasad, 1988). Schemas are particularly relevant for management researchers to understand since 'organizational actions, including the creation and use of knowledge, are structured by the organized systems of constructs [schemas] which organizational participants use to interpret and anticipate events' (Dunn and Ginsberg, 1986, p. 957).

Other investigators have developed the notions of schemas and their effects on the noticing and interpreting of new knowledge and on behavior in more conceptual detail (e.g Weick, 1979; Kiesler and Sproull, 1982; Schwenk, 1984; Feldman, 1986). The relationship has also been the subject of several empirical investigations. Bukszar and Connolly (1988) showed that for MBA students, knowledge about actual events influenced attention to and retention of case material. Porac and Thomas (1988) articulated the hierarchy of competitive categories managers used, and demonstrated that the categories affected the managers' views of competitive boundaries in their market. In examining perceived causes of organizational structure, Ford and Hegarty (1984) showed that managers believed the organizational context was important in designing the structure and that structure was important to organizational performance. These beliefs affected how managers would approach an organizational design problem. Lord *et al.* (1984) found that individuals' ratings of leaders correlated strongly with how closely the leader matched the raters' prototype of a leader. Mapping of nursing supervisors' schemas helped Jolly *et al.* (1988) understand why the supervisors used the categories they did when rating their nurses.

In summing up the present thinking about managerial cognition, Gioia (1986b) presents several benefits and costs to cognitive structuring. Essentially, individuals' schemas allow them to make sense of the world in an efficient way, and thus to interact effectively with the environment; however, individuals' schemas can prevent them from noticing important anomalies and from thinking creatively (p. 346).

Organizational Level of Learning

The organizational schema is a set of knowledge, assumptions, and norms that guide thinking and behavior for organizational members. In some companies it is strong and explicit, in others it is weak and implicit. An organizational schema is the result of interaction among the group of managers who determine the direction of the organization, usually the top management team. Organizational schemas have been explored much less intensively than individual schemas; however, some researchers have begun to develop an understanding of the phenomenon. From a cognitive perspective, the organizational schema has been defined as some type of aggregation, either shared or collective, of individual schemas (e.g. Bougon et al., 1977; Duncan and Weiss, 1979; Prahalad and Bettis, 1986; Walsh et al., 1988; Crossan, 1989). Other authors have used a more interpretive perspective, and see the organizational schema as an ideology representing the shared cultural values of the organization (e.g. Smircich, 1983).

The role organizational schemas play in influencing the actions of managers has been examined by a few investigators. Argyris and Schön (1978) described many instances in which organizational theories-in-use, or norms about behavior, prevented managers from learning from each other. Meyer (1982) found that the ideologies of hospitals in the United States affected their response to a strike of anesthesiologists, and concluded that ideologies partially determine what information the members of the organization will notice and what they will do with it. Dunbar et al. (1982) related a case study of change at a business school. The older, established members of the business school had ideologies that prevented changes the new dean wanted to make. In his study of organizationally based environmental disasters, Gephart (1984) explained unresolvable disputes by showing how different stakeholder groups interpreted disasters from different perspectives. Taking another point of view, Sutton and Callahan (1987) demonstrated how a society-level shared meaning about filing for bankruptcy attached a stigma to firms that have done so; this stigma affected how other stakeholders interacted with the firm and its top managers. These investigations have shown that understanding organizational (or higher) level schemas can help explain the behavior of organizational members.

Changing the Organizational Schema

Since dimensions of the organization and environment are continually changing, the organizational schema must correspondingly change if an organization is to remain aligned with its environment (Duncan and Weiss, 1979; Shrivastava, 1983; Stopford and Baden-Fuller, 1990). The process of changing schemas is the least researched of organizational learning components.

Argyris and Schön's (1978) single- and double-loop learning processes result in changes in organizational schemas. Huff's (1982) description of how concepts are dropped from and added to a stream of strategy echoes Argyris and Schön's analysis. Gray *et al.* (1985) suggest that coincident meaning (a shared schema) depends on the use of the same concepts in the presence of the same causal schemas, as well as from sharing values, or deep meaning structures. Some studies have concentrated on how collective sense-making of shared experiences develops the organizational schema (Bartunek, 1984; Isabella, 1990). Others have emphasized the role of the leader in changing the organizational schema (Sutton, 1987; Stopford and Baden-Fuller, 1990).

The research on subprocesses of organizational learning is synthesized in a model in FIGURE 1.1. Individual managers act

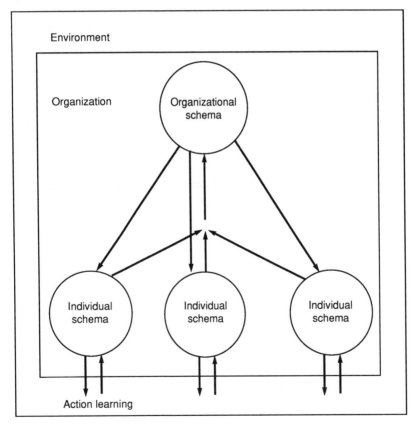

FIGURE 1.1 Organizational learning model

upon the environment and learn from their actions. Actions on and interpretations of the environment are influenced both by managers' own schemas and by the organizational schema. When managers interact with each other, they share experiences and build a common interpretation, thus influencing the organizational schema.

The Present Study

By showing that behavior, stories, and present interpretations of past events change over time, research has shown that organizational schemas change; however, there is still little insight into how a top manager or management team with a vision for the future can deliberately change the organizational schema to match the requirements of the vision. The present study applies the rigor of cause map analysis to this question at an exploratory level. We limited the study to causal relationships, since it is these relationships that are most directly associated with decision-making and behavior. Causal relationships can be shown clearly in maps' interconnecting concepts, and these maps can be aggregated in many ways (Huff, 1990). At the organizational level, we limited our analysis to consensual relations to identify the content and complexity of core assumptions upon which managers acted in a unified way.

In accordance with grounded theory methodology (Glaser and Strauss, 1967), no specific hypotheses were made before beginning this study except that: (a) the 1987 organizational schema would be different from the 1990 organizational schema, and (b) these differences could be traced partially to intervening actions and events.

EMPIRICAL STUDIES

In this section, the organization will be described, then the methodologies, results and discussions of the 1987 and 1990 studies will be reported separately. The two cause maps will be compared in the general discussion.

Constructing cause maps must address two major challenges. First, what individuals report now as being their interpretation of events in the past, while important for understanding how they make sense of events (Isabella, 1990), is not necessarily an accurate description of what their understanding was then (Nisbett and Wilson, 1977). Second, there is often a discrepancy between actual and espoused causal relations. The relationships stated by managers may be the 'socially desirable' responses rather than the actual determinants of their behavior (Argyris and Schon, 1978). The study was designed to meet these challenges as well as possible.

THE ORGANIZATION

The organization studied was the head office of a small life insurance company with 50 employees. The management group consisted of 12 managers, including the president and chief executive officer (CEO). Only one manager from the 1987 management group remained in 1990. Since the unit of analysis was the organization and not the individual, high turnover was a legitimate cause of change in the organizational schema, and not a mortality threat to internal validity (Cook and Campbell, 1979).

Operations within the company included product development, marketing, policy underwriting and service, and claims payment. The company's policies were sold to the end customer by a broker, who carried policies from other life insurance companies. The broker, in turn, worked for a general agent, who liaised with the life insurance companies they represented. General agents took policy data collected by brokers, organized it and sent it to the insurance company, negotiated any options with the insurance company, then sent the completed policy back to the broker. Most general agents represented over 100 brokers.

This organization was chosen because of the CEO's vision for the future of the company. Soon after he entered the organization as CEO in 1987, he introduced a vision for global operations by 1995 (called '5×95'), facilitated by the development of personal computer technology. We were interested in observing how his vision had influenced the organization's causal schema. The entire management group participated in the study: all members were active on task forces and were involved in initiatives around the vision, so it was decided that the causal assumptions of the group as a whole were important to understand.

1987 ORGANIZATIONAL CAUSE MAP

Methodology

The data used to build the 1987 cause map were a set of SWOT (strengths, weaknesses, opportunities and threats) analyses conducted by managers in January of 1987. Just prior to announcing his global vision, the president engaged in a strategic exercise with the members of the management group. All managers were asked to fill out a SWOT analysis on as many of 16 specific topics as they were able to comment on. These data were used because they fulfilled two important criteria for the study. First, they were recorded prior to the announcement of the vision and thus reflected assumptions held prior to the intervention being studied. Second, it was felt that they represented actual theories more closely than formal reports would have: the CEO's stated emphasis was obtaining people's *thoughts* on the company, and not what they believed was the 'party line'; ideas were jotted quickly and in point form suggesting that managers wrote from stream of consciousness without careful phrasing; no manager completed all 16 analyses, indicating that they did not feel obliged to make an 'espoused' comment on every topic. Undoubtedly the managers were conscious of making an impression on their new president, but this bias would have been present in any data collected at that time. Unfortunately, the CEO did not complete the analysis himself.

The SWOT analyses were screened twice to ensure that the final data represented as reliably as possible the actual, consensual causal relations. Since the format of a SWOT analysis (2×2 matrix) encourages inclusion of four items, it was felt that any analysis with four or fewer items was likely to have been completed based on espoused theories and/or was of little importance to the manager. These SWOT analyses were eliminated from the data set. The second screening eliminated categories to which fewer than half of the managers had responded, based on the assumption that there was little consensus around these issues. The final set contained 52 SWOT analyses from 11 managers on seven issues: new business opportunities, technology, market opportunities, accounting and reporting, personnel development, administrative processes and customer service, and products and services.

The analyses were aggregated and then examined for important themes, and six themes were chosen for content analysis (Berelson,

1971, pp. 138–140): product, service, broker relations and distribution, staff/personnel, internal operations, and technology. Each statement was categorized by its theme. If the statement could fit into two categories (e.g. our *products* are limited by our *technology*), the item was categorized by its *goal* (e.g. product), but the causal relationship was also noted. A straight content analysis was performed, aggregating frequencies of the themes over the 11 managers, on the assumption that frequency of statement reflects importance (Berelson, 1971; Erdener and Dunn, 1990). Although causal links among the themes were not always stated explicitly, we assumed that the frequency of explicitly stated causal relationships proportionally represented the strength of actual relations. Thus another content analysis was performed on the data, this time on explicit causal relationships among the six themes plus 'company success'. The 1987 organizational cause map was constructed from these frequencies of themes and causal relationships.

Results

The results of the content analyses are shown in TABLES 1.1 and 1.2, and the 1987 consensual cause map is shown in FIGURE 1.2. From the SWOT analyses, a total of 397 of the 431 statements were categorized as reflecting one of the six themes. In the map, the size of a concept's circle is proportional to the number of statements related to it, in accordance with the content analysis assumption that frequency reflects importance. Non-consensual causal relationships (8 or fewer explicit connections) are not shown on the map. Weak-consensual causal relationships (17 or 18 explicit connections) are shown with broken arrows and strong-consensual (26 or more explicit connections) are shown with full arrows.

TABLE 1.1 Results from content analysis for themes, 1987

Theme	Aggregate frequency
Product quality	116
Employee quality	103
Internal operations	66
Technology	47
Service quality	43
Broker relations/distribution system	22
Other categories	34
Total	431

TABLE 1.2 Results from content analysis for causal relations, 1987

Cause	Effect						
	Product	Service	Employees	Internal operations	Technology	Distribution	Company success
Product quality	x	0	0	0	0	2	45
Service quality	1	x	0	0	0	4	17
Employee quality	0	3	x	26	0	1	5
Internal operations	0	1	2	x	0	4	1
Technology	5	8	0	36	x	2	6
Broker/distribution relations	1	1	0	0	0	x	18

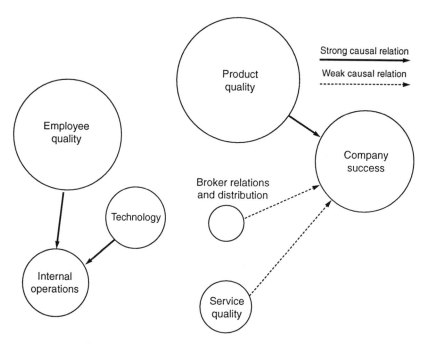

FIGURE 1.2   Organizational cause map 1987

Discussion

There are three important points to note with this 1987 cause map. First is the existence of two sets of relationships with no consensual connection between them. As a group, managers in 1987 perceived no causal connection from internal operations, such as accounting efficiency measures, to company success either through a direct or an indirect route. This point was validated by the CEO, who remarked that when he arrived managers' greatest concern was receiving accurate budget-to-actual reports and reducing variations. He gave an example of managers reducing employee overtime to remain within budget although service was adversely affected.

The second interesting characteristic of the 1987 cause map is its stark simplicity. This simplicity can be attributed partly to the methodology of aggregating themes and using data that were not collected specifically for causal analysis, but discussions with the managers suggest that some of the lack of complexity reflects the actual situation. The previous CEO was described by those who knew him as being very authoritarian: he made all decisions and required only that the managers and employees carry them out. Although this management style would not preclude managers having complex cause maps, it suggests that the managers in 1987 did not *need* to have complex cause maps on which to base decisions. Furthermore, several managers remarked in 1990 that they felt they understood the interconnections among different aspects of the business now more than they ever had, implying that at one point they did not make as many causal connections between some of the concepts.

The third point is the relative importance of product and service quality and their relative impact on company success. Every manager noted many times (an average of more than one per SWOT analysis) the direct causal relationship between product quality and the success of the company. Managers emphasized having a full portfolio of products, developing products quickly, incorporating agents' and brokers' ideas into new product design so these people would be more likely to sell them, and developing specialty products. Virtually all 'new opportunity' ideas concerned developing a new product for a specific market (emphasis on product, not market – no one suggested bringing a present product into a new market). On the other hand, few managers noted the importance of service quality, and even fewer described a causal relationship between service quality and company success. The components of service quality were articulated by very few managers and not frequently even by them. Some managers reported in 1990 that when they joined the organization they found a great lack of service infrastructure, such as policy manuals and systems for updating customers' policies.

When these results were presented to the managers in 1990, they were shocked at the importance of internal operations and lack of emphasis on service. Four managers who were not in the company at the time but who interacted with it then (e.g. as general agents or consultants) agreed that the map was an accurate representation of what they saw as the company's priorities. At that time, they said, the company had a couple of excellent products, but paid no attention to its agents or service.

In the general discussion these points will be compared with the 1990 organizational cause map.

1990 ORGANIZATIONAL CAUSE MAP

Methodology

The 1990 methodology was designed with specific criteria: to obtain a detailed actual cause map for each manager, then to aggregate the cause maps based on consensus. We wanted to capture actual, as opposed to espoused, relationships for each manager. We did not want to limit managers to a restricted set of concepts, or to present them with concepts for which they would describe salient relationships *even if there were none they would act upon*. We also wanted to obtain a high level of detail so that we could trace the roots of subsequent changes. To match these criteria, previously used methods such as analyses of written statements (e.g. Huff and Schwenk, 1990; the 1987 data in this study), repertory grid (e.g. Dunn and Ginsberg, 1986), and self-Q (Bougon, 1983) were not used here and a new methodology was developed.

Semi-structured, two-hour interviews were conducted with each manager. The interview protocol was designed to cover three areas: what is important/significant about this company; what the key success factors for the industry are and how the company attempts to achieve them; and the globalization vision. Questions about these topics were asked indirectly so that espoused answers were avoided as much as possible. The complete protocol is included as Appendix A. All interviews were tape-recorded and transcribed fully. Interview transcriptions were used to generate a list of causal inferences (Axelrod, 1976; Loflin, 1978) for each person. An $m \times m$ matrix was constructed for each person with all concepts mentioned on each axis. Their causal relationships were mapped inside the matrix, with the cause on the vertical axis and the effect on the horizontal axis.

Summaries of salient relationships were made for each person. Any concept that was mentioned in at least four causal relationships over the interview was included in the summary. It was felt that a lower limit on frequency was necessary for two reasons: (a) a manager would be likely to mention a concept in an espoused relationship at least once, but only actual relationships were likely to be mentioned several times; and (b) it was impossible to handle all concepts mentioned in a coherent way (the average number of concepts per person was 131.4, with a range from 101 to 255). This subset of concepts will be referred to as the 'important concepts'.

Each important concept was listed as a cause with all its effects or as an effect with all its causes, depending on the type of relationship it reflected, in questionnaire format (Appendix B). This summary was returned to the manager for a reliability check. The manager was asked to amend each list as necessary, and the researcher worked through the first two questions with each manager to ensure the task was understood. No manager left the questionnaire unamended; this was considered indicative that the managers completed it thoughtfully. The average change was 10.1% (89.9% reliability). Managers were also asked to rate each item on a three-point scale of importance in causing the relevant effect. These ratings were not used to aggregate data in this study but will be a basis of comparison in the longitudinal study. The data returned by the managers are summarized in TABLES 1.3 and 1.4.

To construct the consensual cause map, they were aggregated by first identifying all important concepts mentioned by at least five managers. A lower limit was necessary for two reasons: (a) by a conservative definition of the organizational cause map a concept must at least have some consensus in order to be considered 'organizational'; and (b) there were 68 such important concepts, and not all could be included in a final map in a meaningful way. The limit of five was chosen because there seemed to be a qualitative difference in the types of concepts that were important to five or more people and those that were important to fewer than five people: the less-consensual concepts reflected more 'micro' scale phenomena. This procedure resulted in 11 consensual concepts.

Each of the 11 concepts was analyzed further to determine their consensual causes and effects. Again, if a cause or effect was mentioned by at least five people* it was included in the consensual map. This procedure was repeated until there were no linking concepts important to at least five people. The 1990 organizational cause map was constructed by linking the consensual concepts together based on the causal relationships elicited from managers.

---

*However, for items that were already on the map for some other relation, and which had consensus of 4 with something else already there, the connection is also drawn, for example Agent Compensation/Commissions; Product Quality; and Sales. Management Quality is represented to emphasize the contrast between espoused importance and actual emphasis in interviews.

TABLE 1.3   Important concepts and consensus, 1990

Important concepts	Consensus
Company success	12
Service quality	12
5×95 Success	11
Administrative system and technology	9
Sales	9
Management quality	7
Product quality	7
Employee commitment to vision	6
Training and development	6
Agent compensation and commissions	5
Employee quality	5
Company size	4
Customer Service Rep Quality	4
Leader quality	4
Personal satisfaction	4
Experience	3
Future success of the company	3
Having a 'One Person Insurance Company'	3
Morale	3
Speed of issuing new policies	3
Balance present and future priorities	2
Breadth of responsibility	2
Change speed	2
Competitive advantage	2
Customer service unit success	2
General knowledge	2
International success	2
Management quality in the Customer Service Unit	2
Price/rates	2
Profit	2
Recruiting quality	2
63 other concepts	1

TABLE 1.4   Consensus of causes and effects of important concepts

Direct causes and effects of important concepts	Consensus
A. *Direct causes of company success* (12 managers)	
Service quality	12
Product quality	10
Agent compensation/commissions	7
Balance present and future priorities	5
Vision and strategic direction	5
Service to the agent/broker	4
Controlling costs	4

continued overleaf

TABLE 1.4   (*continued*)

Direct causes and effects of important concepts	Consensus
Employee quality	3
Parent company support	3
Employee commitment to the vision	3
Employees making decisions, taking responsibility	3
Individual contributions of employees	3
Innovative capacity	3
Leadership	2
49 other causes	1
B. *Direct causes of service quality* (12 managers)	
Speed of issuing new policies	9
Administrative system and technology	8
Service accuracy	6
Service speed	5
Employee quality	4
Management quality	4
Size of customer base	4
Underwriting quality	4
5×95 Success	4
Speed of issuing commissions	4
Attitude of being committed to service	4
Employee's technical knowledge and ability	4
Quality of phone contact	4
Treatment of internal customers	4
Turnover	3
Quality of communication	3
Service consistency	3
Morale	3
General responsiveness	3
Responsiveness to agents	3
Sending out company reports	3
Having a sense of urgency	3
Training	2
49 other causes	1
C. *Direct causes of 5×95 success* (11 managers)	
Systems, technology	8
Developing a 'One person insurance company'	6
Employees' commitment to the vision	5
Employee quality	3
Incremental change implementation	3
Employees working together on a common goal	3
Having a general agent test site	3
Having a good implementation plan	3
Having good leadership in the company	3
Having good leadership on the management team	3
Having a model office	3
Training	2
48 other causes	1

TABLE 1.4 (*continued*)

Direct causes and effects of important concepts	Consensus
D. *Direct causes of sales* (9 managers)	
Agent compensation, commissions	8
Service quality	6
Price/rates	4
Product promotion, product marketing	4
Product quality	4
Term length of compensation	4
Loyalty of general agents	4
Effort of brokers and general agents	4
Speed of issuing new policies	4
Relationships with brokers/agents	2
14 other causes	1
E. *Direct causes of management quality* (7 managers)	
Manager's growth/personal development	3
Manager's ability to plan	3
Manager's commitment	3
Manager's ability to deal with employees	3
Manager's general knowledge	3
Company's recruiting	3
Company's training and development	2
34 other qualities/attributes intrinsic to manager	1
11 other company-related factors	1
F. *Direct causes of product quality* (7 managers)	
Knowledge of market needs	6
Prices/rates	5
Agent compensation, commission	4
Actuarial input	4
General agent input	4
Parent company support (financial)	4
Having a full portfolio, good product mix	3
Having new products	2
10 other causes	1
G. *Direct causes of employees' commitment to the vision* (6 managers)	
Seeing results, delivering technology	5
Systems and Technology	4
Motivation/encouragement from management	3
Getting 'daily problems' solved	3
Having a detailed plan	2
11 other causes	1
H. *Direct effects of administrative systems and technology* (9 managers)	
Service quality	8
Service accuracy	4

continued overleaf

TABLE 1.4   (*continued*)

Direct causes and effects of important concepts	Consensus
Speed of issuing new policies	4
5×95 success	3
Accurate payment for agents	3
Innovation	3
Morale	3
Developing a 'One person insurance company'	3
Service speed	3
Customer Service Unit success	2
28 other effects	1
I. *Direct effects of training and development* (6 managers)	
Employee quality	6
Employees' general knowledge	4
Employees' technical knowledge	4
CSR's ability to perform all functions	4
Employees' attitude towards service	4
Service quality	2
8 other effects	1

NOTE: there was no consensus on causes or effects of Agent Compensation and Commissions or Employee Quality, therefore they are not listed here.

Results

The company's 1990 cause map is shown in FIGURE 1.3. The size of the circle is proportional to an index of importance, which was defined for each concept as the larger of (a) the number of managers who agreed the concept was important, and (b) the number of managers who agreed it was a cause or an effect of an important concept. The arrows linking the concepts show causal relations; the numbers on the arrows show the number of managers who articulated that connection. For example, five managers felt that 'Agent compensation and commissions' was an important concept; four believed it directly influenced product quality; seven believed it directly influenced company success; and eight believed it directly influenced sales. The index of importance for 'Agent compensation and commissions' was therefore eight.

Discussion

There are four important characteristics of the 1990 cause map to note. The first, and most obvious, is the complexity relative to the

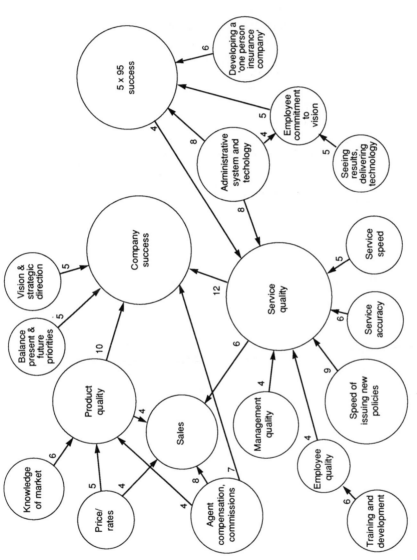

FIGURE 1.3 Organizational cause map 1990

1987 cause map. Part of this can be attributable to methodology: the 1990 methodology was designed specifically to capture the complexity of causal relations. However, the CEO and other managers believe that the phenomena is not entirely an artifact. For example, all managers articulated at least some of the shown components of service quality, whereas they did not in 1987. Two new 'peripheral' variables were perceived to have a direct influence on company success by some managers: the company's ability to balance today's and future priorities, and the vision or strategic direction of the company.

The second important point is the relative importance of product and service quality. Service quality was an important concept to more people than was product quality; in fact service quality was the only concept, other than company success, with complete consensus. The relationship between service quality and company success was unanimous, and the relationship between product quality and company success was the second most consensual connection.

The third characteristic is the existence of a future-oriented component. Eleven managers believed that 5×95 success was an important concept. This is partly because managers were specifically asked about the 5×95 vision if they did not mention it themselves; however, even with this manipulation, one manager refused to discuss the vision. Consensus around the influences of 5×95 success was lower than for company success, but there is general agreement that technology is important in two ways: directly, and indirectly through 'developing a "One person insurance company"', which is a technological initiative designed to improve processing of applications.

A final interesting point is the relative lack of consensus about the importance of managers and employees. Management quality is important to seven managers, but only four of those managers see it as directly influencing anything. Employee (i.e. non-management) quality is important to only five managers. Both management and employee quality are perceived as directly influencing service quality, but not company success, sales, the 5×95 vision, or other possible concepts. This is one area in which the organization's actual cause map differs from its espoused cause map, although some managers also asserted that once the proper computer systems were developed, anyone could 'push the buttons'. All managers were surprised when they saw the lack of consensus here, but most admitted that it was probably true.

GENERAL DISCUSSION

The organizational cause maps from 1987 and 1990 will be compared here on four dimensions: complexity, relative importance of product and service, addition of a future component, and influence of management and employee quality. Causes for the differences, particularly with respect to interventions made by the CEO, will be explored. These causes are drawn from interview data, discussions with the CEO and participants after they were presented with the two cause maps, and general observations. The discussion is summarized in TABLE 1.5.

TABLE 1.5   Differences and similarities between 1987 and 1990 organizational cause maps

Changes from 1987 to 1990	Possible explanations

Complexity:
  Increase in individual's
  complexity
	Methodology
	Turnover, Recruiting
	Decentralized decision-making

Increase in consensus	Turnover, Recruiting Increased interaction among managers
Relative importance of product and service quality	New marketing managers Structural change: service now part of marketing 5×95 initiatives aimed at service
Addition of future-oriented component	Presentations on vision Task forces
Effects of management and employee quality (little change from 1987 to 1990)	Emphasis on technology Turnover May change soon with task forces on human resources systems

COMPLEXITY

As noted in the individual study sections, there was a noticeable increase in the complexity of the cause maps, from 1987 (seven concepts, five relationships) to 1990 (20 concepts, 25 relationships). It is accepted that some of the increase is due to methodology, but not all of it. The increase probably reflects two phenomena: (1) an increase in the complexity of individuals' schemas, and (2) an increase in the consensus around organizational causes and effects.

Two specific reasons can be suggested for the increase in individuals' complexity. First, and most simple, is the turnover in management staff. Only one manager remained in 1990 from the 1987 group. Many of the managers who left had been unable to adjust to the new climate, and the CEO tried to replace them with people who were open to changing their assumptions about the industry. In other words, it is likely that many people with simple cause maps left and many with more complex cause maps entered. Second, decision-making had been decentralized a great deal since 1987. The CEO, in the words of one manager, 'lets us run our own show'. This is partly because of his personal style, and partly because his background is not in the insurance industry and he believes that the managers are more 'expert' in their areas that he is. The CEO suggested that perhaps managers are able to articulate more concepts and connections simply because they must now think about those connections to make their decisions. Other possible reasons for the increase in complexity of individuals' cause maps include increased competition in the industry, requiring greater understanding of the levers for enhancing company success, and a change of ownership of the company.

The greater consensus can likewise be traced specifically to two factors. The first is the high turnover: the CEO is likely to have hired more managers who reflect his cause map that managers who do not. Furthermore, new managers often had a great deal of input into hiring subsequent managers, producing a possible snowball effect in replicating a particular organizational schema. As well, interaction among managers has increased. All managers serve on management teams and task forces to solve interfunctional problems. This interaction probably leads to a greater understanding among managers of how other areas contribute to the success of the company.

RELATIVE IMPORTANCE OF PRODUCT AND SERVICE QUALITY

There is no doubt that the company was heavily product-oriented in 1987 and had a more balanced product and service orientation in 1990. One explanation is the greater authority of the new marketing managers and the emphasis they have placed on service. They have held meetings and discussions for all managers to help them understand the importance of fast, accurate and consistent service to general agents, and have had a general agent visit the company to speak with the managers about service. The Vice President of Marketing is a former general agent himself. The emphasis on service was reinforced with a structural change in the organization: at the time of the study, the VP Marketing recently had been assigned responsibility for the service function in the company as well as the marketing. A second explanation is the direction of the 5×95 vision. Until the time of the study, the initiative was aimed specifically at improving service. While this direct connection was recognized by only four managers, the discussions surrounding development of the vision tended to concentrate on service aspects and their improvement with technology.

ADDITION OF A FUTURE COMPONENT

This change has the most obvious cause of all the comparisons. The CEO had given several explicit presentations about the 5×95 vision and encouraged managers to think about how the vision could be realized. Several managers had been working on projects dealing specifically with elements of the vision, including developing an expert underwriting system and cross-training customer service representatives. What is most surprising is that given all the attention the vision receives, there is not more consensus about its causes and effects. Some managers suggest that because development time is lengthy and few initiatives had materialized by the time the 1990 interviews took place, it was difficult to know what the vision was *actually* about.

INFLUENCE OF MANAGEMENT AND EMPLOYEE QUALITY

This is one area in which change would have been welcome from 1987 to 1990, but did not materialize. In 1990 there was still little consensus about how the quality of managers and employees contributes to the success of the company. One reason for this could be the emphasis on technology. While managers recognized that employees would need to be trained to perform new functions, they also agreed that 'you can't train people on technology you haven't got' and that technology development, at that point in the vision implementation, was more important than training. There was also a sense, as noted earlier, that once the technology was developed the person operating it would not be important. It was perceived that the computer would make almost all decisions and perform almost all functions. Also, turnover at the company was very high; it was over 50% in 1989. Although it is unclear whether this is a cause or effect of the perceptions that people are not important, it is certainly related.

Just before the 1990 interviews were conducted, a series of task forces were initiated by the VP Human Resources to cover issues such as performance evaluation, employee recognition, and career development. The mandates of these task forces were to develop new human resources systems directly tied to three company goals of innovation, being customer-driven, and having unmatched quality. As the researchers visited the company over the next five months, it was evident that the task forces were taking their mandates seriously. It is possible that a repeat of the study would show a stronger relationship between people quality and company success.

CONCLUSION

LIMITATIONS

One of the limitations of this study was its single location, thus restricting external validity. The study is also being conducted at a larger, technology and research-oriented firm. Although direct comparisons will be limited because of the different industries, the diverse settings will help us develop a more universal theory of organizational learning.

A second limitation here was the nature of the 1987 data. It is difficult to be certain how much of the change between the two cause maps was due to actual changes and how much due to different methodologies. The 1990 study was repeated at both organizations in 1991, and the data from these new studies will provide a more valid comparison to the 1990 studies. We will also have some idea of how much cause maps change over six months, given certain levels of organization and environment change. With this information, we will know what level of detail is needed in future research to understand changes over a short period of time.

A third limitation of the study is the lack of performance data and connection between cause map changes and performance changes. The assumption of the study was that if causal assumptions change then behavior and decision-making changes, and thus company performance changes as well. This assumption, obviously, must be tested in subsequent research.

RESEARCH CONTRIBUTIONS

Despite the limitations, the study makes several contributions to research on organizational learning and organizational cognition. One contribution is the development of a methodology for eliciting and constructing rich, actual cause maps of individuals and organizations – the methodology used for the 1990 study. Although the method is intense and cannot be used efficiently with large samples, it addresses many construct validity concerns for building cause maps (Cook and Campbell, 1979). In particular, a close approximation of the individual's actual cause map was obtained by in-depth probing around inferred cause–effect relations, including eliciting from managers what they would do in a given situation and thus matching causal assumptions with behaviors. The cut-off points for frequency of statements helped ensure that concepts mentioned only once, possibly out of a sense of obligation, would not be included in the final map. Finally, the validation of the assumptions in a different form from that in which they were elicited provided additional confidence in the validity of the data. As well, the level of detail obtained in the cause maps, although not reflected in the consensual cause map, will allow us to trace the roots of changes observed in the 1991 maps.

Other contributions relate to the findings of the study. First is the simple conclusion that the elements and dimensions of the organizational cause map changed over time and that these changes helped us understand variations in managers' behavior. While managers could validate the changes in cause maps after seeing them, managers could not specifically generate changes when asked. We have also found that the changes over three years were quite dramatic. This suggests that changes over even a short period of time may be substantive and result in significant changes in behavior. The views on how the maps changed in response to vision implementation could be used in refining theory on the process organizational learning, and could be tested in a simulation or experiment to determine their internal validity. The study could then be expanded to other organizational settings.

MANAGEMENT IMPLICATIONS

Managers can use the individual and organizational cause maps in several ways. First, the maps can be used as a conflict resolution tool. Instead of arguing conflicting viewpoints as 'right' and 'wrong', these perceptions can be seen as representing different points of non-consensus in the organizational cause map. The reasons for this non-consensus can then be explored. Managers should be cautioned, however, that non-consensus is not necessarily dysfunctional. In fact, it is in non-consensual areas where new ideas are most likely to enter the organizational cause map.

Cause maps can also be used as a diagnostic tool. The actual relationships, as mapped, can be checked against espoused relationships and 'industry wisdom' to gain insights into operations. When this research was reported to the participating managers, they described the 1987 cause map as a 'recipe for suicide in this industry'. They declared that any organization that operated under the 1987 assumptions would either have to change or would fail. After validating the 1990 consensual cause map, they engaged in a dialogue about concerns such as: How can we change our attitude towards people? Why aren't there more financial indicators on here? There is nothing here about understanding competitors – why not? Do we really not understand why we're working towards the 5×95 vision? They discussed the relative merits of complexity and simplicity in cause maps in terms of vulnerability to competition. A process was initiated whereby each manager would construct her or his own map as an overlay on the organizational map and examine the differences to better understand their own behavior in the company. At the end of the session, managers were enthused about the new understanding they had gained through the process.

Cause map analysis is especially useful for the CEO implementing a vision. The organizational cause map is a picture of how the managers have made meaning from the vision. In this organization, we helped the CEO compare his own cause map with the organizational cause map to identify areas where the managers had not assimilated the vision. Again, it was important to recognize that non-consensus is not necessarily dysfunctional for implementation of visions, but should at least be examined. This activity will help the CEO implement the vision more effectively.

SUMMARY

In this study we used a developing field of theory, organizational learning, to help us understand a specific practical phenomenon, the implementation of a leader's vision. This match has been very fruitful: organizational learning theory has directed our attention to how managers draw meaning from interventions in their company, and analyzing the vision implementation process has helped us understand how managers' meanings change as an organization learns. We anticipate that the second phase of this project will bring even greater insight into both organizational learning and vision realization.

ACKNOWLEDGEMENTS

The authors thank Mary Crossan, Harry Lane, Betty Vandenbosch, and Honorio Todino for input and discussion. Funding from the Plan for Excellence and Social Sciences and Humanities Research Council of Canada (Fellowship 452-90-2685) is gratefully acknowledged.

APPENDIX A

INTERVIEW QUESTIONS

Section One – Background

1. How long have you been at this company?
2. Your position now is _____? What are your responsibilities? What do you spend your day doing?
3. What other positions have you held here? How were they different?

4. Where did you work before you came here? What positions did you have there?
5. How does this company compare with others you have worked with/for?

Section Two – Company Operations

6. To succeed in the life insurance industry, what are the few things that any company must be able to do extremely well? What makes a life insurance company successful?
7. What does this company do well to compete in the life insurance industry? (Relate to answers for (6).)
8. Who are your competitors? What makes this company different from its competitors?

Section Three – Vision

9. What *is* this 5×95 vision? What does it mean to you?
10. How will the company achieve the vision?
    e.g. What will the company have to change? Why?
        What are the key functions for achieving the vision? Why?
        What is your role in implementing the vision?
        What are the roles of other managers? What will they have to change? Why?

Appendix B

Examples of Validation Questionnaire Items

A. Important Effect Listed with Causes

Managers adjusted list as necessary and rated causes from 1 (somewhat important for causing the effect) to 3 (critical for causing the effect).

The success of the company is influenced *directly* by:

—balancing present and future priorities

—employees' commitment to the vision

—agent compensation and commissions

—financial backing from the parent company

—product quality

—service quality

—knowledge of the industry

B. Important Cause Listed with Effects

Managers adjusted list as necessary and rated effects from 1 (often leads to result) to 3 (almost always leads to result).

The quality of systems/technology *directly* influences:

—service quality

—company growth

—service speed

—success of the 5×95 vision

REFERENCES

Argyris, C. and Schon, D. (1978). *Organizational Learning: A Theory of Action Perspective.* Reading, Mass.: Addison-Wesley.

Axelrod, R. (Ed.) (1976). *Structure of Decision: The Cognitive Maps of Political Elites.* Princeton, NJ: Princeton University Press.

Bartunek, J. M. (1984). Changing interpretive schemes and organizational restructuring: The example of a religious order. *Administrative Science Quarterly,* **29,** 355–372.

Berelson, B. (1971). *Content Analysis in Communication Research.* New York: Hafner Publishing Company.

Bougon, M. G. (1983). Uncovering cognitive maps: The self-q technique. In G. Morgan (Ed.) *Beyond Method: Strategies for Social Research* (pp. 173–187). Beverley Hills, CA: Sage Publications.

Bougon, M. G., Weick, K. and Binkhorst, D. (1977). Cognition in organizations: An analysis of the Utrecht Jazz Orchestra. *Administrative Science Quarterly,* **22,** 606–639.

Bukszar, E. and Connolly, T. (1988). Hindsight bias and strategic choice: Some problems in learning from experience. *Academy of Management Journal,* **31,** 628–641.

Cook, T. D. and Campbell, D. T. (1979). *Quasi-experimentation: Design and analysis issues for field settings.* Boston, MA: Houghton Mifflin Company.

Crossan, M. (1989). A learning perspective on strategic decision-making. University of Western Ontario, unpublished manuscript.

Cyert, R. M. and March, J. G. (1963). *A Behavioral Theory of the Firm.* Englewood Cliffs, NJ: Prentice Hall.

Daft, R. L. and Weick, K. (1984). Towards a model of organizations as interpretation systems. *Academy of Management Review,* **9,** 284–295.

Dunbar, R. B., Dutton, J. M. and Torbert, W. R. (1982). Crossing mother: Ideological constraints on organizational improvements. *Journal of Management Studies,* **19,** 91–108.

Duncan, P. and Weiss, A. (1979). Organizational learning: Implications for organizational design. *Research in Organizational Behavior,* **1,** 75–123.

Dunn, W. N. and Ginsberg, A. (1986). Sociocognitive network approach to organizational analysis. *Human Relations*, **40**, 955–976.

Erdener, C. B. and Dunn, C. P. (1990). Content analysis. In A. S. Huff (Ed.) *Mapping Strategic Thought* (pp. 291–300). Chichester: John Wiley.

Feldman, J. (1986). On the difficulty of learning from experience. In H. P. Sims Jr and D. A. Gioia (Eds) *The Thinking Organization* (pp. 263–292). San Francisco, CA: Jossey-Bass.

Fiol, M. C. and Lyles, M. A. (1985). Organizational learning. *Academy of Management Review*, **10**, 803–813.

Ford, J. D. and Hegarty, W. H. (1984). Decision makers' beliefs about the causes and effects of structure: An exploratory study. *Academy of Management Journal*, **27**, 271–291.

Gephart, R. P. Jr (1984). Making sense of organizationally based environmental disasters. *Journal of Management*, **10**, 205–225.

Gioia, D. A. (1986a). Symbols, scripts, and sensemaking: Creating meaning in the organizational experience. In H. P. Sims Jr and D. A. Gioia (Eds) *The Thinking Organization* (pp. 49–74). San Francisco, CA: Jossey-Bass.

Gioia, D. A. (1986b). The state of the art in organizational social cognition: A personal view. In H. P. Sims Jr and D. A. Gioia (Eds) *The Thinking Organization* (pp. 336–356). San Fransicso, CA: Jossey-Bass.

Gioia, D. A. and Manz, C. C. (1985). Linking cognition and behavior: A script processing interpretation of vicarious learning. *Academy of Management Review*, **10**, 527–539.

Glaser, B. G. and Strauss, A. L. (1967). *The Discovery of Grounded Theory*. Chicago, IL: Adline Publishing.

Gray, B., Bougon, M. G. and Donnellon, A. (1985). Organizations as constructions and destructions of meaning. *Journal of Management*, **11**, 83–98.

Huber, G. P. (1991). Organizational learning: The contributing processes and the literatures. *Organization Science*, **2**(1).

Huff, A. S. (1982). Industry influences on strategy reformulation. *Strategic Management Journal*, **3**, 119–131.

Huff, A. S. (1990). Mapping strategic thought. In A. S. Huff (Ed.) *Mapping Strategic Thought* (pp. 11–49). Chichester: John Wiley.

Huff, A. S. and Schwenk, C. R. (1990). Bias and sensemaking in good times and bad. In A. S. Huff (Ed.) *Mapping Strategic Thought* (pp. 89–108). Chichester: John Wiley.

Hurst, D. K., Rush, J. C. and White, R. E. (1989). Top management teams and organizational renewal. *Strategic Management Journal*, **10**, 87–105.

Isabella, L. A. (1990). Evolving interpretations as a change unfolds: How managers construe key organizational events. *Academy of Management Journal*, **33**, 7–41.

Jolly, J. P., Reynolds, T. J. and Slocum, J. W. Jr. (1988). Application of the means–end theoretic for understanding the cognitive bases of performance appraisal. *Organizational Behavior and Human Decision Processes*, **41**, 153–179.

Kiesler, S. and Sproull, L. S. (1982). Managerial responses to changing environments: Perspectives on problem sensing on social cognition. *Administrative Science Quarterly*, **27**, 548–570.

Loflin, M. D. (1978). Discourse and inference in cognitive anthropology. In M. D. Loflin and J. Silverberg (Eds) *Discourse and Inference in Cognitive Anthropology*. The Hague: Mouton.

Lord, R. G. and Foti, R. J. (1986). Schema theories, information processing, and organizational behavior. In H. P. Sims Jr and D. A. Gioia (Eds) *The Thinking Organization* (pp. 20–48). San Francisco, CA: Jossey-Bass.

Lord, R. G., Foti, R. J. and De Vader, C. L. (1984). A test of leadership categorization theory: Internal structure, information processing, and leadership perceptions. *Organizational Behavior and Human Decision Processes*, **34**, 343–378.

Meyer, A. D. (1982). How ideologies supplant formal structures and shape responses to environments. *Journal of Management Studies*, **19**, 45–61.

Nisbett, R. E. and Wilson, T. D. (1977). Telling more than we can know: Verbal reports on mental processes. *Psychological Review*, **84**, 231–359.

Porac, J. F. and Thomas, H. (1988). Taxonomic cognitive structures in managerial competitive sensemaking. Working paper, University of Illinois at Urbana-Champaign.

Prahalad, C. K. and Bettis, R. A. (1986). The dominant logic: A new linkage between diversity and performance. *Strategic Management Journal*, **7**, 485–501.

Schwenk, C. R. (1984). Cognitive simplification processes in strategic decision-making. *Strategic Management Journal*, **5**, 111–128.

Shrivastava, P. (1983). Typology of organizational learning systems. *Journal of Management Studies*, **20**, 7–28.

Smircich, L. (1983). Organizations as shared meanings. In L. R. Pondy, P. J. Frost, G. Morgan and T. C. Dandridge (Eds) *Organizational Symbolism*. Greenwich, CT: JAI Press.

Stopford, J. M. and Baden-Fuller, C. (1990). Corporate rejuvenation. *Journal of Management Studies*, **27**, 399–415.

Stubbart, C. I. and Ramaprasad, A. (1988). Probing two chief executives' schematic knowledge of the US steel industry using cognitive maps. *Advances in Strategic Management*, **5**, 139–164.

Sutton, R. I. (1987). The process of organizational death: Disbanding and reconnecting. *Administrative Science Quarterly*, **32**, 542–569.

Sutton, R. I. and Callahan, A. L. (1987). The stigma of bankruptcy: Spoiled organizational image and its management. *Academy of Management Journal*, **30**, 405–436.

Walsh, J. P., Hendersen, C. M. and Deighton, J. (1988). Negotiated belief structures and decision performance: An empirical investigation. *Organizational Behavior and Human Decision Processes*, **42**, 194–216.

Walton, E. J. (1986). Managers' prototypes of financial terms. *Journal of Management Studies*, **23**, 679–698.

Weick, K. E. (1979). *The Social Psychology of Organizing* (Second Edition). New York: Random House.

2

The Role of Strategists' Ways-of-thinking in Strategic Change Processes

BO HELLGREN, LEIF MELIN

The problems associated with the major shifts in corporate strategy are closely related to the cognitive and cultural dimensions of organizations (Johnson, 1990). Although organization activeness has to do with shared values and collective actions, it is always based on individual, cognitive processes (Gioia and Sims, 1986). This chapter deals with cognitive aspects of leadership. The focus is on the strategic way-of-thinking of CEOs (chief executive officers) in processes that generate strategic action. Strategic ways-of-thinking consist of a number of relatively stable thematic sets of values, assumptions and thoughts about leadership and strategic development in organizations; they reflect the life experience and personality of a leader. As time passes, a specific strategic way-of-thinking may be modified by the different situations a leader is confronted with, but it tends nonetheless to retain a high degree of stability and is resistant to radical rethinking.

A focus on the ways-of-thinking demonstrated by top leadership can give important contributions toward a better understanding of

Strategic Thinking: Leadership and the Management of Change.
Edited by J. Hendry and G. Johnson with J. Newton.
Copyright © 1993 the Strategic Management Society. Published 1993 John Wiley & Sons Ltd.

strategic change process. It can enhance our understanding of the interplay between thinking and acting, i.e. between cognitive processes and what actually happens in organizations. For instance, our own case studies of several Scandinavian firms indicate that the ways-of-thinking of a CEO have substantial impact on corporate reorientation. But strategic change naturally is more than the outcome of the way-of-thinking of an influential individual. Leadership thought interacts with an organizational culture that represents collective values and a worldview from a corporate standpoint. Furthermore, strategic change is influenced by dominating opinions shared by companies and actors in a specific industry – opinions about the rules of the game and freedom of action within the structural confines (Grinyer and Spender, 1979; Spender, 1989; Hellgren *et al.*, 1993).

It is important to note that our cognitive perspective and its emphasis on the top leader does not imply that cognitive aspects are the main impetus for strategic change. In the corpus of research literature, strategic change is often explained as being a necessary reaction to external, environmental forces such as decreased demand, increased competition, and critical financiers (e.g. Grinyer *et al.*, 1988); or sometimes as being due to other internal organizational forces such as power structure, control system, and competence structure (Greiner, 1983; Melin *et al.*, 1983; Pettigrew, 1985; Melin, 1989). The point we wish to make is that a deeper understanding of strategic change requires us to focus on top leaders' ways-of-thinking and related cognitive and cultural aspects; this approach serves as a complement to other traditional explanations found in strategic management literature. In this chapter we will use a cognitive focus to present a case study of a Scandinavian pulp-and-paper company and the long-term strategic change occurring there between 1968 and 1989.

The purpose of the chapter is to describe and interpret the role of two CEOs and the strategic way-of-thinking of each, together with how this affected the long-term strategic change process in a pulp-and-paper company. We will furthermore relate this cognitive dimension to the role that organizational culture and a collective opinion of industry might play in a strategy process. A brief review of literature with emphasis on the thinking-and-acting interplay is followed by the case description. The company twice changed its structure and strategy. The first strategic change was brought about by financial difficulties and the failure of earlier leadership. However, the strategic way-of-thinking of the new CEO was crucial for the direction of change. The second change in strategy was not preceded by any apparent crisis or negative operating outcome. Instead, it was the result of a new strategic way-of-thinking by the corporate leader. The appointment of the second CEO was part of a natural course of events since his predecessor had reached the age of retirement. No basic change in the corporate environment took place at the time. No other internal change agents were operating. No consultants were engaged. The other members of the board were stable in their actions and did not introduce any new option that might plausibly account for strategic reorientation.

The method used to gain an understanding of the change process was a longitudinal in-depth case study. We conducted retrospective studies of the historical development and also followed the progress of the company in real time during two periods: 1974–75 and 1985–88. We have taped 50 interviews and, more important, took part in several meetings with each of the CEOs (and other significant actors) prior to and after their major strategic actions. In this way we were able to get a general picture of the intentions of each before they began to implement their strategic intentions and compare these with their later strategic action.

The analysis has resulted in a conceptual framework for understanding one important dimension of the process of change. This framework highlights the dialectical processes in which an individual top leader's way-of-thinking, organizational culture, and industrial wisdom interact.

THE COGNITIVE PERSPECTIVE: A BRIEF COMMENTARY

Individuals tend to have some type of cognitive structure in which information is assimilated and organized. Cognitive structures operate as interpretive frameworks and consist of '. . . conceptually related representation[s] of objects, situations, events, and of sequences of events and actions' (Markus and Zajonc, 1985, p. 143). They fill in information gaps and attempt simplification when information overload occurs. Cognitive structures help us achieve a more coherent environment, shape our own reality, and guide our own actions.

There are at present a number of partially overlapping concepts that capture different aspects of cognitive structures. Concepts such as beliefs (Donaldson and Lorsch, 1984), implicit theories (Downey

and Brief, 1986), interpretive schemes (Ranson *et al.*, 1980; Bartunek, 1984), maps (Weick and Bougon, 1986), and schema (Gioia, 1986a) are all suggested as conceptualizations of mental structures. These concepts indicate a relatively tight connection between managers' mental structures, their interpretations of the world, and their actions. Although there is congruity, there is also discrepancy (Gioia, 1986b). Some authors (e.g. Ranson *et al.*, 1980; Donaldson and Lorsch, 1984; Downey and Brief, 1986; Isenberg, 1986) assume that mental structures are thought-driven; in other words, they are the result of thinking processes that precede action. In this view, thinking and acting are more or less separate from one another and are step-by-step processes. An opposite view is to regard mental structures as action-driven, and thereby assume that thinking and acting are two simultaneous and intertwined processes (Weick, 1983; Bartunek, 1984). According to this latter school of thought, managers learn while they act, and not through rational stage models of decision-making. A further disagreement concerns whether mental structures are more or less stable assumptions that rarely change (Donaldson and Lorsch, 1984) or structures that continually change to accommodate new experience (Weick, 1983).

Organizational research on strategic change does not focus its interest on thinking *per se*. On the contrary, focus is on the interplay between cognitive processes and what actually happens in organizations. Although the cognitive perspective has contributed important items of knowledge about change, we believe there remains a need for continued conceptualization to further develop our understanding of strategic action and change. At least two arguments support this statement.

First of all, the importance of the cognitive dimension is not restricted to the individual level (e.g. of top leaders). Cognitive dimensions exist on a corporate level as well as an industry level; these are expressed by the notions of organizational change (e.g. Frost *et al.*, 1985) and industry recipe (Spender, 1989). In the field of management theory today there is a dearth of models that capture the cognitive dimension as a multilevel phenomenon. Secondly, individuals do not act purely as cognitive beings in the narrow meaning of cognition. They are influenced by their emotions, values, hopes, etc. Actions take place in an interplay between cognitions and emotions. A strategic actor thinks and acts as a whole human being, not driven by any single map or scheme, but rather by a far more holistic and complex mind structure that is charged with situational maps and more general assumptions, beliefs and values about the external world. Therefore we need conceptualizations that cover the individual leaders' cognitive and emotional structure as a whole – a structure which molds and in turn is molded by the leaders' actions in an interplay with other collectively held cognitive sets such as industry recipe and organizational culture. Such conceptualizations should enhance the understanding of strategic change. Based on our case study, this chapter presents our initial step in developing such a model.

A CASE STUDY ON MANAGERIAL THINKING AND STRATEGIC TRANSFORMATION

This section presents the strategic development between 1968 and 1988 of a Swedish pulp-and-paper company: Holmen AB. The case description emphasizes critical strategic incidents and major strategic action in the strategy process at Holmen. Due to our interest in top leaders' ways-of-thinking, we will look especially at the two corporate strategists who served as CEO. The first held the post between 1968 and 1983 and the second between 1984 and 1988. Each has put his stamp on two quite different and distinctive strategic epochs of Holmen's history.

The Holmen case illustrates how actual strategic changes in a company are related to dominant ways-of-thinking. It can also serve to contrast the mind sets of strategists and exemplify the cognitive content of strategic ways-of-thinking and their impact on major strategic shifts. Finally, it can help put individual strategists' ways-of-thinking in a broader context in terms of corporate culture and industrial wisdom, and contribute to the discussion of the role of these three cognitively related dimensions in major strategic change.

THE 1968 SITUATION AND THE DELIBERATE STRATEGIC DEVELOPMENT THAT ENSUED

The Holmen paper mill was founded in 1609. Manufacture of handmade paper under the Holmen trademark began in 1633. At an early stage, Holmen became a company based on two main operations: paper manufacture and textile manufacture. In 1968, the firm was approaching a crisis situation. It had one declining

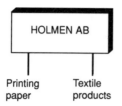

Printing   Textile
paper   products   FIGURE 2.1   Holmen AB: 1968

and nonprofitable textile unit and one pulp-and-paper unit (see FIGURE 2.1), the latter operating in very old factories but still showing a profit. A CEO appointed in 1967 was not successful in managing the firm's structural and economic difficulties. The Holmen board therefore appointed a new CEO in 1968.

The new head of the company decided early on to close down the textile operations and aggressively concentrate the firm's strategic development on printing paper. The entire textile unit was systematically terminated during 1970, and a ten-year long-range plan for the printing paper sector was worked out. The business concept was to supply the market with custom paper for newspapers and magazines, and to expand in pace with the market. This long-range plan was based on careful analysis. The CEO formulated a clear goal – to increase the production capacity of printing paper from 600 000 to over a million metric tons. The strategic plan was one means of reaching this goal. Various versions and parts of this plan were discussed at more than 15 meetings in the company board before being formally adopted in 1971. The key idea was to build increased capacity by investing in new paper machines. A consequence of the realization of the plan was that some old machines were closed down and others converted to production of other printing paper qualities. The CEO himself was heavily involved in creating the optimal paper machine configuration at the three Holmen production mills.

The long-range plan became a device for heavy investment in very large-scale newsprint machines at two sites: one of the old Holmen production plants and one completely new plant on the Swedish east coast. Between 1970 and 1984, Holmen fulfilled its massive concentration strategy and attained the position of largest European newsprint producer; viewed in an overall paper-producing situation, Holmen was the sixth largest paper-producing company in Sweden in 1984. During this period, the company made ineffectual efforts to diversify into product areas outside the forest industry, where the technology base could be further exploited (see FIGURE 2.2).

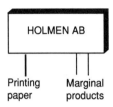

Printing paper   Marginal products   FIGURE 2.2   Holmen AB: 1970–1984

At the time, Holmen was a highly centralized company. The CEO was a powerful and rather autocratic leader. Coming as he did from a forest trade association, he was experienced in the line of business. The personal logic behind his strategic action was substantially anchored in the conventional wisdom of the industry. He had a strong respect for the rules of the game and tried to avoid offending competitors. On the other hand, he had little faith in collaboration with competitors. He wanted Holmen to be self-sufficient. He firmly believed in his mission: the concentration and expansion strategy within the printing paper sector – 'Our plan was to concentrate on what we knew best (printing paper), to concentrate on the business area with the best technological conditions.'

This strategy implied bold decisions about heavy financial investment. At the same time, the strategy was not aggressively competitive. The idea was to retain Holmen's share of a growing market: 'The room for the Swedish forest industry is in itself limited because of limited supply of raw material . . . The primary objective for Holmen is to maintain its position in this industry. This will demand all our energy because of the necessary heavy investments. Both the whole productive apparatus and the administration machinery must be concentrated on a correct realization.'

Once the strategic plan was fulfilled, the CEO saw a future need to diversify outside the forest industry: 'Holmen is in the last development stage of our investments in the forest industry. Now we try to optimize the exploitation of our potential in the pulp-and-paper industry. We don't have any prerequisites for a potential further development in this industry.'

This corporate leader had a very stable strategic way-of-thinking from 1970 to 1984. He accepted some changes in the competitive environment and made some minor modifications of the strategic directions. But he stuck firmly to his general view about Holmen's position and role in the paper industry and steadfastly conducted his strategy of one-legged concentration – from within a highly centralized organization.

A NEW STRATEGIST INITIATES
RADICAL STRATEGIC CHANGE

In 1984, when the new CEO entered the scene, the former CEO moved upstairs as chairman of the board. Despite that fact, the new company head put his personal stamp on developments at Holmen. His leadership style and way-of-thinking on strategic issues were quite different from that of his predecessor.

The new CEO was very action-oriented. He concentrated his efforts on the future structure of Holmen and indeed on a restructuring of the entire paper-making industry. In order to fulfill his visionary role, he refrained from attempting to control the daily operations. His visionary style of leadership helps explain his belief in decentralization. If he were to have enough time to focus on Holmen's strategic development, it was necessary for him to introduce a much more decentralized structure at the company. Consequently, his first major decision was to take steps to decentralize and radically change the 15-year-old organization of the corporate staff and sectors.

In contrast to the former CEO, this man did not believe in formal strategic planning, although a three-year strategic plan was worked out in 1985. Rather than being a direct basis for future strategic action, this planning work was a way for the new president to learn more about the internal strengths and weaknesses of Holmen.

His strategic way-of-thinking soon became apparent through an aggressive growth strategy.

'When I assumed the post of CEO, Holmen was European number one in newsprint paper. On the other hand, our product range stood on a single leg. This restricted our growth possibilities. We could not grow more in newsprint and journal paper. Customers would not allow us to become too dominant; they wanted second source suppliers. So we could not continue indefinitely to expand the newsprint business. We had to find other expansion paths and other products within the range of wood-containing printing paper, and also product areas in other parts of the forest industry which like newsprint are characterized by low-wood usage, steady growth demand and cyclical stability.'

During 1985/86, the strategic orientation of Holmen changed significantly, apparently not because of changes in the company environment. A new strategic view was brought about by the entrance of a new corporate leader. The business idea at Holmen was still based

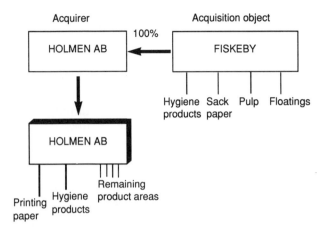

FIGURE 2.3   Holmen AB: 1985–1986

on a growth philosophy, but now a much more aggressive and less limited one. The objective was to become one of the leading pulp-and-paper enterprises in all of Scandinavia and to become a leading European supplier in all Holmen product areas. Initially the strategy was to grow in two business areas: wood-containing printing paper and woodfiber-based hygiene products (i.e. tissue paper and sanitary products). Holmen acquired the latter product group in December 1985 by taking over a Swedish competitor, Fiskeby. Hygiene products met the criteria for strategic investment, which were a high degree of utilization of pulpwood, expected growth in demand and a high degree of stability regarding demand and prices over the business cycle. The other products acquired through the Fiskeby takeover did not meet these criteria and had no priority in the new CEO's strategy. This is illustrated in FIGURE 2.3.

To communicate his strategic vision and the major new strategies of Holmen, the new CEO put a great deal of effort into a project called 'Setting the course – for everyone at Holmen'. This project was a far-reaching 'meaning–selling' process intended to implement his strategic thinking throughout the company. In a booklet given to all employees after participation in a one-day strategic seminar, the CEO clarified Holmen goals and strategies and laid down guiding principles for corporate esprit and form.

> 'Much has happened during the last few years. With the acquisition of Fiskeby we became one of the biggest forest industries in Sweden . . . As a matter of fact, it is a transformation process of great proportions

that we are now implementing in Holmen. The object is to make us stronger. A condition that must be fulfilled if we are going to succeed is that everyone in the company is familiar with the direction we want Holmen to take.' (From the CEO's introduction in the booklet 'Setting the Course'.)

In the product area comprising wood-containing printing paper, Holmen decided to expand not only in newsprint but also in magazine paper and coated printing paper grades, especially low-weight coated (LWC) paper. LWC paper was the fastest growing printing paper quality in Europe during the 1980s.

The growth strategy for printing paper implied further expansion of production capacity. During 1986 the strategic discussion led by the Holmen CEO focused on how to reach increased production capacity for both newsprint and LWC paper. Despite the fact that LWC consumption was growing rapidly, there were reasons to expect an overcapacity of LWC paper in Europe around 1990 because of huge investments in LWC machines throughout the trade. So Holmen had to make a quick decision to invest in a new LWC machine, or as an alternative way to reach LWC capacity, to find an acquisition object. During the spring of 1986, Holmen was contacted by a West German company regarding a possible collaborative arrangement. This company, MD Papierfabriken, had ongoing investments that would make them the largest LWC paper producer in Europe. The Holmen CEO recognized beneficial strategic openings, and in January 1987 he succeeded in acquiring a 25% stake in MD Papierfabriken (see FIGURE 2.4) with an option to increase the ownership share to 50%. Holmen had not only solved its LWC problem, but also got a channel straight to the Common Market – by getting inside it.

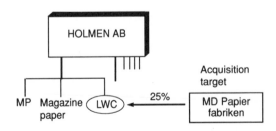

FIGURE 2.4   Holmen AB: January 1987

The next step in the chain of strategic conquests was the acquisition of a business unit containing hygiene products from a Swedish competitor, MoDo.

'It is important to be among the best and the biggest. Our aim is to attain a predominant position for the products we concentrate on. And it is our ambition to grow even bigger and stronger. We can do that by buying additional units or acquiring ownership stakes in other companies or seeking business alliances in the paper-making trade.'

The acquisition took place in September 1987 (see FIGURE 2.5). Holmen acquired MoDo Consumer Products, a division of MoDo that produced hygiene products. MoDo, one of Holmen's main competitors in the Swedish forest industry wanted an ownership stake in Holmen as payment for the division they divested. But the Holmen CEO rejected that solution since one of his overall objectives was to preserve Holmen's independence. Instead he had to pay a rather high cash price for MoDo Consumer Products. The acquisition made Holmen's Hygiene Division the third largest in Europe and an important producer of sanitary products. All told, Holmen Hygiene became Scandinavia's second biggest producer of hygiene articles.

This CEO believed in related diversification. He regarded growth possibilities in newsprint as being rather limited. During this period Holmen started a new business area (hygiene) and expanded the existing printing paper business into LWC quality. He pursued his aggressive dominance strategy on two fronts, emphasizing the

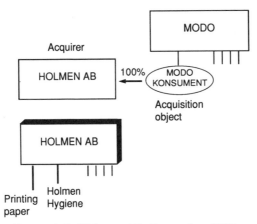

FIGURE 2.5   Holmen AB: September 1987

importance of becoming market leader in Holmen's main business areas, and the crucial need for Holmen to be big enough to protect it from outside takeover. He believed aggressive acquisition and collaborations necessary in the plan to restructure Holmen and allow it to play an active role in restructuring the industry.

This CEO's way-of-thinking was colored by his personality and by his earlier professional experience. He often referred to how the then leading pulp-and-paper company in Sweden had achieved its position. His first ten years after graduation from university were spent at that company, whose strategic development during the 1970s showed many similarities with the strategic action taken by the Holmen CEO ten or 15 years later. He was also a member of an informal but quite well-known group of Swedish top managers aged in their late forties and all with the same business mentor. (The group was dubbed the Bear Gang after the name of their mentor, Björn, the Swedish word for Bear.)

Through the CEO's aggressive restructuring and growth of the Holmen group, he was in part challenging the conventional wisdom of the pulp-and-paper industry. He threatened the negotiated order in the field where each company had a given position. In modern times and before the entrance of this CEO, Holmen had always been a medium-sized firm without ambition to take an active and leading role in structuring the industry. At the same time, however, other players aspired to the role of leader in the Scandinavian part of the pulp-and-paper field.

After a surprise acquisition of a minority stake in Holmen in October 1987, MoDo achieved 100% ownership of the company in June 1988 (illustrated in FIGURE 2.6). The Holmen CEO had already left his post in March. Near the end of 1988, the structure of the new MoDo group was presented, where two of the eight strategic business units were Holmen Paper (the former printing paper division) and Holmen Hygiene (the former hygiene division).

To conclude, it is interesting to note that shortly after MoDo's acquisition of Holmen, the latter's hygiene division was put up for sale. In February 1989, Holmen Hygiene was acquired by a Finnish

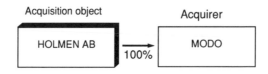

FIGURE 2.6   Holmen AB: June 1988

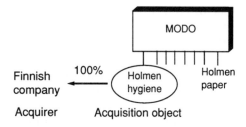

FIGURE 2.7 MoDo: February 1989

company, Metsä-Serla (illustrated in FIGURE 2.7). Holmen Hygiene suffered from a profitability bind, due in part to a lengthy and problematic integration process following the merger of Holmen's hygiene division and MoDo Consumer Products. But the main reason for the sale of Holmen Hygiene seemed to be the strategic way-of-thinking of the CEO at MoDo. As recently as 1987 he had sold his hygiene business unit, MoDo Consumer Products, to Holmen because of his lack of confidence in future growth and profitability for this business sector, an opinion he had long held.

Furthermore, the new Finnish owner soon resold the sanitary products part of Holmen Hygiene to another competitor, concentrating its business on tissue paper with a focus on the Nordic markets. This latter orientation meant that they divested their non-Nordic plants for tissue production which were located in two EC countries. This new domestic orientation was not in line with the original and aggressive strategic vision of the former Holmen CEO.

TWO STRATEGISTS THINK AND ACT

The introduction of a cognitive dimension in strategy research can result in new understanding of dynamic change processes. However, as mentioned earlier, it is not the cognitive dimension *per se* that is interesting. Our reason for introducing the way-of-thinking concept is to gain a better understanding of the complex and crucial relation between managerial thought and strategic action. The way-of-thinking concept is used to try to capture the strategist's cognitive and emotional mind structure as a holistic phenomenon. A strategic way-of-thinking consists of a number of thematic sets of values, assumptions, beliefs, ideas, and thoughts about leadership and strategic development in organizations. Each particular way-of-thinking represents deposits from the total life experience and the personality of a leader; in other words, way-of-thinking is more than an expression of a leader's professional experience.

In strategic management literature, strategic change is often seen as a necessary reaction to a mismatch between the external situation and the strategy and structure of the focal firm. Triggering cues for change include negative financial outcomes, obvious crises, ownership changes and suchlike. In our case, the CEO who stepped up in 1968 introduced radical change as a result of such a process. However, the strategic direction of future action was not given, and his choice, to concentrate his business during a time when diversification was in fashion, was stamped by his personal way-of-thinking. His strong belief in careful strategic analyses and in organic growth, through investments in new production capacity, were two aspects of his strategic way-of-thinking that turned out to be very important.

The second major shift in strategic orientation at Holmen cannot be explained through the traditional view as a result of external change and/or internal crisis. The reorientation and transformation between 1984 and 1987 occurred without any obvious change in the competitive environment. Nor was the ownership structure or the board make-up changed. Performance as expressed in terms of profit and ROI was not at all bad. The only major difference was the replacement of the CEO. The strategic way-of-thinking of the new CEO seems to have been very influential and the dominant reason for the strategic changes implemented during this period. His belief in being one of the biggest, market dominance, and growth through acquisitions and alliances were all important and influential aspects of his way-of-thinking. When he left Holmen in 1988, he became CEO of a Swedish medium-sized bank. During his two years there he acquired the biggest stockbroker firm in Sweden and was an architect behind a major merger with another Swedish bank. These and other strategic actions during his short stay in this bank were oriented towards increased size and volume. Today this bank has financial problems. The present CEO has publicly criticized his predecessor: 'The top management in the bank at the end of the 1980s was too eager to be as big as the two dominating Swedish banks and expanded too fast.' Without evaluating the strategic steps in this bank by the former Holmen CEO, the quotation gives some evidence of a rather stable pattern of strategic action.

The first conclusion based on our case is then quite natural: A strategic way-of-thinking is quite stable over time. In our case, the two CEOs each represent a way-of-thinking that is distinctive on a number of themes. In the Holmen case we have identified a number of evident themes that were related to both thoughts and actions of the two CEOs:

- the growth philosophy
- the opinion about market leadership
- the opinion about necessary size of the company
- the beliefs about economy of scale and size of (paper) machines
- the view on diversification
- the control philosophy
- the role of formal strategic planning
- the means for expansion and growth; to build versus to acquire increased capacity
- the opinion about the structural freedom of action for the company in the global industry.

Each CEO expressed opinions, views and actions along all these themes that were individually stable and distinctive, without showing any strong tendency to vary with the situation. The ways-of-thinking represented by these two top leaders differ on almost all of these themes.

Furthermore, we hold the opinion that a top leader's way-of-thinking is shaped by his/her own personality, history and early managerial experiences. This proposition has support in research. Mitroff and Mason (1983) have shown that different personalities regard the same problem in different ways and have different assumptions about what issues are of importance. The significant point of this proposition is that it contradicts the traditional view on strategic decision-making, which implies that strategic choices are based on analytical and objective analyses. Mitroff and Mason mean that a complex environment is interpreted in a way that fits the preferences of the type of personality in question. Their proposition is in line with our findings: a top leader interprets the environment and its threats and possibilities in accordance with his personal strategic way-of-thinking (compare Miles and Snow, 1978; Weick, 1979). Observations by Argyris (1983) about the role of a leader's individual theory-in-use supports this conclusion. A leader interprets situations and events in a way that confirm his or her own theory-in-use. It is not especially surprising that different individuals have different ways-of-thinking. What is much more interesting is the fact that two top leaders may act strategically in quite different ways in the same situation.

Another related conclusion is: A strategist's way-of-thinking may dominate over the actual environmental situation, i.e. an established way-of-thinking is not easily changed by new situations. However, at the same time we emphasize the stability dimension of a strategist's way-of-thinking (compare Donaldson and Lorsch, 1984), we must consider the processual characteristic inherent in thinking, acting and learning. In a longer time perspective, one can assume that a way-of-thinking is continuously changed through small, incremental modifications, because of new actions and new enactments. This interpretation contrasts the opinion by Weick and Bougon (1986) that cognitive maps are modified significantly by the situation.

The next conclusion relates to the dynamic stability of a strategic way-of-thinking and expresses a paradox: When a new leader, with an established and stable way-of-thinking, enters a mature company the result may be radical strategic change. On the contrary, a top leader who has successfully acted in a company for a long time will have major problems in recognizing a need for strategic reorientation because of the leader's stable strategic way-of-thinking. This propostion is given support by Nystrom and Starbuck (1984), based on their studies of severe strategic crises in a number of companies.

Our propositions about leaders' ways-of-thinking and their influence on strategic change are based on two fundamental conditions. The top leader in question is supposed to be a significant actor in the strategic development of the firm (though this is not always the case). The top leader gives expression to his or her way-of-thinking through strategic actions (a point questioned by some students of managerial cognition). In conclusion, the top leader must have the power to realize his or her way-of-thinking in strategic actions.

Our last proposition on the role of strategists' ways-of-thinking summarizes this section: In order to initiate radical strategic change in a mature organization, a new strategic way-of-thinking must be introduced and given freedom of realization.

THE COGNITIVE DIMENSION OF STRATEGIC CHANGE

The emphasis in this chapter on individual top leaders' ways-of-thinking does not imply that this aspect is the main reason behind

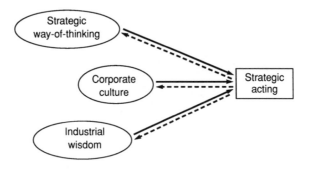

FIGURE 2.8　Three cognitive spheres in strategic change processes

strategic reorientation. Instead, a focus on the cognitive dimension gives a supplementary understanding in addition to more traditional explanations of strategic change, such as change in demand and competition and other external forces.

Cognitive impact is not only to be found on the individual level, i.e. the cognitive dimension is not restricted to strategists' ways-of-thinking. On the contrary, the multilevel dimension of cognition in strategic change processes must be recognized. We use the notion 'cognitive spheres,' to differentiate between cognitive structures on different levels of aggregation. Based on our empirical studies, we suggest that there are three cognitive spheres that have crucial impact on strategic change processes. Alongside individual ways-of-thinking, we wish to introduce two collective thought structures (see FIGURE 2.8).

Within every industrial sector there seems to be a dominating industry recipe, which we label *industrial widsom*. This conventional wisdom expresses dominating opinions, shared by companies and actors, about the rules of the game and the freedom of action within the structural confines of a sector (compare with the recipe notion of Spender, 1989).

Also on the company level, there is a cognitive sphere that is important to strategic change. The *corporate culture* represents the way-of-thinking of the collective, through its shared worldviews, values and beliefs.

Finally we have the individual leader's *strategic way-of-thinking* that consists of a number of thematic sets of values, assumptions, beliefs, ideas and thoughts about leadership and strategic development of organizations.

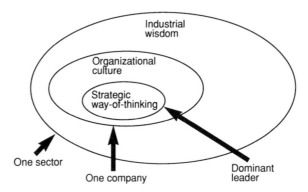

FIGURE 2.9   The cognitive dimension of industrial sectors – three different cognitive spheres

These three spheres all influence strategic change on the company level. They are three mutually dependent spheres that make up the *cognitive dimension* of industrial sectors. See FIGURE 2.9.

In the Holmen case, it is obvious that each CEOs' way-of-thinking affected the firm's transformation in a significant way, while the impact of the other two cognitive spheres is not as evident. Both CEOs related their analyses of the industry and their strategic actions to the more generally held opinions in the industry that we call industrial wisdom. The first CEO's thinking and acting lay within the prevailing industrial wisdom, apart from his heavy concentration strategy. On the other hand, the second CEO seems to have challenged the prevailing industrial wisdom when activating his way-of-thinking in Holmen. (The empirical evidence regarding the industrial wisdom is not fully presented in the brief case description in this paper. See Hellgren *et al.* (1992) for more detailed descriptions of the industrial wisdom in the printing paper part of the European pulp-and-paper industry.) The strategic way-of-thinking of this CEO seems to have triumphed over the industrial wisdom, i.e. he did not 'walk the industrial wisdom line'. His strategic actions did more than challenge competitors. They contributed – together with other radical strategic changes in the industry in the mid 1980s – to a reorientation of a number of opinions and beliefs within the body of industrial wisdom (Hellgren *et al.*, 1992).

Strategic change, materialized in new strategic actions, is probably preceded by change of prevailing worldviews and frames of thought. An emerging strategic way-of-thinking presumably replaces an earlier one. A penetration of a new strategic pattern in the company will also initiate changes in the prevailing organizational culture. In some situations, an old culture that counteracts change will be able to win the battle against a new strategic way-of-thinking.

When the second CEO introduced his way-of-thinking, one could have expected a conflict with the old culture (partially shaped by the former CEO). But that did not occur at Holmen. There are two plausible interpretations of why the new way-of-thinking and the corporate culture were so smoothly integrated. The idea of far-reaching decentralization, which was one main ingredient in the new CEO's way-of-thinking, was heavily supported by nearly all members of the organization. Furthermore, the new CEO managed to communicate and get acceptance for his way-of-thinking in terms of corporate mission, strategies, and leading values. The CEO was successful in his attempt to shape and interpret situations, and to guide organizational members to a common interpretation of reality (Smircich and Morgan, 1982), without challenging other core values of the organizational culture.

To summarize, these three cognitive spheres are characterized by a state of dynamic stability. They are all products of long-term evolution. When activated in the short term, their stability will be emphasized. In comparison, the Holmen case indicates that the individual way-of-thinking of an experienced top leader will show a higher degree of stability than the two collective spheres of beliefs and assumptions, the corporate culture and the industrial wisdom. New companies may enter a sector, as did Japanese car manufacturers, an action that may lead to a totally changed industrial wisdom. A new generation of employees in an organization may also change the corporate culture.

STRATEGIC CHANGE: A MATTER OF MANAGERIAL THOUGHT AND POWER

We have found that a top leader's strategic way-of-thinking is characterized by a high degree of stability, and that a stable way-of-thinking can initiate rather radical change. But radical change is only one of several possible outcomes of an entrenched strategic way-of-thinking. A firm with an established culture operating in an industry with a rather static industrial wisdom and with a dominating strategic way-of-thinking that agrees with the prevailing culture and industrial wisdom, will have severe problems in initiating radical strategic change. At the other extreme, we find a truly turbulent situation when a new way-of-thinking is introduced while both the culture and the industrial wisdom are adrift. Such conditions for change are not so common, and create a situation where it is hard to predict the outcome of the change process. Many East European countries are confronted with such conditions in the early 1990s.

The mind-set of a top leader can play rather different roles in strategic change processes, since the mind-set can act either as a stabilizing force or can initiate strategic change. Whether change is initiated or not is a matter of the degree of similarity (or difference) between a top leader's way-of-thinking and the dominating opinions and values expressed in other cognitively loaded spheres of importance, for instance, the organizational culture and industrial wisdom of the surrounding sector. A replacement of the top leader can be a means toward radical change since the new leader's way-of-thinking can be a counterforce to the prevailing culture that most often impedes change in organizations through its converging character.

However, the role of a strategist's way-of-thinking is not just a matter of the interplay between several cognitive spheres. It is also a matter of power. On the one hand, the power of the top leader internally to get strategic freedom of action and enable change that is based on his or her way-of-thinking. On the other hand, the power of the firm externally to use or increase the structure freedom of action in the industrial sector to change the firm's strategic position without being subjected to strong competitive counteraction.

All in all, our conclusions raise the general question of whether leadership really matters or not. There are several schools of thought on this. Selznick (1957), for instance, is one of those who believe that leadership matters, while Pfeffer (1977) represents the doubtful faction. Among the factors that affect a company's performance, many remain outside the leader's control. Costs determined by labor markets, the rate of demand, and government politics are all important areas that the business leader can little influence. However, apart from this, the Holmen case shows that a leader, at least in certain circumstances, can significantly influence the corporate strategy, and thereby also influence the performance of the firm. In general, we need more knowledge about situational variables that tend to more or less accompany influence of leadership on strategic change. Research on strategists' ways-of-thinking is one way to enhance the knowledge about the impact of leaders on the overall development of organizations.

In this chapter, we have argued for the importance of top leaders' strategic ways-of-thinking in change processes. Further research should specify the meaning and role of this concept and develop knowledge about the dynamic interaction between dominant ways-of-thinking, organizational cultures and industrial wisdom in different sectors. This direction of strategy research implies a deeper interest in strategy-making as a learning process. However, to further increase our understanding of strategic change, we should also put much more emphasis on strategy processes as being political games, i.e. to include issues of power as an integral part of our descriptions and analyses. A final aspect that calls for greater interest is the time factor, in two senses. There is a need to look more closely at the role of timing in encounters between leaders, organizations and sectors in a strategic change process. There is also a need to take a long-term view in studies of the change process since the true significance of strategic epochs often does not present itself until ten years or more have elapsed.

REFERENCES

Argyris, C. (1983). Productive and counterproductive reasoning processes. In S. Srivastra *et al.* (Eds) *The Executive Mind: New Insights on Managerial Thought and Action*. San Francisco, CA: Jossey-Bass.

Bartunek, J. M. (1984). Changing interpretive schemes and organizational restructuring: The example of a religious order. *Administrative Science Quarterly*, **29**, 355–372.

Donaldson, G. and Lorsch, J. W. (1984). *Decision Making at the Top*. New York: Basic Books.

Downey, H. K. and Brief, A. P. (1986). How cognitive structures affect organizational design: Implicit theories of organizing. In H. P. Sims, D. A. Gioia *et al.* (Eds) *The Thinking Organization: Dynamics of Organizational Social Cognition*. San Francisco, CA: Jossey-Bass.

Frost, P. J., Moore, L. F., Louis, M. R., Lundberg, C. C. and Martin J. (1985). *Organizational Culture*. Beverly Hills, CA: Sage.

Gioia, D. A. (1986a). Symbols, scripts and sensemaking. In H. P. Sims, D. A. Gioia *et al.* (Eds) *The Thinking Organization: Dynamics of Organizational Social Cognition*. San Francisco, CA: Jossey-Bass.

Gioia, D. A. (1986b). Conclusion: The state of the art in organizational social cognition. In H. P. Sims, D. A. Gioia *et al.* (Eds) *The Thinking Organization: Dynamics of Organizational Social Cognition*. San Francisco, CA: Jossey-Bass.

Gioia, D. A. and Sims, H. P. (1986). Introduction: Social cognition in organizations. In H. P. Sims, D. A. Gioia *et al.* (Eds) *The Thinking Organization: Dynamics of Organizational Social Cognition*. San Francisco, CA: Jossey-Bass.

Greiner, G. (1983). Senior executives as strategic actors. *New Management*, **1**.

Grinyer, P. H. and Spender, J-C. Recipes, crises and adoption in mature industries. *International Studies of Management and Organization*, **9**, 113–133.

Grinyer, P. H., Mayes, D. G. and McKiernan, P. (1988). *Sharpbendes. The Secret of Unleashing Corporate Potential*. Oxford: Basil Blackwell.

Hellgren, B. L., Melin, L. and Pettersson, A. (1993). Structure and change in industrial fields – A contextual approach. In S. T. Cavusgil (Ed.) *Advances in International Marketing*, Vol. 5. Greenwich, CT: JAI Press.

Isenberg, D. J. (1986). The structure and process of understanding: Implications for managerial action. In H. P. Sims, D. A. Gioia *et al.* (Eds) *The Thinking Organization: Dynamics of Organizational Social Cognition*. San Francisco, CA: Jossey-Bass.

Johnson, G. (1990). Managing strategic change; the role of symbolic action. *British Journal of Management*, **1**, 183–200.

Markus, H. and Zajonc, R. B. (1985). The cognitive perspective in social psychology. In G. Lindzey and E. Aronson (Eds) *Handbook of Social Psychology*. New York: Random House.

Melin, L. (1989). The field-of-force metaphor. In I. Johansson and L. Hallén (Eds) *Advances in International Marketing*, **3**, 161–179.

Melin, L. *et al.* (1983). Structure and change, corporate strategies and local actors. Linköping University, Department of Management and Economics, Research report 131 (in Swedish).

Miles, E. M. and Snow, C. C. (1978). *Organizational Strategy, Structure, and Process*. Paris: McGraw-Hill Kogakusha.

Mitroff, I. I. and Mason, R. O. (1983). Stakeholders of executive decision making. In S. Srivastra *et al.* (Eds) *The Executive Mind: New Insights on Managerial Thought and Action*. San Francisco, CA: Jossey-Bass.

Nystrom, P. and Starbuck, W. (1984). To avoid organizational crises, unlearn. *Organizational Dynamics*, Spring, 53–65.

Pettigrew, A. (1985). *The Awakening Giant – Continuity and Change in ICI*. Oxford: Basil Blackwell.

Pfeffer, J. (1977). The ambiguity of leadership. *Academy of Management Review*, **2**, 104–111.

Ranson, S., Hinings, B. and Greenwood, R. (1980). The structuring of organizational structures. *Administrative Science Quarterly*, **25**, 1–17.

Selznick, P. (1957). *Leadership in Administration*. New York: Harper & Row.

Smircich, L. and Morgan, G. (1982). Leadership: the management of meaning. *The Journal of Applied Behavioral Science*, **18**, 257–273.

Spender, J-C. (1989). *Industry Recipe – An Enquiry into the Nature and Sources of Managerial Judgement*. New York: Basil Blackwell.

Weick, K. E. (1979). *The Social Psychology of Organizing*. Reading: Addison-Wesley.

Weick, K. E. (1983). Managerial thought in the context of action. In S. Srivastra, *et al.* (Eds) *The Executive Mind: New Insights on Managerial Thought and Action*. San Francisco, CA: Jossey-Bass.

Weick, K. E. and Bougon, M. G. (1986). Organizations as cognitive maps. Charting ways to success and failure. In H. P. Sims, D. A. Gioia *et al.* (Eds) *The Thinking Organization: Dynamics of Organizational Social Cognition*. San Francisco, CA: Jossey-Bass.

3

Emergent Industry Leadership and the Selling of Technological Visions: A Social Constructionist View

MICHAEL LEVENHAGEN, JOSEPH F. PORAC,
HOWARD THOMAS

Much of past research in industry structures and competition has tended to present markets as domains with objectively real boundaries, with clearly cut lists of players, and with well-defined products and services being traded among market participants.

However, markets and competition are not always as objectively real as they may seem. Research Studies using a cognitive analysis of competition suggests new insights into the nature of industry structures. In particular, in emergent industrial settings, we can observe that first-mover entrepreneurial firms can provide industry leadership and influence the structures of new competitive domains towards their own ends and means, thereby creating potentially sustainable competitive advantages.

Porac *et al.* (1989) argue that a fuller understanding of markets and competition can be enhanced with the addition of market

Strategic Thinking: Leadership and the Management of Change.
Edited by J. Hendry and G. Johnson with J. Newton.
Copyright © 1993 the Strategic Management Society. Published 1993 John Wiley & Sons Ltd.

participants' perceptions of each other, their perceptions of market boundaries, and their perceptions of the products or services within those market boundaries. (This set of perceptions we call competitive definitions – without which, strategy formulation cannot reasonably occur.) In brief, Porac *et al.*'s argument is that market participants' perceptions in and around value chains underlie and form the bases for stable transactions in the 400-year-old Scottish knitwear industry. There, material transactions within that market – and the understandings of those transactions – reciprocally structure and reinforce one another so that, to its participants, the market seems highly structured, real and, to a large extent, without external threats. Using these authors' study as a basis for departure, this chapter extends their stipulations and evidence to a model of market formation.

First, an explication of traditional conceptions of transactions and market domains will be presented. Following that review, a cognitive view of transactions and market domains will be used to augment the more traditional (and material) conceptualizations. Then, a life-cycle approach will be used as a framework to combine both material and cognitive perspectives of transactions to explain how market domains form. The thesis of our present argument is that market domains arise through social-construction processes initiated by frame-making and frame-breaking entrepreneurs. Last, central challenges are suggested for managers wishing to instigate the formation of new markets.

TRADITIONAL VIEWS OF MARKET DOMAINS AND TRANSACTIONS

There are two traditional views of transactions and market domains. The first view, fostered by economics, industrial organization, and marketing, is basically a bidimensional conceptualization (FIGURE 3.1). Firms match their outputs (products or services) to extant homogeneous demand schedules, generally in value chains. Transactions are exchanges of firms' products or services with customers' cash flows, and the products or services within value chains are generally believed to be substitutable commodities. Markets are intersections of firm-level resources (namely, using a resource-based view of the firm) with customer needs in defensibly segmented domains. Competitive spaces, then, are similarly configured firms

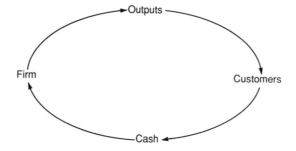

FIGURE 3.1   An economic model of markets and transactions

trading with similarly demanding customers. Competition essentially becomes a question of price.

The second traditional view of transactions and market domains – a more multidimensional view – has been proposed by population ecologists (FIGURE 3.2). Firms not only exchange outputs for cash with customers but also other sorts of 'outputs' with other kinds of stakeholders. For example, in the software markets, firms trade paperwork for regulatory legitimization with governments, equity for starting capital with venture capitalists, as well as output for output with strategic – alliance partners. By population-ecology arguments, market domains are multidimensional resource spaces partitioned by species of firms, whose survival and proliferation of forms are limited by available resources. (Resource dependency arguments further support this view – see Pfeffer and Salancik, 1978.)

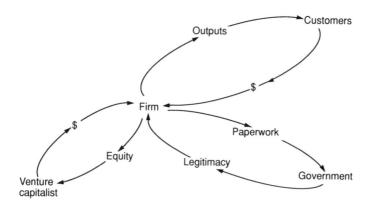

FIGURE 3.2   A population ecology view of markets and transactions

Population ecologists also emphasize legitimacy and competition as factors that enhance or limit firms' survival rates. In the earliest stages of market-domain development, increased firm densities in resource spaces lead to increased legitimacies of firms and to their increased abilities to appropriate needed resources. At some point, however, competitive rivalry begins to clear species of firms poorly matched to the resource spaces. It is posited that firms' organizational structures (and the implementation of their strategies) unfortunately cannot be changed as resource spaces change, and organizational forms perish as environments change. Strategic choice – the ability of firms to adapt to changing environments – largely does not exist (compare Penrose, 1959; Wholey and Brittain, 1986). Competing successfully within resource spaces is a matter of historical accident (Lippman and Rumelt, 1982) and luck (Barney, 1986).

COGNITIVE VIEWS OF TRANSACTIONS WITHIN MARKET DOMAINS

Both the economic view and the population-ecology view are 'materialist' views. Both viewpoints see firms as black boxes substantially incapable of influencing their own resource configurations or the resource spaces within which they find themselves.

These materialist descriptions are surface descriptions. The items of exchange between stakeholders within resource spaces are items that can be seen and measured objectively: cash, products and services, regulation, paperwork, etc. Furthermore, these theoretical viewpoints do not completely explain why material resource transactions do, in fact, occur among firms. Price may clear markets, but additional links are needed at the firm level to explain why firms trade with some partners as opposed to others.

Theories in finance and economics argue that exchange decisions depend upon the expected values of outcomes between trading partners. These expected values are usually expressed in terms of prices. Yet prices are forever unstable and subject to fluctuations and variations for a multitude of reasons. Even in commodity markets, the fixing of the value of highly standardized products is uncertain among all participants – established only for a short time by market pricing and clearing.

The ambiguity of competitive structures and domains (Day *et al.*, 1979; Wensley, 1991) and the uncertainty of prices in all markets provide empirical bases for the use of a social-construction viewpoint. Stakeholders' perceptual understandings of each other, of their competitive domains, and of their varied transactions (i.e. competitive definitions) are the deep-structured underpinnings of material resource transactions. In turn, material transactions (or the lack of them) among stakeholders provide cues for stakeholders' perceptions. Both help to structure market domains. To illustrate, a few examples are offered.

In FIGURE 3.3, a generic transaction between a firm and a resource provider is represented using both materialist and cognitive perspectives. In the diagram, a firm provides an output to a resource provider in exchange for its resource. Underlying the transaction, however, are four understandings (mental models) of the exchange. The firm has a set of beliefs about what it is providing to the resource provider (embodied by the output) as well as a set of beliefs about what it is being provided in exchange. The same can be said from the resource provider's point of view. These 'mental models' need not match between stakeholders on either side of an exchange, but it seems reasonable to assume that the trade between the two partners engenders some shared beliefs of equity.

FIGURE 3.4 represents a more specific example taken from ongoing research in software development markets, and it assumes no intermediary between the end user and the firm. In the diagram, it is assumed the software development firm has some understanding of the end user's needs. From this understanding, the firm makes a product that it believes embodies and satisfies those needs. Also shown in the diagram is a line from the end user

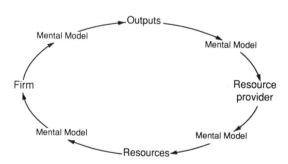

FIGURE 3.3 A cognitive view of markets and transactions

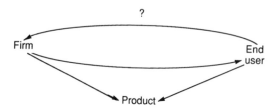

FIGURE 3.4   A cognitive representation of a transaction between a software firm and an end user

to the product indicating some mental model of the firm's product. Should the mental models construct the best available, mutually beneficial understanding to both these parties, the material trade of product for cash is likely to ensue. At this point, it is unclear whether the end user needs an understanding of the firm.

FIGURE 3.5 presents a more complex transaction between a software firm and a venture capitalist (VC), and it shows how different exchange partners may have significantly different underlying knowledge structures. In an exchange of high-risk capital for equity, these two partners are likely to construct beliefs concerning a number of different issues.

Both the firm and the venture capitalist have beliefs about each other. The firm needs to understand the VC's goals, objectives, typical deal structures, and connections within the product market. The VC, however, seeks knowledge about the firm's financial health, its financial projections, its team composition, and its future competition. The VC also develops insights about the product the firm produces and what the end users will buy in sufficient quantities to generate positive cash flows. A clear and consistent

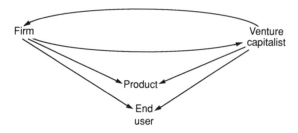

FIGURE 3.5   A cognitive representation of a transaction between a venture capitalist and a software firm

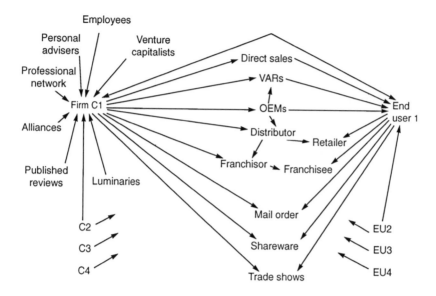

FIGURE 3.6   A cognitive representation of a software development value chain

conception of its product and a framework of what end users would want in terms of benefits should result from this analysis. In this reduced-form description of the transaction, only six mental models are presented. The real situation is assuredly much more detailed and complex than portrayed. For example, FIGURE 3.6 is a representation of the important 'players' in the software markets under investigation by Michael Levenhagen of the Western Business School, University of Western Ontario. Among each value-chain participant, external stakeholder, and observer are multiple mental models as FIGURE 3.5 suggested.

In sum, cognitive views of transactions complement materialist views of transactions. Both views of transactions and market domains are inextricably tied to each other. Each interacting party has an important perceptual view of the other and of the relevant aspects of the perceived environment based upon apparent dealings (or the lack thereof) within the market domain. Each interacting party's perceptions act as the basis for material transactions between trading partners.

From both cognitive *and* materialist points of view, then, market domains are multidimensional sets of resource flows embedded in a matrix of beliefs about products, suppliers, technologies, etc.

within stakeholders' areas of interest. Participants' material transactions and their sensemaking processes maintain (and destroy) old market domains and the competitive 'rules of the game' (see Spender, 1989) that stakeholders use to guide their activities. Moreover, both viewpoints can be used to explain the developments of competitive rivalry in new market domains.

THE LIFE CYCLE OF MARKET DOMAINS

Markets today are changing fundamentally, and new markets are emerging. New markets intrigue stakeholders and hold out the promise of huge strategic gains for firms that successfully stake out and defend these new territories. Furthermore, these domains offer the opportunity for such firms to influence the establishment of the 'competitive rules of the game'.

The analytical approach used to present a cognitive and materialist perspective on the formation of market domains is that of a life cycle, but it is used simply as a pedagogical device. No linear, lock-step, sequential set of events is implied. Such an approach would be a contradiction of the basic theoretical stand taken by social constructionists that cognitive and transactional events interact continually with one another.

Four stages of market domain development are proposed. Each stage has both short-run and long-run implications associated with it. To ground the following theory contextually, examples will occasionally be provided from research conducted by the authors in the software development industry.

THE BACKDROP: PRECOMPETITIVE KNOWLEDGE DEVELOPMENT

A life cycle of market domains presupposes changing technological environments. Here, technology is conceptualized broadly, that is, as the development of different streams of knowledge in industries, markets, cultures, science, etc. Knowledge streams are commonly perceived as independent and disconnected from one another, and they seem to develop at different rates, at different times, and in different places. The trajectory of any particular technology is largely unpredictable, due to bounded-rationality constraints.

The movements of technology trajectories intersect with one another constantly and open and close knowledge gaps. When knowledge gaps open, uncertainty and ambiguity are perceived. When knowledge gaps close, uncertainty or ambiguity is perceptually reduced, as is the case when one knowledge-stream development informs another. Examples of independent technological developments that later provided the bases of the computer industry are Jacquard punchcards, symbolic logic, the audion tube, and binary theory (Drucker, 1985).

STAGE 1: CONCEPT FORMATION

The life cycle of market formations assumes the existence of Schumpeterian entrepreneurs. The theory views entrepreneurs as cognitive agents who first perceive ambiguous and uncertain knowledge spaces and who then discover or create frame-making or frame-breaking ideas. Such entrepreneurs may conceive of future directions of knowledge streams, or they may see conceptual linkages between disconnected knowledge streams. In so doing, these creative cognitive agents reduce perceived uncertainty by bridging and closing gaps between different streams of knowledge. Second, and no less importantly, market-creating entrepreneurs envision new resource combinations (business systems) that can implement novel insights to create altogether new kinds of throughput functions within conceptual market domains.

Such 'grand entrepreneurial ideas' (Hughes, 1983) must be genuinely novel. They cannot simply be incremental modifications based upon ideas found in existing market domains, and they must reduce potential stakeholders' perceived uncertainty or ambiguity significantly. A good measurement of the worth of entrepreneurs' ideas for creating new market domains is the extent to which their ideas can be expressed within existing languages. If new market-domain ideas are not dissimilar enough to those in other market domains, then preexisting languages will be able to articulate the new ideas. Extant market domains and their stakeholders could expand their operational boundaries to appropriate the novel ideas. The novel idea would not create a new market domain but would find itself soon incorporated into competitive spaces already established and occupied. New languages will signal the new ideas to others and distinguish them from other existing languages and concepts.

To continue the example presented earlier, the independent technologies of audion tubes, binary theory, Jacquard punchcards, and symbolic logic were brought together conceptually to create the first computer. The concept of a computer later created a new language that linked together the four previously independent knowledge streams linguistically and conceptually. No previous language could have described the computer concept adequately. Later, the primary knowledge streams – hardware and software – each split off and became independent streams in their own right. Two new market domains were created. In each domain, the cognitive, the linguistic, and the real (in terms of products and services) were united and enacted interactively with each other over time.

STAGE 2: CONCEPT CHAMPIONING: THE DEVELOPMENT OF COGNITIVE INFRASTRUCTURES

Often, what the entrepreneur lacks is the new product or service itself. There may be no prototypes for stakeholders to perceive and evaluate because it may take resources to produce them. Instead, the novel concepts themselves will have to be sold to potential stakeholders.

Selling visions to potential stakeholders may require cycling back to Stage 1 (concept creation) because novel ideas must critically link to stakeholders' existing economic mental models. The novel concepts need to imply economic gains through the suggestion of a significant reduction of uncertainty in stakeholders' markets (Tushman and Anderson, 1986). As a securities analyst said to us concerning successful software developments: ' . . . key factor of success number one: find a market where you change the functionality in how people do their jobs; it must make their lives dramatically easier . . .'.

Entrepreneurs need to acquire a perceived legitimacy for their new concepts. Although legitimacy can be assumed to exist from extensive or stable material transactions, legitimacy can also be acquired through persuasive efforts aimed at creating a consensus among potential stakeholders. Market-creating visions must be sold to potential stakeholders, who in turn will influence others: there is no other way to material enactments of novel ideas.

Completely novel ideas, and the products or services that embody them, must be adopted and used to some extent to realize their full value. Few buyers of such products feel secure enough to buy novel products or services without intersubjective signals (signs indicating confidence and beliefs) from others that the products or services are legitimate (and thus worthy) in the eyes of others. Buyers and distributors in the software industry use a number of surrogate indicators to establish the worth of products and services. The quantity and quality of capital resources, the reviews of products in the trade magazines, what industry luminaries say about directions of technological developments, what key competitors have bought, market shares, the management team compositions, the firms' strategies and marketing plans, and the firms' alliances with key partners are all intersubjective signals that stakeholders use to judge the value of new software ideas.

Shared beliefs in new economic ideas will bring markets together cognitively and provide the basis for material transactions among stakeholders. The greater the number of stakeholders who 'buy into' firms' visions, the more legitimate and credible those visions are in the eyes of other stakeholders, and the more new ideas are likely to succeed economically. Research into successful intracorporate innovation processes has suggested that no new idea can rely upon technical excellence alone (Schön, 1963). New ideas are implemented more through informal networks of personal contacts than through formal investment – evaluation processes; the championing activity of entrepreneurs and managers translates new ideas and sells them to others (Bower, 1970; Burgelman, 1983). This line of research also emphasizes the importance of intermediate management positions in innovative organizations (Kanter, 1982, 1983). Domain-creating entrepreneurs assume intermediate positions as a matter of course when they bring stakeholders together.

Shared beliefs about new ideas, in and around value-chain systems, are the cognitive infrastructures of market domains, upon which material infrastructures are based. For example, after the creation of the first computer, the English Electric Iliac, budding computer enthusiasts in large research and development labs convinced their organizations that computers should be investigated. The organizations 'bought into' the idea, which hardly had much economic value at the time. These 'buy ins' contributed to the idea's development and legitimization, and hence to its eventual present-day enactment.

Cognitive first-movers also create new categories in stakeholders' minds in value-chain systems. Research into competitive group and category-identification processes (Rosch and Mervis, 1975; Tang and Thomas, 1992) suggest that prototypes and exemplars are powerful cognitive framing devices used for comparisons of similarity and difference. Assuming that entrepreneurs choose important areas of ambiguity and formulate new mental models to link centrally and critically to potential stakeholders' existing mental models, then new category-creating first-movers can encourage stakeholders to compare all later providers to the first-movers. Potential competitors who consider entry must do likewise; they must consider the domain exemplars and be forced to position themselves against them in the minds of the stakeholders (see Hotelling, 1929; Ries and Trout, 1981).

STAGE 3: CONCEPT APPROPRIATION BY SELF AND OTHERS

The degree to which a novel concept is easily sold is a measure of the cognitive fit of the novel concept in Stage 1 and the pervasiveness of its sale in Stage 2. The way in which it is materially enacted is also important to sustain a competitive advantage. Again, the reason is cognitive: ideas cannot be kept proprietary once exposed to the marketplace. Of all assets, ideas are the most appropriable. Entrants can imitate cognitive first-movers' concepts through a number of means. Devices can be reverse-engineered, firm behaviors can be mimicked, patents can be technically analyzed and ingeniously circumvented, and trade or scientific journals can be perused for competitive intelligence purposes (Fuld, 1985).

Cognitive first-movers must surround their novel concepts with isolating mechanisms and mobility barriers to protect their newly staked territories from imitators with stronger skill sets and deeper pockets. An example of concept appropriability in software might be MicroSoft's creation and dominance of the microcomputer operating system market, which turned on historical accident. When the makers of RPM missed a meeting with IBM to discuss its possible use in the upcoming IBM-PC, IBM – not to waste its trip to the West Coast – called on a competitor, Bill Gates of MicroSoft. The rest of the story is history. IBM's adoption of MicroSoft's DOS led to its standardization, instantaneous credibility, and exemplar status for all PC-compatible microcomputers. MicroSoft reaped a huge installed base, an exemplar reputation, and a long-term cash flow that funded the development of later successful products in other segments. Compare what a CEO of a software development firm said of his own firm's efforts to establish itself in its market:

'[We are] trying to get some essentially lateral advertising for the product, because it adds to our credibility immensely when you have someone like a major instrumentation manufacturer featuring your software for their system. You know, our name is not Lotus, our name is not MicroSoft, and so [we] have a credibility problem . . . And so [we] have to buy credibility . . . And the only way to prove that a [software] company [will] exist in a year or two is (1) either be a company who's been around a long time, or (2) be linked to a company who's been around for a long time'.

While later entrants themselves try to appropriate novel concepts, attracted to the success and excitement of new entrepreneurial opportunities, the originally enacted ideas are likely to undergo incremental improvements from additional dialogues. Later entrants initiate their own dialogues with domain stakeholders and with new stakeholders also drawn to the opportunities. Domain boundaries may widen as more stakeholders enjoin novel mental-model discourses. Resource pools enrich, niche densities increase, and general legitimacy for all members of new 'communities' tends to rise.

STAGE 4: INSTITUTIONALIZATION OF MARKET DOMAINS

A number of existing lines of research describe this stage in detail in organizational behavior and strategy. In sum, market domains become reified, and material transactions tend to stabilize. Mobility barriers continue to be erected as specialized assets are developed by competitors in domains over time, and firm-specific isolating mechanisms are established. Material costs to entry tend to rise for new entrants in this latter stage.

Languages of domains becomes routinized, and industry recipes begin to appear. Organizational routines become embedded and perhaps automatic, unconsciously perceived, and believed to be *the right way*. Shared jargon arises in domains, and important terms become shortened to one-word lengths. As material transactions stabilize, firms' time horizons lengthen as exchange partners' understanding of one another become more subtle and detailed. Long-term relationships and trust arise between exchange partners (Zucker, 1986). As predicted by population ecologists, domain densities increase to levels where shakeouts occur, usually because dominant technologies are chosen and the value of exchanges between partners are believed to be more fully understood. Ambiguities and uncertainties are reduced in domains because consensus forms concerning competitive and technological standards. Important stakeholders not directly involved in value-chain transactions (e.g. expert observers) become less influential than they were in stage 2 because their beliefs are no longer valued or needed intersubjectively.

As novel concepts become more standardized, a shift to process technologies may become more evident. Initially, firms' strategies focus on strategies that emphasize defining the competitive definitions in resource spaces (effectiveness). Later, firms' strategies turn to fine-tuning the rules of the game and to more efficient organizational resource configurations. The latter domain activities are not frame-making or frame-breaking changes but rather incremental changes easily described and communicated by language within the domain.

Last, cognitive specialization appears more evident. The knowledge base and the discourse between participants within domains increasingly specify and concern themselves with more operational detail. Knowledge becomes more focused to micro-level actions as firms become immersed in day-to-day, tactical and operational issues. In other words, the technology streams evolve to boundaries dictated by physical science limitations (Foster, 1986), as firms seek to squeeze the last few percentage points out of the concepts that unify a domain. Thus, the process returns full circle to stage 1.

Examples of this stage in the software markets are not easy to provide, for in many instances, continuing technological developments may deny cognitive first-movers access to some tactics indicated above. Even though the dominance of Lotus 1, 2, 3 in spreadsheets and WordPerfect and Word in word processing may come to mind, a more obvious example would be the US steel industry's adherence to 'tried and true' recipes of industrial production and product – before the introduction of mini mills.

KEY LEADERSHIP CHALLENGES IN THE COGNITIVE LIFE CYCLE OF MARKET DOMAINS

There are many strategic challenges facing managers who wish to become domain-creating first-movers – too many to discuss here. Instead, a few key challenges are indicated for each stage.

During precompetitive knowledge developments, entrepreneurial leaders must find ways to stay abreast of fundamental technological/ knowledge changes, especially outside their own domains. This direction for environmental scanning is a question of balance, for leaders must also, of course, stay abreast of the important knowledge developments in their own domains. Entrepreneurial leaders need to remain versed in perceived areas of ambiguity and uncertainty as they are created and reduced by independent knowledge streams and their intersections.

In stage 1 (concept formation), entrepreneurial leaders must learn to suspend judgment in 'the accepted' ways of doing business in their own markets, as well as that in others. Only when leaders can challenge preexisting conceptualizations and their underlying assumptions can they possibly generate new conceptualizations and recombinations of knowledge and resources. Here, there are a number of creativity-process generators available for use described by existing literature: scenario planning, brainstorming, force-field analysis, morphological analysis; etc. (Miller, 1987). But first, leaders must not become too wedded to existing conceptualizations because, from a social constructionist point of view, no conceptualization is objectively real; all are subject to radical change sooner or later.

It should be reemphasized that frame-breaking entrepreneurs must take great care in novel-concept formulations. If novel concepts do not critically link to potential stakeholders' present economic mental models and reduce uncertainty or ambiguity significantly, then potential stakeholders are likely not to pay much attention to the novel concepts. Instead, 'normal' expectations will not be met, trust will be breached, and confusion can ensue for potential stakeholders (Garfinkel, 1963). Furthermore, distrust of the novel concepts can ensue if the suspicion arises that potential transactions will disrupt other transactions within stakeholders' value chains and systems (Zucker, 1986).

In stage 2 (concept championing), leaders must consensually reduce ambiguity and uncertainty and gain legitimization and credibility by exercising interpersonal influence with potential stakeholders. Leaders must learn to provide arguments, 'stories,' or scenarios to express their novel concepts to potential stakeholders in such ways as to suggest new and increased value for stakeholders' futures. Domain-creating entrepreneurs may have to provide new data to disprove old mental models or sell new mental models to 'explain away' market ambiguities or uncertainties. At times, a good 'new story' with all the right elements may strike an emotional chord in a number of potential stakeholders and establish an independent life all its own. As Victor Hugo once said, 'Not all the armies in the world can defeat an idea whose time has come' – perhaps even if it is wrong.

It is likely that personal and informal networks with potential stakeholders are very useful in this stage of development. The perceived trust, reputation, and integrity of domain-creating entrepreneurs are important personal attributes that can be used to circumvent formal investment evaluation processes used by stakeholders' organizations. Perhaps potential stakeholders can be made into 'assistant product champions', themselves.

In stage 3 (concept appropriation by self and others), domain-creating entrepreneurs must ensure that their own execution abilities reinforce the concept competitively. Can cognitive first-movers actually implement the novel concept? Do firms have the right skill sets and assets? Can they erect the right mobility barriers and isolating mechanisms? Competitive inimitability is important, but first-movers may not wish to remain absolute monopolists. As population ecologists have suggested, new domains' survivability depend upon legitimacy, and legitimacy may be a function of firm densities within markets. Having more than one firm may increase legitimacy within new domains; there may be optimal levels of firm densities from first-movers' perspectives.

First-movers must ensure that their exemplar status remains intact and unblemished because cognitive-category dynamics will influence entrants to play 'the game' by the first-movers' rules. This suggests that the worst thing cognitive first-movers can do is fail early. If, say, a first-mover's mental model has an important technical flaw that goes unnoticed until the concept goes into production and sales, its exemplar status can vanish overnight with a perceived failure. Unseated by their own mistakes, exemplars can find their leadership positions quickly usurped by entrants with untarnished and related reputations. Once novel domains and their firms have established a perceived legitimacy, however, exemplars should have accumulated large enough stocks of reputation to weather stakeholders' disappointments successfully. MicroSoft's late delivery of Windows deteriorated its reputation somewhat for a while, but its exemplar status remained secure enough to influence its partners and customers to wait until its products were finally introduced. Indeed, MicroSoft has erected unique exemplary barriers to entry by insinuating itself and its designs deeply into the strategies (mental models) of its exchange partners.

In stage 4 (institutionalization of the domain), cognitive first-movers will have to find ways to build and expand upon those novel concepts' key attributes that are valued by resource providers. Firms cannot rely upon single-product developments. Cognitive first-mover firms must determine what attributes stakeholders have come to value in their products and continue to develop more products that embody those attributes. This refers to firms' distinctive competencies based upon firms' asset configurations – but *not* from the firms' points of view. Firms must know *what and how value-chain participants distinctively perceive and value them,* and learn to cultivate their skills to continue to produce those product attributes in new products.

All throughout new-product developments, domain-creating firms must assiduously protect their exemplar statuses. As an exemplar in a cognitive category, image is the name of the game. Staying on the top rung of the mental ladder in stakeholders' minds is as important as any material first-mover advantage. As indicated earlier, the cognitive and material aspects of any competitive community are reciprocally reinforcing and cannot be easily disentangled, because each influences the other. Yet all the while, especially in this last stage, all cognitive exemplars need to stay well aware that the next domain-creator may be amassing a stakeholder critical mass for the next round of frame-breaking developments. The next cognitive frame to be broken may be the present exemplar's new concept frame.

CONCLUSION

There is more to leadership than the internal leadership of firms. There are important opportunities residing in and between all industrial domains for *industry leadership* as well. These opportunities exist at all times in almost all markets because market domains are not 'real' in any objective sense. They are 'constructed' through implicit agreement by their participants. In that markets have important cognitive and perceptual elements that influence what and how material transactions occur among stakeholders, almost any market can be maintained or destroyed through persuasive industrial leadership efforts – but *not* without good economic reasons. Since uncertainty and ambiguity reside in all market domains, good economic reasons are always in abundance.

The crux of industry extrepreneurial tasks, then, is the persuasive sale of visions. This is no more evident than in emergent industrial settings, where uncertainty and ambiguity are at their greatest and where new visions can most easily take hold.

REFERENCES

Barney, J. B. (1986). Strategic factor markets: Expectations, luck, and business strategy. *Management Science*, **32**, 1231–1241.

Bower, J. L. (1970). *Managing the Resource Allocation Press*. Boston, MA: Harvard.

Burgelman, R. A. (1983). A process model of internal corporate venturing in the diversified major firm. *Administrative Science Quarterly*, **28**, 223–244.

Day, G. S., Shocker, A. D. and Srivastava, R. K. (1979). Customer-oriented approaches to identifying product markets. *Journal of Marketing*, **43**, 8–19.

Drucker, P. F. (1985). *Innovation and Entrepreneurship*. New York: Harper & Row.

Foster, R. N. (1986). *Innovation: The Attacker's Advantage*. New York: Summit Books.

Fuld, L. (1985). *Competitor Intelligence*. New York: John Wiley.

Garfinkel, H. (1963). A conception of and experiments with 'trust' as a condition of stable concerted actions. In O. J. Harvey (Ed.) *Motivation and Social Interaction: Cognitive Determinants*. New York: Ronald Press.

Hotelling, H. (1929). Stability in competition. *Economic Journal*, **39**, March, 41–57.

Hughes, T. P. (1983). *Networks of Power: Electrification in Western Society, 1880–1930*. Baltimore, MD: Johns Hopkins University Press.

Kanter, R. M. (1982). The middle manager as innovator. *Harvard Business Review*, July–August, 95–105.

Kanter, R. M. (1983). *The Change Masters*. New York: Simon & Schuster.

Lippman, S. A. and Rumelt, R. P. (1982). Uncertain inimitability: An analysis of interfirm differences in efficiency under competition. *Bell Journal of Economics*, **13**, 418–438.

Miller, W. C. (1987). *The Creative Edge*. New York: Addison-Wesley.

Penrose, E. (1959). *The Theory of the Growth of the Firm*. New York: John Wiley.

Pfeffer, J. and Salancik, G. R. (1978). *The External Control of Organizations*. New York: Harper & Row.

Porac, J. F., Thomas, H. and Baden-Fuller, C. (1989). Competitive groups as cognitive communities: The case of Scottish Knitwear Manufacturers. *Journal of Management Studies*, **26**, 397–416.

Ries, A. and Trout, J. (1981). *Positioning: The Battle for Your Mind*. New York: Warner.

Rosch, E. and Mervis, C. B. (1975). Family resemblances: Studies in the internal structures of categories. *Cognitive Psychology*, **7**, 573–603.

Schön, D. A. (1963). Champions for radical new inventions. *Harvard Business Review*, March–April, 77–86.

Spender, J-C. (1989). *Industry Recipes*. Oxford: Basil Blackwell.

Tang, M. and Thomas, H. (1992). The concept of strategic groups: Theoretical construct or analytical convenience. *Managerial and Decision Economics*, **13**, 323–329.

Tushman, M. L. and Anderson, P. (1986). Technological discontinuities and organizational environments. *Administrative Science Quarterly*, **31**, 439–465.

Wensley, R. (1991). The state of marketing strategy: What do we know? Warwick Business School, University of Warwick, working paper.

Wholey, D. R. and Brittain, J. W. (1986). Organizational ecology: Findings and implications. *Academy of Management Journal*, **11**, 513–533.

Zucker, L. G. (1986). Production of trust: Institutional sources of economic structure, 1840–1920. In B. M. Staw and L. L. Cummings (Ed.) *Research in Organizational Behavior*, Volume 8, Greenwich, CN: JAI Press.

4

The Importance of Organizational Identity for Strategic Agenda Building

JANE E. DUTTON, WENDY J. PENNER

Janet Hill, manager of the Port Authority (PA) Bus Terminal in New York City sat in her office perplexed. Joe Bourden, her customer service representative, had just left her office, reporting that in last night's count, homeless persons sleeping in the bus terminal had reached the phenomenal level of 500 persons in a single night! The outside weather was excruciatingly cold (windchill factors put the temperature at -35 degrees Fahrenheit). Janet felt in her bones the draw of the bus terminal's facilities for persons who had to face sleeping outdoors in the cold, but as a manager, she knew that the presence of homeless persons in the terminal was severely affecting the level of service that this terminal could provide for its customers. However, she felt her hands were tied by the limited set of options that the PA had for effectively dealing with the homeless issue, and management's continual claim that the PA was *not* in the business of providing social services. She had tried before, both on her own, in meetings with her directors, and in conjunction with other terminal managers, to get the 'top guns' of the organization to see and feel that the issue of homeless persons present in bus terminal was a significant strategic issue for the organization. However, in her mind, to date her efforts to get the homelessness issue on the agenda of the PA had been futile. She was concerned and desperate, and called in a friend who was a management researcher at a local university to see what advice could be gleaned from the 'literature'. With a note of desperateness

Strategic Thinking: Leadership and the Management of Change.
Edited by J. Hendry and G. Johnson with J. Newton.
Copyright © 1993 the Strategic Management Society. Published 1993 John Wiley & Sons Ltd.

in her voice, she asked: 'How *do* you get an issue on an organization's strategic agenda?' (Names and facts used in this opening example are fictitious, although subsequent references to the Port Authority of NY and NJ's struggle with the issue of homelessness are taken from a case study reported in Dutton and Dukerich, 1991.)

This chapter develops a framework for understanding the importance of an organization's identity in the process of strategic agenda building. The purpose of the chapter is three-fold. First, we establish the importance of the strategic-agenda building processes in organizations, and briefly review previous work on factors affecting how and when issues 'make' an organization's strategic agenda. Second, we focus on the concept of organizational identity as a critical component of the organizational context that affects strategic agenda building. We describe what the organization's identity is when conceptualized as an organizational and as an individual-level construct. Finally, the major focus of the paper is on articulating the process by which an organization's identity affects strategic agenda building. In pursuit of this last purpose we describe two paths by which organizational identity affects strategic agenda building. Path one pertains to the process by which the organization's identity systematically affects organizational members' perceptions of issues and their motivation to invest in (e.g. spending time to understand an issue), and act on (e.g. willingness to 'go to bat' to get others to see the issue as important) the issue. Path two describes how an organization's identity gets embedded in routines and programs that shape the processes and create the outputs of agenda building. By the chapter's end, we hope to be able to provide one set of answers for Janet Hill's query: How does one get an issue on the organization's strategic agenda? Our answer says understanding the organization's identity is an important keystone for understanding this process.

AN ORGANIZATION'S STRATEGIC AGENDA AND THE PROCESS OF STRATEGIC AGENDA BUILDING

An organization's strategic agenda (Dutton, 1988b) or issue portfolio (Pondy and Huff, 1988) refers to the set of issues that consumes top decision-makers' collective attention at any one time. Where attention in organizations is a limited and relatively scarce resource (March and Shapira, 1982), and where attention allocation is an important precursor to decisions and action (McCall and Kaplan, 1985), knowing how and when strategic issues consume attention is a key lever to understanding how and when organizations change (Dutton and Duncan, 1987a, b).

For example, in the 1970s, top management in US car manu-facturers varied in terms of the timing and degree of attention that they invested in the issue of changing consumers' preferences for small cars. The relative absence of attention paid to this issue had a significant effect on corporate performance and the level and type of strategic change that these firms eventually undertook (Yates, 1983). In a more contemporary example, organizations vary considerably in the degree to which top management sees workforce diversity as a legitimate or important strategic issue, with discernible effects on the level and type of organizational response to this issue (Milliken *et al.*, 1990). Two definitional issues arise from these examples: (1) what are strategic issues? and (2) how does one know an issue is receiving collective attentional investment?

Strategic issues refer to events, developments or trends that are perceived to have the potential to affect organizational performance (Ansoff, 1980). What events, developments or trends are perceived to be issues, and how they are interpreted are not objective facts but are social constructions created in an organizational context (Weick, 1979; Daft and Weick, 1984; Feldman, 1989; Weiss, 1989). Thus, what is considered a strategic issue in one organization may be seen as tactical or irrelevant by managers in another. Given the ambiguity (e.g. lack of clear information; see March and Olsen, 1976) and equivocality (e.g. existence of conflicting meanings applied to issues; Weick, 1979) that mark most strategic issues, the process by which managers try to claim the attention of top management (here called strategic agenda building) is particularly important.

Evidence that top management has an issue 'on the strategic agenda' is indirect and hard to specify exactly. The allocation of an organization's information processing capacity or resources to an issue (Simon, 1971) is one important indication of agenda placement. Evidence that attention has been allocated can be simple and informal: (1) the naming of an issue; (2) time investment in an issue; and/or (3) the collection of information about the issue (Dutton, 1988b, p. 127). Alternatively, evidence that attention has been allocated can be more complex and formal. For example, the creation of a taskforce or a particular role that has responsibility for an issue are strong evidence an issue is consuming vital attentional revenues. In a case study of a chemical firm's evolving response to issues of the natural environment, the creation of an environment committee and formal creation of a role called 'chemical hazards engineer' were structural indicators that the environmental issue had become part of the organization's strategic agenda (Mylonadis, 1991).

When an issue is part of the strategic agenda, the issue has been labeled so that individuals may converse about it. For example, in a study of 12 strategic issues over a five-year time period, Dutton (1988a) found that managers used labels for issues to denote that a particular strategic issue was legitimate for the organization. However, beneath the common label, managers often did not agree about the issue's boundaries or its core substance. Although the issue's label had different meanings for various individuals, there was some common focal point that had been legitimated as a concern for the organization. It was this commonality that defined the issues as strategic agenda items.

Strategic agendas are built in at least two ways. One is through the actions of individuals who, through communication and influence tactics, attempt to get others to see, believe, and agree that some controversy, event, development, or trend is an issue for the organization. Individuals' actions that fit this description will be called *issue-selling* behaviors (Dutton and Ashford, 1993). Issue selling has been described indirectly by innovation and change researchers who have identified the significant roles that particular individuals play in creating momentum for action through legitimation of an idea or solution. They suggest that these individuals' actions are criticial for explaining the timing and substance of ideas that are given attention by others. For example, Dean (1987) calls these individuals 'architects' – they are persons who have the right combination of credibility and commitment to push successfully an idea. Other researchers have called individuals playing similar roles 'champions' (e.g. Schon, 1963; Chakrabarti, 1974; Burgelman, 1983; Howell and Higgins, 1990), or in the case of congressional docket setting, 'policy entrepreneurs' (Kingdon, 1984). These are individuals who, through the right means of communication and interpersonal influence, and through sensitivity to the importance of timing, are able successfully to focus top management's attention onto an issue. In the words of Kingdon (1984), they are able to see and act upon policy windows.

The second way that agendas are built is through collective or group-level actions. These actions come closest to what strategy researchers have described as coalition mobilization around issues (e.g. Narayanan and Fahey, 1982; MacMillan and Guth, 1985). In contrast to the issue selling that focused on individual promotion of an issue, *coalition mobilizing* emphasizes the processes by which issue attention is focused and activated by a group of individuals. It resembles what political sociologists have described as resource-mobilization processes, where groups in organizations try to affect priorities, policies and actions outside of conventional political channels (Zald and Berger, 1978). Coalition mobilizing around issues (as opposed to around alternatives or solutions) is relatively understudied within the strategic change literature. While there is a common assumption that coalition formation and mobilization are issue-sensitive (e.g. MacMillan, 1978), we know very little about the dynamics of the processes by which a group of individuals negotiate, align, and convince top management that an issue requires attention.

Both issue selling and coalition mobilizing describe processes that are involved in the 'making' of strategic issues. Both processes emphasize the bottom-up forces at work forming an organization's strategic agenda, where momentum and action are developed by persons and groups outside of the top management team. This work builds on arguments of previous researchers who claim that the actions and involvement of middle or nonmanager employees are criticial to strategic change and performance (e.g. Bower, 1970; Burgelman, 1983; Schilit, 1987; Westley, 1990; Woolridge and Floyd, 1990).

In trying to isolate what accounts for an issue being placed on the strategic agenda, previous researchers have focused on two sets of factors: (1) the issue context, and (2) the organizational context (Dutton, 1988b). The issue context refers to how characteristics of an issue and characteristics of the political context shape and direct the level of exposure to and level of interest in a particular issue. For example, Dutton (1988b) has argued that issues that are perceived as more important and that are more abstract and simple, are better able to gain the exposure and interest necessary for an issue to 'make' the strategic agenda. However, in order to understand *why* individuals and groups perceive issues in particular ways (assuming that issues are not objective facts but are an amalgam of attributes constructed and emphasized by others), it is important to understand how the organizational context shapes and directs these perceptions. For example, why in some liberal arts colleges was the decline in the number of 18–20 year olds seen by administrators as a legitimate and important issue, feasible to resolve, while in other colleges, the same issue was seen as irrelevant or impossible to resolve (Milliken, 1990)? Alternatively, why, in some hospitals facing a doctors' strike was this event seen as a major threat to survival, while in others, the same issue was seen as an opportunity to innovate and reduce costs (Meyer, 1982)?

Evidence from previous research suggests that the organization's context, and in particular the substance of beliefs held by organizational members, is pivotal for determining perceptions of how legitimate, how important and how feasible to resolve an issue will be (Meyer, 1982; Dutton and Duncan, 1987a; Milliken, 1990). Where these perceptions are key to explaining agenda placement for an issue, we need to consider what organizational beliefs are important and how these beliefs motivate individuals and groups to 'go to bat' for an issue. We assert that the idea of organizational identity captures beliefs that are critical for shaping the timing and success of strategic agenda building. We represent the different pathways by which organizational identity affects agenda building in FIGURE 4.1. Before describing how organizational identity affects strategic agenda building, we first need to develop a workable definition of identity beliefs.

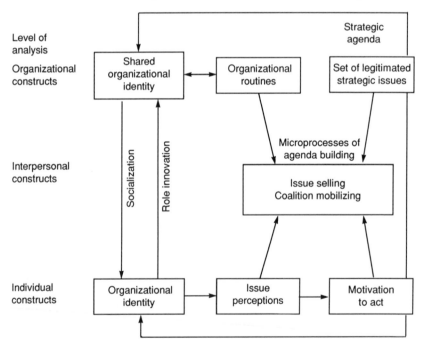

FIGURE 4.1   The multi-level connection between organizational identity and strategic agenda building

DEFINING ORGANIZATIONAL IDENTITY

What members perceive as enduring, central, and unique about their organization describes an organization's identity (Albert and Whetten, 1985). At the individual level, an organization's identity describes an individual member's schema for what that person believes are core attributes shared by members of the organization.

Organizational identities vary in terms of the attributes that individuals believe uniquely characterize an organization. Individuals in one organization may see their organization identity as containing the characteristics of social responsibility, technical expertise and democracy. Individuals in another organization may see the content of their organization's identity as conservative, providing superior service, and bureaucratic. As this simple example illustrates, an infinite set of attributes can be used to characterize or distinguish one organization from another when viewed through the eyes of organizational members. However, a central assumption of this chapter is that organizations do have identities or sets of attributes that individuals believe others share in distinguishing one work organization as a social group from another (Albert and Whetten, 1985). Viewed in this way, organizational identity is a subset of the collective beliefs that constitute an organization's culture (Beyer, 1981). Thus, we assume that, on average, there is less variance in what is believed to be central, enduring and distinctive about an organization between organization members, than between organization members and nonmembers. However, scholars of organizational culture remind us that there is considerable variance in the degree to which any set of organizational beliefs or values are shared (Meyerson and Martin, 1987). Nonetheless, we presume that organizations can be described as having an identity (with acknowledgment that the content and structure of that identity is highly variable across organizational and environmental contexts).

Several ideas support the claim that organizations possess identities. First, it is common practice for organizational leaders to articulate and claim what is unique, central and enduring about their organization (Pfeffer, 1981; Albert and Whetten, 1985). Whether or not these claims of uniqueness are empirically valid (e.g. Martin *et al.*, 1983) is less important than the fact that prominent and powerful organizational members engage in communication and influence processes that try to articulate and disseminate the identity of an organization to insiders and outsiders. In fact, the use of organizational identity as a basis for collective understanding increases as organizations institutionalize the identity creation and dissemination process through public relations and external affairs offices, as well as through formalized socialization practices (Alvesson, 1990). Second, organizations have a broad repertoire of cultural forms beyond leader behavior (e.g. rituals, symbols, ceremonies, stories) that encode and reproduce shared patterns of behavior and interpretation in organizations (Allaire and Firsirotu, 1984). Thus an organizational identity is created and distributed through the cultural and sociocultural systems in an organization, which both shape and are shaped by individuals' beliefs and actions.

Organizational identity has both an individual and an organizational manifestation. At the organizational level, organizational identity describes the collective beliefs that individuals share about what is distinct, unique and central about the organization. Collective identity beliefs are sustained through socialization and institutionalization processes. Shared identity beliefs are communicated to individuals in formal and informal socialization processes, when individuals acquire 'the social knowledge and skill necessary to assume an organizational role' (Van Maanen and Schein, 1979, p. 227). Thus, individuals acquire their sense of an organization's identity through formal orientation programs and informal, personal encounters with members. These programs and persons shape individual expectations about the centrality and distinctiveness of particular attributes of an institution, and by association, characteristics of members who belong to it.

When an organization's distinctive, central and enduring characteristics are institutionalized and preserved in cultural artifacts such as rituals, ceremonies, sagas and routines, then individuals are likely to exhibit consensual beliefs about the organization's identity (Clark, 1979). The shared identity puts boundaries around what an individual's sense of the identity is likely to be. Thus, while different groups in an organization may have different interests and vantage points for understanding the organization's identity, the shared characterization puts limits on the level of differentiation that will be tolerated (Young, 1989).

Depending on an individual's tenure with an organization, their role or departmental location, they may vary in the degree to which their individual beliefs about the organization's identity map onto others' beliefs. While some aspects of an organization's identity may be highly institutionalized, other dimensions may be subject to change by individuals. Individuals enter organizations with different values and beliefs. These different values and beliefs can be expressed in ways that help to transform an organization's identity over time. For upper-level managers, this effect is most apparent when new managers enter an organization. Because top managers are in positions of formal power, their new viewpoints may be implemented by changes in organizational strategy, reward systems, or in the ways that an organization is structured. Alternatively, individuals in less powerful positions may try to alter the organization's identity through role innovation and the promotion of new ideas, which when legitimated as part of the organization's agenda may initiate actions that transform what employees view as distinctive and enduring about the organization. These possibilities are represented in FIGURE 4.1 by the arrow that connects organizational identity at their individual level with organizational identity as an organizational construct. It is also the relationship implied by the feedback loop that occurs between the set of legitimated strategic issues and organizational identity as an individual and organizational construct.

This general description of identity can be linked to important behaviors in organizations. Organizational identity is important for understanding the process and outcomes of agenda building. Organizational identity matters at two levels of analysis. First, at the individual level, organizational identity influences members' perceptions of issues and their motivations to act on and invest in these issues. Second, at the organizational level, a shared organizational identity activates routines and programs that shape the processes and create the outputs of agenda building. Each of these links is developed in more detail below.

THE IMPORTANCE OF IDENTITY BELIEFS AT THE INDIVIDUAL LEVEL

There are two major ways the identity beliefs affect individuals in their strategic agenda building activities. First, the organization's identity affects the perception of issues. These issue perceptions, in turn, affect both issue selling and coalition mobilizing (the two microprocesses we've described are central to agenda building). Second, the organization's identity affects individual's willingness to act on an issue via two paths. First, organizational identity affects actions *through* issue perceptions. Second, identity beliefs affect motivation to act more directly, through the link between an organization's identity and a member's self-concept. Each of these links is described in more detail below.

IDENTITY BELIEFS AND THE PERCEPTION OF ISSUES

An individual's beliefs about the organization identity shape an individual's perception of an issue's legitimacy, its importance and the feasibility of resolving an issue. When issues are perceived as legitimate, important and feasible to resolve, they have a greater chance of securing collective attention of top management (Dutton and Duncan, 1987a).

Organizational Identity and Issue Legitimacy

We propose that the organization's identity affects whether or not an issue is seen as legitimate. The process of issue legitimation is one of social construction, where actions of individuals at all levels interact and create a sense that an issue is acceptable and warrants resource investment (Neilsen and Rao, 1987). When an issue is not perceived as legitimate, it is often discounted, downplayed, or side-tracked so that scarce attentional resources are not devoted to it. For example, in one study of the Port Authority of New York and New Jersey's (PA) struggle with the homelessness issue, at an early stage top management viewed the issue as not in the domain of issues the PA should have to resolve. Individuals at all organizational levels expressed a concern that they were not in the social service business, and therefore this issue was an unacceptable and inappropriate corporate concern (Dutton and Dukerich, 1991). However, when the problem worsened to a level where the costs of not taking action became intolerably high, the issue became a legitimate corporate issue (signaled by its appearance in business plans and in top management conversations about the issue), and the organization responded with a significant investment of time and money in the issue (Dutton and Dukerich, 1991). In this example, the PA's identity defined how and when the homelessness issue was seen as a legitimate and acceptable concern for investing scarce corporate resources.

Individuals' beliefs about the organization's identity serve as important reference points for judging whether or not an issue is a legitimate organizational concern. Individuals' beliefs about the organization's identity filter or sort issues into those that are safe to discuss and safe to act upon, and those that are not. The organization's identity also creates expectations for individuals inside and outside of the organization about what issues are the organization's duty or responsibility to act upon. These expectations create incentives for organizational members to see issues that are identity-consistent as both safe to converse about, and desirable to act upon. Sometimes organizational members reluctantly take ownership of an issue because not doing so would create problems with maintaining a desirable organizational identity.

Returning to the case of the PA's struggle with the issue of homelessness, we saw how members' sense of the PA's identity constrained the PA's issue response, particularly in the early issue period (1982–86), when the PA debated over whether homelessness was a legitimate strategic issue for the agency. During later periods in the PA's struggle with this issue, decision-makers reluctantly assumed ownership of the issue, because not doing so violated the expectations of insiders and important outsiders (Dutton and Dukerich, 1991).

The discussion leads us to propose the following hypothesis:

H1: The more that members perceive an issue as identity-relevant (e.g. as affecting the characteristics of the organization's identity), the greater the perceived legitimacy of the issue.

Organizational Identity and Issue Importance

Beliefs about an organization's identity affect individuals' assessments of an issue's organizational importance or perceived value to the organization, as well as importance to one's own self-concept (Dutton *et al.*, 1991). The central point being made here is that what individuals see as distinctive and unique about an organization will affect individuals' assessments of an issue's organizational and personal importance.

Two examples illustrate this relationship. In Meyer's (1982) study of how hospitals responded to a doctors' strike, beliefs about the hospital's identity influenced how administrators interpreted the strike (e.g. as an ideological dilemma, an opportunity to test organizational dexterity, or an aberration). The issue was viewed as more important when the strike forced organizational actors to consider actions that contradicted the organization's identity (e.g. questions about laying off workers had to be considered by administrators in a hospital that cherished predictability, self-reliance and its ability to ignore changes in its environment).

The PA's struggle with the issue of rising numbers of homeless persons spending time in PA facilities provides a second example (Dutton and Dukerich, 1991). PA decision-makers initially classified the presence of homeless persons as a police/security problem, and as such, not directly relevant to their major transportation service business. In the eyes of PA members, the homelessness issue became much more important when it threatened to destroy central components of the PA's identity. For example, PA employees saw themselves as working for a first-class, highly professional organization. When the 'homeless problem' spread from the PA's bus and train locations to the 'PA flagships' – its high-class facilities such as the World Trade Center and the Airports – PA members saw the issue as much more important and urgent. Similar to the hospital administrators' interpretations of the doctors' strike, organizational identity became a critical reference point for seeing the issue of homelessness as an important PA problem. This reference point became more significant when decision-makers were forced to consider the possibility that their actions were inconsistent with the organization's identity (Dutton and Dukerich, 1991). In both examples, the identity defined areas of economic and political vulnerability for the organization, that made attending and acting on the issue more critical and urgent for organizational members. It seems that an organizational identity helps individuals to locate motives and skills that others will agree should take precedence (Gephardt, 1984).

Individuals' beliefs about the organization's identity also relate to their perceptions of an issue's personal importance. When an organization's identity is threatened by an issue-related action, then an individual's self-identity is potentially compromised. This reaction occurs because of the potentially close affiliation between an individual's self-concept and the organization for which they work (Ashforth and Mael, 1989; Dutton et al., 1991).

Visible organizational issues reflect directly on individuals, particularly those who define themselves based on their organizational affiliation. These types of individuals personally feel the costs of identity-inconsistent issues (e.g. 'the dirty homelessness issue' for a high-class, high-quality organization like the PA). For individuals who derive a large part of their own self-definition through affiliation with the organization, these costs are very painful, making the issues appear more important and urgent. The power of this connection is revealed in a quote from a PA manager observing how the presence of the homelessness issue affected the members' personal reactions:

> 'You know, that guy that's running the Lincoln Tunnel doesn't have a full perception of how the [PA] Bus Terminal, or the homeless impact what he does on a day to day basis. But the minute he leaves and goes to a cook-out in his neighborhood and meets somebody, and this person says, "What do you do for a living?" "Oh, I work for the Port Authority." They say, "How can you stand the Bus Terminal?" What can you do? That's the name. That's the symbol of the Port Authority. It's the standard-bearer. And you know, so personally everybody that's involved in any aspect of working for the Port Authority is identified with that place and with that issue [the homelessness issue].' (Dutton and Dukerich, 1991, p. 538)

These arguments support the following two hypotheses:

H2: The greater the members' perception that an issue is prompting actions that are inconsistent with the organization's identity, the greater their perception of the importance of the issue.

H3: The greater members' perception that an issue will affect valued characteristics of the organization's identity, the greater their perception of the importance of the issue.

Organizational Identity and Issue Feasibility

Individuals' senses of an organization's identity also affect perceptions of the feasibility of resolving issues. For example, Milliken (1990) found that university administrators who perceived their institution as effective and who perceived a strong institutional identity interpreted changing demographic trends as having less effect on their institution (lower effect uncertainty), and had greater confidence that their institution would respond effectively (less response uncertainty). Based on personal results, individual beliefs about organizational identity may reduce effect certainty and inflate response certainty, making an issue appear less important. In this way, organizational identity beliefs contribute to organizational inertia by constraining individuals' issue interpretations to be identity-consistent. When strategic issues are identity-consistent, individuals are more likely to believe that they have the skills and competencies for dealing with the issue. When issue feasibility is high, then individuals are more willing to expend scarce resources on understanding the issue because they are more certain that this investment will produce some type of payoff (Dutton and Webster, 1988).

This line of argument suggests the following hypothesis:

H4: The greater the members' perception of an issue as being identity-relevant, the greater their perception of the feasibility of resolving the issue.

IDENTITY BELIEFS AND THE MOTIVATION TO ACT

Individuals' willingness to exert effort in selling and resolving a strategic issue reflects their motivation to act on an issue. These effects are related to issue perceptions. One can envision issues and contexts that excite individuals to invest in making an issue an organizational concern. Similarly, one can see how for other sorts of issues, or in different contexts, it might be very difficult to get individuals to invest scarce resources in an issue (such as time or financial resources). For example, in one study of coalition formation around issues (where larger more diverse coalitions are evidence of greater collective issue motivation), researchers found that issues that were perceived as feasible to resolve, and which arose in contexts that were more certain, generated greater motivation to act (Dutton and Webster, 1988). In another study, researchers found that individuals were more willing to invest their own time, and corporate agenda space and money to issues that were perceived as more urgent and more interdependent with other issues (Dutton *et al.*, 1990). Both studies provide evidence that how an individual perceives an issue relates to that person's motivation to invest in it.

Because organizational identity relates to issue perceptions, the way that individuals see an organization's identity will affect their motivation to act. The sentiments of organizational members more easily resonate with issues that are identity-consistent (Neilson and Rao, 1987). Thus, if an issue is perceived as legitimate and important, for example, expectancy–valence models of motivation (e.g. Vroom, 1964) would predict that they would be more willing to expend effort to understand and promote action on the issue. If, however, an issue is identity-inconsistent, individuals can choose to reframe the issue to be identity-consistent, take actions to try to revise the identity, or decide not to invest further in the issue.

In addition to the indirect relationship between organizational identity and motivation to act (i.e. through its link to issue perceptions), there is a more direct way that the organizational identity excites individuals to exert effort on an issue. An organization's identity does more than provide reference points for assessing an issue's importance or legitimacy. For some individuals it provides a type of character mirror for individuals to build identities for themselves (Dutton and Dukerich, 1991; Dutton *et al.*, 1991). The attributes that make up an organization's identity, by association, are transferred to individuals who work there, which in turn affect members' decision-making (e.g. Cheney, 1983), and motivate them to display their organizational affiliations at different times (Cialdini *et al.*, 1976). An organization's identity helps individuals to give meaning to themselves as social beings (Ashforth and Mael, 1989). Another facility manager at the PA conveys this relationship in a description of how issues and an organization's identity are related to one's self-image.

> 'But I've also felt that the Port Authority is – and part of our self-image as I put my fingers on it – is that we do things a little bit better than other public agencies. There's a whole psyche that goes with that. That is why, when there's time like now [referring to the severity of the homelessness issue], when times are tough, people are nervous a little bit, because that goes to their self-image, which is that the Port Authority does things first class.' (Dutton and Dukerich, 1991)

Given the association between the content of the organization's identity and individuals' self-concepts, members should be more motivated to push for issues that strengthen valued parts of the organizational identity, issues that add new, attractive components of the organization's identity, and issues that revise unattractive elements of the identity. Support for this relationship was again evident in the study of the PA's struggle with the homelessness issue. This study documented that individuals' motivations to invest in the issue of homelessness were heightened when they incurred a personal stigma by their association with the PA, and the PA's association with a negatively viewed issue such as homelessness (Dutton and Dukerich, 1991).

Thus, from this discussion, we add two more hypotheses:

H5: The more that members view an issue as consistent with attractive components of the organization's identity, the greater their motivation to act on the issue.

H6: The more that members view an issue as prompting actions that revise unattractive components of the organization's identity, the greater their motivation to act on the issue.

THE IMPORTANCE OF ORGANIZATIONAL IDENTITY AT THE COLLECTIVE LEVEL

Shared organizational identity is the collective version of organizational identity. It describes what individuals agree is unique, enduring and distinctive about an organization. Walsh's (1990, p. 16) review of the organizational literature on knowledge structures documents the variety of names that have been applied to supra-individual beliefs in organizations – including collective cognitive maps (Axelrod, 1976), hypermaps (Bryant, 1983), dominant logics (Prahalad and Bettis, 1986), negotiated belief structures (Walsh and Fahey, 1986), and organizational minds (Sandelands and Stablein, 1987). However, the concept of a collective or shared organizational identity defines a much narrower domain of knowledge content than the constructs mentioned above because the relevant beliefs are limited to those that define central, enduring, and distinctive organizational attributes.

As with other collective organizational beliefs, collective beliefs about an organization's identity are embodied in different organizational routines and programs (e.g. March and Olsen, 1989). Organization routines refer to 'patterns of behavior that are engaged in by more than one person oriented to a common stimulus' (Feldman, 1989). These routines are closely related to the skills of an organization (Nelson and Winter, 1982). As such, these routines constrain the process and content of strategic agenda building in ways that are described below.

Organizational scholars have acknowledged links between systems of beliefs, routines and procedures in organizations by describing systems that contain both. For example, Shrivastava and Mitroff (1983) call these systems 'frames of reference', Johnson (1987) calls them 'paradigms', and Hinings and Greenwood (1988) call them 'archetypes'. Whatever the label, these researchers call attention to the strong link between an organization's belief system and the routines, programs or structures that perpetuates it. It is this relationship that is often used to explain patterns of organizational inertia. Johnson's (1987) research provides an example of the link between collective organizational identity and routines that affect agenda building. In his study of the Foster Brothers retail organization, he characterized the firm's identity as nurturing and paternalistic. These beliefs, in turn, were linked to human relations routines (e.g. promoting from within) and socialization routines. These routines were partially responsible for decision-makers' resistance to identity-inconsistent information. Also at Foster Brothers, marketing routines consistent with the 'pile it high, sell it cheap' identity perpetuated this blindspot, even when it was deleterious for organizational performance. Thus, critical organizational beliefs about an organization's identity become crystallized in routines and programs, which generate action in particular directions (Starbuck, 1983). Thus, 'actions are fitted to situations by their appropriateness within a conception of identity' (March and Olsen, 1989, p. 38).

The organization's identity is associated with routines that create informational and political resources and processes that affect agenda-building processes and outcomes. At least two sets of routines are important in this regard. First are the routines for data collection that determine what issue-relevant information is available organizationally to make claims that in fact an issue is important and 'deserving' of scarce organizational attention. In organizations with formal environmental scanning or issues management systems, the operation of these routines is transparent, and relatively easy to observe. Daft and Weick (1984) make a similar point when they describe organizational interpretation modes that have embedded in them differing degrees and types of routines for information collection and interpretation. However explicit and transparent these data collection routines are, they affect the availability of substance and support for issues that are competing for agenda inclusion.

A second set of routines that relate to a collective or shared identity concern communication and participation routines. Communication routines refer to the general bundle of programs that specify when, where, what, and to whom individuals can communicate about strategic issues. Organizations have very different communication routines that encourage or discourage issue selling or coalition mobilizing by individuals at lower organizational levels. Communication routines are one way that 'strategic ideologies [here as manifested in a collective sense of organizational identity] guide discourse about strategic initiatives [in this case, issues], by constraining how individuals can frame issues, where, and when and to whom they can sell the issues, and how they are likely to feel about those efforts' (Westley, 1990, p. 25). As a result, certain forms of issue selling and coalition mobilizing are likely to become institutionalized in organizations. For example, Cobb and Elder (1972) identified four different means by which individuals and coalitions in Congress create legitimate docket issues: (1) readjusters who base their claim that an issue exists based on a logic of redressing imbalances; (2) exploiters who 'manufacture the issue for their own personal gain' (p. 83); (3) circumstantial reactors who build an issue by jumping on the focus and attention devoted to an unanticipated event; and lastly, (4) do-gooders who advocate an issue for reasons related to the public interest. Within organizations more generally, different roles or patterns of issue selling and coalition mobilization may emerge and be supported based on the communication routines that are tacitly guiding the agenda building process.

The communication and participation routines are similar to what proponents of garbage-can models of decision-making call decision structures – procedures and programs that connect decision-makers and choice opportunities (Cohen *et al.*, 1972). These routines facilitate or block the formation of coalitions around issues by easing or constraining access to information that suggests that an issue is important, by making it more easy or more difficult to gain access to arenas for expressing issue support, and by affecting the allocation of issue responsibility to particular groups or individuals in an organization. Thus, these routines connect particular issues to particular individuals or groups, which affect the probability that the issue will 'make' the strategic agenda. For example, organizations with a collective identity in which paternalism and lifetime employment are central features are likely to have routines in place that attach higher-level human resource managers to a broader range of strategic issues than in organizations where these attributes are less central or not present at all.

Communication and participation routines have a major effect on the content, occasion and outcomes of issue selling and coalition mobilizing. For example, if communication routines regulate who is entitled to initiate claims that an issue is 'strategic', and these routines make middle managers feel excluded, then the rate of interaction between superior and subordinate is likely to be lower and energy levels around issues is likely to dissolve (Westley, 1990). These effects, in turn, are likely to decrease the frequency with which new issues are pushed by individuals or coalitions, and as a result, the content of the strategic agenda changes at a slower rate.

CONCLUSIONS

This chapter follows in the general stream of work that examines the individual and group-level processes underlying patterns of strategic change. It asserts that organizational identity, as both an individual and organizational construct, shapes and directs strategic change *through* its links to the processes involved in agenda building. In particular, we have described how organizational identity influences issue perceptions and individuals' motivations to invest and act on issues. We have described how the collective organizational identity activates routines that systematically affect information collection, communication, and participation in agenda-building processes. Together, these contextual conditions activate different political interests, and different cultural meanings that direct patterns of organizational attention, and hence, patterns of strategic change.

Returning to the original question posed by Janet Hill of the PA – how do you get an issue on an organization's strategic agenda? – our account has provided several insights. First, managers outside the top decision-making team should be aware of what others see as distinct, enduring and central about the organization – i.e. they should know what the organization's identity is. The identity serves as a cognitive filter and motivational lever for getting others to see and believe that an issue warrants attention. Thus, as a starting point, they must understand what members see the organizational identity to be. Second, they must try to relate the issue to consequences and actions that are organizationally identity-relevant. In particular, an issue seller or coalition will see an issue's legitimacy more easily, perceive its importance and believe they are more equipped to resolve it, if they see the issue as tied to the organization's identity. The momentum to place an issue on the agenda will be even greater to the extent that issue sellers or coalitions interested in promoting an issue can get others to see that actions on the issue either enhance valued parts of the organization's identity or alter unattractive aspects of the identity. As this simple example illustrates, we believe an understanding of how organizational identity affects agenda building equips managers with new insights on how to work the organizational context in service to placing an issue on the strategic agenda.

Our depiction of agenda building and its relationship to organizational identity also underlines several themes that are central to strategic change researchers. The approach makes context a keystone to understanding the emergent processes that produce patterns of action. The approach weaves together political and cognitive processes to describe how context molds process. It makes issue interpretation a central step in creating momentum for change. The approach is distinctly multilevel, involving processes and forces evolving at the individual, interpersonal and collective organizational levels in order to account for the content and change in strategic agendas over time.

However, the chapter does more than reemphasize themes that others have already uncovered. The focus on organizational identity and its link to agenda building is particularly promising for several reasons. First, the tie between individuals' senses of an organization's identity and their own sense of who they are and what they stand for, provides a powerful motivational link for connecting organizational context to individual and collective issue investment. Individuals' beliefs about the organization's identity create or destroy energy and excitement about certain strategic issues. This energy and enthusiasm, or apathy and indifference, can translate into attention and investment in some strategic issues and ignorance or purposeful avoidance of others. Thus, by linking organizational identity and individual motivation, we uncover part of the engine that derives momentum for strategic change.

Second, the links between collective organizational identity, organizational routines and the processes of issue selling and coalition mobilizing provide important insights into institutionalization processes in organizations. It suggests that shared beliefs about what distinguishes an organization constrain what issues are defined as 'strategic' by automatically engaging routines that constrain the processes of issue selling and coalition mobilizing. The routines that are attached to the collective identity bound the domain of issues that are sold and the way that they are sold so that the strategic agenda stays fairly constant or is filled with the similar issues over time. Such a connection suggests that organizational inertia is quite likely – a claim that is pervasive in the organizational literature (e.g. Hannan and Freeman, 1984). However, it suggests that inertia is perpetuated by the forces of institutionalization that operate on the allocation of attention in organizations.

This conclusion raises an important practical question for researchers and practitioners. Practitioners' and academics' advice to create 'strong organizational cultures' and 'clear organizational visions' are prescriptions that lead to conformity, stability and conservatism in organizations. These prescriptions are consistent with the conclusion that the relationships between organizational identity and agenda building contribute to patterns of organizational inertia. Thus far we have avoided the prescriptive and normative question of whether this is good or bad for organizational performance or desirable or undesirable for the individuals who work there. While these questions cannot be answered here, it seems appropriate to ask whether or not this link between organizational identity and agenda building allows for the ambiguity that typifies many organizational contexts (Meyerson and Martin, 1987), and whether the existence of a strong, and consensual organizational identity silences voices on issues that are identity-inconsistent, but are potentially significant to organizational members. If the perceptual, motivational and political forces that link identity and agenda building resemble the ones we have described here, then the issues that individuals are willing to promote, and the way that they see them are channeled in directions that are identity-consistent. Individuals who define themselves to be different from the prevailing organizational identity are constrained to frame issues in ways that link them to the current organizational identity, to be silent, or to exit the organization (Hirschman, 1970). Alternatively, individuals may unite forces with other individuals and work outside of the conventional political channels, to create a type of social movement in the organization (Zald and Berger, 1978). At a minimum, these possibilities encourage serious consideration of the normative and ideological implications of this description of how identity and strategic agenda building are related. From a managing change perspective, these questions invite consideration of how the processes through which individuals are motivated to interpret and sell issues could be designed to encourage or discourage the variety of issues that consume collective attention in organizations.

The link between organizational identity and strategic agenda building suggests several important research questions. First, a focus on strategic agenda building encourages research on the process by which issues are identified and legitimated in organizations. Studies of these processes need to represent the perceptual and political forces at work in activating individuals and groups to mobilize resources aimed at directing the attentional investments of key organizational channels (Zald and Berger, 1978). Second, it encourages research on the substance of individual and collective beliefs about an organization's identity, and the connections between these beliefs and individual and collective motivation to interpret and act on issues in particular ways.

ACKNOWLEDGMENTS

Thanks to Janet Dukerich, Marlene Fiol, C. V. Harquail, Don McCabe, Debra Meyerson, Frances Milliken, Robert Hooijberg for comments on earlier drafts of this chapter, which was originally presented at an SMS–Cranfield Workshop on Leadership and Strategic Change.

REFERENCES

Albert, S. and Whetten, D. (1985). Organizational identity. In L. L. Cummings and B. M. Staw (Eds) *Research in Organizational Behavior*, volume 7 (pp. 263–295). Greenwich, CT: JAI Press.

Allaire, Y. and Firsirotu, M. (1984). Theories of organizational culture. *Organizational Studies*, **5**, 193–276.

Alvesson, M. (1990). Organization: first substance to image? *Organization Studies*, **11**, 373–394.

Ansoff, I. (1980). Strategic issue management. *Strategic Management Journal*, **1**, 131–148.

Ashforth, B. and Mael, F. (1989). Social identity theory and the organization. *Academy of Management Review*, **14**, 20–39.

Axelrod, R. (1976). *The Structure of Decision: The Cognitive Maps of Political Elites*. Princeton: Princeton University Press.

Beyer, J. M. (1981). Ideologies, values and decision making in organizations. In P. Nystrom and W. Starbuck (Eds) *Handbook of Organization Design*, volume 1 (pp. 166–202). London: Oxford University Press.

Bower, J. L. (1970). *Managing the Resource Allocation Process: A Study of Corporate Planning and Investment*. Boston: Harvard University Press.

Bryant, J. (1983). Hypermaps: A representation of perceptions in conflicts. *Omega*, 11, 575–586.

Burgelman, R. (1983). A process model of internal corporate venturing in a diversified firm. *Administrative Science Quarterly*, **28**, 223–244.

Chakrabarti, A. K. (1974). The role of champion in product innovation. *California Management Review*, **17** (Winter), 58–62.

Cheney, G. (1983). On the various and changing meanings of organization membership: A field study of organizational identification. *Communication Monographs*, **50**, 343–362.

Cialdini, R. B., Borden, R. J., Thorne, A., Walker, M. R., Freeman, S. and Sloan, L. R. (1976). Basking in reflected glory: Three (football) field studies. *Journal of Personality and Social Psychology*, **34**, 366–375.

Clark, B. R. (1979). Academic culture. Yale University, working paper. Cited in Sproull, (1981).

Cobb, R. and Elder, C. D. (1972). *Participation in American Politics: The Dynamics of Agenda Building*. Boston, MA: Allyn and Bacon.

Cohen, M. D., March, J. G. and Olsen, J. P. (1972). A garbage can model of organizational choice. *Administrative Science Quarterly*, **17**, 1–25.

Daft, R. L. and Weick, K. E. (1984). Toward a model of organizations as interpretation systems. *Academy of Management Review*, **9**, 284–295.

Dean, J. W. (1987). Building the future: The justification process for new technology. In J. M. Pennings and A. Buiteendam (Eds) *New Technology as Organizational Innovation* (pp. 35–58). Cambridge, MA: Ballinger.

Dutton, J. E. (1988a). Perspectives on strategic issue processing: Insights from a case study. In P. Shrivastava and R. Lamb (Eds) *Advances in Strategic Management* (pp. 223–244). Greenwich, CT: JAI Press.

Dutton, J. E. (1988b). Understanding strategic agenda building and its implications for managing change. In L. R. Pondy, R. J. Boland and H. Thomas (Eds) *Managing Ambiguity and Change* (pp. 127–144). Chichester: John Wiley.

Dutton, J. E. and Ashford, S. (1993). Selling issues to top management. *Academy of Management Review*, forthcoming.

Dutton, J. and Dukerich, J. (1991). Keeping an eye on the mirror: The role of image and identity in organizational adaptation. *Academy of Management Journal*, **34**, 517–554.

Dutton, J. E. and Duncan, R. B. (1987a). The creation of momentum for change through the process of strategic issue diagnosis. *Strategic Management Journal*, **12**, 76–90.

Dutton, J. E. and Duncan, R. B. (1987b). The influence of strategic planning on strategic change. *Strategic Management Journal*, **8**, 103–116.

Dutton, J. E. and Webster, J. (1988). Patterns of interest around issues: The role of uncertainty and feasibility. *Academy of Management Journal*, **31**, 663–675.

Dutton, J., Dukerich, J. and Harquail, C. V. (1991). The organizational self: Linking organizational image and identity to individuals' feelings, beliefs and behviors. University of Michigan, working paper.

Dutton, J. E., Stumpf, S. and Wagner, D. (1990). Diagnosing strategic issues and the investment of resources. In R. Lamb and P. Shrivastava (Eds) *Advances in Strategic Management*. Greenwich, CT: JAI Press.

Feldman, M. P. (1989). Understanding organizational routines: Stability and change. University of Michigan, working paper.

Gephardt, R. P. (1984). Making sense of organizationally based environmental disasters. *Journal of Management*, **10**, 205–225.

Hannan, M. and Freeman, J. (1984). Structural inertia and organizational change. *American Sociological Review*, **49**, 149–163.

Hinings, C. R. and Greenwood, R. (1988). *The Dynamics of Strategic Change*. New York: Basil Blackwell.
Hirschman, A. O. (1970). *Exit, Voice and Loyalty: Responses to Declines in Firms, Organizations and States*. Cambridge, MA: Harvard University Press.
Howell, J. M. and Higgins, C. A. (1990). Champions of technological innovation. *Administrative Science Quarterly*, **35**, 317–341.
Johnson, G. (1987). *Strategic Change and the Management Process*. Oxford: Basil Blackwell.
Kingdon, J. W. (1984). *Agendas, Alternatives, and Public Policies*. Boston, MA: Little, Brown and Company.
McCall, M. and Kaplan, R. (1985). *Whatever It Takes*. Englewood Cliffs, NJ: Prentice-Hall.
MacMillan, I. (1978). *Strategy Formulation: Political Concepts*. St. Paul, MN: West Publishing.
MacMillan, I. and Guth, W. D. (1985). Strategy implementation and middle management coalitions. In P. Shrivastava and R. Lamb (Eds) *Advances in Strategic Management* (pp. 233–254). Greenwich, CT: JAI Press.
March, J. and Olsen, J. (1976). *Ambiguity and Choice in Organizations*. Bergen: Universitetsforlaget.
March, J. and Olsen, J. (1989). *Rediscovering Institutions*. New York: Free Press.
March, J. and Shapira, Z. (1982). Behavioral decision theory and organizational decision theory. In G. R. Ungson and D. N. Braunstein (Eds) *Decision Making: An Interdisciplinary Inquiry*. Boston, MA: Kent.
Martin, J., Feldman, M., Hatch, M. J. and Sitkin, S. (1983). The uniqueness paradox in organizational stories. *Administrative Science Quarterly*, **28**, 438–453.
Meyer, A. D. (1982). Adapting to environmental jolts. *Administrative Science Quarterly*, **27**, 525–537.
Meyerson, D. and Martin, J. (1987). Cultural change: An integration of three different views. *Journal of Management Studies*, **24**, 623–646.
Milliken, F. J. (1990). Perceiving and interpreting environmental change: An examination of college administrators' interpretations of changing demographics. *Academy of Management Journal*, **33**, 42–63.
Milliken, F. J., Dutton, J. E. and Beyer, J. M. (1990). Adapting to a changing workforce: Organizations and work-family issues. *Human Resource Planning*, **13**, 91–107.
Mylonadis, Y. (1991). Environmental concerns as a source of organizational learning. In G. Hauptman and N. Nohria (Eds) *Navigating Amidst Uncertainty: Deciding and Organizing Technology Rich Contents*. Working paper.
Narayanan, V. K. and Fahey, L. (1982). The micro-politics of strategy formulation. *Academy of Management Review*, **7**, 5–34.
Neilsen, E. H. and Rao, M. V. H. (1987). The strategy-legitimation nexus: A thick description. *Academy of Management Review*, **12**, 523–533.
Nelson, R. and Winter, S. G. (1982). *An Evolutionary Theory of Economic Change*. Cambridge, MA: Harvard University Press.
Pfeffer, J. (1981). Management as symbolic action. In L. L. Cummings and B. M. Staw (Eds) *Research in Organizational Behaviour*, Volume 3 (pp. 1–52). Greenwich, CT: JAI Press.
Pondy, L. R. and Huff, A. S. (1988). Budget cutting in Riverside: Emergent policy reframing as a process of analytic discovery and conflict minimization.

In L. R. Pondy, R. J. Boland and H. Thomas (Eds) *Managing Ambiguity and Change* (pp. 177–200). Chichester: John Wiley.

Prahalad, C. K. and Bettis, R. A. (1986). The dominant logic: A new linkage between diversity and performance. *Strategic Management Journal*, 7, 485–501.

Sandelands, L. and Stablein, R. E. (1987). The concept of organization mind. In S. Bacharach and N. DiTomaso (Eds) *Research in the Sociology of Organizations* (pp. 135–162). Greenwich, CT: JAI Press.

Schilit, W. K. (1987). An examination of the influence of middle-level managers in formulating and implementing strategic decisions. *Journal of Management Studies*, 24, 271–293.

Schon, D. A. (1963). Champions for radical new inventions. *Harvard Business Review*, 40, March–April.

Shrivastava, P. and Mitroff, I. (1983). Frames of reference that managers use: A study in the applied sociology of knowledge. In R. Lamb (Ed.) *Advances in Strategic Management*, 1, Greenwich, CT: JAI Press.

Simon, H. (1971). Designing organizations for an information rich world. In M. Greenberger (Ed.) *Computers, Communication and Public Interest*. Baltimore, MD: Johns Hopkins Press.

Sproull, L. (1981). Beliefs in organizations. In W. Starbuck and P. Nystrom (Eds) *Handbook of Organizational Design*, pp. 204–224. Oxford: Oxford University Press.

Starbuck, W. (1983). Organizations as action generators. *American Sociological Review*, 48, February, 91–102.

Van Maanen, J. and Schein, E. H. (1979). Toward a theory of organizational socialization. In B. Staw and L. L. Cummings (Eds) *Research in Organizational Behavior* (pp. 209–264). Greenwich, CT: JAI Press.

Vroom, V. (1964). *Work and Motivation*. New York: John Wiley.

Walsh, J. P. (1990). Knowledge structures and the management of organizations: A research review and agenda. Dartmouth College, working paper.

Walsh, J. and Fahey, L. (1986). The role of negotiated belief structures in strategy making. *Journal of Management*, 12, 325–338.

Weick, K. (1979). *The Social Psychology of Organizations*. Reading, MA: Addison-Wesley.

Weiss, J. (1989). The powers of problem definition: The case of paperwork. *Policy Sciences*, 22, 97–121.

Westley, F. (1990). Middle managers and strategy: microdynamics of inclusion. *Strategic Management Journal*, 11, 337–351.

Woolridge, B. and Floyd, S. W. (1990). The strategy process, middle management involvement and organizational performance. *Strategic Management Journal*, 11, 231–241.

Yates, B. (1983). *The Decline and Fall of the American Automobile Industry*. New York: Empire Books.

Young, E. (1989). On the naming of the rose: Interests and multiple meanings as elements of organizational culture. *Organization Studies*, 10, 187–206.

Zald, M. N. and Berger, M. A. (1978). Social movements in organizations: Coup d'Etat insurgency and mass movements. *American Journal of Sociology*, 83, 823–861.

5

Strategy Development and Implementation: Cognitive Mapping for Group Support

COLIN EDEN

I believe . . . that in deciding where you would like to be, as opposed to where you are probably going to end up, you need a great deal of discussion and a great deal of development of new thinking and new processes. The idea of doing this through the planning department, or through a paper on strategy presented to the board, seems to me to be quite inadequate. This process involves large amounts of time and constant discussion with those involved lower down the line who will actually execute the strategies on which the whole picture relies. This sort of circular debate, frequently widening out to involve others within and without the company, goes on until all are satisfied that the result is as good as they are going to get. (Harvey-Jones, 1988)

This chapter is about the role of cognitive mapping and special-purpose computer software in facilitating the type of discussion Harvey-Jones talks about. The role of the computer is twofold – to help groups in the organization with the discussion of strategy through the provision of a group decision support system (GDSS) that can represent, manipulate, and analyse cognitive maps; and

Strategic Thinking: Leadership and the Management of Change.
Edited by J. Hendry and G. Johnson with J. Newton.
Copyright © 1993 the Strategic Management Society. Published 1993 John Wiley & Sons Ltd.

secondly to provide members of the executive team with a sort of executive information system that can help with the implementation of strategy.

One of the greatest difficulties facing the chief executive involved in creating a sound strategy for an organization is not the development of the strategy, but rather making the strategy have any real impact throughout the organization. The resolution of the difficulty rarely lies in making the strategy more correct from the point of view of its content, but one of gaining commitment, ownership, and appropriate strategic control. The key lies in being able fundamentally to change strategic *thinking* in the organization – the way senior managers construe their world. 'Decision conferencing' (Phillips, 1990) and other GDSSs (Rosenhead, 1989; Vogel and Nunamaker, 1990) are making progress through locking together the processes of strategy development and implementation. That is, computer and facilitator-aided group processes are allowing cognitive data to be used analytically within the context of the sort of group activities that promote higher levels of ownership. The strategy is expected to be robust because it has absorbed more of the experience, wisdom and judgements of a wider cross-section of the organization. That is, the strategy pays attention to the cognitive maps that guide the strategic thinking of each member of the management team. The cognitive maps that are of interest are those that reflect the way in which the managers 'make sense of and give meaning to the managerial world which they inhabit'.

Their participation in an overtly analytical process for elaborating and structuring their wisdom, and the consequent belief that they have had an opportunity to influence the strategy, generates high levels of cognitive ownership of strategy. Importantly, by bringing to the surface the realities as seen by those who will enact strategy, it not only provides ownership but counters the risks of locked in perspectives that derive from the 'mind of the organization'.

Returning to the introductory quote from John Harvey-Jones, this chapter will now consider some of the characteristics of strategy development. In the light of these characteristics it will consider the role of cognitive mapping and computer assistance (group decision support) that allows a group to 'play with' their cognitive maps about strategy through the real time interaction with graphical computer representations and analyses of their maps.

The Nature of Strategy Development

Strategy development usually involves some or all of the following group activities:

- articulating *strategic vision*
- identifying major *strategic issues* facing the organization
- *option* generation and *scenario* building
- identification of *stakeholders* and their possible response in relation to their own goals.

These activities represent the groundwork of strategy building, followed by:

- developing an appropriate *goal system* for the organization
- setting *strategies* within the context of the goal system
- establishing a series of *strategic programmes* related to the strategies and representing an action package
- the creation of a *mission statement* in relation to the above
- developing a *strategic control system* involving a review of strategic performance and the performance of strategy.

If attention is paid to the major problems of implementing strategy – making it work for the organization – then these processes often involve large numbers of staff within the organization. Indeed, it is typical for our own work with organizations, in both the private and public sector, to use a cascading series of strategy workshops that might involve upwards of 200 staff. At several stages the senior executive team will come together to evaluate and analyse the content generated by these workshops. Indeed, as we shall see, the cognitive maps of the executive team provide the initial framing for the contributions of other staff. Later, the executive team may work with the output of 10–20 workshops, on other occasions the team work only with the content generated by themselves.

The executive team are central to whatever processes are used for strategy development and it is they who are likely to gain the most benefit from computer-aided group decision support. The 'composite cognitive map' of the members of the executive team, combined with 'group maps' of other participants, and the support system forms the basis of strategy development. The process has been used within organizations such as Reed International (Eden and Ackermann, 1993). Shell (Eden, 1990a), BT, the Prison Service (Eden, Cropper and Train, 1990), government departments, NHS (Telford, Ackermann and Cropper, 1990), and multi-organizational settings (Pizey and Huxham, 1991). It has also been used in a wide variety of different formats, depending upon the nature of the organization – culture, personal style of the chief executive, level of sophistication in strategic management, and time and money available.

COGNITIVE MAPPING AS THE BASIS FOR SUPPORT TO GROUPS

The conceptual framework described above is founded upon the notion that strategy development is about discovering how to manage and control the future. It is concerned with capturing the experience and wisdom of organizational members about how they believe an attractive vision of the future can be attained. Strategic thinking is thus action oriented and concerned with identifying how to intervene in the incrementalism of the organization itself and its relationship with the environment. The data is the outcome of managers thinking about the future, and thinking about the future involves creating new theories (Spender, 1989) about the relationship between the organization and its environment. These theories are based on experience and wisdom rather than precise forecasts or quantitative analyses. Judgements are made about how the market and the organization will be working, and these judgements are seen within the cognitive maps of the decision-makers.

The data of strategic thinking will, therefore, be dominated by a qualitative *belief system*, which represents 'theories' about why the world works and thus how it can be changed. The need to recognize the complex interaction between the multiple beliefs of organizational members reflects the reality of every goal being qualified by others and every strategy being constrained and enhanced by a network of other strategies.

The assertions made above relate closely to those encompassed by personal construct theory (Kelly, 1955) – those of peoples' attempts to make sense of their world through anticipating and differentiating events, and to seek out ways of managing and controlling their futures. In summary, personal construct theory sees 'man as a scientist', constantly trying to make sense of the world in order to act within and upon that world. Therefore, at the core of the method, is the technique of 'cognitive mapping'. Although cognitive mapping has a variety of interpretations in practice (Axelrod, 1976; Huff, 1990), this particular form of cognitive mapping is uniquely based on personal construct theory. It has been developed, following extensions to the use of repertory grids, for the purpose of capturing a 'personal construct system' (Eden *et al.*, 1979; Eden and Jones, 1984; Eden, 1988). The analyst, using the technique of cognitive mapping, seeks to elicit the beliefs, values, and so embedded expertise of decision-makers. These are then captured as a model of a part of the person's construct system, and the model is a cognitive map. The cognitive map is made up of constructs linked to form chains of action-oriented argumentation.

In sympathy with personal construct theory it is important to note that maps are coded so as to be action-oriented representations of the world – argumentation about policy issues is coded so as to reveal or highlight the implications for 'managing and controlling' through the way the strategic issues are 'anticipated' (examples of mapping argumentation in this way are given in FIGURES 5.1(a) and (b)). This type of cognitive map demands that assertions have consequences or implications (which reveal the answer to the 'so what?' questions) – and so the map is made up of 'constructs' (or concepts) and arrows indicating the direction of implication embedded in the belief system. In particular, the arrow shows the implied possible action and its possible outcome as suggested by the theories used to explain the world. Thus meaning is given to a construct not only by its content, but also from the consequences attributed to it (forming the chains of consequences for a value system) and from the explanatory constructs that support it (the belief chain). In gathering data and in building the model, the central questions guiding the coding are: (1) what are the implications of *using* the 'theory or belief about the world' as a basis for intervening in the world so as to protect or support values?, and (2) what might explain or support the assertion?

Thus an assertion is questioned by considering why the manager is making it – what does the manager expect someone to do as a result of knowing the assertion? For example, if the manager asserts that 'customer loyalty is the result of developing long-term personal relationships with particular individuals', and that 'helping the customer solve problems is one important aspect of getting the right relationship instead of always treating the customer to a sales pitch,

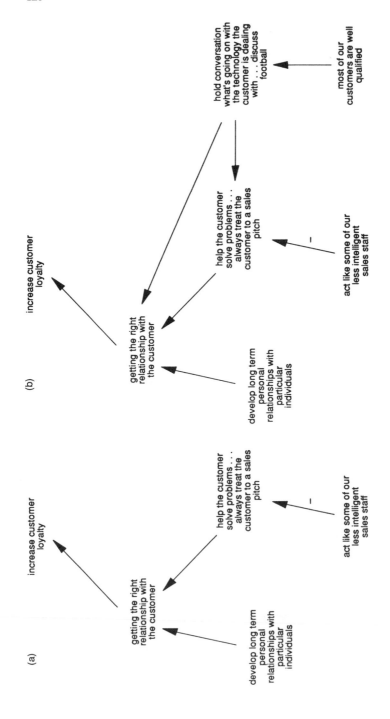

FIGURE 5.1 (a) Part of a cognitive map; (b) Extension to the part of a cognitive map shown in (a)

as some of our less intelligent sales staff do', then we might code this part of the cognitive map as FIGURE 5.1(a). In the same manner, when a manager makes an assertion such as 'most of our customers are well qualified', then it becomes important to review the context of the assertion, within the holistic sense of the manager's view, to discover, and so state, the way in which this data is regarded as significant. Clues derive from other statements such as those made above and others such as 'many of our salesmen can discuss only football – the last thing they might do is hold together a conversation about what's going on with the technology our customers deal with'. These contextual assertions might lead to an extension of FIGURE 5.1(a) to create the part of the map in FIGURE 5.1(b).

THE DISCOVERY OF A STRATEGIC BELIEF SYSTEM

As indicated above, the process of collecting experience and wisdom is through a series of interviews with members of the executive team. Each interview (or two) generates a cognitive map that belongs to a particular manager. These maps are verified by each manager so that they are a reasonable representation of the thinking that the manager declares about strategic issues that are relevant to the development of strategy.

It is important to be clear about distinction that can be made about the status of different types of cognitive map. The discussion above argues that this particular form of cognitive mapping (of the form depicted in FIGURES 5.1(a) and (b)) is supposed to be a reasonable way of formalizing a body of cognitive theory (personal construct theory). It is designed to be so, and the coding guidelines (Ackermann *et al.*, 1990) have been developed so as to be faithful to Kelly, and the process of elicitation as a development of the repertory grid method. A cognitive map is not supposed to be a model of cognition but rather a faithful interpretation of personal construct theory.

Secondly, a cognitive map is taken to be a device that translates this theoretical framework into a practical tool by acting as a device for representing that part of a person's construct system they are able and willing to make explicit – thus whilst Kelly is clear that a construct is not the same as a verbal tag it is nevertheless *useful* to collect verbal tags as if they were constructs. So a cognitive map, in practice, is dependent upon the notion that language is a common currency of organizational life and so can be used as the dominant medium for accessing a construct system.

Thirdly, for many perfectly good reasons a person will not make explicit many beliefs to another person, let alone a strategy consultant. This is the case even if the manager believes that the interview is totally confidential. Thus, the cognitive map, developed in strategy development, is significantly biased by the necessary social interaction, or social gaze, that is the basis of elicitation through interview.

Lastly, the manager will not necessarily be prepared to validate a cognitive map so that it can be used as a contributor to a vehicle within group activity.

Thus, the so-called cognitive map that a strategy consultant can work with is always likely to be significantly different from cognition, but at least it will be in the spirit of Kelly and in the spirit of working with a manager's own theories about his or her world. More significantly it can be a tool to facilitate negotiation about different possible strategic futures for the organization; a negotiation that can take place between those managers who have the power to act, and a negotiation that starts from the individual subjective worlds of the participants to the negotiation.

This initial set of interviews and the associated cognitive maps form the foundation for continuing strategy development work which seeks to involve as many others as is practicable. The involvement of others as participants rather than decision-makers is designed to both increase ownership and to elicit expertise that can influence strategy. It is this process of exploring 'organizational cognition' as it is framed by the cognitive maps of the executive team that has become known as SODA (Strategic Options Development and Analysis – Eden, 1989a), and which involves building a composite cognitive map or 'strategic map' (a map in the spirit of cognitive map but that signifies only the cognition of the organization as a reified entity!).

> One reason why you should try to develop the direction in which you think the company should go from both ends of the company at once is that in the process you gain the commitment of those who will have to follow the direction – and 'make it happen' – and in a free society you are unlikely to get this commitment without a high degree of involvement and understanding of both where the ultimate goal is, and the process by which the decisions regarding that goal have been reached. (Harvey-Jones, 1988)

The six stages of working with 'cognitive/strategic maps' is depicted in FIGURE 5.2 (stage 1 having been discussed above).

STAGE 1
The Interviews

STAGE 2
Computer Modelling and
Analysis using COPE

STAGE 3
The Focus Group Meeting

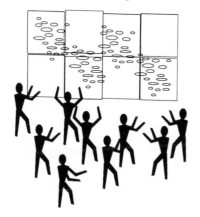

STAGE 4
Computer Modelling and
Analysis using COPE

STAGE 5
Group Decision Support System Workshop

STAGE 6
Control & Review

FIGURE 5.2 The six stages of SODA

After the initial round of one or two interviews with members of the senior executive team the process shifts to work with groups in a workshop setting. The composite cognitive map is analysed (in stage 2) to help identify emerging strategic issues – the software has a number of analysis methods that detect clusters of constructs, central constructs, organizational values, core beliefs, etc. (Cropper *et al.*, 1990; Eden, 1991; Eden *et al.*, 1992). The emerging issues form the agenda for, and so frame, workshops with other members of the organization. Usually each involves between 6 and 24 people who will be invited to influence the strategy of the organization through the further elaboration of strategic issues and emerging goals.

This 'focus group' work is generally a combination of 'nominal group techniques' (Delbecq *et al.*, 1975), the use of 'dominoes/sno-cards' (Eden *et al.*, 1983; Backoff and Nutt, 1988), and the use of the special-purpose cognitive mapping software for recording, analysis and display purposes. Participants work in groups of 10–15 people and are encouraged to use 'dominoes' (20×10 cm cards shaped as ellipses) to record and publicly display their own views of the strategic issues facing the organization within the context of the views of other members of the group. The group is provided with 'triggers' that are labels for the emerging issues from the analysis of the composite cognitive map of the executive team. This 'starter pack' is designed to focus the group on further elaboration of issues of importance to the group who will finally decide, but is not intended to constrain the group from the identification of new strategic issues.

As participants display their ellipses on the wall in front of them they are continuously organized by the facilitator, with help from participants, into clusters of related statements. They are implicitly arranged by the facilitator into an hierarchically arranged cognitive map so that the most superordinate outcome is at the top and the most detailed means or option at the bottom of the cluster. Each cluster of statements represents an emerging 'strategic issue' identified by the group. The group members are encouraged to elaborate and contradict the emerging view of issues being displayed on the wall. FIGURE 5.3 shows an example of a developing cluster.

The clusters, their content, in the interrelationship between content within clusters, and between clusters is added to the existing composite map using the computer software. Thus the organizational cognitive map is continuously elaborated as each workshop unfolds. In practice the recorder will modify the wording of what is written on the ellipses in order that the assertion indicates an intervention

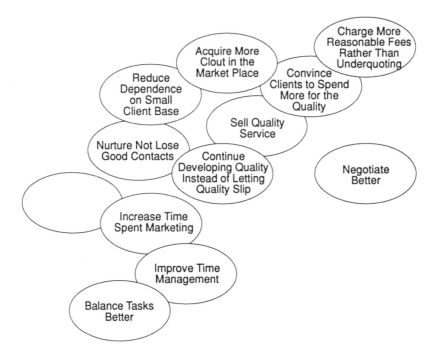

FIGURE 5.3   An example of a 'Domino' cluster

to change the world – that it suggests a 'call to action'. FIGURE 5.4 shows a cluster being recorded and represented on the computer screen using COPE.

The request to focus on issues is designed to grab the attention of participants by allowing them to express 'firefighting' concerns (Eden, 1990b) they each have about the future. This may promote a temptation to continually refer to the present (and thus past) nature of the world as it is expressed by the 'corporate rain dance' of the annual planning process, rather than make explicit theories that are genuinely prospective. However, the use of dominoes to record discussion is aimed at encouraging individuality whilst developing creativity and synergy alongside synthesis and reducing the probability of 'groupthink'. In practice participants in a workshop have different ways of construing strategic issues – some contrast or differentiate (in a Kelly sense) the past with the present, some the past with the future, and others the future with the present.

Focusing on strategic issues rather than the development of idealized scenarios or preferred goals is deliberately designed to

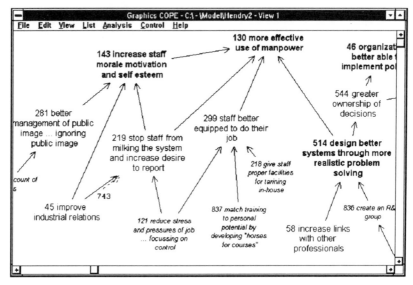

FIGURE 5.4   A cluster recorded by COPE

ensure that strategy is not 'motherhood and apple pie'. The clusters are specific theories that apply to the world of the participants' specific organization rather than *any* organization. It also reduces the possibility of participants discussing 'espoused theories' derived from attendance of management courses, rather than the 'theories of action' that will drive future decision-making (Argyris, 1983; Bartunek and Moch, 1987).

EMERGING STRATEGIC GOALS

The next stage of work with a group is focused on the identification of emerging strategic goals. Participants are encouraged to take an holistic view of each cluster and consider the goals that are implicit through the identification of a cluster as a strategic issue. When members of the group have emotionally and psychologically envisioned issues that must be resolved, then they will be implicitly or subconsciously presuming a desired direction for the organization, this stage of the workshop is designed to make explicit these assumptions about direction – hence they are the emerging strategic goals/values of the organization.

These goals are usually written on to self-stick notes (to differentiate them from the issue content) and are organized hierarchically in relation to each cluster in turn. It is at this stage that the clusters become explicitly related to one another, for each goal informs others, some of which are superordinate, thus relating to several clusters. The software is used to record these goals. The large amount of material generated and cross linkages can be collated into a single model. The group now becomes increasingly dependent upon COPE and the computer display to manage the complexity of their strategy development. The display can be used to focus upon any part of the model and show its linkage upwards to superordinate 'end' and downwards to subordinate 'means'. Attention of the group gradually shifts from material on the wall to the aggregated model on the computer display. Thus the group absorbs the use of computer-aided group support in a 'natural' rather than directed manner – the use of the computer appears obvious and transparent.

COMPLETING THE GROUNDWORK OF STRATEGY DEVELOPMENT AND REFINING STRATEGY

Strategy development follows work with participant groups by shifting to active group decision support with the executive team (stage 5). Thus the executive team is encouraged to consider those statements that are most subordinate, within the strategic issues, as possible strategic options. The software is used to help locate potential options that might be particularly significant. For example, not all of the most subordinate concepts need be considered in the first instance, those that have a single chain of ramifications are likely to be less important than those with many ramifications. The software finds those potential options that are either 'potent' or 'key' (potent options are those that have ramifications for a large number of goals, key options are options that are most subordinate within the model having more than one consequence). As the group addresses these possible options they are encouraged to develop 'actionable' means to resolving the strategic issue being considered and so add new concepts to the model. As possible strategic options are identified they are given a typeface/colour that will clearly indicate them on the computer display, on a printout, and as an analysable set within the model.

Similarly, the possible reaction of stakeholders to 'key options' are noted within the model, both as responses that could damage or support the strategy and as stakeholder goals that might encourage them to respond in the manner predicted.

REFINING STRATEGY

The stages described above may be undertaken many times with a variety of groups within the organization. When working with any specific group a choice will be made about whether they are to build their own model of issues, goals, options, and stakeholder responses or whether it is appropriate to aggregate their views with those recorded from previous groups. The choice is mostly resolved by considering the time available to work with the increased complexity of an aggregated model set against the potential for increased ownership of a broad organizational perspective on strategic issues.

Although it is possible for the executive team to consider the model after the backroom work of aggregating the material has been carried out, it is not possible for the groups generating the material to work with it all unless the software can be used in 'real time'. This is especially true if a series of groups are working on the material, as they will not only want to be able to review what previous groups have contributed but add their own comments and insights directly to it. Thus using 'real time' software will enable them to grasp hold of the direction of other groups whilst adding their own. This facility also enables the executive team to work on the material interactively if they should so choose.

Whichever route has been chosen, the executive team will have come together at stage 5 (see FIGURE 5.2) to consider a large amount of qualitative data – typically 1000–1500 concepts, made up of 40–50 issues, 80–90 potential goals, and 200–300 potential strategic options. Their task, with the help of two facilitators and the computer support, is to refine the goal system, agree appropriate strategies to meet these goals, evaluate options and create a programme of action to support the strategies, and so write a mission statement that will act as an inspiration to members of the organization.

Two facilitators are used so that one facilitator can act mostly as a 'process manager' in front of the group and the second facilitator act predominantly as a 'content manager' in front of two computer screens (one screen working as a preview for the main screen refresh or for exploratory analysis). The large screen used by the group is either the display from a three-colour projector, or a large 37" colour VGA monitor. With one facilitator paying attention to process and the other to content it becomes possible to allow the analysis of content to be contingent upon the social processes of the group and the social processes of the group to be contingent upon the analysis of content (Eden, 1990c). The facilitators are able to act in concert, and the social needs of the group and content of the issue are also able to be in concert with one another so that effective negotiation occurs (Eden, 1989b).

The group decision support task in relation to the executive team is to provide help in the management of cognitive complexity. COPE is designed to provide this help in a number of ways. Cognitive mapping, because of its basis in Kelly's 'management and control' orientation, enables the computer software to offer support that is coherent as between *personal* constructs, a negotiated *organizational* cognitive map, and a model of potential *strategy* that is amenable to analysis informed by a framework of strategic *management*:

- each of the different *categories* of data, or all of the data, can be identified and displayed separately
- clusters can be formed where concepts are grouped so that there is a minimum number of bridging links to other clusters, thus *identifying manageable parts* of the model and suggesting *emerging features* of the strategy
- clusters can be formed based upon an *hierarchical analysis* of the model, thus sets can be formed that relate to particular parts of the goal system, allowing the exploration of possible strategic programmes
- particular parts of the model can be chosen to depict an *overview* by 'collapsing' the overall model down to, for example, the relationship between key options and certain goals
- *'central' concepts* can be isolated through a sequence of analyses that identify those concepts with a dense domain of other concepts, or alternatively highly elaborated support (subordinate chains of 'means' to a selected 'end').

These analyses allow the structure of the strategy model to be explored so that the emerging characteristics of the data can be identified. It is through the 'playful' use of the model in this way that the executive team are able to get a feel for the model as a whole. Subsequently the team is able to focus on the task of reducing the goal system down to a manageable size – about 10–12 core strategic goals (strategies) supported by 15–20 other goals (strategic objectives). The process is a combination of analysing goal centrality with merging of goal statements to capture the essential features, of maybe four adjacent goal statements, into one goal (this merging process is easily managed with the help of the software, so that all interrelationships are maintained). FIGURES 5.5 and 5.6 show a typical merging of three goals. The process is cyclical, involving various analyses to provide an agenda of displays. These displays are focusing on 'central' concepts and subsequent rewording, merging, and 'deleting' (concepts are never deleted in practice but rather reduced in typeface size and coloured deep blue so they become insignificant; this is because they sometimes resurface as significant as the cycle proceeds).

An executive team seems able to make use of the support system with remarkable ease. They quickly become accustomed to the power of the software so that facilitation shifts from highly

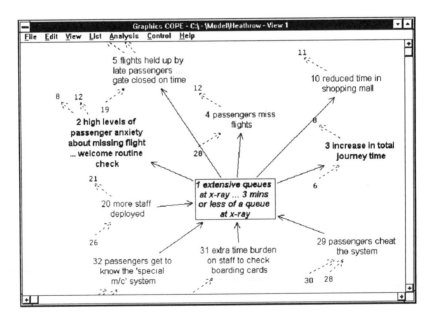

FIGURE 5.5   A part of a goal map prior to merging

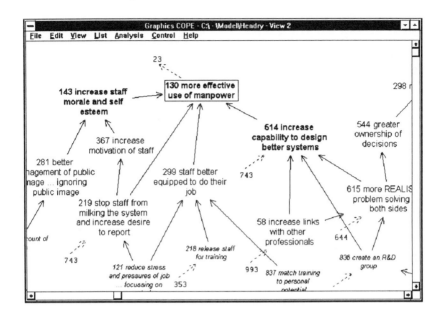

FIGURE 5.6   A part of a goal map after merging

FIGURE 5.7   An executive team working with COPE

directed conceptual and technical guidance to collaborative support. The use of the computer mouse within a 'windows' environment allows members of an executive team to grab control of the software so that the GDSS is transparent rather than technical 'magic'. FIGURE 5.7 shows an executive team at work.

STRATEGIC CONTROL

The strategy model developed by multiple groups and refined by the executive team is the agenda for strategic action. For it to be successfully implemented an effective strategic control system is absolutely essential (Goold and Quinn, 1990). While a significant element of strategic control is the process of strategy review on a regular six-month and twelve-month basis (Eden and Ackermann, 1993) a fundamental element is the problem-solving support the strategy framework is expected to provide to executives on a day-to-day basis. In this respect the model is used in a variety of forms as a type of executive information system.

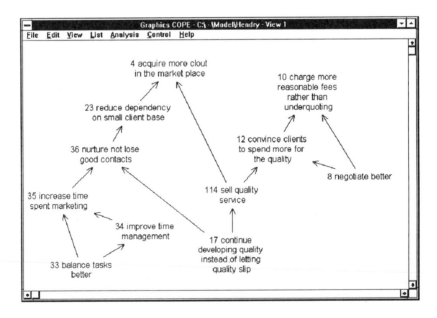

FIGURE 5.8   An example of a review display

First, the model resides on the personal computer of senior staff as the basis for 'problem framing', resource acquisition, acquisition and new product evaluation, and as the basis for 'vertical cut' in relation to task groups. Strategic control is established through the requirement that all requests for major decisions must be made by direct reference to the strategy model; by so doing, decisions are more likely to be coherent in relation to the detail of strategy and in relation to one another. A strategy that cannot be referred to in its full complexity allows decisions to be justified against strategy statements that are so superordinate, and therefore 'motherhood', they are open to multiple interpretations to suit the needs of the manager requesting resources.

Secondly, the model becomes the basis for the review of all subordinate staff. Agreed strategic actions are recorded in the model with respect to the manager responsible for delivery and the date of delivery. All managers are able to use COPE to search for all actions designated to a particular individual or team and not only check on progress, but much more importantly check that progress is being designed to achieve the ends that the strategy originally determined. It is common for individual managers to claim successful implementation of a particular strategic action without undertaking the task in such a manner that the strategic aims of the action are achieved. COPE forces such considerations simply because all displays of actions show the supporting actions and expected consequences (FIGURE 5.8) – the manager is expected to demonstrate the attainment of the consequential arrows as well as the action itself. The review process is not restricted to the use of the model to check implementation of detailed actions but also as a part of the annual performance review of senior staff. Here the model becomes a structured prompt for asking staff to explain their performance and the performance of their staff in building the strategic future of the organization.

CONCLUSION

I believe . . . that in deciding where you would like to be, as opposed to where you are probably going to end up, you need a great deal of discussion and a great deal of development of new thinking and new processes. The idea of doing this through the planning department, or through a paper on strategy presented to the board, seems to me to be quite inadequate. This process involves large amounts of time and constant discussion with those involved lower down the line who will actually execute the strategies on which the whole picture relies. This sort of circular debate, frequently widening out to involve others within and without the company, goes on until all are satisfied that the result is as good as they are going to get. (Harvey-Jones, 1988)

Computer-aided GDSSs must be able to support this activity as it continues and yet also provide an effective 'transitional object' (De Geus, 1988) or 'organizational memory' that carries forward the essence of the discussions. While the SODA method and COPE software aim to do this they are only the beginning of a revolution in the use of computers for helping groups and individuals think creatively – 'such models have exhausted empiricism and placed no bounds on rationality' (Rohrbaugh, 1987).

In the approach discussed in this chapter, cognitive mapping has been used as the basic technique for both understanding and exploiting the experience and wisdom of managers. Unless the richness and subtlety of this data is to be ignored by working with summary cognitive maps that are therefore relatively small, as is predominantly the case for the maps reported in Huff (1990), then computer software and computer-aided group decision support are presently the only practicable way of exploiting expert knowledge about strategy. The combination of individualism through cognitive maps, and group work through 'composite cognitive maps' seems to provide an organization with the opportunity to create a strategy that has a high level of ownership across all levels of the organization.

References

Ackerman, F., Eden, C. and Cropper, S. (1990). *Cognitive Mapping – a user's guide*. Working Paper No. 12, Dept. of Mgt Science, University of Strathclyde.

Argyris, C. (1983). Action science and intervention. *The Journal of Applied Behavioural Science*, **19**, 115–140.

Axelrod, R. (1976). *The Structure of Decision*. Princeton, NJ: Princeton University Press.

Backoff, R. W. and Nutt, P. C. (1988). A process for strategic management with specific application for the nonprofit organization. In J. M. Bryson and R. C. Einsweiler (Eds) *Strategic Planning: Threats and Opportunities for Planners*. Chicago: Planners Press.

Bartunek, J. M. and Moch, M. K. (1987). First-order, second-order, and third-order change and organization development interventions: A cognitive approach. *The Journal of Applied Behavioural Science*, **23**, 483–500.

Cropper, S., Eden, C. and Ackermann, F. (1990). Keeping sense of accounts using computer-based cognitive maps. *Social Science Computer Review*, **8**, 345–366.

De Geus, A. (1988). Planning as learning. *Harvard Business Review*, April–March.

Delbecq, A. L., Van de Ven, A. H. and Gustafson, D. H. (1975). *Group Techniques for Program Planning*. Glenview: Scott Foresman.

Eden, C. (1988). Cognitive mapping: A review. *European Journal of Operational Research*, **36**, 1–13.

Eden, C. (1989a). Strategic Options Development and Analysis – SODA. In J. Rosenhead (Ed.) *Rational Analysis in a Problematic World*. London: John Wiley.

Eden, C. (1989b). Operational research as negotiation. In M. Jackson, P. Keys and S. Cropper (Eds) *Operational Research and the Social Sciences*. New York: Plenum.

Eden, C. (1990a). Strategic thinking with computer. *Long Range Planning*, **23**, 35–43.

Eden, C. (1990b). Cognitive maps as a visionary tool: Strategy embedded in issue management. In R. G. Dyson (Ed.) *Strategic Planning: Models and Analytical Techniques*. London: John Wiley.

Eden, C. (1990c). The unfolding nature of group decision support – two dimensions of skill. In C. Eden and J. Radford (Eds) *Tackling Strategic Problems: The Role of Group Decision Support*. London: Sage.

Eden, C. (1991) Working on problems using cognitive mapping. In S. C. Littlechild and M. Shutler (Eds) *Operations Research in Management*. London: Prentice Hall.

Eden, C. and Ackermann, F. (1993). Evaluating strategy – its role within the context of strategic control. *Journal of the Operational Research Society*, **44**.

Eden, C. and Jones, S. (1984). Using repertory grids for problem construction. *Journal of the Operational Research Society*, **35**, 779–790.

Eden, C., Ackermann, F. and Cropper, S. (1992). The Analysis of Cause Maps. *Journal of Management Studies*, **29**, 309–324.

Eden, C., Cropper, S. and Train, C. (1990). Performance and coherence: The strategy review process. Paper presented to Strategic Planning Society, February.

Eden, C., Jones, S. and Sims, D. (1979). *Thinking in Organizations*. London: Macmillan.

Eden, C., Jones, S. and Sims, D. (1983). *Messing About in Problems*. Oxford: Pergamon.

Goold, M. and Quinn, J. J. (1990). The paradox of strategic controls. *Strategic Management Journal*, **11**, 43–57.

Harvey-Jones, J. (1988). *Making it Happen*. London: Collins.

Huff, A. (Ed.) (1990). *Mapping Strategic Thought*. New York: John Wiley.

Kelly, G. A. (1955). *The Psychology of Personal Constructs*. New York: Norton.

Phillips, L. (1990). Decision analysis for group decision support. In C. Eden and J. Radford (Eds) *Tackling Strategic Problems: The Role of Group Decision Support*. London: Sage.

Pizey, H. and Huxham, C. (1991). 1990 and beyond: Developing a process for group decision support in large scale event planning. *European Journal of Operational Research*, **55**, 409–422.

Rohrbaugh, J. (1987). Paper presented to the International Symposium on Future Directions in Strategic Management, Toronto, September.

Rosenhead, J. (1989). *Rational Analysis for a Problematic World: Problem Structuring Methods for Complexity, Uncertainty and Conflict.* Chichester: Wiley.

Spender, J. C. (1989). *Industry Recipes, and Enquiry into the Nature and Sources of Managerial Judgement.* Oxford: Basil Blackwell.

Telford, W. A., Ackermann, F. and Cropper, S. (1990). Managing quality. In R. O'Moore, S. Bengtsson, J. R. Bryant and J. S. Bryden (Eds) *Medical Informatics Europe '90 – Proceedings*, Glasgow, August.

Vogel, D. and Nunamaker, J. (1990). Group decision support impact: Multi-methodological exploration. *Information and Management*, **18**, 15–28.

6

Strategic Vision at Work: Discussing Strategic Vision in Management Teams

KEES VAN DER HEIJDEN

Strategy emerges under the influence of the driving force of a strategic vision in an ever-changing and uncertain business environment. For the individual entrepreneur this is a personal process of decision-making. The entrepreneur can consult others, but personally decides and takes the risk of failure. In larger, more mature companies professional management takes over the role of the entrepreneur. In most cases the responsibility for strategic decision-making becomes shared in a management team. The underlying driving force is no longer a personal, but a shared vision, arrived at through communicating and modifying personal views in the team through a conversational process.

The strategic vision requires adjustment in times of change. When important outside parameters change, the corporate direction may have to change with it, if the organisation is to survive. When change is rapid the vision-sharing process needs to speed up too.

Strategic Thinking: Leadership and the Management of Change.
Edited by J. Hendry and G. Johnson with J. Newton.
Copyright © 1993 the Strategic Management Society. Published 1993 John Wiley & Sons Ltd.

Some teams have proven more skilful at arriving at commonality of view than others. A lot depends on the composition of the team. Roles in management teams are often divided along functional lines and managers come to the team from very different backgrounds. The different views brought to the management table can be the source of enhanced corporate awareness of environmental change, if the process is successful, or it can be the source of political in-fighting and decision paralysis.

This chapter discusses the conditions for an effective strategic conversation process in a management team, resulting in a suggested format of a vision statement, which enhances the chances of success.

PERSONAL AND CORPORATE VISION AS DRIVING FORCES

In day-to-day language vision is associated with notions such as broad world-view, deep understanding/insight and future orientation. 'Vision' is mostly attributed to individual people, although a common or shared vision is often associated with a cohesive group of people, for instance a management team.

Individual vision is closely related to the tendency of the conscious human mind to mentally rehearse 'pathways into the future'. These establish in the mind what David Ingvar has called 'memories of the future'. Ingvar's (1985) research shows that these act as filters to incoming information, and determine how the world around is understood. In this model every human being is visionary, albeit in different degrees of breadth. (As Ingvar has shown, mental health break-down often seems related to a pathological impoverishment of the set of 'memories of the future' available for interpretation of the world. A broad repertoire of 'memories of the future' seems a prerequisite for effective functioning in the world.)

Entrepreneurs bring their envisioning to the business situation. Schumpeter (1947) defined entrepreneurship as the activity to develop new profitable business opportunities by combining resources in a new way. This implies an *a priori* vision in the mind of the entrepreneur of a 'new world' after the application of the entrepreneurial invention, advantageous to the entrepreneur on the basis of a novel business.

In larger, more mature companies professional management takes over the role of the entrepreneur. In most cases the responsibility for strategic decision-making becomes shared in a management team. The underlying driving force is no longer a personal, but a shared vision, arrived at through communicating and modifying personal views in the team through a conversational process.

The power of this driving force is encountered by strategy analysts employed by management. Interestingly, it is often experienced by them as standing in the way of implementation of new strategy. From the analyst's perspective, they have been hired in order to contribute to a better understanding of the relevant world of business, but management seems to be reluctant to feel committed to specific strategies derived on the basis of such expert analytical understanding. For example, the danger of strategic rigidity is a popular theme for chief executive officers 'CEOs' speaking at strategy conferences (e.g. C. J. Van De Klught, CEO of Philips, at the SMS conference in 1988, and P. Barnevick, CEO of ABB at the SMS conference in 1990).

Quinn (1980) observed that most important strategic decisions are made outside the formal planning structure. Mintzberg (1987) described strategy, as he observed it, as emergent, mostly not planned. Donaldson and Lorsch (1983) observed that sudden and rapid major strategy shifts do not occur very often. The process is incremental and each step is relatively small: 'Managers draw upon their experience and judgement, shaped by shared beliefs, which include those passed on to them by their predecessors. Their decisions reflect non-rational aspects, because they have been filtered through these belief systems.'

Our observations in many years of strategic research confirm these views. Decisions are strongly influenced by the shared visions of the managers involved, and rational strategic analysis is by no means the only determinant of the outcome.

OTHER INTERPRETATIONS OF THE VISION CONCEPT

The term 'strategic vision' is used in many different connotations. The following are examples that contrast with the meaning adopted in this chapter.

VALUES

Vision is often discussed in terms of a set of predispositions and values in a broad sense that lead to the proposal or acceptance of one set of ideas rather than another. In this chapter we adopt a somewhat narrower definition in which the vision contains an entrepreneurial idea. The term 'strategic vision' here denotes a view of the future of the company in terms of its business idea, size, scope, success formula, etc. In this sense vision is an entrepreneurial notion, something that will indicate direction for action. Although often tacitly held it can in principle be expressed rationally, based on 'potential for surplus creation' which can be analysed, discussed and improved.

Often a vision statement is designed more as a cultural artefact in the company, to provide a unifying concept of cultural unity and cohesion in the organisation and to increase motivation and commitment. In this interpretation alternative words used include 'values', 'credo', 'code of conduct', 'ideals', 'a dream', often containing business ethics overtones (Campbell and Yeung, 1991). A feature of such statements is often that they contain self-evident truths, which are nevertheless held to have cultural value, but which do not contribute to rational decision-making processes. For example:

- a company that our people are proud of (e.g. Levi Strauss)
- duty of the manufacturer to serve man's happiness (e.g. Matsushita)
- constant respect for people (e.g. Motorola)
- contributing to public good and quality of life (e.g. Sainsbury)
- be the customer's first choice (e.g. Norske Shell).

In this chapter a more directionally significant model is aimed at. In order to be useful, a vision statement, in the sense used here, must meet the test that its opposite would also be meaningful as a vision statement.

DRIVING FORCE

Tregoe and Zimmerman (1989) argue that a vision should identify a driving force, a governing concept or mind-set that provides focus in making choices. A company must make a decision on the perspective from which the strategic vision will be approached, which can be one of four:

- offered product driven
- served market driven
- asset/capability driven
- return/profit driven.

From the account Tregoe and Zimmerman give of their work these categories inspire powerful questions for strategists to ponder. However, making a choice of perspective in the way they propose does not constitute defining a strategic vision in the sense used in this chapter. What is missing is the explicit causal link with entrepreneurial surplus creation potential, i.e. how the choice of driving force leads to such a potential.

STRATEGIC INTENT

Hamel and Prahalad (1989) have introduced another element in the debate about strategic vision with the notion of 'strategic intent', which they contrast with 'strategic fit', as follows:

Strategic fit	*Strategic intent*
Search for niches	Search for new rules
Portfolio of businesses	Portfolio of competences
Products/channels/customers	Core competences/relationships
Find sustainable advantage	Accelerate learning
Trim ambitions to resources	Leverage resources to reach goals
Financial targets	Strategic challenges

The message here is that in devising strategic vision one should avoid being unconsciously curtailed by traditional concepts. The strategic vision needs to be grounded in an entrepreneurial idea, which cannot be found in the traditional thinking style of 'strategic fit', but which needs to be newly invented.

While strategic intent makes an important contribution to the understanding of strategic vision, it is not the same thing, as long as it does not give an account of how the intent statement will lead to a structure with surplus creating potential.

INTERACTION IN MANAGEMENT TEAMS

A corporate strategic vision is defined here as an image of the enterprise in the future after realisation of its entrepreneurial idea. Its effectiveness in guiding the decision-making process will depend on the degree to which it is subscribed to by all key contributors to decisions, i.e. the people with the power to act.

Most strategic decision-making in corporations is a group activity. Many contribute towards building the case, defending positions and questioning assumptions.

Members of the same management team will initially have different views of where to go. Even if a political compromise on action is reached this does not imply an alignment of visions. Vision cannot be changed by force but only by a change of insight. For this reason attempts in organisations to align strongly held personal visions tend to be based on appeals to rational resolution of differences. If management teams fail to do this, individuals will resort to 'political' means to pursue their own vision, leaving the company as a whole without a sense of direction, and therefore less skilful in reacting to environmental change.

Alignment of strategic visions through rational argumentation is achieved through a conversational process. People continuously influence each other's 'memories of the future'. Strategic management therefore is concerned with many visions active and interacting at the same time. This is often a complex process:

- Visions tend to be tacit, taken for granted, they are seldom made explicit, they operate in the background.
- Visions are resistant to change. Because they filter outside signals by providing the framework for attributing meaning, those signals indicating a need for significant change often will tend to stay outside the field of view. Generally only the experience of 'pain' can override this feedback loop, and create the circumstances for a real and dramatic change in view.

People who have come together to run a business transfer elements of their views of the future of the corporation to each other. Through networked communication, elements of vision circulate among them in an iterative process. If this is strong enough, vision becomes a cultural phenomenon. However, the sharing process is time-consuming, depending on how successfully conversation on long-term vision competes with dealing with day-to-day problems. A shared vision will change even more slowly than an individual vision.

If the business environment changes faster than the vision consensus building process, a divergence will open up between required and actual speed of response. In these circumstances the corporation's ability to learn faster than competitors will create competitive advantage (De Geus, 1988).

The evolution of the shared vision results from a conversational process. The speed of evolution depends on the effectiveness of communication, driven by external pressures or by the joint determination to achieve alignment. Faster change requires more dynamic alignment of visions, through a more effective process of communication. Individual visions as such need not be rational, but attempts in organisations to make others change theirs are mostly based on appeals to rationality (in terms of making conscious choices among alternatives following deliberation). Processes designed to achieve alignment within a team tend to be drafted on rational argument. This requires making the vision explicit and thereby more amenable to discussion and joint analysis.

Such a conversational process requires a shared vision language in which the vision can be expressed. For this language to emerge a few conditions need to be met:

- The power of vision as the major driving force in the corporate strategic decision-making process should be commonly appreciated.
- There should be agreement on the categories in which the vision needs to be expressed.
- There needs to be a common meta-level world-view on purpose and meaning, through which shared reasons why one vision might be better than another can emerge.

THE WORLD-VIEW SUPPORTING STRATEGIC VISION

Rational discussion requires a common understanding of meaning based on a shared world-view. In this section we explore the question of the world-view of people coming together to develop an entrepreneurial idea in a corporate organisation.

It seems plausible that at a deep level common ground can be found in most organisations, whatever the diversity in opinion at a more superficial level. Douglas (1986) has argued that institutions could not persist unless established by such a shared cognitive device. Mutual convenience in multiple transactions does not seem enough to cause the degree of commitment that institutions typically require from their members. Convenience alone does not create enough certainty about the other person's strategies to justify the degree of trust required. This trust needs to be established on the basis of a deeper assumption on how the institutional world works.

Generally, metaphor is used to understand one element of experience in terms of another. Douglas has found that stable institutions require a shared understanding of the institutional world based on analogy between the structure of its social relations and a structure found in nature.

Morgan (1986) gives examples of how many of our taken-for-granted ideas about organisations are metaphorical, allowing people to quickly perceive how to act skilfully in otherwise complex and paradoxical organisational life. Some grounded-in-nature metaphors in common use include: machines, cultures (in terms of growing a crop), instruments of domination, self-organising brains, living organisms. If the organisation is interpreted as a machine or as a culture, strategic vision becomes a design concept, a predetermined blueprint to be exactly implemented. If it is seen as an instrument of domination, strategic vision is an authoritarian statement of political will. If it is seen as a self-organising brain, strategic vision is an emerging property.

Dominant metaphors tend to change over the lifetime of a company. In the early stages, when ownership and entrepreneurial idea are closely linked, the organisation tends to be seen as an instrument serving the purpose as defined by its owner. Purpose is defined outside the organisation itself. In more mature companies where ownership and management become separated, purpose is no longer based on the external owner, but becomes generated and defined internally. Metaphors evolve towards either power-related or organic models.

The subject of this chapter is the management team attempting to come to a shared vision as a basis for action. The underlying model for this behaviour is the organic metaphor, as distinct from more power or aesthetics driven analogues. Characteristic for the organic metaphor is harmonious co-operation between semi-autonomous functions, serving the internally generated dual purpose of self-development, unless threatened, when survival becomes dominant. For example, organisations adopting the organic metaphor will give priority to the organisation's ability to be aware of it's environment, in order to perceive developing threats as early as possible.

The organic institutional metaphor generally provides a common world-view as a basis for rational conversation of strategic vision. The dual objective set – survival/self-development – provides an effective rationale for discussing the relative merits of alternatives.

RENT-DRIVEN VISION

A rational discussion of a strategic vision in an organically oriented management team will focus on assessment in terms of scope for company development (or survival) as a first priority. In a competitive market development is not guaranteed. How can management think about shaping the company to enhance its developmental chances?

Development implies the creation of a surplus. This excess of income over cost can find its way into financial or into hard and/or invisible assets, with the potential of increasing the company's strength and enhancing its chances in a competitive world.

In the context of strategic vision we are particularly interested in the longer-term structural underpinning of the surplus creation potential, not its operational implementation. In this chapter we use the term 'economic rent' for this longer-term structural potential. Forces of competition drive to destroy rent, but encounter friction forces in many different forms, generally slowing down the process.

Rent can be a feature of a market or industry, if the friction forces are of an industry structure nature. Individual companies may exploit rent related to such industry structures.

We therefore come to the conclusion that an effective and convincing vision expression will clarify the relationship between the desired developmental direction and end-stage of the company on the one hand, and its surplus creation potential, or rent, on the other. Comparison between two visions then takes the form of assessing their relative rent potentials, and the higher-quality vision will be the one with the superior rent expectation.

As we see the vision as a conversational tool in an institutional dialogue, the vision statement needs to go beyond an assertion of rent potential, to give an account of how the proposed structure will enhance the potential for surplus. The vision needs to have the power to convince people that the proposed future is not a 'pipe-dream' but that a feasible process can be envisaged which will cause its realisation.

STRUCTURAL SURPLUS POTENTIAL (RENT)

To meet the effectiveness criteria developed in this chapter, a vision needs to contain an entrepreneurial business idea, which addresses the rent question. For the purpose of this discussion it is convenient to distinguish two elements in this: (1) the identification of an area of economic activity or market, where economic rent will occur due to specific supply/demand features; and (2) the development of a business positioned to exploit this rent area.

Social change and entrepreneurial invention cause new market rent areas to emerge continuously. On the other hand, rent areas do not survive forever, but erode over time. Rumelt (1987) has identified the conditions creating a new market rent area:

- The emergence of an entrepreneurial invention, either in the Schumpeterean sense of a new combination of resources, or in the form of creation of a new market (new combination of demand).
- The business idea must be socially efficient, providing an increment in value over substitutes.
- The envisioned business must be able to resist appropriation of rents by buyers, sellers, owners of cospecialised assets and government.
- The envisioned business must have some protection against competitive imitation.

Rent implies 'friction forces' in the market protecting against such competitive imitation. Rumelt (1987) suggests these can take the following forms:

- property rights
- barriers to knowledge leakage
- producer learning, experience effects
- response lags, particularly when competitors are reluctant to 'cannibalise' existing businesses

- economies of scale, relative to size of market
- buyer evaluation and switching cost
- reputation
- channel crowding.

The combination of (1) a socially efficient entrepreneurial idea, and (2) a market with friction forces against imitation, will create a market rent area in which an individual business can try to develop a position that will give it a structural surplus potential.

COMPANY RENT

Teece (1986) has shown that friction forces as listed above ultimately derive from two sources: (1) sunk irreversible investments, and (2) uncodified institutional knowledge and skill, embedded in its networked people and processes. The two factors together constitute the company's set of visible and invisible assets that are the basis of its distinctive resources and competences. Because these are specific to the company, they cannot be copied by the competition, and therefore protect entrepreneurial ideas against rent-destroying competition and/or appropriation.

Exploitation of a rent area takes the form of increasing the value creation potential of customer systems (social efficiency, see above) by bringing to bear such competences. Because these are distinctive the company makes a unique value contribution to its customers, for which a rent price can be charged. Therefore creating company rent means building and maintaining distinctive resources/ competences.

How can a company go about building distinctive competences? It is obvious that there cannot be a codified method of doing this. Knowledge that is available to everybody cannot be a source of rent. For example, it does not seem possible to acquire rent by buying distinctive resources/competences (e.g. by acquisition) without paying a price which negates it (Schoemaker, 1990). On the other hand, a deficiency in knowledge that is generally available may be a source of 'negative rent'. Companies need to deploy all relevant available knowledge as a strategic necessity. But it does not lead to the generation of positive rent, on which a strategic vision can be based.

We may set out to invent new unique competences, but others try to do the same thing. We may be more lucky than our competitors – there is no doubt that luck is an important factor in rent creation. The ability of the company to be more open to unexpected developments that its competitors can be a rent-creating distinctive competence. A company may consider its distinctive creative culture as a source of rent. But luck as such is not a useful component in the rationale for a strategic vision. Vision needs to leave room for the unexpected, but it cannot entirely depend on it. The assumption of serendipity as such seldom convinces others.

By definition the only source of uniqueness in the company are its existing distinctive competences. Therefore new distinctive resources/competences can intentionally be created only by means of entrepreneurial ideas using and building on whatever existing distinctive resources/competences are available (Collis, 1990). A company setting out to develop new rent areas needs first of all to develop a clear idea of what its existing distinctiveness is, and then develop ideas to build on that.

This notion of developing distinctive competences on the basis of building on existing distinctive competences is the key towards creating a high-quality strategic vision. It needs to show the relationship between:

- the business idea
- the existing distinctive resources/competences
- the use of these for the development of new distinctive resources/ competences
- through this principle the building of sufficient isolating mechanisms around the new business to ensure a sound rent structure.

Intentional ex-ante creation of rent out of nothing does not seem possible. It has to result from the combination of a business idea with the existing unique elements already present in the existing state of the company. In this sense history is important in strategic vision.

Large companies are likely to have a larger stock of distinctive competences than small ones and consequently may find it easier to build on this larger base in an evolutionary process. On the other hand, small companies may find it easier to maintain a culture open to the unexpected and be more competent in recognising and developing the unexpected rent areas emerging from discontinuities in societal development.

THE ELEMENTS OF STRATEGIC VISION

Following this line of thought the following elements need to be discussed in a constructive institutional vision debate:

- Description of the perceived business environment, in particular societal developments leading to discontinuities and new rent ideas.
- Business definition, specifying surplus creation potential in terms of the market rent areas that the company intends to exploit. This needs to be defined as the value creation potential of a customer base that the company will leverage through its distinctive resources/competences.
- Description of the distinctive resources/competences existing now in the company, or capable of development through the use of the existing set.
- Understanding of the constraints to imitation, making the resources/competences distinctive, and this distinctiveness sustainable.
- Understanding of a feasible path through time from now to where we hope to arrive, always building new distinctiveness through the use of existing distinctiveness (the 'formula for success').

All this to lead to a definition of a successful high rent future 'end-state' of the company, which can serve as a feasible and communicable target to aim for.

Normally, in an institutional context there will be a number of competing entrepreneurial vision proposals to compare. The above format provides a language in which relative merits can be discussed focusing on the rent structure expectations of the proposals. In this way objective and rational criteria are used to measure the potential towards the shared goal of survival/development of the company. Through this process the chances of converging towards a common understanding, and therefore institutional learning and progress, are enhanced.

The basic point of this chapter is self-reflexive. It is suggested that the strategic vision might itself address the ability to develop a better strategic vision, as a distinctive competence in its own right, leading to rent. Companies may consider how, through the use of the methodology suggested here, they can build on their existing capabilities to develop strategic visions, including:

- skilful perception of the outside world and business environment
- rational expression and sharing of business ideas
- building on existing distinctive competences.

ACKNOWLEDGEMENT

The author wishes to acknowledge the contribution to this chapter by members of Group Planning in Shell International Petroleum Co., London, through numerous in-depth discussions of the subject.

REFERENCES

Campbell, A. and Yeung, S. (1991). Creating a sense of mission. *Long Range Planning*, **24**, 10–20.
Collis, D. J. (1990). A theory of profit. Paper presented to SMS conference.
De Geus, A. (1988). Planning as learning. *Harvard Business Review*, **66**, 70–74.
Donaldson, G. and Lorsch, J. W. (1983). *Decision Making at the Top*. New York: Basic Books.
Douglas, M. (1986). *How Institutions Think*. New York: Syracuse University Press.
Hamel, G. and Prahalad, C. K. (1989). Strategic intent. *Harvard Business Review*, **67**, 63–76.
Ingvar, D. (1985). Memories of the future, an essay on the temporal organisation of conscious awareness. *Human Neurobiology*, **4**, 127–136.
Mintzberg, H. (1987). Crafting strategy. *Harvard Business Review*, **65**, 66–75.
Morgan, G. (1986). *Images of Organisations*. Beverly Hills, CA: Sage Publications.
Quinn, J. B. (1980). *Strategies for Change: Logical Incrementalism*. Illinois: Irwin.
Rumelt, R. P. (1987). Theory, strategy and entrepreneurship. In D. J. Teece (Ed.) *The Competitive Challenge* (pp. 137–158). Cambridge MA: Ballinger Publishing Company.
Schoemaker, P. J. A. (1990). Strategy, complexity and economic rent. *Management Science*, **36**, 1178–1192.
Schumpeter, J. A. (1947). *Capitalism, Socialism and Democracy*, 2nd rev. edn. London: Allen and Unwin.
Teece, D. J. (1986). Firm boundaries, technological innovation and strategic management. In L. G. Thomas (Ed.) *The Economics of Strategic Planning*, Lexington, MA: Lexington Books.
Tregoe, B. B. and Zimmerman, J. W. (1989). *Vision in Action*. London: Simon & Schuster.

Section II

Strategic Action

7

Strategic Management and Organizational Learning: A Meta-theory of Executive Leadership

R. THOMAS LENZ

When persons in positions of leadership are asked about what they do to lead their organizations, the answer is more often than not, 'Well, it all depends . . .'. Further questioning about individual actions and tasks usually results in the distinct impression that the work of top-level executives is so varied and situation-specific that it has no order or regularities.

The purpose of this chapter is to contribute to the body of theory about the nature of managerial work at the most senior levels of organizations. It is suggested that there is, in fact, an underlying structure in the day-to-day work activities of top managers. The major thesis is that seemingly independent actions and tasks of persons in such positions invariably exhibit one of only five basic patterns. Each pattern can be thought of as a distinct type of influence process that has a particular effect on the rate and nature of organizational learning.

Strategic Thinking: Leadership and the Management of Change.
Edited by J. Hendry and G. Johnson with J. Newton.
Copyright © 1993 the Strategic Management Society. Published 1993 John Wiley & Sons Ltd.

The five patterns postulated are not all equally effective. One of these, 'officeholding', has been defined previously by Thompson (1967). It is a pattern of *in*effective leadership that occurs as persons in top management positions take actions that constrain organizational learning and, thereby, impair the adaptive capacities of their enterprises. A contingency framework is used to identify and explain four additional patterns. All of these are effective, though quite different in the way they influence learning among members of organizations and external constituents.

Before discussing patterns exhibited in the work of senior-level executives and their implications for the task of leading strategic change, it is necessary to establish some basic assumptions about the work context, and administrative function and responsibilities of top management.

THE ADMINISTRATIVE FUNCTION AND WORK OF ORGANIZATION LEADERS

The work of leaders is inherently prescriptive in nature and, in contrast to that of managers, is concerned with fostering more or less continuous change (Burns, 1978; Kotter, 1990). It involves diagnosing situations, determining what needs to be done and marshaling collective effort sufficient to achieve a desired future or avert significant problems. The specific actions involved in leading vary from one context to another.

DECISION PROCESSES: THE ARENA OF EXECUTIVE WORK

With respect to the unique role of senior-level executives, Thompson (1967) suggests that the primary function of leadership is to reach and sustain coalignment among a few factors that are critically important to the long-term growth and development of an enterprise in a changing environment. Among these are resources, strategy, and the administrative structure and operating technology or technologies of a firm. In this way of thinking, performance of this administrative function is the rationale for the existence of top management and the principal means by which senior-level executives 'add value' to the ongoing life of an organization.

Leaders work to foster change within the continuous flow of decision-making that occurs throughout a hierarchy, and among organizational members and other stakeholders. It is here, via debate, dialogue, and 'enactment' (Weick, 1979) that individuals and groups formulate problems and opportunities and determine how these can be solved or exploited. This process of defining both adaptive and preemptive strategic actions is incremental, and informed by a succession of shared beliefs and values (Quinn, 1980; Hedberg, 1981; Lyles, 1981). Conceived in this way, organizations are problem-finding, problem-solving entities, and inter and intraorganizational decision-making processes are the central mechanisms of change and adaptation. This continuous flow of decision-making is the arena in which leaders exert leadership and organizational learning occurs. From it originates the impetus for collective action that is basic to organizational survival (Cyert and March, 1963; Thompson, 1967).

If decision-making processes are the central mechanisms of organizational change and if top management is primarily responsible for managing change, what is executive leadership?

Executive Leadership: As Influence Processes

Executive leadership can be defined as an influence process. It entails two closely related activities: (1) the use of power and persuasion to define and determine the changing constellation of problems and opportunities that comprise the working agenda of an organization, and (2) the solutions produced and actions taken by individuals and groups both inside and outside an organization to cope with such issues. The process of leadership is manifest in day-to-day actions taken toward the realization of top management's preferred goals (see Greiner and Bhambri, 1989; Westley and Mintzberg, 1989).

If executive leadership can be usefully thought of as an influence process revealed in the performance of discrete but related tasks, two matters of theoretical and very 'practical' importance become apparent. First, what is the spectrum of discretionary factors that can be legitimately employed by leaders to influence an organization's agenda of problems and opportunities and the outcomes of decisions its members make with respect to these? Identification of such factors makes possible informed speculation about the relative intensity, or invasiveness, of leaders' actions in organizational decision processes. A second, and equally important, matter is learning whether the tasks and actions that comprise influence processes exhibit regularities or recurring patterns. Should such patterns exist and be few in number, they might serve as starting places for continued theory-building about the phenomenon of executive leadership, and improvements in leadership development and administrative practice.

THE EXERCISE OF DISCRETION IN ORGANIZATIONAL DECISION-MAKING PROCESSES

The purpose of exercising influence in organizational decision-making processes is to foster learning on behalf of organizational members and facilitate change. Strategic change, in any practical sense, requires modifying 'behavior programs' (Simon, 1976; Starbuck, 1984) of individuals and groups. This, in turn, involves altering shared goals, understandings, and expectations.

Generally, learning occurs in one of three ways: (1) replace some or all organizational members; (2) employ logic and reasoning to convince persons to change what they do; and/or (3) alter contingencies of the work environment to provide organizational members with new experiences that result in changed expectations and definitions of desired behavior. Sustaining coalignment within a changing institutional context involves the use of discretionary variables to accelerate, decelerate or stabilize the rate of learning that occurs in accordance with prevailing environmental conditions (Nystrom and Starbuck, 1976). By implication, then, effective leaders must at different times be more or less aggressive and invasive in decision-making processes in order to affect the rate and nature of organization-wide learning.

DISCRETIONARY VARIABLES

For the most part, leaders have discretion over two general spheres of action that can affect the magnitude of influence they exert. The first is their *personal role* in organizational decision processes, and the second sphere is the extent to which they alter the *work environment* of organization members. (For a fuller explication of the concept of managerial discretion see Hambrick and Finkelstein, 1987.)

There is a wide spectrum of roles organizational leaders can play as they seek to influence the agenda of an organization and the outcomes of multilevel organizational decision processes. At one extreme is that of a coach and teacher who remains deep in the administrative background and works through others in seeking to manage a broad-based learning process. In this mode of action, senior-level executives deflect credit for achievements away from themselves. Organizational successes are attributed to empowered role models and described as accomplishments stemming from the efforts of all. At the other extreme is a leader who takes on the mantle of 'hero' or 'messiah'. Such an individual positions himself or herself as the central protagonist of organizational drama and origin of ideas and actions crucial to the future of an enterprise. Successes are made to be seen as personal, not organizational, achievements.

A second discretionary sphere pertains to factors comprising the daily work environment of organization members. These include, but are not limited to: formal organization structure, the operational distribution of power, reward systems, information and reporting systems, formal decision-making processes (e.g. strategic planning, budgeting, capital investment, human resource planning), staffing assignments, standing and *ad hoc* committee structures, definition of role models, and organizational ideology. The more invasive a leader is in exercising influence on the work environment, the more of these factors are likely to be changed and to a greater degree. An evolutionary approach to fostering learning and change entails gradual adjustments to such factors. In contrast, radical alteration usually produces organizational revolution.

Since leaders can, of their own volition, vary the degree of invasiveness in decision processes and, thereby, the rate of organizational learning and change, what factors account for these variations?

A CONTINGENCY FRAMEWORK

Two relatively independent factors account for most of the variation in the degree of invasiveness of effective executives in organizational decision processes: (1) the *density of administrative and technical competence* among managerial and technical personnel, and (2) a *leader's sense of urgency* for initiating change. By joining these factors, it is possible to construct a contingency framework. FIGURE 7.1 consists of four patterns of leadership (i.e. influence processes). Each pattern involves a set of discrete yet related actions in which a leader's role and degree of aggressiveness in altering the work environment of organizational members differs. Common

		Orchestrated learning	Execute now
Density of administration and technical competence	Sufficient	● Managing interacting processes ● Contributing ideas ● Building vocabularies, shaping understandings ● Empowering role models ● Serving as coach, teacher, confessor	● Setting a vision and goals ● Defining a strategic agenda ● Moving quickly ● Encouraging learning by doing ● Intense personal involvement ● Emphasis on implementation
		Orderly transition	Shock treatment
	Insufficient	● Cultural evolution ● Signaling the need for change and its implications ● Arranging succession to new role models ● Encouraging graceful exits ● Protecting operating core and external dependencies	● Cultural revolution ● Quickly replacing key personnel ● Centralizing decision-making ● Establishing performance goals and responsibilities ● Redirecting resources
		Low	High

LEADER'S SENSE OF URGENCY

FIGURE 7.1   Alternative influence processes for leading organizational change

to each process is fostering learning. However, the manner in which this occurs, its effect on the rate of learning, and the risks associated with each approach vary greatly.

The 'density of administrative competence' of an enterprise is central to organizational success (March, 1974). It is individuals in key managerial and technical positions who provide creative energy, execute essential behavior programs, and function as 'leverage points' (Gergen, 1968) for the control of resources. Of central importance is whether the capabilities of individuals in such roles are sufficient for formulating and resolving emerging issues, problems and challenges. If requisite competence exists, or can be fostered via learning, it may not be necessary to replace personnel in order to effect change. On the other hand, if the capabilities of such persons are insufficient for tasks ahead and new learning is not feasible, replacement may be necessary.

A second factor that can be used to discriminate among influence processes is a leader's perceived sense of urgency for making change. Generally, one's sense of urgency varies in accordance with the magnitude of problems and opportunities confronted, considered in the context of the estimated period within which these must be resolved or exploited. The expectation of long lead times for altering factors such as corporate culture, operations technology, external institutional dependencies, and financial resources, coupled with a limited 'window of opportunity', typically increases the sense of urgency. When such circumstances do not prevail, one's sense of urgency is less and leaders can proceed at a more deliberate pace.

ORCHESTRATED LEARNING

Orchestrated learning is a leadership influence process in which the primary focus of senior-level executive work is the administrative system or 'design' (Nystrom and Starbuck, 1976) of the organization. It is recognized as interacting processes that foster continuous, organization-wide learning. Leaders concentrate most of their 'executive work' (Barnard, 1938) on evolving a system that attracts and retains talented persons, elicits commitment and creativity, and produces actions necessary for continuous adaptation.

Orchestrated learning is viable when there are managerial and technical personnel whose capabilities are sufficient for formulating and solving relevant problems, and when a leader's sense of urgency is rather low. Such conditions are typical of a well-managed, profitable enterprise that has significant lead-time and financial resources for making necessary changes. Organizations of this kind are usually managed within a relatively sophisticated ideological system; have widely shared values that assure a sufficient level of administrative competence; an organization structure and reward system that results in individual and organizational goal congruence; and effective and efficient multilevel decision processes.

This leadership process places senior-level executives in the roles of teacher, coach and consultant. Of especial importance is adding value as an idea generator who helps individuals and groups develop concepts and vocabularies that lead to new understandings (Nonaka, 1991). This more-or-less continuous reframing process depends on patient coaching, providing encouragement, teaching and a willingness to absorb the occasional sense of ambiguity and self-doubt experienced by others.

Organizational learning is fostered via participation in decision processes designed to involve a broad base of persons. The intent is to help both individuals and groups discover emerging strategic problems and opportunities *for themselves*, formulate viable solutions and undertake collective action. In this way, capabilities are continually transformed and organizational adaptation occurs.

Leadership of this type is decidedly aheroic. Thus, those employing it are often unrecognized outside of their organizations for their skill. Their work is behind the scenes, directed at affecting the work environment, and making other individuals highly visible role models. Despite their frequent anonymity, such leaders may be among the most effective leaders.

EXECUTE NOW

This leadership pattern is suited to circumstances in which there is a high density of managerial and technical competence and when a leader senses a high degree of urgency to take action. These conditions typically exist in a well-managed organization whose competitive situation is threatened. Such change could originate from market entry of a product or service substitute; the introduction of a new process technology or raw material; rapid restructuring of up and/or down stream industries; a change in the regulatory environment; or sudden elimination of mobility barriers. A leader has talented personnel to work with, but very little time to implement necessary strategic changes.

Due to the perceived sense of urgency, there is little or no time to initiate broad-based organizational learning processes. Yet, there is a need to emotionally and mentally engage key persons in decision processes central to adaptive organizational responses. Thus, in the execute now influence process, senior management itself defines the initial agenda of strategic problems and opportunities, and quickly focuses key personnel in implementing solutions.

The role of a senior-level manager is that of intense personal leadership – assertive, directive, supportive and deeply involved (see Noel, 1989). The leader's attention centers primarily on a top management team that learns by doing. Major elements of a strategic vision for the organization are explained and made tangible and credible as problems and opportunities related to its implementation are confronted and resolved. This influence process is goal-oriented, concentrated, and usually fast-paced. Leaders depend on the top management team to marshal support and cooperation in their respective areas and, thereby, quickly move implementation throughout an organization's new or existing administrative system.

In this mode, top management originates an organization's strategic vision. Typically, only the top management teams and, perhaps, a few key middle-level managers are empowered to act. Other organization members are considered to be, essentially, implementors of senior management's vision. Execute now is an influence pattern that assumes a leader can originate a succession of strategic goals suited to evolving institutional and competitive contingencies. Hence, the proximate locus of strategic learning is the leader or top management team.

Orderly Transition

In this condition, a leader's sense of urgency is low and the current and potential capabilities of key personnel are clearly *in*sufficient for coming to grips with what will be demanded of them to effect strategic change. Organizations whose adaptive capacity has atrophied, though these still maintain prominent or even dominant market positions, are often associated with an orderly transition influence process.

Successful execution of this type of leadershp requires considerable skill, an acute sense of timing, persistence and patience. The central administrative challenge is to manage a complex cultural evolution. Key personnel must be replaced – usually with individuals from outside the organization. This is accomplished while avoiding a disturbance of the culture and day-to-day operations that would disorient other organizational personnel and, thereby, adversely affect market image, external institutional dependencies, and profitability. If this transition is not orderly, in this sense, employee morale declines, suppliers and customers lose confidence, and the organization, instead of going forward, may suffer a setback.

Since managerial and technical competence is insufficient for managing change, participatory decision processes are not a viable option. A leader cannot adopt the role of teacher and coach. Instead, he or she must play a twofold role: (1) signaling about the emerging strategic challenges and their implications, as well as (2) counseling individuals in senior and middle-level management positions targeted for outplacement.

Executives take every opportunity to signal to organizational members that emerging competitive realities indicate that business cannot go on as usual. Every effort is made to identify 'weak signals' (Ansoff, 1980), and interpret and amplify their strategic and career implications for organizational members. To lend credence to such revelations, selective reductions in force and curtailment of certain noncritical expenditures are usually made. Leaders, to sustain their own credibility, must make such changes in ways that show they 'had no choice'. Irresistible competitive pressures, not personal administrative choice, must be seen as necessitating such 'painful decisions'. The point of all of this is to undermine the past without declaring overtly that it was deficient or reflected incompetent management practices (despite the fact that both may be true). With these tactics, desirable aspects of the current culture can be carried forward as a basis for evolving a new, more resilient enterprise.

The task of counseling those destined for outplacement is time-consuming and uncertain. It must be kept in mind that, unless there is widespread sentiment that current management is incompetent, replacement of top managers is equivalent to destruction of corporate role models. Such individuals are of great symbolic importance and typically associated with a firm's previous achievements and future prospects. It is necessary, therefore, to create conditions in which those to be replaced choose to leave – i.e. the goal is graceful exits in which dignity is preserved. If this can be done, a leader's reputation as a well-intentioned, magnanimous, forward-looking individual grows.

SHOCK TREATMENT

Shock treatment is a leadership pattern suited to circumstances in which the density of administrative and technical competence of an enterprise is *in*sufficient for finding and solving emerging strategic issues, and when a leader's sense of urgency is high. Such circumstances are often present in turnaround situations when a new leader from outside an organization is appointed chief executive officer (CEO). Usually, the adaptive capacity of an organization has atrophied; slack resources are exhausted; competitors are eroding market share; and suppliers are losing confidence in an organization's ability to survive. A scenario such as this requires dramatic action.

There is no time for unlearning and new learning via broad-based participatory decision processes. Instead, top management must replace key managerial personnel as a means for unlearning and avoiding total collapse. Leaders in such situations typically move very quickly. Their goal is to get all of the 'bad news' out of the way as rapidly as possible, so that the new management team's attention and energy can be directed toward formulating and implementing strategic change. If the leader has a viable strategic vision in mind, the new management team is usually hired and told to implement. If a CEO does not have a fully developed strategy, newly hired managers are first charged with conducting in-depth assessments of their areas of responsibility and bringing forth proposed action programs. The leader becomes immersed in detailed operational and strategic assessments, but not in a way that would usurp the authority or administrative discretion of the newly hired management team.

The basic challenge of this process is to undertake a rapid revolution of corporate culture. In this section, a series of shocks are usually delivered to the prevailing culture – otherwise, it is impossible to establish leadership and demonstrate that fundamental change is coming. Actions typically center on dismissal of existing role models, reprioritizing budget allocations, redirecting capital investment plans, setting new goals, reductions in force, reorganization and changes in reward systems, and aggressive participation in formal organizational decision processes. The purpose of these actions is to temporarily disorient organizational members and rapidly introduce elements of a new, more responsive work environment and culture before vested interests can marshal opposition. As such steps are taken, they must be accompanied by articulation of a compelling, new strategic vision. If these processes of destruction and creation are not simultaneous, persons will not be willing to make sacrifices necessary for achieving strategic change.

DISCUSSION

The foregoing is not a theory about leaders. It is instead, a rudimentary meta-theory about *leadership* – in which leadership is defined as an influence process. This process is manifest in the performance of individual actions coordinated in such a way as to affect organizational learning about the agenda of problems and opportunities that must be confronted, and the outcomes of decision-making throughout a hierarchy and among key external stakeholders. It is rooted in assumptions about the nature of organizations, the most important of which are: (1) that inter and intraorganizational decision-making processes are the central mechanisms of adaptation and the most important arena of executive action, and (2) that the primary responsibility of leaders is to sustain coalignment by fostering learning and change.

The ideas presented derive from a heretofore unstated premise that theory-building about strategic management can fruitfully proceed by engaging in concept development (i.e. conjecture) regarding the phenomenon of influence processes whose empirical referents are the day-to-day, goal-directed tasks (behaviors) of senior-level executives. It is from this premise that the thesis of the chapter derives: there exist regularities that take the form of patterns in the various tasks performed by top management. These are associated with differing degrees of invasiveness initiated by leaders into the decision-making processes of an enterprise. Variations of invasiveness, reflected in top management's role and alteration of the work environment, affect the rate of organizational learning.

A contingency framework is offered that uses two variables – density of administrative and technical competence, and a leader's perceived sense of urgency – to predict the occurrence of four different patterns of leadership. These four, when joined with Thompson's (1967) notion of 'officeholding', are postulated as the universe of underlying patterns of leadership behavior. If this is so, these patterns account for virtually all of the effective and ineffective goal-directed actions of leaders of any type of formal organization. Assertions of this sort, if correct, have potentially far-reaching implications for both scholars of leadership and senior-level executives.

IMPLICATIONS FOR SCHOLARLY RESEARCH

Popper (1968) argued that for a theory to be regarded as scientific, it must be subject to testing and refutation. Employing this criterion, the validity of the ideas offered can be determined, in part, by tests of four hypotheses and examination of several derivative research questions.

HYPOTHESES

Hypothesis 1: Organization leaders employ an *orchestrated learning* influence process when the density of administrative and technical competence is sufficient and perceived urgency is low.

Hypothesis 2: Organization leaders employ an *execute now* influence process when the density of administrative and technical competence is sufficient and perceived urgency is high.

Hypothesis 3: Organization leaders employ an *orderly transition* influence process when the density of administrative and technical competence is *in*sufficient and perceived urgency is low.

Hypothesis 4: Organization leaders employ a *shock treatment* influence process when the density of administrative and technical competence is *in*sufficient and perceived urgency is high.

THE PROSPECT OF INCOMPLETE SPECIFICATION

If this contingency theory fails to have descriptive and predictive power, it may be either incompletely specified or misspecified. Should this be the case, the following are some of the more obvious variables which could moderate the predicted relationships.

POWER AND ITS LEGITIMATE USE: NATIONS, CORPORATE CULTURE AND ORGANIZATION TYPE

The legitimate use of power is known to vary systematically with the culture of nation states, industries and organizations. This factor may, as a consequence, moderate the efficacy of the two variables appearing in FIGURE 7.1. In the case of Japan, for example, it may be that effects of behavioral norms associated with national culture are so powerful that shock treatment is not a viable influence process. In some Western countries, such as the United States, where individualism and the heroic myth are prevalent, this type of leadership process may be widespread and regarded as the accepted means for inducing rapid organizational change.

In the case of corporate culture, as opposed to national culture, deeply seated values regarding the legitimate use of power may affect the range of leadership processes that are acceptable. Similarly, the distribution of power is known to vary systematically with the type of organization. In universities, hospitals, and professional firms, such as law practices and consulting organizations, power is usually widely shared and the only viable leadership processes may be associated with the low urgency conditions of FIGURE 7.1. Thus, 'execute now' and 'shock treatment' are not within the range of leaders' discretion. Comparative research on matched pairs of organizations or nations may shed light on these issues.

ETHICAL IMPLICATIONS OF THE EXERCISE OF INFLUENCE

Many leaders, though by no means all, have a 'theory' about leadership, its prerogatives and responsibilities. Theories of this sort usually incorporate beliefs about the nature of man and a means for rationalizing or justifying moral implications of the theory when it is applied. Nature of man assumptions are usually reflected in statements such as '. . . the only way to change an organization is to . . . because people simply will not respond to other means of change . . .'. These positions usually take one of two well-known and extreme forms: (1) organizational man is self-serving and will resist any attempt to make meaningful change; therefore, key people must be replaced and steps taken must be rapid and dramatic; or (2) most persons want to do the 'right thing' and the role of leadership is to remove organizational constraints that inhibit the creative energy and organizational learning.

The moral dimension of the first position is typically reflected in the view that previous management is at fault for letting circumstances deteriorate to a critical point. Therefore, current management is not culpable, and the only humane and moral thing to do is to make painful changes quickly (e.g. shock treatment). Persons holding this view will often argue that any other alternative is irresponsible. It will only delay the inevitable and place the organization at greater risk, thus raising the prospect of total collapse that would harm all involved. It is better, therefore, to sacrifice the few than to endanger the many.

The moral dimension of the second position is usually based on the belief that organizational members should not be made to pay the price for the 'sins of the past'. Thus, the humane thing to do is to strive to sustain high employment, redevelop the capabilities of as many current personnel as possible and slowly grow the organization out of its present difficulties. If this is a leader's belief, shock treatment is considered to be morally repugnant and not within the realm of responsible executive action.

LEADERS AND ORGANIZATIONS: INTERACTING LIFE CYCLES

Leadership involves fostering change in organizational life, and both leaders and organizations exhibit life cycles. These cycles can have a profound effect on the exercise of leadership. Of particular interest here is the life-cycle phase of a leader.

One aspect of any executive's assessment of a potential organization-wide change process is a calculation of the personal career risk involved. The outcomes of processes of this sort are often difficult to predict. Therefore, if a leader perceives the risks to be excessive, he or she may opt for a change process that appears to involve lower uncertainty. For example, a CEO near the end of a career with an organization may employ a change process associated with a 'low' sense of urgency, regardless of his or her private assessment of the degree of urgency. This tactic provides the necessary appearance of action being taken, without prompting significant changes whose outcomes could prove difficuilt to manage and may have a deleterious effect on corporate earnings used to calculate bonuses, stock options and/or retirement benefits. This is an effective way to preserve face with the board and others, without placing too much at risk.

BOARD OF DIRECTORS

It is unlikely that a CEO would initiate a significant change process without first discussing it with an executive committee of a board and, subsequently, its full membership. As such discussions occur, it may become clear that members have strong opinions about the type of actions employed. These views can be motivated by a myriad of factors, such as loyalty to certain tenets of corporate culture, personal relationships with particular executives whose future status may be affected by change, a financial position in the corporation, or a member's own 'theory' of organizational change. These and many other considerations can alter the range of discretion of an organizational leader to execute a particular type of leadership process.

RESOURCE AVAILABILITY

Each of the four patterns described is based on implicit assumptions about the availability of human and financial resources; hence, some are more expensive to initiate than others. A CEO's range of discretion is often limited, in particular, by financial resources.

Shock treatment would appear, *ceteris paribus*, to be the most expensive approach to change. It often involves costly write-offs of severance pay, plant and equipment, and other extraordinary financial and accounting charges. In addition, hiring managers from outside the organization can require payment of substantial salary and bonus premiums and the need for temporary redundancy of managerial personnel. In contrast, the alternative of 'orchestrated learning' may be the least expensive and, therefore, a more viable option for a company of limited means. There is also, however, the matter of subjective estimates of long versus short-run costs. For example, shock treatment may be more expensive in the short-run but less so in the long-run. This matter is controversial, and often used as a *post hoc* rationalization of a preferred course of action.

DERIVATION RESEARCH QUESTIONS

In addition to the hypotheses are a few related research questions. Among the more important are the following.

1. *What is the range of applicability of this meta-theory?* This meta-theory was cast at the level of a whole enterprise. Does it, in addition, have descriptive and predictive power at the level of nation states, for example? If we were to consider the cases of the Soviet Union, Hungary and Poland, there appear to be distinct differences in the influence processes employed by political leaders to effect change and variation in their degrees of success. If the hypothesized patterns hold at this higher level of aggregation, the theory may have a broader scope than originally envisioned.

2. *What is the range of the behavioral repertoire of effective executives?* The task of coalignment is more or less continuous and, necessarily, the need to accelerate, decelerate or stabilize organizational learning varies with the passage of time and changing circumstance. Logic suggests that leaders whose tenure spans organizational periods characterized by significantly different contingencies would employ whatever influence process is suited to prevailing conditions. This should also happen concurrently in different divisions of large, multibusiness enterprises. But, does this actually occur?

Weick (1979) suggests that individuals 'enact' their environments. In this way of thinking, the meaning of events and experiences are assigned by individuals, they do not exist in some objective sense that makes them subject to discovery. If this is so, empirical tests may reveal that some leaders are oblivious completely or in part to the contingent variables in FIGURE 7.1.

This possibility raises an interesting implication: Do some (or all) leaders merely enact conditions that call for influence processes that they have mastered and used previously with considerable success? If so, one would expect to find that leaders are specialized in the type or range of influence processes they can successfully execute. Should such behavior occur among a large portion of the population of leaders, it would render the notion of contingent behavior as expressed previously as either irrelevant or evidence of deficiencies in leader development and training. Conversely, it may be that some leaders exhibit a behavioral repertoire that encompasses all four types of influence processes. In either case, it is important to learn why these occur and what portion of the total leader population exhibits range restriction in its leadership repertoire.

3. *Are 'orchestrated learning' and 'execute now' steady-state leadership influence processes, and 'orderly transition' and 'shock treatment' transitional processes?* Some would argue that an organization cannot survive under the continued uncertainty produced by the latter two. Therefore, these are effective only as transitional leadership processes. By implication, then, 'transformational leadership' (Burns, 1978; Tichy and Devanna, 1986) may not be a sustainable influence process, and probably should not be exalted as ideal or depicted as desirable in all circumstances.

4. *What is an ideal leadership influence process?* The steady-state and transitional issues are inherently associated with questions about the ideal type of continuous leadership process and its implications for organizations. A case can be made that 'orchestrated learning' is the epitome of leadership excellence: the establishment of an enterprise that is capable of continually renewing itself, regardless of who occupies positions of top management. By implication, the work of March (1974) suggests that leadership that sustains a density of administrative competence and well-oiled decision-making processes has done all it can to assure organizational learning and adaptation necessary for survival. Certainly, this is consistent with the conception of orchestrated learning. Thus, this may be an ideal type of leadership.

On the other hand, a case can be made that 'execute now' is ideal, though inherently more risky and difficult to sustain. Organizations whose ideologies place a premium on individual accomplishment consistent with the concept of 'the hero' in Western civilization may consider this pattern to be sustainable and ideal. This way of thinking about leadership philosophy and practice is often found in consumer product, retailing, and advertising organizations, and entrepreneurial companies. It is here that ideas and actions of 'great' individuals implemented by others are seen as primary sources of organizational success.

Myth and ideology may be the final arbiter concerning leadership that is considered ideal, or even acceptable. From a more detached point of view, however, this is more than a mere value judgment – there are significant implications for organizational performance. Survival of organizations in which 'orchestrated learning' is dominant is dependent on an effective organizational design: success derives from the administrative system, not a particular individual or top management team. In contrast, 'execute now' is an influence process that depends on the more-or-less continuous production of 'great' individuals to fill key roles, sustain strategic vision and facilitate adaptation. These are radically different burdens for organizations to bear. Which is more successful in the long run is a research issue that deserves more attention.

5. *What is ineffective leadership?* It may be that leadership effectiveness, from a *behavioral perspective*, takes one of two basic forms. The first, as noted previously, is 'officeholding'. Thompson (1967, p. 152) suggests that the most widespread limitation on organizational decision processes occurs when managers define administration as merely holding office, rather than facilitating organizational accomplishment. The consequences of this are impaired learning and other deleterious side effects (see Badaracco and Ellsworth, 1989).

If FIGURE 7.1 is correct, a second type of ineffectiveness may occur when senior-level executives cannot or do not conceive and execute one of the four relatively coherent and purposeful patterns identified. An error in assessing the density of administrative competence of an organization could give rise to inappropriate and/or insufficient actions. Alternatively, mixing elements of distinctly different influence patterns could result in contradictions that confound and confuse organizational members. Finally, executing only a portion of a coherent, internally consistent set of tasks and actions could lead to ineffectiveness.

Leadership effectiveness is often assessed with financial criteria (e.g. return on expenditure, return on assets). Literature on corporate decline and failure indicates that such measures are 'lagging indicators'. Use of behavioral referents affords a means to evaluate leadership with 'leading indicators'. This may open the way for more rapid corrective action, if deficiencies are present, and afford more timely information about one harbinger of organizational decline and failure.

IMPLICATIONS FOR FORMAL EDUCATION AND ADMINISTRATIVE PRACTICE

Executive leadership is described as the exercise of influence by senior-level managers within inter and intraorganizational decision-making processes with the intent of effecting strategic change. This is accomplished by affecting the agenda of problems and opportunities confronted by an enterprise, as well as the actions taken to resolve problems and fully exploit opportunities. Implicit in this way of thinking is an assumption that effective leadership is dependent on the ability of an individual or top management team to execute successfully, on a contingent basis, the related tasks and actions comprising the four distinct patterns of influence presented in FIGURE 7.1. These notions, when considered in the context of extant research on the phenomenon of strategic management and the nature of managerial work, have implications for both the role of formal education in the development of future leaders, and for human resource development and day-to-day administrative practice.

THE ROLE AND POTENTIAL CONTRIBUTIONS OF FORMAL EDUCATION FOR LEADERSHIP DEVELOPMENT

No explicit assumptions have been made about personality traits, psychological profiles, life experiences, administrative styles, or genetic endowments of successful leaders. Instead, effective leadership is conceived in terms of the ability to diagnose prevailing circumstances and execute tasks and actions necessary to achieve desired organizational outcomes. Thus, leadership is assumed to be largely comprised of learned behaviors – some proportion of these involve higher-order cognitive abilities, while others involve interpersonal and other related types of skills (e.g. verbal and written communication).

This is not to suggest that the development of future leaders and the improvement of ineffective leaders merely entails behavior modification. Such a position is naive and, from an educational perspective, potentially irresponsible. Clearly, there are other powerful variables at work which are not subject to control in educational settings. For example, the lives of many successful leaders are marked by personal experiences central to their capacity to lead that are beyond the purview of formal education (see Zalesnick, 1977). There is also some empirical evidence and much common experience that suggests that leadership depends on self-development. This process occurs as individuals consciously place themselves in a succession of contexts, each of which gives rise to an ever-growing repertoire of leadership behaviors (see Bennis, 1989). Despite these qualifications, conceiving the phenomenon of leadership in terms of distinct tasks, actions, and responsibilities that can be described, defined, taught, learned and practiced, helps with the problem of determining the relevant domain within which formal education can contribute to leadership development.

THEORETICAL COMPREHENSION

Few would argue that theory is not an important contributor to successful leadership. But this leaves unanswered the matter of 'theory about what'? At least two areas come to mind: (1) understandings of organizations as whole entities embedded within institutional contexts, and (2) the nature and chief characteristics of inter and intraorganizational decision-making processes.

Many contemporary courses about executive leadership focus on leaders, without adequately addressing environmental and organizational contexts. The latter are often considered to be abstract and, therefore, far removed from the 'realities' of leadership. Programs of study involving primarily biographies of leaders, ghost-written accounts of personal achievements of individual leaders, and/or topical surveys of subjects related to leading modern enterprises may not be sufficient. Unless there is also taught a conceptual framework that relates such subjects to various contextual conditions in which influence processes are executed, there may be no way to grasp important connections between context and administrative action. Thus, the range of discretion and feasibility of alternative actions cannot be understood. This problem may account for some of the criticisms that schools of business confront when chided for training technicians, not men and women who can size-up situations that are inherently ambiguous in nature, and take appropriate, goal-directed actions requiring cooperation of many persons.

There is a need to begin the study of strategic management not with the studies of leaders, but with considerable education about the nature and functioning of organizations and their institutional contexts. There are many different and potentially useful theoretical systems for doing so. Porter's work can be helpful with both economic and competitive characteristics of industries, as well as rivalries among nation states (Porter, 1980, 1990). Much remains to be accomplished, however, with respect to developing powerful conceptual frameworks for dealing with nonmarket forces. The research of Doz (1986), Freeman (1984), and Williamson (1985), among others, provide important beginnings on this subject. Further developments within this area of inquiry will undoubtedly give rise to more complete conceptions of these forces.

There are many theories of organization and research that lend themselves to study about the context of leadership and much literature about how organizations learn about and respond to change. Those with most promise provide considerable insight into the nature and workings of inter and intraorganizational decision-making processes (see, for example, Mintzberg *et al.*, 1976; Burgelman and Sayles, 1985; Cyert and March, 1963). Conceptions of these basic mechanisms of organizational learning and change can provide an understanding of linkages between and among individuals and groups. These processes are the proximate contexts of executive action. The absence of a viable conception of their nature and workings may severely limit the effectiveness of individuals in positions of leadership, by impairing insight into the means by which organizational members and constituents arrive at shared goals, define meaningful work activity, and commit to an enterprise. In the absence of such understanding, it is virtually impossible to take steps to unleash and direct the creative energies of organizational members in the achievement of institutional purpose.

SKILLS DEVELOPMENT

Mastery of concepts may be a necessary, though certainly not a sufficient, condition for preparing individuals for positions of leadership. There is, in addition, the need to hone certain skills; but, as above, there is the question of which skills?

Considerable knowledge about basic leadership skills exists and can be found throughout the curricula of most schools of business.

One implication for the meta-theory presented here is that it may provide a framework to draw together knowledge about relevant skills into more or less coherent categories or groups that relate to a particular type of influence process. For example, it might be useful to define skills that are peculiar to the four patterns of influence presented in FIGURE 7.1. When taken together, these may be used to configure a 'program' of training and/or educational experiences that advance an individual's ability to execute successfully one or more of the four patterns of influence. True, many would be generic and, therefore, would be associated with all patterns. But others may not be. More important than this issue is that of providing some order to the presentation of subject matter about which skills need to be mastered and how these are used to stimulate learning and adaptation throughout an organization. An overarching conception of leadership may provide a conceptual framework for relating subject matter taught rather than independently in a variety of courses and training experiences.

IMPLICATIONS FOR ADMINISTRATIVE PRACTICE

There are two implications for administrative practice. The first pertains to the problem of evaluating alternative courses of action for leaders of an organization, and the second concerns human resource development activities within large organizations.

EVALUATION OF ALTERNATIVE INFLUENCE PROCESSES FOR LEADING STRATEGIC CHANGE

The influence processes described in FIGURE 7.1 are, in fact, four different ways to stimulate learning among members of an enterprise. The effects of some are more severe and risky than others. Only one, shock treatment, is consistent with much prevailing practice (especially in the United States) that seems to derive from the myth of the hero. What some describe as the 'John Wayne' or 'Rambo' school of thought regarding leadership is only one course of action. Other, less invasive, less risky, though equally effective options exist.

In the search for managerial discretion and the need to manage risks, FIGURE 7.1 affords practitioners a framework for evaluating a wide array of options for exerting leadership. With it, an individual confronting the need for change has a means for selecting a course of action and recognizing, in advance, the demands that will be placed on him or her and the competence they must possess to fulfill successfully the role of leader. It might also be used by boards of directors when evaluating a CEO or confronting the matter of leadership succession.

HUMAN RESOURCE DEVELOPMENT

At the risk of oversimplification, it would seem that the primary function of human resource development is to reach and sustain a density of managerial and technical competence necessary to ensure survival and adaptation of an organization. Does this rudimentary meta-theory speak to the issue of how this might be accomplished?

In most organizations, the human resource function is charged with the responsibility for developing future leaders. The approach taken is usually that of sending persons off to seminars that address issues pertinent to their area of responsibility, as well as rotating job assignments. The by-product of these joint actions is supposed to be leadership development. Rarely are these actions, however, framed by a coherent concept related to specific skills or effective performance as a leader in different situations. They are, more often than not, merely imitative of other organizations that also have no overarching conception of leadership development. The influence patterns identified in FIGURE 7.1, when joined with extant research concerning cognitive and skill training, may provide a framework for guiding the actions of human resource organizations in the task of leadership development.

If the influence patterns in FIGURE 7.1 define the scope of effective contingent-based leadership practices, human resource professionals may be able to use these to define programs of development. These would involve the relevant leadership behaviors to be learned and how to execute the tasks and actions comprising each pattern. As one is mastered, via formal education and direct administrative experience, an individual would be moved on to another. With this approach, candidates for higher-level organizational assignments could be told in advance what they are expected to do and learn on each successive assignment and they could be 'measured' on how well they did against the relevant set of tasks to be mastered. In this way, leadership development is not a hoped-for outcome of a hodge-podge of formal executive programs and rotational assignments. It is, instead, a targeted activity conducted within a conceptual framework, with defined areas for development, standards of performance, and shared expectations. Further, it provides a coherent means for linking formal educational programs with ongoing administrative assignments. Such a scheme may be feasible only in large, multidivision organizations. At this time, the feasibility of such ideas and the potential scope of their applicability are conjectural (see Kerr and Jackofsky, 1989).

CONCLUSION

Early research about the nature of managerial work culminated in conceptions of a few generic administrative processes. Among the more widely accepted were: planning, organizing, directing, controlling, and coordinating. By the early 1960s, the credibility of this way of thinking as a full explanation of managerial conduct was under serious challenge. Due, in part, to these circumstances, the preponderance of subsequent research focused on development of fuller, richer descriptions of day-to-day work activities (e.g. Mintzberg, 1973; Kotter, 1982). These descriptions, as well as more recent conceptual and quantitative research, attest to the potential importance of identifying an underlying structure of leader behavior as a next step in development of a theory of strategic management (see Hart, 1991; Shrivastava and Nachman, 1989). Only time and empirical testing will reveal the value and limits of this approach to theory-building about relationships among strategic management, organizational learning, and organizational adaptation within changing environments.

REFERENCES

Ansoff, H. (1980). Strategic issue management. *Strategic Management Journal*, **1**, 131–148.

Badaracco, J. and Ellsworth, R. (1989). *Leadership and the Quest for Integrity.* Boston, MA: Harvard Business School Press.

Barnard, C. (1938). *The Functions of the Executive.* Cambridge, MA: Harvard University Press.

Bennis, W. (1989). *On Becoming a Leader.* New York: Addison-Wesley.

Burgelman, R. and Sayles, L. (1985). *Inside Corporate Innovation.* New York: The Free Press.

Burns, J. (1978). *Leadership.* New York: Harper Colophon Books.

Cyert, R. and March, J. (1963). *A Behavioral Theory of the Firm.* Englewood Cliffs, NJ: Prentice-Hall.

Doz, Y. (1986). *Strategic Management in Multinational Companies.* Oxford: Pergamon Press.

Freeman, E. (1984). *Strategic Management: A Stakeholder Approach.* Boston, MA: Pitman.

Gergen, K. (1968). Assessing the leverage points in the process of policy formation. In R. Bauer and K. Gergen (Eds) *The Study of Policy Formation* (pp. 205–238). New York: The Free Press.

Greiner, L. and Bhambri, A. (1989). New CEO intervention and dynamics of deliberate strategic change. *Strategic Management Journal,* **10**, 67–86.

Hambrick, D. and Finkelstein, S. (1987). Managerial discretion: A bridge between polar views of organizational outcomes. *Research On Organizational Behavior,* **9**, 369–406.

Hart, S. (1991). An integrative framework for strategy-making processes. Graduate School of Business, University of Michigan, working paper, May.

Hedberg, B. (1981). How organizations learn and unlearn. In P. Nystrom and W. Starbuck (Eds) *Handbook of Organizational Design,* Vol. I. Oxford: Oxford University Press.

Kerr, J. and Jackofsky, E. (1989). Aligning managers with strategies: Management development versus selection. *Strategic Management Journal,* **10**, 157–170.

Kotter, J. (1982). *The General Managers.* New York: The Free Press.

Kotter, J. (1990). What leaders really do. *Harvard Business Review,* May–June, 103–111.

Lyles, M. (1989). The formulation and nature of strategic problems. *Strategic Management Journal,* **2**, 61–75.

March, J. (1974). How we talk and how we act: Administrative theory and administrative life. In M. Cohen and J. March *Leadership and Ambiguity.* Boston, MA: Harvard Business School Press.

Mintzberg, H. (1973). *The Nature of Managerial Work.* New York: Harper & Row.

Mintzberg, H., Raisinghani, D. and Theoret, A. (1976). The structure of unstructured decision processes. *Administrative Science Quarterly,* **21**, 246–275.

Noel, A. (1989). Strategic cores and magnificent obsessions: Discovering strategy formation through daily activities of CEOs. *Strategic Management Journal,* **10**, 33–49.

Nonaka, I. (1991). The knowledge-creating company. *Harvard Business Review,* **69**, 96–104.

Nystrom, P. and Starbuck, W. (1976). Interacting processes as organizational designs. In R. Kilman, L. Pondy and D. Slevin (Eds) *The Management of Organization Design,* Vol. I. New York: Elsevier North-Holland.

Popper, K. (1968). *Conjectures and Refutations: The Growth of Scientific Knowledge.* New York: Harper & Row.

Porter, M. (1980). *Competitive Strategy*. New York: The Free Press.

Porter, M. (1990). *The Competitive Advantage of Nations*. New York: The Free Press.

Quinn, J. (1980). *Strategies for Change*. Homewood, IL: Irwin.

Shrivastava, P. and Nachman, S. (1989). Strategic leadership patterns. *Strategic Management Journal*, **10**, 51–66.

Simon, H. (1976). *Administrative Behavior*. New York: The Free Press.

Starbuck, W. (1984). Acting first and thinking later: finding decisions and strategies in the past. School of Business Administration, University of Wisconsin, Milwaukee, working paper.

Thompson, J. (1967). *Organizations In Action*. New York: McGraw-Hill.

Tichy, N. and Devanna, M. (1986). *The Transformational Leader*. New York: John Wiley.

Weick, K. (1979). *The Social Psychology of Organizing*. Reading, MA: Addison-Wesley.

Westley, F. and Mintzberg, H. (1989). Visionary leadership and strategic management. *Strategic Management Journal*, **10**, 17–32.

Williamson, O. (1985). *The Economic Institutions of Capitalism*. New York: The Free Press.

Zalesnick, A. (1977). Managers and leaders: Are they different? *Harvard Business Review*, May–June, 67–78.

8

Social Structures and Strategic Leadership

RICHARD WHITTINGTON

This chapter examines how three entrepreneurs fashioned from their social contexts the powers and visions that constituted their strategic leaderships. These three men were not just 'top managers': they were leaders in the sense of being able to motivate and inspire (Burns, 1978). But, though remarkable as individuals, their character as leaders cannot be explained simply in individualistic terms. For all three, their leadership qualities can be traced back to their positions in society at large. As entrepreneurs, they incarnated the revitalised 'enterprise culture' of 1980s' Britain; as Jewish business-men, they had access to an ethnic tradition of informal, expansionist and committed business behaviour; for two of them at least, within a patriarchal society, they were able to wield the unaccountable and intimidating authority of the older male.

This stress on the societal foundations to leadership adds a dimension to the psychology preferred in contemporary leadership studies (Burns, 1978, p. 24). The psychological approach to leadership focuses on a potential internal to human beings, one that can be called forth from most of us given the right opportunities and training (Bass, 1990). The sociological perspective adopted here draws attention rather to the leadership resources provided by society. As our resources vary by social background, we are not equal in our leadership potential, and we differ in the kinds of qualities we may possess as leaders. The implication for managers

Strategic Thinking: Leadership and the Management of Change.
Edited by J. Hendry and G. Johnson with J. Newton.
Copyright © 1993 the Strategic Management Society. Published 1993 John Wiley & Sons Ltd.

is that they should look not just inside themselves for their leadership potential, but look also to the capacities afforded by their positions within society at large. It is by recognising frankly the social advantages of their class, their ethnicity or their gender, that managers will make the most of their leadership potential.

This sociological perspective on leadership has implications also for the recent concern for 'organisational learning'. With its roots in cognitive psychology, the learning approach emphasises changing the 'mental models' or 'master programs' (Senge, 1990; Argyris, 1991) that govern our behaviour. The sociological perspective, by focusing on social resources and social rules of conduct, puts limits on the learning approach to change. In this view, social rules of conduct, frequently acquired and reinforced outside of the organisation, are often little susceptible to learning programmes confined to an organisational level. From this perspective too, resources are also interests, and entrenched interests are hard to 'unlearn' away.

The chapter begins by reviewing the contrasting approaches of social elite theory and leadership studies, proposing a reconciliation in the 'structurationist' perspective of Giddens (1984). The next section introduces the three leaders in question, and identifies particularly the structural rules and resources made available to them by their social backgrounds. Following the structurationist perspective, we next consider how exactly these men drew from their social structural positions the powers and ideals that informed their leaderships. The conclusion is that the 'charisma' of leadership, far from being the divine endowment of tradition (Bass, 1985), is in fact a very worldly phenomenon.

INDIVIDUAL LEADERS AND SOCIETY

Investigators of social elites have found fairly substantial regularities in the characteristics of top management cadres. Whether in the USA, the UK or France, top managers tend to come from upper-class backgrounds, be educated in exclusive schools and universities, and share close religious, ethnic and kinship networks (e.g. Mills, 1956; Stanworth and Giddens, 1974; Scott and Griff, 1984; Bauer and Bertin-Mourot, 1987; Barsoux and Lawrence, 1990). Those who, though themselves not upper class in origin, do manage to penetrate into the upper echelons, become merged with the established elite through exclusive clubs, appropriate marriages and the elite institutions of the corporate world itself (Whitley, 1974; Useem, 1984). Whatever the class origins, corporate elite members are almost all male (Scase and Goffee, 1989; Barsoux and Lawrence, 1990).

These, then, are the characteristics of the strata from which a great deal of our corporate leaders come. But to establish such general social characteristics of top management is not, of course, to describe leadership qualities *per se*. It is a cliché now to differentiate 'leaders' from 'managers' (Bass, 1985; Kotter, 1990). The men at the top – and men they mostly are – may occupy leading positions, but they need not be 'leaders'. As Burns (1978, p. 880) pointed out, leadership involves not simply the power of control, but the power to motivate: like detectives, 'one must look for motives as well as the weapon'. Accordingly, identification and true understanding of managers as leaders requires analysis and interpretation of them as personalities.

It is here that the elite theorists fail. Rather than close interpretive understanding, they have preferred to deal in the generalities of social strata. Motives are adduced from positions, and actions from interests (Medding, 1982). Though other social structural features are admitted into analysis, finally the singular characteristic of class is too often allowed unambiguous determination of all else (see Hindess, 1982). Actors are defined by broad social category, rather than recognised in their particular social groups or even in their actual individuality (Pahl and Winkler, 1974).

The strength of contemporary leadership studies is that they start right with the individual. By contrast with the aggregates of elite research, the prevalent method of leadership investigations is the accumulation and comparison of individual biographies – from Gandhi to Iaccocca. The focus is on the personal qualities of such leaders – their self-confidence, their self-determination, their innovativeness, and so on (Bass, 1985). Seen as someone obsessed with change (Kotter, 1990), the leader's personal 'vision' is paramount (Westley and Mintzberg, 1989). These visions are often approached through close interpretive understanding of individual motives, and careful ethnographic documentation of their activities (e.g. Noel, 1989). The origins of these visions are explained in psychological, or even psychoanalytic terms (Kets de Vries, 1989). Breaking with deterministic obsessions with social and economic structure, these visions are portrayed as enacted through the creativity and effectiveness of individuals' own efforts (Burns, 1978, p. 442).

This reassertion of the active, potentially transformatory capacity of the individual is something to be retained. But the leadership tradition involves a loss too. Leadership studies often combine a naïve idealism about leaders with a blindness to the social origins of their powers. The capacity for leadership is attributed too widely (Bass, 1990), while the psychological need for leaders is too trustingly accepted (Kets de Vries, 1989). Focused on individuals, the social is admitted into analysis only in so far as it may have contributed to the early psychological formation of leaders (Burns, 1978) or as it defines particular contexts (i.e. crises) in which leadership activity may be promoted (Roberts and Bradley, 1988). In presenting such characters as Henry Ford or Kemal Attaturk (Bass, 1985), neither the social resources that empowered these leaders – capitalist or political – nor the social ideals that inspired them – entrepreneurial or patriotic – are exposed to any commentary. Personal qualities, not social positions, dominate all.

There is a middle way. Following Giddens' (1984) structurationist approach, social structures can be seen as enabling rather than simply determining (see Pettigrew, 1987). Society provides both the social resources, material and symbolic, that empower our actions, and the social rules of accepted behaviour that actually guide them. Though powers and motives are drawn ultimately from social structures, there is no necessary determinism. Everyone occupies a diversity of social structural positions – manager, parent, citizen – all of which offer a variety of rules and resources by which to act. According to this structurationist perspective, therefore, the study of particular leaders requires both sociological analysis of their polyvalent social structural potential and a more interpretive, psychological understanding of how they individually choose to exploit it.

This structurationist perspective gives particular insight into the two key elements of leadership identified by Burns (1978) – power and motive. Leaders assemble their powers from the various social resources their positions in society afford them, and they draw their motives from corresponding social rules. The synthesis may be unique, and their stamp personal, but ultimately both empowerment and inspiration are social.

Thus the next section, in introducing the three leaders, will also stress their sociological backgrounds. These backgrounds gave them access to the diverse and divergent rules and resources of three sets of social structures in particular: capitalist, ethnic and familial. These social structures provided them with the potential for leadership, but it was up to the three individuals themselves to translate possibility into actuality.

SOCIAL STRUCTURAL FOUNDATIONS OF LEADERSHIP

The argument so far is that social structures provide the raw materials of leadership – both the social resources (symbolic and material) that empower and the rules that guide and inspire. This section will briefly introduce the three leaders and their companies, stressing the diverse social structural positions they occupied and therefore the richness of the rules and resources available to them. The following section will examine how these three individuals transformed these materials into actual leadership practices.

But first a word on method. The three companies and their leaders were investigated using both internal and external documentary data and a series of 33 extended interviews with (mostly) senior managers (see Whittington (1989) for a fuller account of these and competitor managers from a different perspective). At two companies, Rose and Exemplar, the two crucial leaders, Sir Ben Rose and Jo Stone, were recalled by their followers (respectively three years and one year) after their deaths. The vividness with which they were remembered is testimony in itself to their leadership qualities. At Kremer's, the leading figure, Bernie Kremer, was interviewed twice.

Rose Electrical Industries was a large British conglomerate founded by Sir Ben Rose, an Austro-Jewish entrepreneur, in 1926. By the early 1980's, Sir Ben had moved over from the chairmanship to the presidency of a company with a total turnover in excess of £2 billion. The focus of the research was on the Domestic Appliances Division, which had been established at the start of the 1950s and grew to become the largest UK manufacturer of cookers and refrigerators, with a 1980 turnover approaching £200 million.

Jo Stone was another Austro-Jewish migrant, who had fled to England just before the start of the war. In the post-war period, he had built up a successful furniture company and later became managing director and part owner of another leading domestic applicance company, Exemplar. It was Exemplar, with a turnover of around £100 million, that provided the original context of this research.

Bernie Kremer's company was much smaller, with only £20 million turnover. None the less, within the fragmented furniture industry in which it operated, this was enough to give it a leading position. Son of an East End Jewish immigrant, Bernie had founded the company in 1952 by selling furniture out of a London garage. However, the company had expanded rapidly, going public in 1971 and establishing subsidiaries in France and the United States.

What then were the social structural rules and resources available to these men? To start with, capitalist structures empowered them in a number of ways. Though none of these three started with the class advantages stressed by the elite theorists, over the course of their careers they did acquire substantial financial resources. In all three cases, their organisational power was underpinned by dominant shareholdings – for Jo Stone, 17% of the company's shares; for Bernie Kremer, 35%; and for Ben Rose, around 11%. These resources were confirmed in the three cases by hierarchical position – respectively, chief executive, chairman and president.

But capitalist structures offered them symbolic as well as material resources. The three men were entrepreneurs in their own right, creators of large and successful businesses. Within a capitalist society, they had access therefore to an entrepreneurial ideology cultivated since the earliest days of the industrial revolution (Bendix, 1963), and being actively renewed in the Britain of the 1980s (Morris, 1991). This entrepreneurial ideology afforded them, as the embodiments of a revitalised 'enterprise culture', a legitimate authority that went beyond that simply of ownership or hierarchical position. For their followers, they could become symbols of enterprise and success. In their eyes, moreover, entrepreneurial status could legitimate otherwise eccentric behaviour. As entrepreneurs, a degree of arbitrariness, informality and daring could only be expected.

Yet they also had a completely different set of social rules and resources potentially available to them. These men – and their followers – were all members of a wider society in which the family, as well as the enterprise, provides models of authority and conduct. Weber (1964) has shown how in politics older males can hijack familial codes of patriarchal behaviour to establish what he terms 'patrimonial' leadership over hand-picked gangs of youthful followers. The same can be true in business. The Victorian capitalist George Courtauld reinforced his legitimacy in the factory by portraying his workers as his 'family', with him as 'father' and 'patriarch' (Lawn, 1983). Even today, patriarchal models of authority and conduct survive not only in many small family enterprises (Scase and Goffee, 1982), but also – at least vestigially – in such large corporations as Marks & Spencers and Cadbury, where paternalistic codes of practice still resonate (Anthony, 1986). The family is not an unambiguous model, however: the fraternal ideal can clash with patriarchal authority. In Goffee and Scase's (1982) small building firms, a fraternalist model prescribed relationships between employers and employees based on mutuality and equality. There, leadership had to be far more consensual.

Thus, even within business, familial social structures can provide a variety of rules and resources for leadership. The three entrepreneurs here were well placed to exploit these. All three were family businessmen – even if Rose Electrical Industries had become a large public company and Jo Stone was working in partnership with another conglomerate. Needless to say, they were also men. Moreover, by the early 1980s, they were quite old: in 1980, Stone was 62, Kremer 58 and Sir Ben a venerable 80 years old. Male and senior, the three had open to them the possibility of supplementing their capitalist powers by exploiting familial structures to gain as well a patriarchal supremacy.

There is one more social characteristic that these three men shared, giving them access to still other social codes of conduct. All three were Jewish. For many ethnic communities, ethnicity is closely bound with business life. As traditional outsiders, for Jewish people business success has often been crucial for gaining social status within otherwise exclusive societies. Accordingly, Kosmin (1979, p. 53) observes of the Jewish businessmen she studied: 'Their whole sense of identity – indeed their whole life – is involved in business and work.'

Thus their ethnicity could offer these three men certain distinctive social patterns with which to guide their business conduct. For example, Kosmin (1979) found of her Jewish businessmen a stubborn, almost perverse optimism, learnt perhaps through survival of terrible oppression and epitomised in the Hebrew phrase *hiye-tov* – 'it will be good, it will come right'. As well as preserving this optimism, many of the Jews who had found in Britain a refuge from Nazi persecution adopted a patriotic gratitude, becoming 'more British than the British' (Berghahn, 1984, p. 175). Despite the importance of business success to regaining social standing in the wider community, within the Jewish firm itself relations between boss and workers are traditionally informal and personal, with everyone on first name terms (Aris, 1970, p. 237). In return, however, the Jewish boss expects complete obedience, often acting in autocratic and domineering fashion (Aris, 1970, p. 21).

Stone, Kremer and Rose were cosmopolitan and intelligent men, by no means slaves to some ethnic stereotype. However, what their shared ethnicity did offer them was a certain code of behaviour over which they had easy command and which could license, in their own eyes and in the eyes of others, conduct that might otherwise seem eccentric. Moreover, this was not the only code to which they had access. Their social positions gave the three men a range of social rules and resources. They could play the parts of entrepreneur, principal shareholder, patriarch or Jewish boss. The next section will examine exactly how these three men chose to manipulate these various social materials into the foundations of their personal leaderships.

TRANSLATING STRUCTURAL POSITION INTO PERSONAL LEADERSHIP

Thus the three Jewish, male entrepreneurs occupied diverse social structural positions – capitalist, ethnic and familial. This diversity gave them access to a luxuriant plurality of social structural rules and resources from which to build their idiosyncratic leadership styles. This section will examine how precisely they translated social structural potential into the actuality of personal leadership. Recalling Burns' (1978) distinction between powers and motives, it will consider first the diversity of social resources from which they constructed their authority and then the various social rules that informed their strategic visions.

POWERS

All three of these men had enormous personal authority amongst their followers. To his managers, Bernie Kremer was known simply as 'the Governor'. His standing was unquestionable: 'He's obviously captain of the ship . . . He's just Bernie Kremer. You know, what can one say? . . . He's chairman of the company; he built the company up.'

Sir Ben Rose was given the same respect:

'We saw him as a paternal figure, as somebody that had built up a very big business, and had made a lot of important decisions and was responsible at that time for employing 75 000 people – and that was from, you know, literally from selling lamps off a stall in a market. I mean, it was the proverbial . . . rags to riches and success to those who go out and look for it. We believed in him.'

As for Jo Stone at Exemplar, he was described as 'a patriarch', 'an enlightened dictator', and 'the saviour' of Exemplar.

The foundations of this authority lay in more than simply hierarchy and ownership. As the quotations above make clear, the legitimacy of Sir Ben and Bernie Kremer stemmed as well from their entrepreneurial statuses as the creators of the companies they ran. The position of Jo Stone was slightly more complex, in that Exemplar was an ailing subsidiary, for which he had been brought in by the holding company to rescue. Nevertheless, Stone's success with his own furniture company was well known, and it was as an 'entrepreneur' that Exemplar's managers most often characterised him: he was 'an entrepreneur, a self-made man'; 'he was a natural, seat-of-the-pants businessman, an entrepreneur'.

To their managers, this entrepreneurial status excused a common informal, spontaneous way of business. At Kremer's, everything worked within 'a free-wheeling structure'. At Rose, 'managerial jargon' was denounced and the favourite expression was 'seat-of-the-pants'. Jo Stone kept no filing cabinets, and believed 'analysis was for the birds'. All three were known, and admired, for having made bold, apparently reckless decisions – Sir Ben, impulsive acquisitions; Bernie Kremer, radical product innovation; Jo Stone, counter-cyclical investments. But, as entrepreneurs, this conduct was legitimate. Jo Stone indeed was accorded near-papal infallibility: 'You're in the presence of a genius. Now geniuses can make mistakes; they can go up a wrong alley and get destroyed. But it so happened that all the things he tried to do at Exemplar, every single one of them clicked.'

But for Jo Stone and Sir Ben in particular, appeal to entrepreneurial ideologies was not enough. The two men also exercised a domineering patriarchal authority over their younger managers. By the 1970s, Sir Ben's original contemporaries had more or less retired, and he was able to exercise a strangely intense dominion over his younger managers. One subsidiary board member recalled:

'You can have many husbands, but you can have only one father; you can have many chairmen and managing directors of a company, but you can have only one founder. And you have this almost unique sort of ability when you are the boss. It is your idea, you have created it. You become very much the *father* of not only the company . . . but also you are the father of all the people in it. And his [Ben Rose's] was a very strong paternal attitude . . . He regarded everybody as sort of children. "They are very good lads", he would say, "They are marvelous lads". But you were never more than a lad.'

Jo Stone's patriarchal position had been deliberately created. On his arrival at the company he had replaced the existing senior management with a hand-picked team of young managers who closely resembled a Weberian patrimonial gang:

'A personalised team was created. Not really like forming a Praetorian Guard, in that respect, the Stone men as opposed to the non-Stone men. There wasn't that sort of thought in mind – to form a gang loyal to Stone. But it develops that way of course, because Number Twos promoted are obviously very loyal. It was a very virile team, very young.'

This youth was important. Several senior managers had been in their twenties on their first appointment, and still in 1980, when Stone was 62 years old, the average age of the top ten managers was only 38. These managers well understood the patriarchal basis of his authority: he was 'that odd mixture of paternalist and autocrat'; 'He was the man in charge . . . He was the father-figure'. Another recalled his autocratic style with his young managers thus:

'He was very difficult to work with because his ideas had to be the dominant ideas. He'd got to have his own way. But I found it a tremendous experience, basically because of my age . . . If I'd been 44, maybe I'd have said, "Well, I don't really want to sit down and be told how to do it . . ." . . . I mean, he did have difficulty with people who were older than me who were here, because they didn't want to be told how to do it . . . Say ten years on, having had ten years' experience, then maybe you'd want to be a little more your own man.'

It is important to recognise how Stone had acted deliberately to exploit the structural potential of his age and gender in order to create this patriarchal authority. Coming into Exemplar from outside, like George Courtauld Jo Stone had propped up his shakey capitalist authority by resort to a familial model.

But simple age and gender did not, of course, dictate this conduct. Bernie Kremer, for instance, was of the same generation as Jo Stone and yet found himself not with patriarchal authority but enmeshed in the sort of fraternal relations described by Goffee and Scase (1982). Bernie's managers, many recruited from the same East End background, remembered him loading the lorries himself and, all from the same generation, identified the company's growth with their own advance to maturity and managerial status: 'We grew together; we grew, we moved up the line together; . . . we've all grown up together.' For these managers, Kremer's itself was their 'family'. Explained one: 'The family is a family of people working together as a team.' By retaining this generation of managers, Bernie accepted both the absence of rational, well-ordered capitalist hierarchy and the lack of unchallengeable patriarchal supremacy. Managers claimed the right to give him 'stick', and described their style of debate by direct appeal to the fraternal model: 'We fight like brothers and sisters. That's how we fight.'

None the less, despite the fraternalism, authority was wielded ultimately with the same directness that Aris (1970) ascribed to his Jewish businessmen. Within his firm, Bernie Kremer was at least a wrathful oldest brother: 'He's the sort of guy who would haul somebody out for something quite trivial – but to his mind important – and reduce that bloke to nothing. But he'd go back in half an hour and ask him how his wife and kids are. It's that type of atmosphere – very much family orientated.'

Jo Stone was even more domineering. Asked what it was like to disagree with Stone, one senior manager laughed: 'It could be bloody stormy. You could see your P45 (dismissal form) sliding over the desk on many occasions. But you either agreed to differ and go off and do it his way or you agreed to differ and got out. It was as simple as that!'

MOTIVES

The motives that guided the businesses of these three men were expressed in the 'strategic visions' (Westley and Mintzberg, 1989) which they had evolved through their experience and which also enthused their followers. Here too their social backgrounds informed their leaderships. Just as they had built and wielded their powers on social structural bases, they found in a similar mixture of capitalist, ethnic and familial structures crucial materials informing their strategic visions.

The motives of these men were not crassly economic: their whole lives were closely bound up with their businesses. Sir Ben hung on long after normal retirement age, Bernie Kremer struggled back to work after a near fatal illness, while, according to one of his managers, Jo Stone 'gave his all to [his] two companies . . . He didn't seem to have any other interests in life'. Indeed, Stone died within one year of retiring from Exemplar in 1983.

Rather than crude financial reward, at the heart of all three men's strategic visions appeared to be a commitment to growth, with little regard for rational capitalist caution. Here entrepreneurial values again coincided with Jewish dispositions, especially optimism and the concern for social status through business success.

Both Bernie Kremer and Jo Stone were known as optimists. One Exemplar manager described Stone as 'a born optimist . . . [with the] rather endearing characteristic that he only wanted to hear the good news'. This optimism supported growth. One manager recalled of Jo Stone: 'Profitability naturally always is a priority. But he wanted this through penetration, volume as opposed to making Rolls Royces at low volume and making a nice big profit. He wanted to be the biggest and the best.' Growth could provide the social recognition so cherished by Jewish outsiders. Bernie Kremer was utterly frank about the vision underlying his business career:

'Growth is what we all want in business . . . Run a small business? That wasn't me . . . One wanted the business to grow, one was young and ambitious, and having smelt a bit of success, you wanted a bit more, let the thing develop . . . It's an ego trip. If you run a public company, if you're managing director or chairman of a public company, it's an ego trip. It's a bit of pride – that you've arrived.'

As reward for his business success, the once penniless Jewish immigrant Ben Rose finally received the exclusive accolade of the upper classes, a knighthood.

This growth was not just egomania. The patriarchal authority of Jo Stone and Ben Rose also seemed to oblige a paternalistic care for employees. For Rose, a paternalistic concern for his managers' careers reinforced his inclination towards growth: 'Sir Ben very much believed in developing his mates in the business. He was very much against bringing people in from the outside.' His managers well understood how this paternalism could cross-cut simple capitalist rationalities: Sir Ben 'virtually never sacked anybody [from his senior management] . . . That attitude cost the company a bit of money, but boy oh boy, it made people feel that here was a man with a heart'. Stone's paternalism was more widely spread. He was remembered as having 'an almost God-given responsibility to look after the hourly-paid workers . . . He attached very much more importance to *their* well-being than he did to his overhead [staff]'. Indeed, his paternalistic welfare measures were praised in a National Economic Development Organisation report of the late 1970s.

Growth had a patriotic inspiration too. The UK-oriented nature of both Ben Rose's and Jo Stone's strategies may well have reflected the Jewish gratitude for refuge from Nazism identified by Berghahn (1984). One Rose manager identified Sir Ben's vision thus: 'Like a lot of people who are not British but who come to Britain and then become more British than the British, his whole concentration was on the United Kingdom . . . He saw himself very much as a man who wished to grow within the United Kingdom.'

Jo Stone was similar, dedicating himself to defending the home market against imports rather than exporting himself. One of his managers summed up the elements of his underlying strategic vision thus: 'His real interest was not in making money. His real interest was in production, the British economy and the people who worked for Exemplar.'

CONCLUSIONS

Each in their own way, these three leaders possessed personal visions that had driven them to the construction of large businesses and enabled them to inspire the deep loyalty and respect of their subordinates. Though their achievements were individual, they relied on social backgrounds for enablement and motivation. The high authority and regard these men enjoyed was not built simply on personal charisma, but also on a creative mix of social structural resources – capitalist property rights and hierarchy, entrepreneurial ideology, and patriarchal domination. The visions that drove them were idiosyncratic in detail, yet were infused with common ethnic ideals of growth and patriotism, familial codes of paternalism or fraternalism, and capitalist models of entrepreneurial informality and daring. It would be hard indeed for any woman, gentile or mere manager, to have acted as Jo Stone, Bernie Kremer and Ben Rose did.

Using the structurationist perspective developed by Giddens (1984), this account of the three men has recognised both the diverse structural rules and resources afforded them by society and the individual means by which they interpreted and exploited these social materials. In this sense, the chapter has acknowledged and developed the neglected contribution of elite theory to leadership studies. Although elite theory may be too insensitive to idiosyncracy to give insight into particular individuals, by establishing the general characteristics of people in leading positions, it has brought out the importance of certain kinds of social structural materials for the exercise of leadership (Whittington, 1992).

From this perspective, therefore, leaders can be portrayed as building their personal powers and strategic visions from the various social structural rules and resources they have access to. To understand the leadership phenomenon, research needs to examine the social structures that underpin it. There is no essential determinism in this recognition of the social: the focus is on how individuals mould the divergent opportunities of social structural position to their own purposes. But neither is there too exclusive a reliance on the personal: strategic visions are informed not just by individual psychology, but also by the rules of the society in which they participate.

This importance to leaders of social advantages, and skill in manipulating them, has implications for the cultivation of leadership capability generally. Because we have differential social endowments, we are both unequal in our leadership potential and various in our leadership styles. The development of leadership capability entails, therefore, clear appraisal of the social advantages and disadvantages each individual possesses. Some – because of gender, class or ethnicity – will be relatively disabled in the leadership stakes, but even these may find aspects of their social characteristics to turn to their advantage. For example, Rosener (1990) shows how 'feminine' experiences and skills can be exploited by women positively to construct 'transformational' leadership styles that are highly effective even in a still male-dominated world. Thus the teaching of leadership, as well as its study, can be enhanced by frank recognition of the importance of social background.

This more sociological perspective adds a further dimension to the current 'cognitive turn' (Huff, 1990; Johnson, 1990) in strategic management. While the influence on managerial cognition of interpretive schemes generated at the organisational or even industry level is now well recognised, this chapter has drawn attention to the importance of symbolic resources at the level of society as a whole. In these firms, the symbolic figures of patriarch or entrepreneur, entrenched deep within the collective consciousness of our society, were powerful influences on the authority of individual leaders and the perceptions of their followers.

This shaping of cognition by social structures has implications for the phenomenon of organisational learning (Pucik, 1988; Argyris, 1991). The challenge posed to managers by societal codes and symbols is that, compared to organisational or even industry 'interpretive environments', they are relatively inaccessible to organisation-based change initiatives. To take the example of Rose, the new top management that succeeded Sir Ben on his retirement tried in vain to instil recognition amongst the older managers of the need for a more professional, disciplined management style. Resistance was strong and effective because these older managers held to an entrepreneurial ideal that was embodied in the figure of Sir Ben and reinforced by the contemporary external promotion of the 'enterprise culture' of 1980s Britain (Morris, 1991). In this sense, 'organisational learning' can be subverted by 'extracurricular learning' within society at large.

To conclude, leadership studies remain in danger of treating such personal qualities as 'charisma' as too literally 'God-given'. The psychological insights being developed in contemporary leadership studies should be complemented by an understanding of the social bases of leaders' powers and the social inspirations for their conduct. The structurationist perspective is proposed here as a means of reconciling leadership and elite theories in a way that recognises managerial leaders as something more than either exceptional personalities or mere creatures of class. Rather, this chapter suggests, leaders are people who enjoy privileged access to, and unusual skill with, the diverse material and symbolic resources, ideals and codes of conduct supplied by their complex positions in society as a whole.

REFERENCES

Anthony, P. D. (1986). *The Foundations of Management*. London: Tavistock.
Argyris, C. (1991). Teaching smart people to learn. *Harvard Business Review*, May–June, 99–109.
Aris, S. (1970). *The Jews in Business*. London: Cape.
Barsoux, J. L. and Lawrence, P. (1990). *Management in France*. London: Cassell.
Bass, B. M. (1985). *Leadership and Performance Beyond Expectations*. New York: Free Press.

Bass, B. M. (1990). From transactional to transformational leadership: Learning to share the vision. *Organizational Dynamics*, **18**, 19–31.

Bauer, M. and Bertin-Mourot, B. (1987). *Les 200: Comment Devient – on Grand Patron?*. Paris: Seuil.

Bendix, R. (1963). *Work and Authority in Industry*. New York: Harper & Row.

Berghahn, M. (1984). *German-Jewish Refugees in England*. London: MacMillan.

Burns, J. M. (1978). *Leadership*. New York: Harper & Row.

Giddens, A. (1984). *The Constitution of Society*. Cambridge: Polity Press.

Goffee, R. and Scase, R. (1982). 'Fraternalism' and 'Paternalism' as employer strategies in small firms. In G. Day (Ed.) *Diversity and Decomposition in the Labour Market*. Aldershot: Gower.

Hindess, B. (1982). Power, interests and the outcomes of struggles. *Sociology*, **16**, 499–511.

Huff, A. S. (1990). Mapping strategic thought. In A. S. Huff (Ed.) *Mapping Strategic Thought*. London: John Wiley.

Johnson, G. (1990). Managing strategic change: The role of symbolic action. *British Journal of Management*, **1**, 183–200.

Kets de Vries, M. F. R. (1989). *Prisoners of Leadership*. London: John Wiley.

Kosmin, B. (1979). Exclusion and opportunity: Traditions of work amongst British Jews. In S. Wallman (Ed.) *Ethnicity at Work*. London: MacMillan.

Kotter, J. P. (1990). What leaders really do. *Harvard Business Review*, May–June, 103–111.

Lawn, J. (1983). Not so much a factory, more a form of patriarchy: Gender and class during industrialisation. In E. Gamarmikov, D. Morgan, J. Purvis and D. E. Taylor (Eds) *Gender, Class and Work*. London: Heinemann.

Medding, P. Y. (1982). Ruling elite models: A critique and an alternative. *Political Studies*, **30**, 393–412.

Mills, C. W. (1956). *The Power Elite*. New York: Oxford University Press.

Morris, P. (1991). Freeing the spirit of enterprise. In R. Keat and N. Abercrombie (Eds) *Enterprise Culture*. London: Routledge.

Noel, A. (1989). Strategic cores and 'management obsessions'. *Strategic Management Journal*, **10**, 33–49.

Pahl, R. E. and Winkler, J. (1974). The economic elite: Theory and practice. In P. Stanworth and A. Giddens (Eds) *Elites and Power in British Society*. Cambridge: Cambridge University Press.

Pettigrew, A. M. (1987). Context and action in the transformation of the firm. *Journal of Management Studies*, **24**, 649–670.

Pucik, V. (1988). Strategic alliances, organisational learning and competitive advantage: The HRM agenda. *Human Resource Management*, **27**, 77–93.

Roberts, N. C. and Bradley, R. T. (1988). Limits of charisma. In J. A. Conger and R. N. Kanungo (Eds) *Charismatic Leadership*. London: Jossey-Bass.

Rosener, J. (1990). Ways women lead. *Harvard Business Review*. November.

Scase, R. and Goffee, R. (1982). *The Entrepreneurial Middle Class*. London: Croom Helm.

Scase, R. and Goffee, R. (1989). *Reluctant Managers: Their Work and Life Styles*. London: Unwin Hyman.

Scott, J. and Griff, C. (1984). *Directors of Industry*. Cambridge: Polity Press.

Senge, P. M. (1990). The leader's new work: Building learning organisations. *Sloan Management Review*, Fall, 7–22.

Stanworth, P. and Giddens, A. (1974). An economic elite: A demographic profile of company chairmen. In P. Stanworth and A. Giddens (Eds) *Elites and Power in British Society*. Cambridge: Cambridge University Press.

Useem, M. (1984). *The Inner Circle*. New York: Oxford University Press.

Weber, M. (1964). *The Theory of Social and Economic Organisation*. Translated by A. M. Henderson and T. Parsons. New York: Free Press.

Westley, F. and Mintzberg, H. (1989). Visionary leadership and strategic management. *Strategic Management Journal*, **10**, 17–32.

Whitley, R. (1974). The city and industry: The directors of large companies, their characteristics and their connections. In P. Stanworth and A. Giddens (Eds) *Elites and Power in British Society*. Cambridge: Cambridge University Press.

Whittington, R. (1989). *Corporate Strategies in Recession and Recovery: Social Structures and Strategic Choice*. London: Unwin Hyman.

Whittington, R. (1992). Putting Giddens into action: Social systems and managerial agency. *Journal of Management Studies*, **29**, 6, 693–712.

9

Leading Change and the Management of Competition

RICHARD WHIPP, ANDREW PETTIGREW

On 7 January 1989 the Business section of *The Economist* began with a cartoon. Arranged across the top of page 65 was a collection of middle-aged men making energetic use of various pieces of gym equipment. Closer inspection reveals that each figure bears the likeness of the head of a major corporation. Prominent among them is Jack Welch of General Electric and Louis Gerstner president of American Express. The article is entitled 'a work-out for corporate America'. Because of the new commercial fitness attained by those such as Welch, the piece goes on to exalt the reader not to apply for Japanese citizenship just yet. Why? Because: 'there are enough success stories to provide guidance on how best to revitalise an American company. On the way, such successes are revealing a new breed of American chief executives.' Similar articles in the UK and European business press abound (see, for example, *Management Today*, May 1986: 19).

The profound challenges to the existence of many traditional Western industries in the 1980s has often led to spectacular changes in the businesses that have survived. The chief executive or business leader has been catapulated to the forefront of national attention. In the UK the names of Halpern, Sugar, or Branson are as prominent

Strategic Thinking: Leadership and the Management of Change.
Edited by J. Hendry and G. Johnson with J. Newton.
Copyright © 1993 the Strategic Management Society. Published 1993 John Wiley & Sons Ltd.

on the front pages as they are in the business sections of newspapers. In the face of epoch-making problems, those who appear able to supply solutions are eagerly lauded. The climate of expectation seemingly has made them into the modern-day counterparts of the mediaeval wizards.

Appreciation of the supposedly magical qualities of such chief executives is by no means universal. Yet most people can appreciate the need for leadership simply from their everday acquaintance with group activities, be it in their work or social lives. Meanwhile, the image of the leader figure is constantly reinforced. The heads of government, political parties, sporting organisations and social movements are convenient targets for the analyst, satirist and layperson alike. In times of crisis the leader figure's role becomes the subject of intense scrutiny. We may not all aspire to the position of leader, but it is one to which most people can relate.

Leadership, though, has proved to be one of the most appealing and yet intractable subjects within management. Two immediate difficulties present themselves. First, leadership cannot be equated only with command, as some would have it. Nor, second, is leadership best understood when it is reduced to the sweeping prescriptions of the ghost-written executive's autobiography. The immense problems that experts have encountered in trying to teach leadership directly, and the lack of commonality in the routes leaders have taken in reaching their positions, only serve to make the subject more elusive.

But it is this elusiveness that has also given rise to such extensive commentary on the subject of business leadership. This chapter begins, therefore, with a summary of the field. It specifies the contribution of the management writers and highlights the range of leadership forms that have been identified. The main conclusion to arise from this synthesis is that the otherwise valuable managerial literature on leadership contains some substantial defects. Most serious of all is the relative absence of studies that connect directly leadership and competitiveness. Comparative studies of leadership in different industries are equally rare. Few have explored the full relevance of process and context to leadership.

After outlining the project from which this chapter derives, some of the main conceptual issues related to the leadership field will be considered. Later sections will examine the role of leadership in managing change and competition in two sectors of the UK economy drawn from the study: book publishing and automobiles. The pattern to emerge from the firms in the study is clear: the problems of dynamics and constraints are ignored by leaders of change at their peril. In particular, this chapter will show how premature or isolated use of the wealth of tools that leaders have at their disposal can be disastrous. Honing the tools in order to match them to the processes and circumstances within which leaders must operate appears far more advantageous.

Our research shows that the ability of an enterprise to compete rest on two qualities. First, the capacity of the firm to comprehend the competitive forces in play and how they change over time. Secondly, there is the linked ability of a business to mobilise and manage the resources necessary for the chosen competitive response through time. Yet irrespective of the strategy adopted, the key intangible asset (Budworth, 1988, 1989) is the capability to carry through the changes implied by the strategy and if necessary transform the strategy through use (Whipp and Pettigrew, 1992). This is the significant message from our research linking managing change to competitive success, and the central mobilising idea of this chapter.

THE STUDY

RESEARCH DESIGN

The study has examined the process of managing strategic and operational change in four mature industry and service sectors of the UK economy: automobiles, publishing, merchant banking and life assurance. All the sectors had reached stages in their life cycles where established products, markets and relationships were undergoing marked alterations. A major attraction of the chosen industries is their range and the way they extend from manufacturing to service.

Two firms were chosen for study in each of the four sectors, making a total of eight. Each pair was made up of, relatively speaking, a higher and lesser performer in the same broad product market – although, as the research showed, these relative positions could vary considerably over time. An important advantage of the use of higher and lesser performers was the avoidance of the general bias in the business literature towards successful organisations. The firms involved were: automobiles – Jaguar,

Peugeot Talbot; merchant banking – Kleinwort Benson, Hill Samuel; book publishing – Longman, ABP; life assurance – Prudential, Anon. The object has been to discover:

- why firms operating in the same industry, country and product markets should record such different performances
- what has been the contribution of the way they manage strategic change.

Longitudinal data have been collected covering the firms' activities in detail over the 1970s and 1980s, guided by a detailed question *pro forma* (see Appendix in Pettigrew, Whipp and Rosenfeld, 1989, pp. 132–136). The sources of data were threefold:

- semi-structured tape-recorded interviews conducted extensively in each firm and related organisations (e.g. government and industry bodies, competitors)
- primary documentary evidence from within the firm, such as board, departmental records and internal reports
- secondary published material, ranging from official government documents to book publications.

In excess of 350 recorded interviews, conducted at all levels of the firms and sectors involved over a three-year period, is an indication of the scale and intensity of the research.

COMPETITION AND STRATEGIC CHANGE: AN INTEGRATED APPROACH

The main feature of the study of competition is that it sees competition and strategic change as intimately linked.

It regards strategic change and competition as joint and inseparable processes. In particular the research contends that these processes occur at multiple levels across time (Whipp, 1987). In other words these processes move forward within their firm, sector and national contexts (Whipp and Clark, 1986; Whipp, 1990). The study's framework is also unusual to the extent that it pays due regard to the way such processes are structured by a trinity of forces. These include not only the objective decisions of managers using information derived from their competitive environment; they also embrace the subjective learning and political dimensions that operate both in and outside the firm. These features can best be understood by examining an outline of the framework.

The central aim of the study has been to link the competitive performance of British firms to their ability to adapt to major changes in their environment. This motivation stems from the way existing literatures appeared to have minimised the role of management in the debates over competition. Little analytical weight in the prevailing accounts of competition has been attributed to the capacity of management to adjust to external change. Most policy discussion of competition in the UK has concentrated on policies at the expense of processes. Comparatively little is said of how such policies should be carried out or in what way the changes that they require might be managed. Too often these processes are assumed to follow (see Langlois, 1986; Hodgson, 1988). In practice the situation is far less straightforward.

The overriding intention of the framework is to capture strategic change and competition as holisticly as possible. FIGURE 9.1 sets out the main constituents of that framework. This implies major judgements about the nature of these twin processes. These have been described at length elsewhere (Pettigrew and Whipp, 1991, ch. 1). Here it is important to explain the central features.

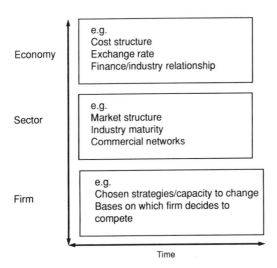

FIGURE 9.1 Competition: Three levels across time (reproduced from Pettigrew and Whipp, 1991, by permission of Basil Blackwell Publisher)

Strategic change should be regarded as a continuous process that occurs in given contexts. The point to appreciate is the richness of these contexts and their simultaneous shaping of strategic change. The hallmark of the processual dimension is that strategy does not move forward in a direct, linear way nor through easily identifiable sequential phases. Quite the reverse, the pattern is much more appropriately seen as continuous, iterative and uncertain.

Competition, similarly, is best appreciated in a multidimensional way (Whipp, Rosenfeld and Pettigrew, 1989). Two dimensions stand out: the levels at which competition operates and the element of time as indicated in FIGURE 9.1. Along the vertical axis are the three major levels with their associated characteristics and measures. The competitive performance of a firm hinges therefore on the recognition that businesses compete not merely against one another but at the same time within the sectoral and the national/international structures and relationships.

The competitive performance of an enterprise is the result of a collection of abilities and modes of action (see Teece, 1987; Rumelt, 1988). One must appreciate therefore the bases on which a firm competes and above all their process of creation. Rarely is there a single base. Most firms develop many tiers of advantages that explain their overall competitive strength. These may combine both price and non-price characteristics.

As the horizontal axis in FIGURE 9.1 suggests, the sectoral and national conditions in which a firm operates and hence the bases on which it competes are quintessentially unstable. They are never static. It is to these changes that management has to respond continuously and which provides part of the major external impulsions for strategic change. Yet there is a critical differential. The ability to perceive those changes and to take necessary action diverges considerably between and within firms. It is those divergences of choice and execution that interest us (Whipp, Rosenfeld and Pettigrew, 1987).

The ability of an enterprise to compete relies on two qualities: (1) the capacity of the firm to identify and understand the competitive forces in play and how they change over time, linked to, (2) the competence of a business to mobilise and manage the resources necessary for the chosen competitive response through time.

Irrespective of the strategy adopted, the capacity to carry out the changes it implies is critical. The need for management to not only assess the environment (at a number of levels), make choices and mount the necessary alterations is vital to explaining contrasting performances between firms. Seldom is there an easily isolated logic to strategic change. Instead that process may derive its motive force from an amalgam of economic, personal and political imperatives. Their interaction through time requires that those responsible for managing that process make continual assessments, repeated choices, and multiple adjustments.

LEADERS AND WIZARDS

Attempts to survey the literature on leadership have reached a common conclusion: its vast scale. Over 100 definitions exist derived from a wide range of perspectives (Bass, 1981). Theories of leadership have proliferated across the social sciences ranging from trait analysis to ethical assessment approaches. One needs to tread very carefully through the thickets of academic specialisation and some brief ground-clearing is required before the contribution of the managerial writers becomes apparent.

Psychologists in the 1950s and 1960s devoted great energy in trying to identify the personality traits of the successful leader (Fiedler, 1967). This work saw leadership in terms of authority and follower relationships. The aim was to discover what differentiated leaders from followers. The programme of research at Ohio State University generated broadly defined categories such as 'consideration' and 'initiating behaviour'. Others concentrated on task-oriented and employee-oriented leader behaviour and sought to locate leaders on the 'autocracy–democracy' scale. Subsequent work has elaborated the theme of behaviour types. These included Bass and Valenzi's (1974) categories of 'direction, delegation, consultation, and manipulation'. One study proposed 19 behaviour types arising out of this field of research (Ropo, 1989).

These attempts at understanding leadership have remained somewhat unfulfilled. The main problem has been the way they placed undue emphasis on personality at the expense of the situation in which leadership occurs.

An entirely different species have grown vigorously though, away from the academic hothouse: the leader as hero seen in the pages of the business biography/autobiography. In many ways the general formula used here shares the main assumption of the psychologists – the centrality of the leader's personality. The success of such volumes, if measured in sales, has on occasions been exceptional (see, for example, Iacocca, 1985). The impact of these books on the lay view of leadership is considerable. Apart from simple curiosity fanned by PR hype, the outpourings of business leaders appear to speak to their times. The social and political tastes of the 1980s seem to have provided a willing audience. Such figures have in many ways assumed the mantle of the self-improving, Smilesian hero of the high Victorian era. In the USA, academic commentators have drawn attention to the appetite for what they describe as the 'romance of leadership' (Meindl *et al.*, 1985). In Europe, too, there seems a ready market for the views of chief executives such as Jan Carlzon of SAS (Edstrom, 1986).

It is easy for academics to be dismissive of this genre, often seen through their eyes as representing the shotgun marriage of the hard sell and journalistic licence. Yet even passing acquaintance with this type of book soon suggests that they have a value beyond self-advertisement. In fact, the more reflective texts can be extremely illuminating.

To be sure, Sir John Harvey-Jones' (1988) book *Making it Happen* is heavily prescriptive and dwells on his own skills of motivation and leadership. Yet at the same time he alerts the reader to leadership as a process. In his case as chairman of ICI between 1982 and 1987 he highlights the critical part of that process: transforming its top executive team from a collection of rival advocates on behalf of individual businesses into a cohesive body of directors of the group's best interests. One of the results was that greater resources were released for ICI's growth businesses.

Careful reading of the more thoughtful (auto)biographies can prove useful in a further sense. Such accounts offer insights into not just leader personality but sometimes the wider set of relations that leaders encounter when managing change. It is significant that the discussions that followed Iacocca's autobiography centred not only on his tempestuous relationship with Henry Ford, but also the internal problems he had to solve at Chrysler. Read carefully, these works offer valuable clues to the practical difficulties of leading change; they also signal the intricacy of the contexts in which change takes place. In this sense the genre has performed a service: it has popularised and opened up the subject. In revealing the scope of the leadership task the authors have reinforced the recent efforts of business analysts in framing a more faithful model of leadership.

Since the late 1970s a much broader approach has been taken to leadership by management writers. The problem is seen more via the situation in which leadership takes place. Some have drawn attention to the requirement to facilitate the work of other managers; to enable them to influence and direct the activities of personnel (Peters and Waterman, 1982). New classifications of leadership have therefore replaced the traditional categories based on personality. Bourgeois and Brodwin (1984) place great emphasis on the leadership styles of companies expressed in the way they implement strategy (see also Kanter, 1989). Their classification extends from the 'commander' (where strategy is forced down to lower levels) to the 'crescive' (where all managers contribute to strategy creation and implementation).

A broader orientation to leadership by management experts is now well established. It is possible, therefore, to separate out three models of leadership that have become accepted: transactional, transformational and representational (for a comprehensive overview see Ropo, 1989).

The transactional leader is one who exchanges money, jobs and security for compliance. The term implies management-by-exception, i.e. the leader intervenes only if standards are not met. The approach is more suited to the accomplishment of routine tasks but is found wanting when the need is for major change. The more recent identification of representational leadership arises from an awareness of the multiple constituencies related to a given organisation. Representational leadership refers to the requirement for leaders to represent some feature of their organisation to those who are by no means their subordinates. This is particularly evident in environmental scanning, resource acquisition and network development (Hunt *et al.*, 1988).

Transformational leadership is quite different. Here the leader motivates others to strive for higher order goals rather than merely short-term interest. It involves, *inter alia*, risk-taking, building commitment and the visionary skills of focusing attention and communication. It does not assume individual exchange relations. In Nancy Roberts' (1985) words, 'the collective action that transforming leadership generates, empowers those who participate in the process'. The collective action is often induced as part of the heightened response to a crisis.

In spite of this widening of the leadership field, conceptual shortcomings persist. Two linked defects stand out: insufficient attention to: (1) leadership as a process (Pettigrew, 1987), and (2) the reciprocal relationship between leadership and context. Above all, nobody has specified what difference leadership can make to competitive performance by comparing firms. Some writers have maintained that situational conditions make leadership irrelevant and unable to effect organisational performance (Pfeffer, 1981). The evidence presented in the following sections will show the opposite is true.

In our view leadership cannot be understood outside of a processual perspective. Too often leadership is treated in a unitary way. In other words, it is the action of a leader at a given moment, or through a single episode (albeit a crisis) that claims attention. The changing nature of leadership across time and through cycles of radical and incremental change is seldom addressed (see Nadler and Tushman, 1988). As Ropo (1989) perceptively notes: 'Although an implicit notion of change and flexibility is inherent in most situational leadership models . . . the issues of time and processes have been totally neglected . . . leader behaviour of managers is abstracted from their concrete contextual settings and investigated in reductionist terms as if it had no past or future.'

To comprehend the dynamics of change processes one has to appreciate the role of energy within the process; its source, means of generation and how it is sustained or dissipated. The contribution of leadership to this aspect is a vital one. We agree with Roberts (1985) that leadership is one key way of creating and redirecting energy within the change process. And it is that energy that makes such a difference when comparing the competitive performance of firms. In book publishing for example, Longman's superior record can be related directly to the way its leadership maintained the level of energy over two decades. That energy level was necessary in order to shift from its editorial preoccupations of the 1960s and 1970s, to the market-oriented competitive bases of the 1980s.

Although this study is at pains to specify how leadership can shape strategic change, one thing should be made quite clear. There is no assumption here of the powerful efficacy of the charismatic leader; no prescriptions being offered for the instant success of the visionary. Quite the reverse, sensitivity to questions of time and process in leadership and change produce the opposite view. It is the unpredictability of the process as it unfolds through time that makes the prospect of control so remote. Assertive action by itself is of limited use and may well be dangerous. Paradoxically this research indicates that the accumulation of more modest preparatory actions is all-important. These might include consideration of the political implications of a given strategy for instance, through problem-sensing and climate setting within the firm. The art of leadership in the management field would seem to lie in the ability to shape the process in the long term rather than direct it only through a single episode.

One of the keys to understanding the process of leading change is to link that process to its contexts. The analytical judgements and resulting action from strategic decisions cannot remain separate from the circumstances in which they are taken. Indeed, it is the tension between these forces that impels the process of change. This relationship demands careful attention in understanding the problems of leading change.

The key to understanding those problems is the extent of the shifting contextual pressures that leaders face through time. The main weakness of the earlier approaches to leadership was their search for almost universally applicable leader behaviour. As the evidence from the research companies in the following sections will show, the flow of alterations in both the organisation and the external competitive environmental call for varying responses, and above all, different types of leadership. Leading change requires action appropriate to its contexts. Different eras produce different leadership needs – leaders have to adapt accordingly. In Jaguar, for example, the type of leadership necessary in the survival year of 1980 was wholly different from that required by the problems of growth after 1985. Indeed, from our evidence, the solidifying of apparently successful leadership behaviour into a sigle mould (as happened at Hill Samuel in the 1960s and 1970s) can become a competitive liability.

Supportive evidence of the need for variation in leadership, rather than the adoption of supposedly timeless principles, is available. In the area of technological innovation Manz *et al.* (1989, p. 633) point to the existence of 'multiple influence procedures' that may be used in that process. For them 'effective leadership combines different types of leadership influence over time as different needs arise'. This does not mean that the earlier categories of leadership outlined above (e.g. transactional or transformational) are of no use in leading change and managing competition. Rather, any category by itself is of limited value. Instead, those alternative types of leadership approaches are better seen as being deployed where and when they best suit the demand (see Goold and Campbell, 1988, p. 180). As Nadler and Tushman (1988) argue, 'magical', heroic, visionary leadership has simply been inappropriate when relatively successful companies have undertaken adaptations in order to sustain their performance. Examples include Xerox, Digital Equipment, NCR and Kodak.

Nor should one forget that leading change is not a one-way relationship emanating solely from the leader. Leaders are themselves affected by the forces that they seek to manage. The relationship is more accurately described as reciprocal. Leaders alter as they attempt to handle change. In the case of Tim Rix at Longman, his leadership triggered a substantial personal development. At Hill Samuel the problems of the market in the 1970s compounded certain problematic traits of Kenneth Keith's style. The observation is simple yet penetrating: it cuts across the familiar assumptions made by many management writers. Otherwise respectable accounts that demonstrate the need for varying forms of leadership fall down when they argue for the need to 'fit' leadership to company character (Goold and Campbell, 1988, p. 246). Attempts in practice to achieve such a static, singular fit almost inevitably come undone as both leader and circumstances change.

One of the strongest features of leadership to arise from our research is that leading change should not necessarily imply a single leader. Change may ultimately involve a number of leaders, operating at different levels in the firm. This becomes all the more likely given the need for a variation in leadership styles to match changing circumstances, whether they originate from environmental threats or the particular needs of implementing strategy. No one person can cover all possible situations. It is noticeable how Prudential, Longman, Kleinwort Benson, Jaguar (and Peugeot Talbot in the 1980s) share a common characteristic in this regard. Alongside their assessment of their competitive environments, great emphasis was placed on two things: (1) creating a broader notion of collective leadership at the highest level, and (2) inculcating over time a complementary sense of leadership/responsibility at lower levels (compare Hambrick, 1987).

The pattern that emerges from the companies in this study is a strong one. Leading change in order to compete is not understood by reference to universal principles carried out by an exceptional individual. More effective in leading change appears to be:

- the use of varying leadership approaches over time
- a combination of practices to address shifting competitive circumstances
- the recognition that leader and context will affect each other reciprocally
- the use of operational leaders at all levels in the firm.

In practice, the more successful companies studied in this research show that the effectiveness of so-called decisive action by their leaders was in many ways more apparent than real. Time and again the companies revealed how extensive yet small-scale conditioning work facilitated strategic changes. These included the less visible asset in leading change of: taking time in fashioning the company's precise competitive choice, creating a capacity for effecting the required changes, and legitimating such acts before undertaking them. These conditioning devices then enabled the full potential of other mechanisms subsequently used by leaders to be released.

In Kleinwort Benson, their seemingly incisive response to deregulation in the City of London in 1987 was not the result of flashes of genius from their leadership. Rather, it was the cumulative result of a sequence of moves in the 1970s. These had set the tone for diversification, had demonstrated the capacity to do so, especially abroad, and had meant that such moves were already well received at various levels in the bank come 1987. In the less successful companies in our sample, it is noticeable how similar decisive competitive acts were made (the Magnum venture at ABP, or the Avenger project in Chrysler UK). Yet those acts crumbled exactly because they did not have the benefit of such conditioning. Such comparisons require inspection at greater length.

BOOK PUBLISHING

The UK-based book publishers ABP and Longman are especially clear examples of the contribution of different styles of leading change to their companies' performance (for a detailed account of the two companies, see Pettigrew and Whipp, 1991, ch. 1). Useful insights can be derived from the similarity of their intentions yet the contrasts in the means they employed to achieve them.

ABP

In ABP the problems of their leadership stemmed from the company's formation. The profitability of the legal specialists Sweet & Maxwell made possible the reverse takeover of the general, academic and specialist publishers Methuen, Eyre & Spottiswoode and Chapman & Hall. The latter's financial weakness meant that the senior management of Sweet & Maxwell occupied the top positions in the new company in 1964. Sweet & Maxwell's managing director, financial director and editorial director became respectively, the new group managing director, group financial director and group editorial director. Therein lay the kernel of a problem that was to grow over the following 15 years. The problem had two main elements. The senior management of ABP had assumed control of a group that now operated across areas of publishing in which they were inexperienced. Second, they went on to attempt to run the hithero family-dominated firms that made up ABP by divisionalisation: a task where they, in common with many other UK firms, had no previous record of achievement.

The aim, as at Longman, was to secure the benefits of separate divisions devoted to particular types of publishing; in ABP's case, law, academic and trade. Yet as management found in the Rootes Group and in other industries (Gospel, 1992) the problems of running such structures for the first time were immense. The constraints of previous fragmentation of demand, the slow emergence of mass markets and the avoidance of formal management techniques in favour of devolved control through payment systems are by now well known. These applied especially to book publishing. ABP registered the considerable achievements of physically uniting the group on the New Fetter Lane site in London by 1970 and establishing, as had Longman, a purpose-built distribution centre on a greenfield site – in ABP's case, at Andover. Book distribution had previously been handled by Book House in Neasden which was part owned by Oxford University Press and Pitman.

The difficulties with the divisional system arose from the way it was conceived and managed by ABP's senior executives in the context of the norms of publishing and the model provided by the rest of British industry. It was entirely logical, therefore, for the leadership of first John Burk and then Peter Allsop from 1972, to concentrate on the most prized asset of any publisher: its editorial strength. Combined with the lack of experience, however, in the trade and specialist areas of ABP, this produced a highly devolved style of leadership. This in turn was reinforced by the problems that arose in the integration of previously distinct businesses in both Canada and Australia and commanded so much of the group executives' attention. Since it occurred at the beginning of the group's existence, the pattern was set.

The result was the separation of senior management – to deal mainly with overseas problems. The divisions became the responsibility of management committees. The aim was to give maximum scope for the entrepreneurship of the publishing lists within each division. It was highly indicative that ABP as a corporate entity was not emphasised. Instead, the brand names – that is the imprints of Chapman & Hall and Methuen – were reinforced both internally and to the trade. Imprint boards remained in place. The outcome was the amoeba-like growth within the divisions in terms of lists (with seven sub-divisions) acccompanied by duplication and weak financial control.

The type of leadership that emerged was closest to the transactional, leadership-by-exception mould outlined above. Apart from the emphasis on the autonomy of the divisions and lists down to 1974, action was directed towards the divisions only where problems arose. Such a style of leadership was consistent with the values and experience of the senior management. It was also made possible by the enduring profitability of Sweet & Maxwell's legal publishing and the satisfaction of the major shareholder the Crossthwaite-Eyre Family Trust. ABP, therefore, did not develop fully as an international company in the manner of Longman. As they noted to themselves in 1979: 'A major reason behind this is that the board has grown from being solely and wholly responsible for the UK, to one formed to operate on an international basis, though so far not made to do so.'

The reliance on a devolved transactional style of leadership meant that the problems of the 1970s were especially hard to face. The reliance on editorial entrepreneurship at the expense of rationalisation was sorely exposed by the fourfold rise in oil prices in 1973–74. As elsewhere, the rapid onset of inflation and the consequent slump in demand required drastic measures. Expenditure in the academic and scientific divisions was cut back by 40%. Commissioning was stopped on many lists for over a year. The damage to the credibility of the lists was severe and took years to recover. An abortive attempt was made to join the academic and scientific divisions under one head.

The outcome for ABP was that the 1970s became dominated by 'fire-fighting'. The company's minimal planning mechanisms, for example, had to deal with the re-pricing of entire lists every three months as well as fending off the investigations of the UK government's Price Commission. The leadership and management was pitchforked into a succession of crisis-like responses. They were therefore unable even to consider much beyond the creation at speed of what change was necessary. Given the accumulated and immediate problems, there was simply no opportunity to build a more sophisticated capacity for change. The failure of moves such as the Magnum mass paperback list from 1976 served to emphasise ABP's lack of financial integration and its inability to move substantially beyond its legal publishing base. A new entrant to the company summarised the outcome well in 1986 when he told his senior executive colleagues how: 'If you are actually going to be an entrepreneur you are going to reach into things that you are not used to and your cash flows are going to be different. And I don't think yet we have got enough nerve to follow this entrepreneur thing the whole way.'

Understanding the nature of ABP's leadership stance from 1964, the circumstances in which it was formed and the way wider economic upheavals then prevented its development, i.e. the process involved, is highly illuminating. This perspective throws light on why by the 1980s ABP had devoted insufficient attention to building the competitive bases which the market now demanded; notably in the areas of marketing and new technology. This is not to argue that there was no change in leadership approach. ABP is a good illustration of the point made earlier concerning the reciprocal effect between leader and situation. Unfortunately for ABP, the response was too late. Above all the new leaders remained within the transactional mode. They were unable to move to a more transformational style that the company needed.

ABP took decisive action in 1979 by separating out the group from the UK operations and appointing an outsider to head ABP UK. Yet the person chosen in many ways symbolised ABP's problems. Alan Miles' skills had been amply demonstrated at Weidenfeld & Nicholson, where he had been managing director. He had managed an illustrious imprint, which none the less relied wholly on the vagaries of trade publishing. His subsequent achievements at ABP were immense. In the short-term he: established a system of financial controls and basic monthly management accounting, which enabled managers to monitor and control performance; purchased a new-generation computer system to enhance systems capability and distribution effectiveness; made key appointments in the form of a new head of the trade division (a colleague of Miles, from Weidenfelds); and the creation of a group marketing director.

These acts provided a sound base for a series of reforms in the 1981–85 period. The aim here was to preserve the experienced publishing teams, maintain the momentum of successful publishing, improve cash flow and profitability by cutting out unprofitable publishing, develop opportunities where they were manageable within current resources, and step up training of managers and staff. The result was a £10 million reduction in costs, a decrease in staff of 25%. ABP's problem divisions recovered with the improvement in demand in the early 1980s, yet overall performance remained flat.

Miles was successful in providing the leadership needed to solve the long-standing problems of ABP centred on integration and financial control. The enthusiasm of managers was clear. As one in the legal division put it: 'He introduced all the modern systems, all the proper modern systems a company should have. Everyone had a cost centre, every cost centre had a manager, every manager a reviewer.' In one sense he orchestrated his own set of conditioning devices and secondary, supportive mechanism. What was lacking was a new set of such devices linked to a conception of the long-term strategic development that would move ABP beyond its traditional products. The result was that ABP's competitive base by 1985 was in many ways only a more sound version of its position in the early 1970s.

LONGMAN

The contribution of the leadership at Longman could not have been more different. The core of that difference has been in the way the company's strategic changes over the past 20 years have been matched by a commensurate alteration in its leadership. Longman had to endure the same economic and market challenges as ABP. In some cases, such as the Nigerian market collapse of 1983, these external shocks were even more acute. However, the sequence of actions taken by Longman's leadership was totally unlike ABP's. This can be demonstrated by considering the distinctive scope of those actions that Longman sustained over almost two decades.

The starting point has to be the way certain strategic decisions were taken early, but then their implications were catered for by a web of interconnecting, smaller supportive actions built up over the long term. The best illustration comes from the way in the 1960s Longman refused to rely on milking its major asset of its overseas operations in British Commonwealth and related markets. The company was already moving to local publishing and joint publishing companies in Europe by the 1970s. In the words of the head of the overseas division they heeded their extensive international networks; they were determined not to be caught in the supposedly 'unchanging world' created by the activities of the 'colonial entrepreneurs in the markets of the old commonwealth'. So when the internationalisation of English accelerated in the 1970s and 1980s, leading to a boom in demand for English language teaching outside the commonwealth, for example, Longman was well placed to respond.

Given these broad early moves, Longman had the advantage of having set in motion a process. Staff became comfortable with this more continuous sequence of building up the direction and major policies of the company. Looking at ABP's and Longman's planning documents is instructive. By the end of the 1970s Longman had moved carefully to a clearly defined position: Longman's overall aim was to become: (1) a major world publisher and the leading British-based publisher in business, professional, reference and information publishing, and (2) to exploit fully its competitive advantage as the leading British-based educational publisher.

ABP, even by 1985, was still trying to move on from its newly-established internal control rather than conceiving a long-range orientation. Longman, however, was in a position to develop supportive secondary mechanisms. Whilst building its strategic goals through an emergent process, Longman's senior management was able, for example, to elaborate and operationalise these aims into a change agenda (e.g. specific targets in North America, or the Third World).

At the same time that Longman built up strategic goals, its leaders were almost equally concerned with fashioning the internal character of the company. Thereby staff might adapt to the implication of such goals more readily. Longman did not try to retain family control and shareholdings as at ABP, but sought out a position within the loosely federated Pearson & Son Ltd in 1968. Nor did Longman attempt to establish a new divisional structure in one go. Unlike ABP, Longman had already become a group of companies in 1966 in order to reflect its spread of overseas publishing units. Longman then embarked on what is best described as a progressive divisionalisation. The aim was to replace the three existing departments of overseas, home and general publishing, sales and production.

Longman did not opt for an instant reduction to three divisions as at ABP. Instead it adopted seven product-based divisions and three geographically related. The mix was deliberate; it set up a more tolerable span of financial control without losing the essential small-scale character of the publishing process at imprint level. It also in time liberated group managers, notably in sales, to take a much wider view. The important point to note, though, is that the structure was gradually adjusted both to meet the needs of diversification and to prevent their ossification. The new sector format by 1986 had opened up greater flexibility across the company. The sectors brought together some earlier divisions and became homes for the new operations that Longman's long-term diversification required.

Moreover, the development of the strategic goals and the preparation of the internal character of the company were not left to operate alone. They were augmented by generation of an appropriate capacity for change within Longman. This entailed parallel shifts effected in the Longman culture. These centred on a refinement of the attitude towards quality, a reworking of the notion of professionalism and a movement in the balance of editorial versus marketing priorities. This necessitated the recruitment of marketing and personnel experts from outside of book publishing. Just as important was the inculcation of specific financial skills of the divisional/sector heads with a view to their identifying and mounting their own acquisitions. It is also worth noting the amount of effort put in over a period of seven years to remoulding the relationship between computing staff and the rest of the company. Without it, many of the advances in the production process and publishing list development in the 1980s would have been still-born.

The pivotal reason for the adoption of these conditioning features in Longman has been the profound change in the style of leadership. Unlike ABP, the senior management of Longman represents a shift over time: from a liberal version of transactional leadership in the early 1970s to a flowering of transformational leadership in the 1980s. It was through the personal development of the chief executive, Tim Rix, that the pitfalls of ABP were avoided. Rix came from the powerhouse division of English Language Teaching, much as his counterparts at ABP came from their legal division. In the first instance, there were a number of more direct exchange relations that had to be worked on, such as the relationship between the emerging group planning system and the newly-created divisions. Yet it has been the progressive movement to a more transformational style from the late 1970s that sets Rix and his senior colleagues apart.

It is worthwhile to dwell on the main aspects of the mechanisms that were used. From 1976 he assembled around him a critical mass of the so-called 'finance committee' and divisional directors who made up the UK board. Rix's extensive international publishing experience gave him the advantage of an early insight into the trends and growth possibilities inherent in the USA, Europe and the Far East. His accomplishments of having achieved growth in the area allied to his personality meant that he was able to transfer many of his techniques piloted and proven in the 1960s and early 1970s. He was able therefore to aim for the altogether higher-order goals outlined above than was the case in ABP's constant need for survival and internal control. What is commonly referred to as 'Tim's vision' did not appear in response to the fashion for mission statements but was forged into a robust form over ten years. Such a vision has, then, provided the basis for collective action at first board and then divisional level. Robert Duncan, head of the medical division was in:

> 'no doubt that there was a two way movement between Tim Rix and myself . . . It appeared to me that there was a lot we could do outside our traditional markets, a lot of opportunities open to us, particularly in America. His feeling was that we should do something to get us out of the dependence on Africa and therefore he encouraged it. It was undoubtedly me and Tim, a joint version.'

The board was relatively stable in the 1980s, augmented by key appointments in computer and production services. The finance committee (Rix and his deputy plus the finance director) grew from its necessary early control and monitoring duties to one where it performs a constant educative role for the heads and then top teams of each division. Much of the basic communication of the ongoing flow of changes is a mature combination of Rix's regular personal appearance in the divisions, a professional communication apparatus across the company and then the home-grown efforts of the divisions. Sector four's 1988 divisional conference on 'planning for development' is a case in point. The result according to a sector manager is that 'there are inter-sectoral problems . . . but it takes time for problem areas to be brought into the open. Its not a secretive culture'.

An easily overlooked yet important mechanism developed under the Rixian mode of leading change has included the balancing of continuity and change. In part this has been accomplished within the interlinked nature of the changes that have been sustained incrementally over a decade and are well expressed in the strategic goals described earlier. The crucial outcome was that Longman retained its most basic assets such as its author loyalty. In contrast to ABP, its strongest product areas were not left to themselves. Perhaps the best illustration of the way this balance was achieved, and to an extent coherence maintained, was in the regrouping of publishing lists. Hence in 1987 the ailing trade and reference lists were moved in alongside the vastly successful ELT division, as part of the sectoral arrangement.

AUTOMOBILES

The experience of Jaguar Cars and Peugeot Talbot are immensely instructive in respect of leading change and competitive performance (for a detailed account of the two companies see Pettigrew and Whipp, 1991, ch. 1). Not only do they expose some of the weaknesses of traditional UK leadership, they also graphically illustrate the interplay of leader and company context. Above all, they demolish any monolithic notion of how to lead change. Both companies demonstrate the wide variation in leadership over the long-term and even in the space of two or three years. The variation in leadership style across the existence of first Rootes, then Chrysler UK and lastly Peugeot Talbot has been startling.

PEUGEOT TALBOT

The direction of the Rootes Group – throughout its existence to 1964 – remained heavily dependent on the Rootes family. Billy and Reginald (sons of William Rootes the founder) provided joint leadership until 1939. Billy won a wide reputation as an entrepreneur while Reginald's skills lay in administration and finance. After World War II their sons joined them. Geoffrey and Brian, sons of Billy, became MDs of manufacturing and overseas operations. Timothy, son of Reginald, was director of sales and service. These family members controlled the boards of each member of the group. As the current success of many West German family-owned firms (including BMW) shows, there is no reason why such enterprises should not succeed. However, in the case of Rootes the perpetuation of family control and executive responsibility resulted in a number of deficiencies. Most important of all, managerial expertise in product planning, finance and training remained underdeveloped by contemporary standards.

In many ways this backwardness provoked the extreme action taken by the new Chrysler UK (CUK) leadership from 1967. On the other hand, such leaps were entirely consistent with Chrysler Corporation's history in the USA of bold innovation and what became known in Detroit as 'panic management'. The response of Chrysler was to import a combination of US managers and those who had come through a US-inspired system in Ford UK. Great faith was placed in the financial and accounting procedures derived from Detroit. The problem was in the way the new system of divisionalisation and procedure manuals was applied. The leadership devoted insufficient time to preparing and conditioning the company for such a massive change. The exasperation of a British project engineer is indicative. As he put it:

> 'Chrysler came over here and plonked a nine foot high stack of manuals on the desk and said "apply that". There was never the manpower to apply that. There was never the experience in a lot of people to apply the things to the letter. It was an attempt to apply certain procedures, certain methods of operating that quite honestly the organisation was incapable of responding to.'

The exceptional actions taken by the new leadership were also undermined by their standing within CUK. The MDs, Hunt (1967–73), Lander (1973–76) and Lacey (1976–78), along with the expatriate US directors of the main functions of CUK, were beset by the common disadvantage of suspicion over their authority. That suspicion was fuelled by their apparent loyalty to those who had appointed them in Detroit, not to mention their intense mode of double reporting to Chrysler Europe and Detroit (a special Atlantic switch had to be installed). The result apparently was: 'A lot of fear in the executive management system. They were very conscious that they were on a month's notice . . . and they were very loyal to their people in Detroit who had put them here in the UK.'

An additional problem was the feeling that the group of exiles were 'rejects' from Chrysler's debacles of the 1960s. Chrysler's lack of experience as a multinational producer also meant that little attention was paid to adjusting their aim of rapid expansion to the British social or competitive circumstances. A hasty, ill-founded strategy was compounded by the leaders' failure to develop the capacity to change or prepare the setting into which such a strategy was to be launched.

The intriguing profile of leading change presented by Peugeot Talbot could not be more different. The position of chief executive has been occupied by two men: George Turnbull from January 1979 to March 1984, and Geoffrey Whalen, assistant MD from October 1981 and MD from 1984 to date. Once the decision had been taken to scale down the UK operations in 1980, a clear continuity appeared in the strategic intentions across the two regimes: the essential rebuilding of the competitive bases of the company as a car manufacturer. Yet with hindsight one can see that in order to achieve the sequence of demanding changes, the wholly different styles of both men were required.

In many ways Turnbull broke the deadlock imposed by the inherited problems of CUK. Whalen then astutely delivered the changes which logically followed. George Turnbull supplied a determined, combative personal style linked to a clear vision of contemporary international competitive standards. Together these provided the impetus to rework the assumptions that had brought the demise of CUK. His precocious rise to become MD of British Leyland in his 40s and his successful stewardship of Hyundai in Korea commanded attention. He rehabilitated the notion of leadership. His manufacturing expertise won him the respect of his staff. A manager of the parts department was clear: 'He knew how to build a car, how to run a manufacturing company, that was his business . . . once he was running the show the meetings for example were very serious, very professional and he was very strong.'

To outside constituencies he was, in the words of a senior DTI officer, unequivocally: 'A first-class car man. He didn't need the money. In other words, he could afford to say his mind and stand up for his corner, which he did in a very firm way both with the government and his French masters.'

Turnbull's re-establishing of managerial authority and basic manufacturing standards was epitomised by his decision to sit out a three month strike in 1979. In Dick Parham's (the assistant MD at the time) view: 'That was a very fundamental point in establishing a new relationship between management and workforce. It allowed the management to manage and the workforce to understand that things had changed, that the era had changed.'

Of course this is precisely the bold action that was discounted earlier in the chapter. The difference was that having established the legitimacy of the new direction and its standards, his successor had the opportunity to develop the capacity to change more fully. Furthermore, Whalen's method of leading change brought into operation a new style of leadership. In the opinion of the director of manufacturing:

> 'We have a managing director in Geoff Whalen who is very good at democratic management. It can't all be democratic but he is very good at a relaxed style of management. So I would never get the feeling, and my plant directors wouldn't (as they certainly would have some years ago) that the central operation is god . . . now the central operation are much more like consultants.'

In addition to this he created a series of supportive secondary mechanisms. These include:

- The judicious shift to a more open, consultative set of relations within senior management, built around the weekly meeting of the operations committee since 1983.
- A vital reshaping of the working and authority relations with Peugeot SA (PSA) so that it became more symmetrical; PSA now accept the expertise of Peugeot Talbot's entirely native management – for example over the peculiarities of the 50% of the UK market taken by fleet sale.
- Rebuilding the confidence of staff (shell-shocked by the horrors of 1975–79) through the necessary contractions that had to occur before the new models and improved standards could bear full fruit from 1983.
- Operationalising the strategic programme of regeneration through an incremental adjustment of internal reporting and communications structures – examples include the termination of the Iranian contract and the Triaxle bus project.

The experience of Peugeot Talbot from 1979 is an excellent example, therefore, of how leading change doesn't have to be associated only with a single leader. The regimes of two very different leaders have combined to produce a transformational leadership. In Jaguar in the 1980s the alteration in performance pivoted on an individual, but one who had to adapt his leadership over time.

JAGUAR

Under William Lyons' leadership and then during the ownership of British Leyland in the 1970s, the problems associated with leadership were almost polar opposites. In the period of post-war growth the system of management at Jaguar relied heavily on Lyons. He maintained a constant level of intervention exemplified by his two tours of inspection per day around the Browns Lane site, his personal stewardship of the US market, his sole right to make new-model decisions and his personal supervision of management salary levels. Lyons' exceptional presence meant that after his absence, and given his distaste for formal management techniques, nobody had been suitably prepared to take his place. 'Lofty' England was MD in 1973 and Geoffrey Robinson from 1973 to 1975. Between 1975 and 1980 the Jaguar management board was disbanded and Bob Knight, the head of engineering at Jaguar was responsible for Browns Lane. Knight had no general management experience. In the light of the confusion within BL after the financial losses and problems highlighted by the Ryder Report in 1975, Knight and Peter Craig the plant directors were forced to devote all their energies to retaining as much as possible of Jaguar's traditional strengths and to thwart the incursions of corporate management.

When John Egan arrived in 1980 leadership had shrunk to this rather negative operational level and was concentrated on survival. One of his main achievements has been the construction of a full version of leadership that was capable of leading strategic change. As with Turnbull at Peugeot Talbot, he had to rehabilitate the position of chief executive. His reputation within the industry (after experience at GM, Unipart and Massey Ferguson) and his natural communication skills were combined with a series of initiatives that established him as a solid point of focus for Jaguar. Many of the actions were modest but well chosen, such as his move to receive customer complaint calls personally in 1980–81. Equally relevant was his openness at not having the technical knowledge about building cars so that: 'I very much had to rely on the knowledge of the people who reported to me. I couldn't invent any of this stuff, because I didn't know. So therefore a non-authoritarian executive regime started immediately simply because the person in charge didn't know the solution.'

In many ways this early orientation to Jaguar's problems was highly indicative of the way the strategic changes at Jaguar were led in the 1980s. Apparently, exceptional measures, such as the stripping out of £20 million of costs in 1980–81 were underpinned by vital parallel adjustments. Immense trouble therefore was taken over what we have called the conditioning features of that process. Hence the effort placed in the demonstration effect of the Black

Museum and the inviting of US dealers to the tracks, which began to loosen the complacency of the previously engineering-led company. What stands out in the Jaguar case is the time taken between 1981 and 1986 to regenerate Jaguar into something resembling a 'fully grown-up car company' (Jaguar was floated successfully in 1984). Before the company reintroduced the series III model in domestic and international markets, for example, care was taken to win back control of Jaguar's sales outlets from British Leyland (BL); to build a new sales and marketing function at Browns Lane vitually from scratch; and to recruit people from outside (as at Longman) who could supply the skills and perspective tuned to the demands of the world car market. This example is indicative of the way the entire change process was approached. In other words as much trouble was taken over creating the capacity to change as in constructing the strategic goals themselves.

Although ultimately baulked in its growth strategy by unpredictable government intervention in 1989, the range of secondary mechanisms that Jaguar mobilised to support its regeneration was formidable. Its methods of communicating the need for the changes in the regeneration programme (Whipp, Rosenfeld and Pettigrew, 1989) and its colourful way of reinforcing success within that programme (e.g. Jaguar national supplier excellence awards) have been widely recognised as establishing new benchmark standards in these areas.

The best example of the use of such supportive mechanisms comes in the way a critical mass, which believed in the regeneration, was assembled. To this end a small senior team was brought together by 1981, a team containing complementary skills. They were notable for their untypically wide engineering qualifications, even in the finance position, as much as for the sporting metaphors that Egan employed to structure their approach. Egan also skilfully included a mixture of ex-BL people desperate for Jaguar to survive (Beasley manufacturing, Edwards personnel and Johnson marketing) as well as outsiders who brought approaches that hitherto had been lacking. Those from within BL were essential for their knowledge prior to Jaguar becoming a private company away from BL.

CONCLUSION

Our central finding in relation to leading change is that no simple universal rules arise. On the contrary. Leadership is acutely context sensitive. This is manifested in a number of ways. The choice of leader, for instance, clearly relates to the those who make the choice and the circumstances in which they do so. The immediate problems the incoming leader faces are largely supplied by the situation that the leader inherits. The zones of manoeuvre open to the new leader in deciding what to change and how to go about it are bounded by the context within and outside the firm.

The critical leadership tasks in managing change appear to be much less heroic and more fragmentary and incremental. Leading change involves action by people at every level of the business. The general preoccupation of the 1980s with the saviours of corporations in crisis was unfortunate. It minimised the even more demanding challenge of sustaining effective leadership over time shown in the companies reported in this chapter.

Moving directly to bold leadership actions can be costly. Instead, the prior need is to build a climate for leading change while at the same time raising energy levels and setting out the new directions to be followed *before* precise action is taken.

We have identified a set of 'primary conditioning' actions, which includes:

- The building of a climate within the firm that will be receptive to change and that involves justifying why the change should take place.
- Similarly, there is little point attempting change without first building the capability to mount that change.
- Equally, establishing a change agenda that not only sets the direction of the business but also establishes the necessary visions and values is by no means simple. It is a process in itself that may take a series of attempts before completion.

Once these conditioning features have been attended to then a more direct set of secondary mechanisms have a better chance of success. These extend from the formation of a core of senior managers (and later operational leaders) who are convinced of the need for change, operationalising the change agenda, communicating the requirements of that agenda, sustaining coherence, through to the reinforcement of successful outcomes in order to build confidence.

The term 'leading change' has been chosen rather than 'leadership'. This seems more appropriate precisely because it suggests the full dimensions of the task facing firms. Leadership, partly for historical reasons, has all the connotations of individualism, and too often, one-dimensional heroism. If the companies here show anything, it is the complexity of the demands that confronted them in leading change. Leading change calls for the resolution of not so much great single issues, but rather a pattern of interwoven problems. The skill in leading change therefore centres on coping with a series of dualities and dilemma.

Longman is a clear example. Its management across the 1970s and 1980s had, among other things, to:

- link continuity and change by preserving existing product strengths while moving into totally new markets
- reconstitute its centre's role while preparing the case for the consequent restructuring of its divisions
- adjust the Longman culture by both surface interventions in the form of swiftly altering the role of financial reporting but at the same time devoting seven years to the remoulding of the computing function.

The problems of maintaining simultaneous action over a long-term process are at their sharpest in leading change. The need appears to be not boldness or decisiveness as much as a combination of planning, opportunism and the timing of interventions.

The result is that leading change necessitates a leadership that can operate with multiple levers and at multiple levels. Nowhere is this better illustrated than in Peugeot Talbot. Since 1983, the regeneration of the company has been founded on a combination of: a new set of open working relations among senior management; a reworking of the authority relations with PSA; rebuilding the confidence of staff shell-shocked after the contraction of 1975, 1978 and 1981–83; and the progressive elaboration of the new model programme through a reworked communications and inter-departmental structures.

As Peugeot Talbot also shows, such breadth of activity cannot be accomplished by one person or through single episodes or programmes. In Peugeot Talbot, the move from survival to re-generation and then growth involved two radically different types of leader in the 1980s, followed by the emergence of complementary leaders of change at lower levels in the company. The example of Jaguar's fall from grace in the late 1980s is interesting in that it had not moved to a new chief executive as occurred at Peugeot Talbot. It also found the development of a capacity to lead change at middle management a problem.

One of the central characteristics of leading change that has arisen from the eight companies under study has been its connectedness; in other words, the way leadership style can have multiple influences on the way an organisation manages change and competition. Here we have concentrated on leading change to shed light on those connections within the process of competition. However, our research indicates that a fuller understanding of that process would embrace four other central factors, namely: environmental assessment, linking strategic and operational change, managing human resources and sustaining coherence (Pettigrew and Whipp, 1991).

REFERENCES

Bass, B. M. (1981). *Stogdill's Handbook of Leadership: A Survey of Theory and Research*. New York: Free Press.

Bass, B. M. and Valenzi, E. R. (1974). Contingent aspects of effective management styles. In J. G. Hunt and L. L. Larson (Eds) *Contingent Approaches to Leadership*. Carbondale, IL: Southern Illinois University Press.

Bourgeois, L. and Brodwin, D. (1984). Strategic implementation: Five approaches to an elusive phenomenon. *Strategic Management Journal*, 5, 241–264.

Budworth, D. (1988). Was Adam Smith right about companies? Paper presented to the conference on Technology, Communication and the Humanities, Edinburgh, 18–21 August.

Budworth, D. (1989). Intangible assets of companies. Mimeo, Science Policy Support Group, London, May.

Edstrom, A. (1986). Leadership and strategic change. *Human Resource Management*, 25, 581–606.

Fiedler, F. E. (1967). *A Theory of Leadership Effectiveness*. New York: McGraw-Hill.

Goold, M. and Campbell, A. (1987). *Strategies and Styles: The Role of the Centre in Managing Diversified Corporations*. Oxford: Basil Blackwell.

Gospel, H. (1992). *Markets, Firms and its Management of Labour*. Cambridge: Cambridge University Press.

Hambrick, D. (1987). The top management team: Key to strategic success. *California Management Review*, Fall, 88–108.

Harvey-Jones, J. (1988). *Making it Happen: Reflections on Leadership*. London: Collins.

Hodgson, G. (1988). *Economics and Institutions*. Cambridge: Polity Press.

Hunt, J. G., Baliga, B. R. and Peterson, M. F. (1988). Strategic apex leadership scripts and an organisational life cycle approach to leadership and excellence. *Journal of Management Development*, 7, 61–83.

Iacocca, L. (1985). *Iacocca*. London: Bantam.

Kanter, R. M. (1989). *When Giants Learn to Dance*. New York: Simon & Schuster.

Langlois, R. N. (Ed.) (1986). *Economics as a Process: Essays in the New Institutional Economics*. Cambridge: Cambridge University Press.

Manz, C., Bastien, D., Hostager, T. and Shapiro, G. (1989). Leadership and innovation: A longitudinal process view. In A. Van de Ven, H. Angle and M. Scott-Poole (Eds) *Research On the Management of Innovation* (pp. 613–636). New York: Harper & Row.

Meindl, J., Ehrlich, S. and Dukerich, J. (1985). The romance of leadership. *Administrative Science Quarterly*, **30**, 78–102.

Nadler, D. and Tushman, M. (1988). What makes for magic leadership? *Fortune*, 6.6.88, 115–116.

Peters, T. J. and Waterman, R. H. (1982). *In Search of Excellence: Lessons from America's Best Run Companies*. New York: Harper and Row.

Pettigrew, A. M. (1987). Context and action in the transformation of the firm. *Journal of Management Studies*, **24**, 649–670.

Pettigrew, A. M. and Whipp, R. (1991). *Managing Change for Competitive Success*. Oxford: Basil Blackwell.

Pettigrew, A. M., Whipp, R. and Rosenfeld, R. (1989). Competitiveness and the management of strategic change processes: A research agenda. In A. Francis and M. Tharakan (Eds) *The Competitiveness of European Industry: Country Policies and Company Strategies* (pp. 110–136). London: Routledge.

Pfeffer, J. (1981). Management as symbolic action. In L. L. Cummings and B. Staw (Eds) *Research in Organisational Behaviour*. Greenwich, CT: JAI Press.

Roberts, N. (1985). Transforming leadership: A process of collective action. *Human Relations*, **38**, 1023–1046.

Ropo, A. (1989). Leadership and organizational change. *Acta Universitatis Tamperensis*, **A**, 280.

Rumelt, R. (1988). The evaluation of business strategy. In J. B. Quinn, H. Mintzberg and R. M. James (Eds) *The Strategy Process: Concepts, Contexts and Cases* (pp. 50–56). Engelwood Cliffs, NJ: Prentice Hall.

Teece, D. J. (Ed.) (1987). *The Competitive Challenge: Strategies for Industrial Innovation and Renewal*. Cambridge, MA: Ballinger.

Whipp, R. (1987). A time to every purpose: An essay on time and work. In P. Joyce (Ed.) *The Historical Meanings of Work* (pp. 210–236). Cambridge: Cambridge University Press.

Whipp, R. (1990). *Patterns of Labour: Work and Social Change in the Pottery Industry*. London: Routledge.

Whipp, R. and Clark, C. (1986). *Innovation and the Auto Industry: Product, Process and Work Organisation*. London. Frances Pinter.

Whipp, R. and Pettigrew, A. M. (1992). Managing change for competitive success: Bridging the strategic and the operational. *Journal of Industrial and Corporate Change*, **1**, 205–233.

Whipp, R., Rosenfeld, R. and Pettigrew, A. M. (1987). Understanding strategic change processes: Some preliminary British findings. In A. Pettigrew (Ed.) *The Management of Strategic Change* (pp. 14–55). Oxford: Basil Blackwell.

Whipp, R., Rosenfeld, R. and Pettigrew, A. M. (1989). Culture and competitiveness: Evidence from mature UK industries. *Journal of Management Studies*, **26**, 561–586.

10

Organization Learning: Theory to Practice

MARY M. CROSSAN, HENRY W. LANE,
TERRY HILDEBRAND

The 'learning organization' has been heralded as the organization of the future. In fact, many have suggested that the only competitive advantage for organizations is their ability to learn faster than their competitors (Garratt, 1987; De Geus, 1988). However, there is virtually no consensus on what organization learning is and how organizations learn (Shrivastava, 1983; Fiol and Lyles, 1985; Bedeian, 1986; Huber 1991).

This paper introduces a sociocognitive model of strategic management that is rooted in an organization learning paradigm. The model is applied to four case studies of Canadian retailers entering the US market to demonstrate from an organization learning perspective why the companies may have succeeded or failed in their endeavours.* As well, evidence from a large-scale empirical study employing 398 graduates and undergraduates, participating in a week-long simulation, is presented to provide further support for the model. Although the case studies relate to

---

*The cases in this paper are condensed versions of longer, more detailed originals that can be found in Evans, Wendy; Lane, Henry; O'Grady, Shawna (1992). *Border Crossings: Doing Business in the United States*. Canada; Prentice Hall.

Strategic Thinking: Leadership and the Management of Change.
Edited by J. Hendry and G. Johnson with J. Newton.

Canadian retailers entering the US, broader implications are drawn for companies seeking to gain competitive advantage through their ability to rapidly adapt or preempt changes in the environment given their capacity to learn.

PRECEPTS OF ORGANIZATION LEARNING

Developing a concept of organization learning is important for several reasons. At the broadest level, organization learning is about how organizations change, a vital process for the vast majority of organizations if they are to survive and prosper. Organization learning, however, is not simply about the management of change, an already well-established field of study. It is about the basic elements and processes by which organizations develop and grow. Growth, not in the physical sense of increased assets or sales, but growth in knowledge or understanding of the organization, its environment and the relationship between the two. Huber (1991, p. 108) states that 'organizational adaption and innovation, both critical in a rapidly changing world, could undoubtedly be improved if organizational designers and administrators knew more about how organizations learn and about how organizations might be guided to learn more effectively'.

The sociocognitive model presented in this chapter is built on three key precepts of organization learning.

1. That organizations learn through individuals, hence understanding individual learning is important.
2. Organization learning is different from the simple sum of individual learning, hence understanding individual learning is not enough.
3. Organization learning is a process of change in behaviors, beliefs (cognition), and other store houses of knowledge such as organizational systems and structures.

The following discussion expands on these three precepts. At the heart of organization learning is individual learning. As Barnard (1938) suggested, organizations are the consciously coordinated activities of two or more people. Therefore, the ability of organizations, which are collectives of individuals, to learn, is dependent upon the learning of its members. Although not necessarily occurring simultaneously, individual learning involves a process of changes in beliefs (cognition) and changes in behavior. However, an individual's beliefs both guide and are a product of the learning process as they undergo modification. Neisser stated that:

> We cannot perceive unless we anticipate but we must not see only what we anticipate . . . Although a perceiver always has at least some (more or less specific) anticipation before he begins to pick up information about a given object, they can be corrected as well as sharpened in the course of looking . . . The upshot of the argument is that perception is directed by expectations but not controlled by them (Neisser, 1976, p. 43).

Neisser's comments demonstrate how beliefs both guide and are a product of the learning process. Although beliefs guide interpretation, Neisser suggested that they do not control the process, and hence there is opportunity to interpret stimuli that may alter one's beliefs.

It is suggested that changes in cognition arise from the detection and resolution of gaps or discrepancies between what one experiences and what one believes.* However, individuals having highly developed belief systems with many concepts and inter-relationships are better able to make subtle distinctions and notice differences others do not. The ability to discriminate sets experts apart from novices as Neisser describes using the example of a chess master.

> The information that the master picks up from the chessboard determines not only where he will move his pieces but where he will move his eyes. Observations show that a good chess player's eye movements are closely related to the structure of the position on the board; he looks at crucial pieces and crucial squares. He quite literally sees the position differently – more adequately and comprehensively – than a novice or a nonplayer would. Of course, even the nonplayer sees a great deal: the chessmen are of carved ivory, the knight resembles a horse, the pieces are (perhaps) arrayed with a certain geometrical regularity. A young child would see

---

*Cognition is broadly defined to encompass knowledge, beliefs, opinions, attitudes and feelings. Although theorists, such as Abelson (1979), have made useful distinctions between many of these elements, Festinger (1957) pointed out that knowledge, beliefs, attitudes and opinions are all elements of cognition. Since individuals do not ordinarily compartmentalize and isolate each element as either a belief or an attitude, etc., it is more important from a cognitive perspective to focus on their similarities than their differences.

still less: that the pieces would fit in his mouth, perhaps, or could be knocked over. A newborn infant might just see that 'something' was in front of him. To be sure, he is not mistaken in this; something is in front of him. The differences among these perceivers are not matters of truth and error but of noticing more rather than less. The information that specifies the proper move is available in the light sampled by the baby as by the master, but only the master is equipped to pick it up. (Neisser, 1976, p. 181)

While the foregoing discussion has highlighted the importance of individual beliefs in the learning process, organization learning is different from the simple sum of individual learning. This chapter highlights two aspects of organization learning not captured by individual learning: (1) the process of integrating individual belief systems to enable the organization to take concerted action; and (2) the influence of nonhuman store houses of beliefs such as systems and structures that endure after individuals have left.

Just as individuals integrate new information into their own belief system, it is necessary for individuals within the organization to have some integration of beliefs in order for the collection of individuals that make up the organization to take concerted action. Recognizing the difficulty and complexity arising from the individual integration process highlights the complexity of the organization experience. For individuals, changes in beliefs arising from the resolution of a conflict or filling a gap, is done within the context of the meaning that they alone attribute to the situation. The added complexity for organizations arises from the integration of a variety of beliefs by individuals who attribute various meanings to that which they are trying to share. Furthermore, the systems and structure of the organization are store houses of beliefs that also guide what individuals interpret and integrate. Walsh and Ungson (1991, p. 66) state that 'rules represent formal and informal codifications of "correct" behaviour that is conditioned by consensual agreement among the participants'. As will be demonstrated in the cases that follow, there are a variety of mechanisms for storing beliefs, from the formal information systems and structure of the organization to the more informal, symbolic mechanisms such as imprinting the corporate mission on coffee cups.

The following section presents an overview of the sociocognitive model and discusses the precepts of organization learning that the model embodies.

OVERVIEW OF THE MODEL

The sociocognitive model of strategic management, shown in FIGURE 10.1 draws on Neisser's (1976) perceptual cycle of the relationship between cognition and reality. Neisser suggested that the 'actual physical world' we encounter, referred to in FIGURE 10.1 as the *environment*, derives its meaning from the belief system through which the individual perceives it. Neisser referred to the belief system as the 'schema'. In FIGURE 10.1, the belief system is referred to as the *individual schema*. Neisser referred to the process of interaction between the individual schema and the environment as the 'perceptual exploration process'. In FIGURE 10.1, it is referred to as the *process of interpreting*.

While Neisser dealt with cognition and reality at an individual level, this conceptual model is extended to a group setting. The *process of integrating* is similar to the process of interpreting, but rather than individuals interpreting stimuli from their environment, a group is attempting to create a shared meaning from their collective

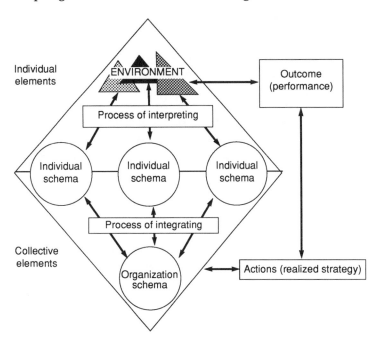

FIGURE 10.1 Sociocognitive model of strategic management

experiences. The result of the process of individual interpretation and group integration is an *organization schema*. The organization schema is the collective belief system which guides *action*. In this model, cognition and behaviors or actions are interrelated: cognition guides behaviors, but behaviors, providing the stimulus for interpretation, may lead to changes in cognition. The collective actions of organization members ultimately result in *performance outcomes*. In turn, performance outcomes affect the environment and become stimuli that are fuel for further interpretation.

The model recognizes both *individual elements* of learning (interpreting and individual schemas) and *collective elements* (integrating and organization schemas). It suggests that individuals have capacities for learning that are distinct yet intertwined with the collective capacity for learning. The model encompasses both the processes of learning (interpreting and integrating) and the products or substance of the learning process (individual schemas, organization schema, and action).

TYPES OF ORGANIZATION SCHEMA

Different levels of interpretation and integration may help explain why some organizational schemas seem to better reflect the environment, as determined by the performance of the organization. This chapter proposes that the organization schema can be categorized into four types based on the *potential level of interpretation* of the members' individual schemas and their subsequent *level of integration* achieved as depicted in FIGURE 10.2. For ease of discussion, references will be limited to high and low interpretation and high and low integration, on the understanding that interpretation refers to the potential provided by individual schemas and that integration refers to the level of integration achieved amongst the individual schemas.

It is submitted that the potential level of interpretation is a function of the complexity of individual schemas and the divergence among them. As previously discussed, individuals having belief systems or schemas with more concepts and relationships are expected to notice differences others cannot. Therefore, it is expected that individuals with a higher level of complexity in their schemas will have a higher level of interpretation. Furthermore, if the individuals in the organization have diverse schemas, they have the potential

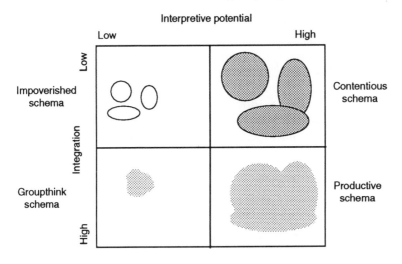

FIGURE 10.2 Organization schema

to interpret different aspects of the environment and therefore have a higher potential level of interpretation.

However, a high level of interpretation will be realized only if accompanied by a high level of integration. Level of integration refers to the level of shared understanding amongst individuals in the organization. Much like a complex puzzle, individuals with different schemas hold different pieces of the puzzle. If the individuals are able to integrate their pieces, they will be able to see a larger piece of the puzzle than they themselves hold. This paper suggests three primary mechanisms for integrating schemas: (1) self-integration; (2) personal facilitation; and (3) artifactual facilitation. With self-integration, individuals with different points of view are able to synthesize the diverse perspectives as a result of the high level of trust and respect they have for other points of view, coupled with an appreciation of and desire for synthesizing ideas. With personal facilitation, one individual may form the linchpin in the organization. As in catalysis, certain elements, unable to react with others without very high temperatures or pressures, require a catalyst to aid the reaction. Likewise, individuals in an organization may need an empathetic individual to help them see others' points of view. With artifactual facilitation, systems, structures, and artifacts such as mission statements and information systems may serve as integrating mechanisms.

It is suggested that low interpretation and low integration will lead to an *impoverished* organization schema, as no shared understanding exists and the individual schemas lack the complexity and diversity to interpret a complex environment. On the other hand, low interpretation coupled with high integration simply leads to a *groupthink* schema. Individuals share a common understanding, but the understanding overlaps and lacks complexity, breadth and depth. However, if there is high interpretation and low integration, a *contentious* schema arises. The contentious schema is a set of diverse and complex individual schemas that are not integrated. Brunsson (1982, p. 41) concluded that 'ideological inconsistencies increase uncertainty and make it extremely difficult to marshall commitments for organizational actions. Conflicts interfere with coordination'. Finally, it is suggested that high interpretation coupled with high integration will lead to a *productive* schema. The productive schema is an organization schema that has integrated diverse and complex views into a shared understanding.

The following section applies the sociocognitive model to four case studies of Canadian retailers entering the US market.

CASE STUDIES

MARK'S WORK WEARHOUSE

Background

Mark's Work Wearhouse (see Hildebrand and Lane, 1990b) was created based on the unique concept of a one-stop shopping place to meet the workwear needs of the working man and his family. The first store opened in 1977 in Calgary, Alberta and was an immediate success. This early success led to an expansion program through joint ventures reaching 33 stores by 1980. The large number of joint ventures became difficult to manage and control and they were eventually combined into one company. The huge success of a public stock offering, compounded by the boom atmosphere in Alberta, gave the company a feeling of 'we can do anything'. The company seemed invincible and embarked on another rapid expansion program doubling the number of stores to 66 by 1981. In that one year sales also increased from $40.7 million to $81.7 million and every store was operating at a profit.

Entry into the United States

In 1980 Work Wearhouse was approached to expand into the United States by an American consultant who told executives in Calgary that nothing like their concept existed in the western United States. Initially, the company was not interested because the Canadian operation and Canadian expansion was the priority. After the successful stock offering the attitude changed to one of 'Why not? We can't be beaten. Bigger is better.' Also, competitors in Canada were beginning to copy Work Wearhouse and the executives felt that expansion would help protect the concept. Mark's management believed that they could operate in the United States without direct competition.

Management was very concerned about protecting the concept. They wanted to open quietly and learn about the market before any major expansion took place. By entering small, remote areas, the company could test the retail concept without attracting the attention of much larger competitors. They wanted to start in areas with similar characteristics to the cities in which they were operating in Canada: cities of less than 50 000 people having a concentration of energy related industries employing blue collar workers.

The consultant investigated nine cities in five states that met the criteria. The analysis revealed that the competitors were more specialized than Work Wearhouse's Canadian competition. Stores were smaller (3000–4000 square feet) and carried a narrower product mix. In addition, sales prices, and profit margins, were much lower in the United States, especially for jeans. The conclusion was, however, that the Work Wearhouse concept was unique and powerful enough to overcome the lower prices with volume sales.

No suitable sites could be found in the company's first choice of a city. In its second choice, Rock Springs, Wyoming, a developer had a site available but he would not lease it to Work Wearhouse unless it also took another site in Pocatello, Idaho where he needed a retailer to anchor the mall he was building. The consultant advised against entering Pocatello because it was a farming community with slow population growth. However, in Calgary the executive committee decided that it was a good idea to test the concept in an agricultural-based economy.

Start-up

The first two stores were opened in November and December 1981. An assistant store manager from Canada was sent to manage the Rock Springs store and a local person was recruited to run the store in Pocatello. A more senior Canadian manager was not sent because no one wanted to live in the remote location. In retrospect the consultant commented:

> 'The Canadian was far too junior in position to be sent to the United States. I was to work with him so I could learn more about Work Wearhouse . . . so I could help them market the concept further. I knew very little about it at this time since we entered the United States only months after the first meeting.'

The consultant continued working with the United States operation and had responsibility for designing and opening stores, leasing the store outlets, hiring the local manager for the Pocatello location, and coordinating the activities of the two US stores since he was located closer to the US operation. As he stated, 'I knew the United States market, they [the executive in Calgary] knew the concept and the clothing industry so we made a good combination.' Although he had no prior retail experience in clothing, he was excited to work with Work Wearhouse because he knew 'nothing like the concept existed in the western United States.'

All key strategic, marketing and administrative decisions were made in Calgary. It was decided to transfer the Canadian concept, without any modifications, including the Canadian marketing campaign to the United States. In addition since the consultant was in the process of learning about the Work Wearhouse concept, the Canadian executives made most of the operational decisions. Canadian management seldom visited the operation in the United States. To keep the executive committee informed, the consultant travelled monthly to Calgary to report on the US activities.

It did not take long for operating problems to appear. The first problems arose from the product line. Due to high Canadian production costs and shipping costs, it was imperative that products be sourced from less expensive American suppliers. However, sourcing in the United States was far more difficult than anyone ever expected. In Canada, Work Wearhouse had very good relations with its suppliers and had no trouble obtaining products when needed. In the United States, the situation was completely different. With only two stores, Work Wearhouse did not have sufficient buying leverage. Buyers had trouble obtaining the desired product lines in the sizes they wanted and at the times they wanted them. This made it impossible to truly reproduce the Canadian concept, and the stores took on a 'sort of' Work Wearhouse look.

The Canadian Operation Experiences its First Set-back

In August 1981, the National Energy Program was introduced by the Canadian Federal government. This program had a dramatic effect on the economy of Alberta, due to the province's dependence on oil and gas. By late 1981/early 1982 the province went into a recession that affected the majority of businesses in the economy. The chief financial officer of Mark's stated: 'When Alberta crashed, so did we.'

For the first time, Work Wearhouse was faced with surviving in difficult economic times. The company discovered that it did not have adequate systems to control and monitor costs. There were no systems for accounts payable, inventory, budgeting or cost control. The company also experienced difficulties in marketing and merchandising. Rapid expansion, without adequate supervision, had allowed stores to be opened that did not accurately reflect the Work Wearhouse concept. During 1982, eight of the worst performing stores were closed, and the management group was rationalized.

The biggest move, however, was to change the marketing strategy from one of a discount retailer to a specialty retailer. The company could not survive difficult economic times by focusing on discounting jeans because the margins were too low. The strategy to sell more jeans than anyone else was no longer working.

The serious operating problems in Canada from 1982 to 1985 meant the majority of Work Wearhouse's resources (financial, management time and energy) were directed to saving the Canadian operation. The consultant still visited Canada monthly to report on the US operations and the executive committee was still involved in all major decisions. However, most agreed the US operation was basically orphaned.

Results in the United States

Initially, Rock Springs experienced good sales volume, but no profit due to higher than expected overhead expenses. Problems with suppliers had constantly hindered the business. The Pocatello store was struggling.

The solution chosen was to expand and to grow out of the problems. With more stores, Mark's Work Wearhouse would be more important to suppliers and would have a bigger base to absorb overhead. Stores were added, sales volume increased to satisfactory levels, but still there were no profits. One reason that profits were elusive was the competition.

Although no American competitor in these areas had the total workwear concept, each of the company's products had competition from at least one retailer. The chief executive officer (CEO) stated, 'It wasn't just competitive, it was a war! . . . Those boys play for keeps.' After Work Wearhouse implemented its low-price strategy, the competition lowered their prices and increased their promotion. The company had to work extremely hard to stay competitive.

The business of promoting discounted jeans, and other low-priced items, was not producing a profit for the company. Margins were too low and stiff competition prevented this from changing. To increase profits, the company decided to go back to the basics of workwear, such as overalls. These products did not sell nearly as fast as jeans. However, the margins were far superior. Concentrating on workwear meant that the company had to give up its goal of fast expansion and attainment of significant market share, since the strategy was now a longer-term approach with slower sales growth and the establishment of long-term customer relationships.

As early as 1984, people associated with the Canadian company were not interested in being involved with the US operation. It became known, but not spoken, that the US operation would not succeed. A board member commented, 'This ended up becoming a self-fulfilling prophecy because the company could not get people to go to the United States. It was viewed as a corporate dead-end. Nobody wanted their hands soiled by being associated with it.' These attitudes became even stronger by 1986.

It was decided in Calgary that resources being used in the United States would be put to better use in Canada. Work Wearhouse decided to close the US operation. On January 14, 1987, the US division of Mark's Work Wearhouse filed for bankruptcy in the United States ending four and one-half years of operation there.

Applying the Conceptual Model

We believe that the Mark's Work Wearhouse experience provides an example of an organization having a groupthink schema evolving into an impoverished schema as it moved into the US market. The two dimensions of the model, interpretation and integration, can be seen clearly in the situation.

Schema complexity was low. Management in Canada knew nothing about the retail market they were entering in the United States. One could argue that their schema regarding the Canadian market, although more complex, was not highly developed and that the company was fortunate to have started and to have grown in strong economic times. Management seldom visited the stores in the United States and really never developed an understanding of the market. The junior Canadian sent to the United States also did not know anything about the market there. The American consultant had no retail experience and did not understand the Canadian concept. He was involved in a learning process as the entry and expansion in the United States was taking place. Although company management and the consultant had different experience bases, no one had an accurate mental map of the competitive territory or what it would take to be successful in the United States.

Schema divergence was low also, and therefore cognitive coverage of the domain was inadequate. There was no initial view divergence. The consultant believed, correctly, that there was no similar concept in the western United States. Mark's management, riding a wave of success, believed that they were invincible and that the concept was extremely powerful. No one raised the question as to why that niche seemed to be empty, or why no similar store existed. No one understood the potential impact of all the indirect competitors that had been identified in the initial analysis.

It may be that the high level of integration evidenced in the Canadian operation shut out any diversity, since individuals were convinced the Work Wearhouse concept was unique and successful. As well, it may have inhibited the integration of the US operation which was viewed as more of an appendage than a central part of the organization.

Although there was agreement about the attractiveness of the retail concept between the people involved in the Work Wearhouse example, we would argue that there was no evidence of integration in the extended management team that included the people in the United States. There was, undoubtedly, high personal integration between the CEO and founder of the company and, possibly, within the executive committee in Canada following the CEO's lead. The consultant's recommendation was not taken in one area with which he was familiar, site selection. There was little, if any, exchange of valid task information and an interaction process that would permit developing a new, and more complex schema shared by the management team.

Integrating mechanisms in Canada were weak since inventory control, accounting, and selection and training systems were not highly developed and routinized. When difficult economic times appeared, Mark's began to see the inconsistencies in the stores and realized that it had inadequate control systems. While there was evidence of a strong personal facilitation on the part of the founder, Mark Blumes, the direction provided by his leadership was based on an inadequate schema of the US domain.

CANADIAN TIRE CORPORATION

Canadian Tire Corporation (CTC) (see Hildebrand and Lane, 1990a), founded in the early 1920s, became a public corporation in 1944. However, John Billes and his brother, Alfred, retained voting control. That same year, CTC diversified the company's product line beyond automobile parts and accessories to include sporting goods, tools and household products. Stores became one-stop shopping outlets. CTC built a reputation for being a company with incredible growth and success. Sales rose from $100 million in 1966 to $1.3 billion in 1981.

Canadian Tire was comprised of two components: the Canadian Tire Corporation, the principal supplier and distributor of merchandise to its dealer network, and a network of associated dealers. The dealer–manager network was considered the cornerstone of CTC's success and a key part of the corporate culture. Across Canada, 404 Canadian Tire stores were operated by associated dealers in 1987.

In addition to the dealer network, key success factors included the concept of power marketing (category dominance, intensive advertising and promotion, and price leadership); the use of state-of-the-art computer and distribution systems; and a commitment to investing in modern, well-located retail stores.

The Decision to Enter the United States Market

In 1977, CTC began developing a master plan for the company's future growth. Projections estimated that by 1985 the maximum Canadian penetration of 400 stores would be reached. Several options for continued growth and expansion were considered. After exploring the possibility of becoming involved in other industries in Canada, the decision was made to develop a retail business in the United States where there could be a transfer of skills.

To achieve an economic mass it was necessary to acquire an existing firm. A list of six existing United States auto parts and service companies fulfilling certain criteria was produced and inquiries were made to see which would be available for sale. At this time, CTC was approached by an American company interested in selling White Stores Inc., one of the six companies being considered. CTC management and board members visited Whites' corporate head office, warehouses and several store locations. Out of this process came the decision to purchase White Stores.

White Stores Inc., based in Wichita Falls, Texas, operated 81 home and auto supply stores in six sunbelt states (mainly Texas), and supplied 420 dealer-owned stores in 12 states. Sales from Whites exceeded $150 million in 1981 and were split 50/50 between corporate stores and wholesale shipments. The operation had been losing money for several years. Half of Whites' corporate stores were located on company-owned real estate while the remainder were on leased premises. The stores' product mix included: auto service products, lawn and garden equipment, sporting goods, hardware, furniture, and major appliances.

Competitive analysis indicated that Texas and the sunbelt markets contained only six major, direct competitors. None of these competitors carried the same product mix as CTC. Therefore, management believed that they had identified a void in the market. The analysis did, however, indicate that Sears, Montgomery Ward and K Mart had significant clout within the market. For example, Sears was heavily involved in auto parts and service, and their outlets often had 16 or more auto bays as opposed to Whites' five or six. However, CTC underestimated the impact of nondirect competition such as Walmart and discount department stores.

Whites' sales per square foot were approximately one-third those of CTC over the same period. The fact that the Whites chain was old, run down and outdated, was considered by retail analysts to explain the significant difference in sales. White Stores did not have a strong management base at the time of the purchase by CTC.

After The Purchase

John Kron, appointed president of White Stores Inc., had been in charge of the marketing, management information systems, and operations in Canada and was considered ideal for the US operation because he was the most broadly based person in Canada. Three additional executives, experienced in advertising, store operations and distribution, were transferred to the Unites States along with several other junior management personnel.

Integration was achieved by CTC president, Dean Muncaster, and the Canadian board of directors being involved in all major strategic and capital acquisition decisions. However, they maintained a distant role to ensure those closest to the market were making decisions.

Prior to the purchase of Whites, it had been decided that CTC would transfer to the United States what the company knew best – the Canadian Tire retail formula. Mr Kron stated that 'Whites will not re-invent the wheel in Texas.'

The strategy to turnaround Whites included: all 81 stores would be refurbished and remerchandised at an estimated cost of $100 million; CTC dealers would be brought in to run some of the stores with a goal of 81 dealer-run stores by the end of 1983; major appliances and furniture would be phased out; Whites would spend more money on advertising than the average US retailer in order to develop a strong, clear consumer image; the independent dealer network would be reduced from the existing 425 to 300 stores by cutting off the outlying dealers. Whites would then reflect CTC's philosophy and corporate objectives.

After each store was reopened, 50–60% of its merchandise was put on promotion and specialty loss leaders were developed and promoted through flyer advertising. The original plan was to reduce the percentage of promotional items as the stores matured; however, it was discovered that the US competitive market forced a higher mix of promotional items than in Canada. To remain competitive, Whites maintained the high level of promotional items.

Performance

The conversion process, which required stores to be closed for up to six weeks, was expensive (estimated at $165 million) and severely hindered profit figures. Whites had a net loss in 1982 of $9.8 million, in 1983 it was $29.2 million, and in 1984 it was $55 million.

Executives realized that they had been too optimistic about the time it would take to become profitable and they discovered that the consumer differences were greater than expected. They underestimated customer loyalty to other stores and the difficulty of changing buying patterns. US customers preferred having lots of choice within a product line to having lots of product lines to select from. CTC also discovered that good store locations were even more important than in Canada. Whites stores were not in prime locations.

Changing Attitudes

Despite the problems, Mr Muncaster and Mr Kron were committed to turning around the US operation. However, at the same time, both were feeling pressure from within the organization to improve Whites' performance. Managers not involved in the United States were concerned because stock they received through the profit-sharing plan was being affected negatively by results in the United States. The new board also was not pleased with the losses. Mr Kron indicated there was a shift in corporate support at this time.

In late 1983 the share structure of CTC was altered. From this time on, Mr Muncaster found it increasingly difficult to operate with the board of directors. The strain caused Mr Muncaster and Mr Kron to start interviewing candidates to take over Mr Kron's job as president of the US operation early in 1985. Mr Muncaster suggested that on several occasions it was difficult to get the board to focus and come to conclusions. This made it difficult to make changes in the United States.

In 1985, it was decided that a strong, experienced marketing manager was needed to improve Whites' performance. John Crowley, VP of Marketing in Canada, was sent to the United States as executive VP of Merchandising. Mr Crowley was an American by birth, with 36 years of retail experience largely in the United States. In May 1985, A. J. Billes (cofounder of CTC), then 85 years old, rejoined the board of directors full-time. Numerous rumours suggested that relations between Dean Muncaster and the Billes family were strained.

It had been obvious for some time that the only products earning money were automotive products and service. After research revealed that no competitor dominated this product area, a new merchandising and marketing campaign was designed to reposition Whites from a one-stop shopping place, to a store focused on auto parts and service. The uncompetitive hardware and houseware product lines were dropped and all other do-it-yourself home improvement products were deemphasized.

In June 1985, CTC's executive committee of the board of directors commissioned a consulting company to do an analysis of Whites. The resulting report recommended downsizing the US operation. White Stores was overextended in relation to its internal operation. The company had too many stores, many of which were in poor locations.

In mid 1985, after announcing losses paralleling 1984's despite repositioning attempts, Mr Muncaster was quoted out of context in a Canadian paper stating that CTC would probably liquidate its US operation. This quote was picked up by US newspapers and resulted in Whites losing bank credit, much of its supplier credit and some employees. On June 15, 1985, Mr Muncaster was asked to leave CTC just prior to the company's annual meeting. John Kron was let go as president of Whites in August, at which time Whites showed a loss of $78.3 million.

It was announced at a United States trade show in October that all franchise contracts expiring on December 31 would not be renewed. This action resulted in a major lawsuit against Whites, CTC, and the executives of both companies by the 22 affected dealers. Half of the 22 dealers were Canadians transferred to the United States by CTC.

In October 1985, Dean Groussman, an American with a strong retailing background, was hired as president. By this time, White Stores was losing approximately $2 million per week and this figure had been increasing rapidly. He concluded that no aspect of White Stores, as it stood, was profitable or capable of becoming so. Downsizing the operation alone would not create profits for many years and the writeoff associated with store closures would only increase the company's losses. Mr Groussman agreed with earlier conclusions that an automotive emphasis was required. Automotive products were the only hope for White Stores' future; however, the stores were too large to convert into exclusive auto specialty stores.

Western Auto Supply Company approached White Stores with an offer to purchase the company. In December 1985, CTC announced its decision to sell the assets of its US operation, White Stores Inc. This marked the end of four years of operation in the United States.

Applying the Conceptual Model

The Canadian Tire example shows a top management group with a groupthink schema that begins developing in the direction of a contentious schema in the process of learning about and trying to adapt to the American marketplace.

Schema complexity was low. Canadian management knew very little about the competition, consumer or markets in the United States. They decided before entering the United States that the Canadian Tire concept and mode of operating would be transferred without modification, assuming that it would work. Divergence also was low. No one questioned whether the concept would work. It had been working since the 1940s!

However, as executives with different backgrounds and experience analyzed the operation, along with external American consultants, it became clear that a different concept had to be developed. At the same time as this increase in divergence was producing learning, changes to the board and the subsequent lack of support and commitment to the US operations created conflict. The lack of integration at the board level made it difficult to make decisions, resulting in a stalemate. It is interesting to note that CTC learned what it had to do to be successful in the United States just before it sold Whites. In the early 1990s, it is engaged in opening a new company in the United States, Auto Source, focusing on the automotive market.

Integration was high, primarily because of the power and success of the CTC retail concept for such a long period of time. CTC had developed sophisticated systems (selection, inventory control, accounting, etc.) and had routinized all its procedures to become extremely efficient in supporting the concept.

Everyone believed in the concept. The degree of sharing of the concept, or its extensiveness, was extremely high. A competent executive team (with the Canadian concept) was transferred to the United States along with 22 dealers. Communication channels were open between the United States and Canada. However, everyone's mindset was to do all the things necessary to make Whites look just like Canadian Tire.

COLES BOOK STORES LIMITED

Suburban shopping centres began springing up across Canada in the latter half of the 1950s through to the mid 1970s, providing Coles (see Evans, 1990) and many other retailers with a vehicle for expansion from coast to coast. Early on, Coles made the decision to become market-dominant by locating in virtually any shopping centre that was presented to them.

The expansion was described as the 'cookie cutter approach' where set assortments of books were slotted into predetermined fixturing and store configurations. As many as three stores were opened in a week. Little attention was paid to regional differences. The product mix, consisting of good value books over a wide range of subjects, school texts, Coles notes for students, and a range of their own published titles and reprints, were right for the market.

Entry into the United States

Eventually, Coles ran out of primary and secondary locations in Canada. By the mid 1960s, Coles had approximately 150 stores and had 'used all the Canadian locations that were viable.' The American market was viewed as a southern extension of the Canadian market and management perceived the US market to be 'very similar, although much larger than that in Canada.'

In 1965 Coles opened its first store in New York State. A new shopping centre 'looked satisfactory' and Coles proceeded with the new store in the same fashion as with any new store in Canada using the 'cookie cutter' approach with identical fixtures and, for the most part, the same mix of merchandise and back sections. Generally the store stocked a broad range of books across a wide number of subjects and selection compared favourably with that of the competition. Since the head office already dealt with United States suppliers, there was no perceived need to duplicate the very expensive purchasing operation. Hence, all the purchasing remained in Canada.

Competing for locations was a major problem. Coles was an unknown in the US market and during this same period, Waldens and Daltons, the two largest book retailers in the United States in the early 1990s were embarking on major expansion programs.

Coles management took the same expansion tactic in the United States as they did in Canada. When a site became available that, in the eyes of the real estate expert and Canadian management, was suitable, they took it. Guidelines did not exist as to which types of locations would be acceptable. There was no preference given to any region. By 1986, 58 stores existed in 24 states and within states stores were generally spread across a variety of markets, with little or no concentration in any one.

Coles' own publishing efforts were expanding in Canada. These books carried high margins and covered a wide range of subjects, not just Canadian content. They were shipped to the United States as well. Some were quite British in flavor, which resulted in poor sales south of the border.

Because the stores were spread across a large number of states, and management spent insufficient time in the United States, very little was known about each individual market. Problems were experienced, for example, in Brownsville, Texas, where Coles had difficulty due to the very high proportion of Spanish speaking population in the area. Regional differences were not taken into consideration in the buying. Downhill skiing books were sent to Florida, European cook books with metric weights, measures and different spelling, were sent to the United States, and the Water Street store in Manhattan had a large section of nature books.

Southam Inc., a large cash-rich Canadian-owned company in the communications and information industries, bought Coles in 1978. The United States company was losing between $1.3 million and $2.0 million per year, and the total loss between the Canadian and United States divisions was approximately $10 million post interest. Under new leadership, the Canadian company was turned around by 1983–84.

Management of the United States Operation

With the turnaround of the Canadian operation, attention turned to the United States.

Long-distance management made negotiations more difficult with stores and suppliers. Inventory control was very poor in the United States stores. In Canada, Coles had been able to negotiate a virtually 'open' returns privilege with Canadian suppliers. They were not geared to the paperwork required to return books in the United States and hence, suffered major overstocks.

Early on as new stores were opened, they were added to Canadian district managers' territories based on north/south proximity. When there were only a few stores, this method worked reasonably well. As the number of United States stores grew and locations were spread across the country, the territories of the district managers became far too large and varied to be effectively managed. American district managers were eventually hired. Although this was an improvement, the districts were still very large and diverse.

All store hiring and firing was the responsibility of the United States district managers. The Canadian company was not involved and Bill Ardell, president of Coles, felt that they (in Canada) were 'so poorly connected to the market that the Canadian operation didn't know whether they were getting good or bad staff'.

On examining the US operation, Coles' management realized that they needed American management to run it. Bill Ardell subsequently hired an American who had been working with W. H. Smith in the United States, to be vice president of the US stores. This person reported directly to Ardell and controlled the whole operation with the exception of finance which was all handled in Canada. A Canadian buyer was sent down to the United States office, and a second buyer was hired from Barnes and Noble, a US discount bookstore chain with over 100 stores. In addition, an advertising manager was hired, also from W. H. Smith in the United States.

The United States office was located in New York City, where there was only one Coles store, located in the central business district on Water Street. All the other stores were located in shopping malls in different markets across the country. It is very important for any buyer to have close access to the stores for which he or she is buying. In this case, the only store to which they had quick access was serving a market that was not representative of the rest of the chain. Though the office was close to the sources of supply, the lack of easy access to the field was a definite drawback.

Rather than the situation improving with the opening of the New York office, it deteriorated further. Bill Ardell stated that the United States office suffered from 'excessive zealousness.' They put in the wrong merchandise, and did not control the quantities of Canadian product. 'The problems were enhanced by the individual in charge'. The inventory situation worsened, and Ardell felt that there was inadequate expertise in the running of the US operation.

Competition

By the mid 1980s the competition had become far more intense than it had been 20 years earlier, when Coles was just entering the market. As previously noted, Daltons and Waldens were the major competition in the early years, both undergoing rapid expansion programs and vying for new locations at the same time as Coles. They had grown into book chain giants with 746 and 940 stores respectively. The growth of the competition over the years left Coles in a middle position, with the full selection, regular-priced chains on one side, and the lower-priced competition on the other.

With the financial and inventory situation worsening in the United States, Coles Canada decided to hire a consultant to provide an assessment of the market position, performance, prospects and recommendations for the US operation. All the options, other than closing or selling the operation, could not solve all of Coles' concerns without a very large investment.

At this point, with the situation deteriorating, Coles made the decision to close the United States office, which had been in operation for only 18 months. In mid 1986, the purchasing was brought back to Toronto. Advertising came under the marketing department; however, very little was done in the US market.

The corporate group, Southam, was deliberating whether or not to remain in the US market. Ardell said that it 'took six to nine months to persuade the corporate group to get out. It was taking too much management time and financial resources'. Finally, in early 1987, the decision was authorized to sell the US operation. Within five months the sale to Walden had been finalized.

Applying the Conceptual Model

The Coles situation is similar to that of Mark's Work Wearhouse and Canadian Tire in that all three companies expanded into the United States with the goal of transferring a retail concept that had been successful in Canada. Management did not understand the differences in the Canadian and American marketplaces.

The interpretive capacity of Coles' management was low. Initially, and for many years, there was no schema complexity or view divergence. Everything was run from Canada in the same way as the Canadian stores. The United States was assumed to be the same as Canada, only larger. It was not until poor results forced Coles' management into recognizing that it needed American management did any view divergence or complexity develop. Unfortunately, the diversity resulted in unresolved differences of how to turn around the US stores.

Initially, there was high integration, except at the staffing level, in that the Canadians ran the US operations. When the organization became more complex and regional managers were hired in Canada to manage the American regions, there was no integration since the Canadian did not know anything about the United States and left most decisions to American store management. The creation of the position of vice president responsible for the US operation brought a different operating philosophy and style into the company from which it never recovered. In the language of the model, we see the development of a contentious schema.

In the three examples so far, impoverished, groupthink, and contentious schemas have led to failure. We now examine an example in which the top management team's mental map led to initial operating and market success.

PEOPLES JEWELLERS LIMITED

The 1970s were boom years for jewellery retailing and Peoples (see Hildebrand and Lane, 1990c) grew to be the second largest jewellery retailer in Canada with 300 stores. By the end of the decade retail growth was over. Rather than opening 20 to 30 stores each year, as had formerly been the case, Peoples was closing more stores than it was opening. In order to revive its previous growth trend, the company turned its attention to the US market.

Peoples' First Entry into the United States

After investigating several possibilities for buying jewellery chains in the United States with no success, Irving Gerstein, president of

Peoples, met an American jewellery consultant, who introduced him to the White chain that had 14 stores in Utah, Montana and San Francisco. An analysis was made of its financial status, including projections of future earnings, as well as an examination of its operations for compatibility with Peoples. In 1978, Peoples purchased 80% of the White chain. The consultant purchased the remaining 20% and became president. Over the next two years, the chain expanded from 14 to 50 stores.

Although the stores were operating at a profit, it was not enough to cover the carrying costs of the investment. In 1982, the US operation was sold at a loss of $8.1 million. The American management was quoted as saying that Peoples failed to understand the key market differences between Canada and the United States, and tried to institute Canadian procedures that did not work south of the border. There were other reasons, such as difficulty getting good locations, and the amount of cash required to build the chain.

The Acquisition of Zale Corporation

Collectively, in 1987, Zale's three retail divisions had approximately 1300 stores, sales of $938.6 million and earnings before interest, taxes and unusual items of $39 million. Despite the fact that Zale was the largest jewellery retailer in the world, it still had only 6.5% of the total US jewellery market as of 1988. The market was extremely fragmented with the four largest jewellers holding only 8.3% of the total market.

In 1981, Peoples purchased 15% of Zale's stock as an investment. In 1985 the company obtained control of Zales. The initial three seats on Zale's board of directors and Gerstein's membership on the company's audit committee gave Peoples a unique opportunity to learn about Zale, its competitive environment, its operations and its key management. Gerstein indicated that once he was on the inside of the company he became very concerned over Zale's ability to achieve growth in the future. He saw that, although the company was the industry leader in the United States, it was plagued with problems. He felt that Zale's performance could be improved significantly if the company became more focused, costs were cut and the organizational structure was simplified.

In 1985, Gerstein and his management team considered Peoples' options with regard to its investment in Zale. They decided the best option was to pursue purchasing Zale.

After the Purchase of Zale

In December 1986, Irving Gerstein took full management control of the company. He called a meeting of the company's senior management to outline the 'new' direction for Zale. During this meeting he indicated that he intended to move aggressively to turn Zale into a more profitable organization. His vision for the company was presented in the form of four principles: (1) Zale is a retail jeweller; retailers make their profits across two feet of counter space; (2) Zale will have a simple organizational structure; (3) Zale will minimize the distance between the customer and the chief executive officer; and (4) the customer is the boss – everything we do is to serve the customer. These four principles laid out the culture that Gerstein wanted to create.

The principles became so prevalent and well known in Zale that coffee cups were created with the principles written on them in gold. As a symbolic move, Gerstein announced that the executive dining-room would be closed immediately. Executives would no longer be separated from the remainder of Zale's staff.

The VP of Store Operations indicated that Gerstein was very interested in 'how things really worked in the company, how people thought and felt about things, and especially what their attitudes were'. Therefore, Gerstein's next step was to interview key executives of Zales. This process allowed him to (1) become more familiar with the company and its management talent, (2) identify problems, opportunities and areas for improvement in the company, and (3) select a management team to run the company. One executive stated that Irving Gerstein's personal style encouraged the change of ideas, 'Ideas that were suppressed in the old system, came out of the woodwork.'

The first change was to simplify Zale's divisional structure. Each division had acted autonomously and very little communication occurred between divisions. The company's organizational structure was changed to a functional structure. This approach allowed the senior management to be reduced significantly and removed redundancies that occurred in the divisional approach.

Next, it was critical to select a person to head each functional area. Almost immediately, it became apparent that personal philosophies and personal chemistry would prevent the existing team from operating smoothly. After several discussions, it was agreed, by all those involved, that some individuals should leave the company. By all accounts it was an amicable 'parting of the ways'.

Peoples' SVP of Merchandising, Marketing and Operations was transferred to the Zale operation as SVP of Merchandising. This person was an American with industry experience in the United States. In addition, two of Zales' executives were promoted into the positions of SVP of Store Operations, and SVP of Finance. Within six weeks of the takeover, Gerstein had his management team in place who, along with himself as president and CEO, and his assistant, were responsible for running the Zale Corporation.

Zales' expenses had to be reduced significantly and its profits increased. During this stage Gerstein relied heavily on input from Zale management. He was quoted in the Zale company magazine as saying: 'I am relying heavily on the expertise and visions of the senior officers who make up our new organizational structure to map out the final details and strategies as we move ahead.'

All members of the management team were encouraged to participate in an exchange of ideas. In fact, Gerstein gave the management team full credit for coming up with the ideas that were implemented. Each of the senior vice presidents felt that they were responsible, as a team, for handling the day-to-day operation of Zale. One manager remarked that 'Irving manages the process, we manage the business'.

During the next months, nonselling staff was reduced by 1600 (35%). Expenses were reduced by approximately $80 million, as a result of wage reductions, the elimination of manufacturing, and a reduction in the advertising budget of $35 million.

The management team also changed the merchandise mix of individual stores. Since previous management had identified department stores as their main competition, they had stocked their stores similar to a department store – broad lines with little depth. To change this strategy to one of a specialty store having narrow lines with depth, the best sellers were identified and slow movers were eliminated from store inventory.

The fact that Irving Gerstein became president of Zale and his Canadian SVP of Finance and Administration became his assistant, made it obvious that Peoples would be active in the management of Zale. The two men continued to spend on average two days a week in Texas. Once a month they would meet with Zale's senior management in a formal meeting that provided a mechanism for the discussion of key issues. Other than this meeting, the remainder of the communication between them was on an informal, *ad hoc* basis. Meetings were set up when necessary.

However, Zale was managed differently from Peoples. Gerstein stated the following soon after the purchase:

> 'I have made it very, very clear. They will be two separate stand-alone operations. We are not taking Canadian management down there . . . I feel strongly that Canada is not the United States and the United States is not Canada. I come with no baggage, and they have an extremely talented professional management team. My role will be to create a framework for them to make Zale Jewellers the most exciting environment for a customer to be in.'

Applying the Conceptual Model

In Peoples we see evidence of a productive schema. The interpretive capacity was high. Complexity was high resulting from the Canadian executives' experience in Canada and, previously, in the United States. Also, the Zale management team was talented, possessing, quite possibly, a higher skill level, and definitely more experience than most of the Canadians. This conclusion was based on the level of experience required to reach the executive levels of Zale, a much larger organization than Peoples. Divergence was high also because of the different backgrounds and experience sets. The executives on the top management team stated that Gerstein's management style and process wanted and expected divergence.

It may be important to differentiate between possible types of divergence. The Peoples example made it clear that compatibility was important and that personal positions and chemistries needed to be managed. However, this probably differs from the professional differences and perspectives of the task that executives indicated that Gerstein wanted. Managing this process and the types of divergence probably makes the difference between contentious and productive schemas.

Integration was achieved through Gerstein's vision, principles, management style, and management process. In terms of extensiveness, belief in the principles was pervasive. An example of efficiency of systems and procedures is Zale's credit system. This credit system was, apparently, the most sophisticated in the industry. Gerstein immediately adopted it for use in Canada.

Postscript: Peoples Jewellers Update

Through March 1989, the results at Zale had been consistent with expectations. At about the same time, Irving Gerstein and Charles Gill became aware that Gordon Jewellery Corp., Zale's major competitor with 625 stores in the United States, was available. Although they were not looking to make such an acquisition, they finally decided to purchase Gordons. Zale stores had been transformed into more high-end jewellery and giftware merchandise, which left a major consumer segment – the lower income customer – open, and Gordon filled this gap, fitting into the company's program to serve the total market. Zale had difficulty with the financing of the Gordon acquisition since the marketplace had changed radically. Whereas previously, raising $100 million had not been too hard, it was necessary to go to three continents to raise the $313 million to acquire Gordons.

The operating results in 1990 were fine for both the Zale and Gordon divisions. In fact, Gordon outperformed its targets and Zale was not far off. Gordon continued to be the most profitable division, especially in the recession. The US operation was under some financial pressure during the early part of 1990, but it was not until August of that same year that the real problems began when consumer confidence began to fade and the economic slowdown reduced traffic in the malls and led to decreased sales.

By March 1991, the difficulties led Peoples' management to sit down with their banks to discuss Zale's financial position, but they still hoped that things would improve. However, consumer confidence continued to erode and as the Christmas season approached, the picture did not improve. The recognition that Zale was not going to meet certain obligations moved its management toward a dialogue with its creditors. One creditor, a Dallas securities dealer, thought it was more appropriate to pursue the discussions within Chapter 11 of the United States Bankruptcy Code, and filed a petition on January 1, 1992. This made it impossible for Zale to continue without the protection of Chapter 11 and therefore management consented to the action. In the fiscal year 1992, Peoples took a writeoff of $149.6 million of its investment in Zale and experienced an overall loss of $159.2 million.

Management raised $450 million which allowed Zale to continue to operate. They then developed a business plan, closed over 400 stores, changed the organization back to a divisional structure, and made a number of changes to operations. As of May 1992, Zale was meeting its obligations. However, the results for the six months ending November 1992 showed a loss of $15.2 million at Peoples and a possible restructuring of the Canadian company was being debated. The future of Peoples and Zale was uncertain.

Does this mean that the Peoples case did not represent a productive schema after all? We think it suggests that different schemas may operate in different domains and that it is necessary to ensure the presence of interpretive capacity (complexity and diversity) as well as integration in all areas of strategic decision-making. It seems that a productive schema was in operation around issues of internal operations and the company's market and customers. However, there may have been a failure in the assessment of financial risk that the new acquisition entailed and the availability of resources to meet it. The most obvious problems were the high level of debt and the major expansion just in time for the recession of 1991. These factors, working together, probably negated all the things that management did do correctly. However, Peoples was not the only retailer that ran into difficulty in the first two years of the decade.

Although the foregoing case studies provide insight into the model, the evidence is anecdotal since there was no intent to actually measure the level of interpretation and integration of schemas. The following section provides a brief overview of a study designed to test the model and some of the salient results.

EMPIRICAL STUDY

The Markstrat simulation involving 398 graduates and under-graduates in business administration was used to examine the difference in performance between 70 groups exhibiting the four types of schema. The added value of the study is that it provides a specific test of the model, establishing links to performance. Cause maps, a representation of an individual's schema, were elicited from the individuals to measure the two elements of interpretation; schema complexity and view divergence. The cause map was elicited by having the individual draw the cause/effect relationship between 18 factors identified as key elements in the Markstrat simulation. Level of integration was measured using a four-item seven-point

Likert scale. Performance was measured as the accumulated profit over the course of the simulation, referred to as 'cumulative net marketing contribution'.

FIGURE 10.3, showing the mean performance and frequency of each of the four schema types, indicates the expected pattern of performance with productive groups having the highest performance ($640.1 million) and contentious groups having the lowest performance ($282.5 million). It was expected that in the absence of integration groups with low view divergence (impoverished groups) would perform better than groups with a high level of view divergence (contentious groups) since lack of view divergence would facilitate taking coherent actions. Contentious groups were expected to either reach a stalemate and therefore fail to take any actions, or take actions that were not internally consistent given the diverse points of view. However, in the absence of integration it was expected that groups with high schema complexity (contentious groups) would perform better than groups with low schema complexity (impoverished groups) since individuals with more complex views were expected to be better able to interpret the environment. However, in this study, the measure of schema

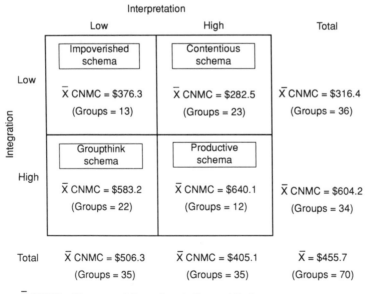

$\bar{X}$ CNMC = Mean cumulative net marketing contribution
in millions of dollars

FIGURE 10.3   Mean performance and frequency of schema types

complexity was weak, as discussed below, and therefore the results are more strongly affected by a group's level of view divergence than their schema complexity.

FIGURE 10.3 also indicates that groups with high integration had higher performance ($604.2) than groups with low integration ($316.4) as expected. However, it is necessary to examine the results from an analysis of variance to determine whether the differences are significant.

The analysis of variance shown in Table 10.1, indicates that level of integration has a significantly positive relationship with performance with an F value of 14.145 significant at 0.000. However, level of interpretation is not significantly related to performance as expected. In fact, a high level of interpretation without integration resulted in very poor performance as found in groups with contentious schemas.

The specific contrasts in performance between each schema type shown in Table 10.2, indicates that four of the six groups have significantly different levels of performance.

As well, a chi-square analysis of the frequency of each schema type indicated that there were significantly more contentious groups (23) than productive groups (12) and more groupthink groups (22) than impoverished groups (13). Since a median split was used to distinguish groups with high and low levels of interpretation, the results indicate that the 35 groups having a high level of interpretation had significantly more difficulty integrating their diversity and complexity than did the 35 groups having a low level of interpretation.

The 70 groups were divided into 14 parallel industries consisting of five groups each. Each of the groups within the industry began

TABLE 10.1   ANOVA: Interpretation by integration by performance

Source of variation	Sum of squares	DF	Mean square	F value	Sig. of F
Main effects	1445918.625	2	722959.312	8.073	0.001*
Integration	1266632.699	1	1266632.699	14.145	0.000*
Interpretation	7067.550	1	7067.550	0.079	0.780
2-way interaction	91122.531	1	91122.531	0.018	0.317
Explained	1537041.155	3	512347.052	5.722	0.002*
Residual	5910120.839	66	89547.285		
Total	7447161.995	69	107929.884		

*Significant at 0.01

TABLE 10.2 ANOVA: Contrasts of schema types

Schema types	T value	T probability
Impoverished–contentious	0.903	0.370
Impoverished–groupthink	−1.976	0.052*
Impoverished–productive	−2.202	0.031*
Contentious–groupthink	−3.369	0.001*
Contentious–productive	−3.355	0.001*
Groupthink–productive	−0.530	0.598

*Significant at 0.05

with different products and product positioning. Therefore, although group 1 in industry 1 began in the same position as group 1 in industry 14, they had different products from groups 2, 3, 4 and 5 in industry 1. An analysis of variance of performance by start position indicated that groups beginning in positions 2 and 4 had significantly higher performance than groups beginning in positions 1, 3 and 5, indicating that groups 2 and 4 had a more favorable start position. It is interesting to note that although groups having a contentious schema, whether beginning in a favorable or unfavorable start position had consistently poor performance, groups beginning in a favorable start position did quite well in spite of having an impoverished or groupthink schema.

Overall, the results of the study provide strong support for the importance of integration, and the difficulty and potential pitfalls of having a high level of interpretation without integration. However, a fixed form approach was used to measure individual schemas which meant that the components of each individual's cause map were derived from the same list of 18 factors. While this approach provided a stronger measure of view divergence since cause maps of different individuals were readily comparable, it weakened the measure of schema complexity since it reduced the variability in the number of constructs and relationships. Therefore, a limitation of the study is that it does not provide a great deal of insight into the relationship between schema complexity, integration and performance.

CONCLUSIONS

This chapter has suggested that a central aspect of organization learning is individual learning, but that organization learning is not simply the sum of the learning of its individual members. Emphasis was placed on the role of an individual's schema in guiding what is interpreted. It was suggested that individuals with more complex schemas, having more concepts and relationships, would be able to interpret things others cannot. Although much of the emphasis in strategic management is on obtaining the 'right information' this chapter has suggested that beliefs rather than information are the primary bottleneck in interpreting the environment since individuals are more likely to 'see what they believe' rather than 'believe what they see'.

Aspects of organization learning not captured by individual learning are the integration of individual beliefs, and the role of systems and structures as integrating mechanisms and store houses of knowledge. Four types of organization schema were proposed based on the potential level of interpretation of the group and the level of integration.

The model was applied to four cases of Canadian retailers entering the US to provide insight into the four schema types. However, schemas were not directly measured in the case studies and therefore empirical support for the model was presented based on the performance of 70 groups participating in a week-long simulation.

Tying together the theory and the analysis from the case studies and the simulation several key implications can be drawn. The first is that in spite of the fact that three of the four companies had difficulty interpreting the US environment, they were all successful in Canada at the time of the US entry. As well, in the simulation, groups beginning in a favorable start position performed quite well. It may be that a favorable economic and competitive environment is more forgiving of schemas that lack complexity or diversity. Alternatively, Miller's (1990) description of the 'Icarus Paradox' in which a company's strengths become its weaknesses may explain the fate of successful Canadian companies who apply the same formula in the US as in Canada when in fact the environments are different.

A second implication is that whether the Canadian companies really understood their key success factors, or blindly applied their strategies in the US, the issue remains that their schemas did not enable them to effectively interpret the US environment. They consistently interpreted information in ways supporting their existing schemas. Therefore, when gaps or discrepancies were identified, they were interpreted within the context of their schemas with no modification, and hence no learning occurred.

Video tapes from the simulation revealed that groups beginning in a favorable start position were quick to take credit for their success. When, late in the simulation, groups in an unfavorable start position gained ground, the favorable groups were not sure how to respond because they had not identified their key success factors.

Thirdly, as born out in both the case studies and simulation, integration is critical. Without integration it is extremely difficult for organizations to take coherent action. It is particularly difficult to deal with diversity in the absence of integrating mechanisms. This chapter proposed three types of integrating mechanisms: self-integration, personal facilitation and artifactual facilitation. In the case studies, Canadian Tire exhibited strong artifactual integrating mechanisms in the form of their systems and structure. Unfortunately, their lack of diversity resulted in a groupthink schema. Irving Gerstein's management style at Peoples is a primary example of personal facilitation where an individual becomes the integrating mechanism. The structure, systems, and guidelines set out by Gerstein were examples of artifactual integrating mechanisms. Furthermore, although it is rare to find, Gerstein's management team appeared to exhibit a degree of self-integration. Given the strength of Gerstein's personal facilitation in the form of powerful leadership, which was also embedded in artifactual mechanisms, the management team actively worked towards synthesizing different points of view. However, the true test of whether in fact the team is able to self-integrate would be to observe them in the absence of Gerstein's powerful leadership.

Finally, a key issue is how companies who have an impoverished, contentious or groupthink schema, develop a productive schema. And furthermore, how do organizations with a productive schema maintain it? Evidence from the simulation suggests that the failure to integrate diverse points of view can be disastrous. The case studies indicated that Canadian Tire's attempt to move from a groupthink to a productive schema through adding diversity was jeopardized by the lack of time and resources required to enable integration to occur and as a result they ended up with a contentious schema.

For organizations with an impoverished schema, the route to developing a productive schema is quite different from the route for organizations with a groupthink schema, as is the case for organizations with a contentious schema. While contentious organizations need to develop integrating mechanisms, groupthink organizations need to develop more complexity and diversity, while impoverished organizations need both. Although groupthink groups need to develop more diversity and complexity, they may also have to alter their strong integrating mechanisms. In particular, artifactual mechanisms may steer the organization in a particular direction and therefore suppress views that deviate from the path. As well, personal facilitation in the form of a strong leader who is unwilling to entertain a new direction for the organization may inhibit learning.

Examining the case of impoverished organizations needing both a higher level of interpretation and integration there are two very different strategies. One strategy adopted by many organizations is to bring in 'new blood'. However, while the newcomers may add diversity and complexity, they may require a higher level of integration than the organization is capable of delivering. Alternatively, the organization can attempt to expand the cognitive coverage of the domain by complicating the understanding of its members and by nurturing diversity. The second approach places fewer demands on organizational integrating mechanisms and greater demands on individual integrating mechanisms. That is, in order for the individual to develop a more complex schema with more concepts and relationships they must undergo an internal process of integrating new information into their schema. Furthermore, by complicating the understanding of individuals, rather than simply bringing in individuals with diverse points of view, the likelihood of self-integration is higher. Greater complexity in an individual's schema may mean greater overlap with the schema of other organization members and hence a higher level of understanding for another's point of view.

In conclusion, the case studies and the empirical study suggest that two key components of organization learning are: the level of interpretation of the organization members and the level of integration of the members' schemas. One dimension of interpretation, schema complexity, is important since it guides what an individual perceives and interprets. The second dimension of interpretation, view divergence, provides for greater cognitive coverage of the domain. However, a high level of interpretation without integration leads to a contentious schema and likely very poor performance. The simulation suggested that it is extremely difficult to integrate diverse and complex schemas and therefore the route to developing a productive schema is a challenging one. Furthermore, maintaining a productive schema is somewhat paradoxical since it requires that organizations nurture diversity while at the same time integrating it. Organizations with strong integrating mechanisms run the risk of slipping into a groupthink schema, if in the process of integration they lose their diversity.

REFERENCES

Abelson, R. P. (1979). Differences between beliefs and knowledge systems. *Cognitive Science*, **3**, 355–366.

Barnard, C. (1938). *The Functions of the Executive*. Cambridge, MA: Harvard University Press.

Bedeian, A. G. (1986). Contemporary challenges in the study of organisations. In J. G. Hunt and J. D. Blair (Eds) *1986 Yearly Review of Management of the Journal of Management*, **12**, 185–201.

Brunsson, N. (1982). The irrationality of action and action rationality: Decisions, ideologies and organizational actions. *Journal of Management Studies*, **19**(1), 29–44.

De Geus, A. P. (1988). Planning as learning. *Harvard Business Review*, March–April, 70–74.

Evans, W. (1990). Coles Book Stores Limited, Research Case 9-91-R006. School of Business Administration, The University of Western Ontario.

Festinger, L. (1957). *A Theory of Cognitive Dissonance*. Standford, CA: Stanford University Press.

Fiol, M. C. and Lyles, M. A. (1985). Organization learning. *Academy of Management Review*, **10**, 803–813.

Garratt, B. (1987). Learning is the core of organisation survival: Action learning is the key integrating process. *Journal of Management Development*, **6**, 38–44.

Hildebrand, T. and Lane, H. W. (1990a). Canadian Tire Corporation, Research Case 9-91-R009. School of Business Administration, The University of Western Ontario.

Hildebrand, T. and Lane, H. W. (1990b). Mark's Work Wearhouse, Research Case 9-91-R008. School of Business Administration, The University of Western Ontario.

Hildebrand, T. and Lane, H. W. (1990c). Peoples Jewellers Limited, Research Case 9-91-R007. School of Business Administration, The University of Western Ontario.

Huber, G. P. (1991). Organisation learning: The contributing processes and the literature, *Organization Science*, **2**, 88–115.

Miller, D. (1990). *The Icarus Paradox: How Exceptional Companies Bring About their own Downfall*. New York: Harper Business.

Neisser, U. (1976). *Cognitive Psychology*. San Francisco, CA: W. H. Freeman.

Shrivastava, P. A. (1983). A typology of organizational learning systems. *Journal of Management Studies*, **20**, 7–28.

Walsh, J. P. and Ungson, G. R. (1991). Organisational memory. *Academy of Management Review*, **16**, 57–91.

11

Patterns of Strategic Change in Health Care: District Health Authorities Respond to AIDS

EWAN FERLIE, CHRIS BENNETT

The strategic change perspective on decision-making within organisations is developing rapidly, but primarily within the context of private sector management, as any perusal of recent editions of management journals indicates. Yet public sector organisations can also provide a fruitful field for such analyses. In particular, the health care sector has perhaps been somewhat neglected in the development of the emerging strategic change perspective, although analyses of health care settings have in the past often been influential in building other organisational theories. For example, the study of an innovative Medical School contributed to the formation of the organisational 'life cycle' perspective (Kimberly, Miles et al., 1980).

It used to be argued that health care organisations were unlikely to exhibit strategic change. The picture painted was one of a complex

This chapter was first published in British Journal of Management, 3, (1992), 21–38, and is reprinted here with permission.

Strategic Thinking: Leadership and the Management of Change.
Edited by J. Hendry and G. Johnson with J. Newton.
Copyright © 1993 the Strategic Management Society. Published 1993 John Wiley & Sons Ltd.

and pluralist organisation characterised by continual negotiation between shifting power blocs (Strauss, 1978), where professionals were more dominant than managers; operating on the basis of collegial norms (Bucher and Stelling, 1977), and where there was also much uncertainty about the real locus of control (Alford, 1975) within the system. The dominant mode of decision-making was thought to be highly incremental (Hunter, 1980), with profound obstacles lying in the way of the expansion of low prestige and powerless services. The hospital perhaps represented the archetype of the professional mode of organisation, which may be in a state of perpetual change at a micro level but extremely stable at a strategic level (Mintzberg, 1990). At worst, stasis could result, or perpetual 'conflict without change' (Smith, 1981).

This view of health service organisations and the way they operate may now be in need of substantial revision. The introduction of general management in the National Health Service (NHS) in the mid 1980s was in part justified by the need to accelerate the pace of strategic change and reduce implementation deficits in sectors such as psychiatry, where long standing policies for change had been implemented only in a very patchy manner (Wing, 1991). There is now evidence to suggest that at least in some localities and in some health care issues, the pace of strategic service change accelerated rapidly in the late 1980s (Pettigrew *et al.*, 1992).

Strategic service change is a particularly fruitful area to study because it represents the cross-over point between management 'means' and service 'ends'. Such a focus helps get us away from examining the managerial process in splendid isolation from end results and connects management with the design of new service systems. This chapter examines the organisational and managerial response by the NHS to the HIV/AIDS epidemic as an interesting example of a strategic change process taking place within health care.

HIV/AIDS first emerged as an issue in the early 1980s, but the epidemic has not abated, nor has a cure been found. Thus, in terms of both timescale and magnitude, the HIV/AIDS issue has 'strategic' implications, and the NHS response to the issue can be usefully used for analysis as a discrete example of a strategic change process. We do not suggest that these responses are 'typical' of the NHS as a whole, but rather represent the experience of management under conditions of high policy drama. Such conditions may, however, expose decision-making processes that otherwise remain hidden.

The chapter contains a major empirical element, drawing on nine intensive, longitudinal, case studies of the organisational and managerial response to HIV/AIDS in different health districts, some of which were key national centres with a high level of prevalence of the virus amongst their patients. Here we attempt to relate these data to some more general strategic management questions.

SOME RELEVANT STRATEGIC CHANGE LITERATURE

The strategic change literature has been usefully reviewed by Johnson (1990), together with a consideration of possible implications for empirical research. He notes first of all the retreat from long-range, formalistic, approaches to strategic management, and a move towards seeing organisations as containing important social, political and cognitive elements.

A number of consequences follow from seeing the world in this new way. One is a new recognition of the importance of antecedent conditions in influencing change, and an increased interest in studying the role of 'change agents', and how they secure change within complex organisations. This directs attention to the micropolitics of decision-making within organisations and how ideas for change are generated and steered through organisations. Stocking (1985) introduces the notion of the 'clinical product champion' as one important facilitator of innovation in health care settings, although this role was not explored in a fully processual manner.

Secondly, attention is directed to the social, political and cultural context of organisations. Organisations may be seen as complex social systems that may be grossly disturbed by a major and sudden change. The distribution of organisational power is crucial in determining whose new issues get on to agendas, and which coalition of interests assumes dominance. Different and even opposing value systems may emerge and do battle, and this is particularly evident in the HIV/AIDS field where different social groupings have advanced very different interpretations of the requisite response. A 'strong culture' has been apparent in the HIV/AIDS issue, often based on value-laden social movements and social movement organisations (Scott, 1990) moving into terrain traditionally occupied by much more value-neutral public sector bureaucracies. The Terrence Higgins Trust, as an early voluntary organisation started by gay people and which has exerted considerable influence on government policy, would be a good example of such an organisational form. There have been pleas for 'strong cultures' as organisational cement (Peters and Waterman, 1982), but less has been said about the dynamics of two culturally dissimilar organisations trying to work co-operatively towards shared strategic objectives.

Crisis management is another important theme. Johnson (1990) sees the emergence of a perceived 'crisis' as providing a pretext around which change agents may usefully mobilise. However, we need to consider this argument rather more fully. Much of the existing literature on organisational crisis (Hermann, 1963; Jick and Murray, 1982) in fact stresses the pathological consequences of 'crisis as threat' which may paradoxically reduce the energy, creativity and flexibility so much needed. Within public sector management, Levine *et al.*'s (1982) analysis of the response within New York City to the fiscal crisis of the mid 1970s found that rapid retrenchment stifled initiative and encouraged errors.

The counter scenario of 'crisis as opportunity' is rather less developed, although Starbuck *et al.* (1978) have advanced this argument. Major change is here seen as much more likely to take place when the perception of a crisis forces awkward issues up agendas: the process of strategic change in ICI would be one example (Pettigrew, 1985), where concern about rapid shifts in traditional market patterns was skilfully orchestrated by new leaders brought in from outside. Under these conditions very different patterns of organisational behaviour may be present. We are likely to see continuing pressure from pioneers, the formation of special groups who evangelise the rest of the organisation, high energy and commitment levels, and a period of organisational plasticity in which anything seems possible. There is, therefore, rapid learning, consciousness raising and mobilisation. In the health care sector, Meyer's (1982) study of an 'environmental jolt' (an unexpected and unprecedented strike by physicians), suggested that: 'by plunging organisations into unfamiliar circumstances, jolts can legitimate unorthodox experiments that revitalise them, teach lessons that reacquaint them with their environments and inspire dramas celebrating their ideologies.'

Where the HIV/AIDS issue is concerned, elements of both scenarios seem to have been present. Strong (1990) argues that the early days of the HIV/AIDS issue were characterised by a very special 'epidemic psychology' where waves of fear and panic spread (particularly as media coverage waxed and waned) both within society as a whole and more narrowly within health care organisations. Some districts went through periods of collective disorientation, with managers demonstrating rapidly changing attitudes to the issue, and great uncertainty about what to do next.

However, change can also potentiate organisational learning. Learning can be defined as a relatively permanent change in behaviour occurring as a result of experience (Bennett *et al.*, 1990), and may take place at three levels: the individual, the small group and the organisational. Shared understanding may occasionally be achieved simultaneously by large numbers of people – for example, during a natural disaster. Normally, however, a collective perception develops through time as some individuals emerge as early learners and then information senders. That learning may then diffuse, first to immediate groups and networks (raising questions about the extensiveness of the networks of the early learners and of their reputation within the wider organisation), and in turn to the larger organisation.

In general, individuals are motivated to learn by the prospect of external or internal reward. But learning may also occur through exposure to new influences, and this process may be helped by the organisational context. Symbolic management is highlighted by Johnson (1990) as a possibly central role of change agents who recognise that within established organisational orders, ritual, ceremony, and myth may play an important role in giving meaning to a particular paradigm (Pettigrew, 1979). HIV/AIDS became a catalyst for the introduction of new ways of addressing the needs of patients experiencing chronic and life-threatening illness. Change agents used symbolic events, as well as other indirect ways of raising people's consciousness of the issue to help to change perceptions, 'images' and stereotypes and construct a new paradigm, but environmental influences were not always controllable and what was learned could be complicated by hidden messages. Other examples of symbolism were collective and emergent, rather than a product of conscious intervention, the development of particular language systems is a case in point. Our case study material provides some good examples of these learning processes.

There are therefore some interesting strategic change questions with which to interrogate the data base. To recapitulate:

• How has organisational history affected the strategic service response to the HIV/AIDS issue?

- Who led change in these case studies and how did they acquire financial resources, political support and organisational attention to put the HIV/AIDS issue on agendas?
- How important are alternative value systems in explaining the push for – and resistance to – change?
- Was there a real or perceived crisis in these organisations around HIV/AIDS? Did such a perception of a crisis help or hinder the process of strategic change?
- What evidence is there of change agents undertaking symbolic management activity and how has organisational learning around HIV/AIDS taken place?

METHODOLOGY

The basic methodology used has been that of the longitudinal and processual comparative case study. As we have argued:

> In summary, despite the substantial literature which now exists on change in health care organisations, we believe that there is a need for more research which is processual (an emphasis on action as well as structure); comparative (a range of studies of local health care agencies); pluralist (describe and analyse the often competing versions of reality seen by actors in change processes); and historical (take into account the historical evolution of ideas and actions for change as well as the constraints within which decision makers operate) (Pettigrew *et al.*, 1988, p. 314).

The case study has been a methodology as much abused as used, so it is important to be clear about method. The approach adopted here has allowed for the analysis of retrospective change as well as considerable real-time analysis. The antecedent conditions and the chronology of change are considered important historical elements, as the past may play a substantial part in shaping the characteristics of the present. The design choice in this study has been to conduct intensive analyses of a relatively few cases, rather than a more superficial analysis of a larger number, since given the complexity of both the issue and the host organisations, super-ficial analyses may be at best limited and at worst profoundly misleading.

A variety of data sources have been used in these case studies. Archival material sensitised the researcher to key questions and supplied a chronology of change. Although minutes have often been

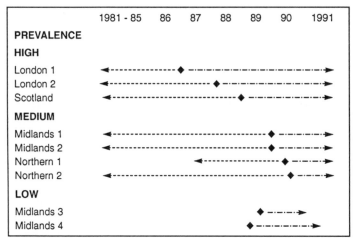

FIGURE 11.1   Organisational and managerial responses to HIV/AIDS

criticised for supplying bland and formalistic accounts, ephemera such as internal memos or annotations in margins could yield interesting insights. Attendance at meetings allowed observation of group dynamics which were different from those of the one-to-one semi-structured interviews conducted (usually about 40 per district). Respondents were selected from those with lead positions within the organisation or because they were directly involved in the change process. They came from different functional groupings and different hierarchical levels, and from outside as well as inside the NHS (such as Social Services). Early analysis concentrated on the single case (Ferlie and Pettigrew, 1990), but we are here moving on to cross-case analysis.

The sample was built up to contain three main groupings of localities as response might be expected to vary according to local caseload (see Figure 11.1). The first grouping includes front line districts in Inner London and Scotland, which were early in identifying large numbers of infected people. The second contains districts in major cities with regional facilities dealing with people with HIV infection; the third, two low prevalence districts. The sample considerably over-represents high and medium prevalence districts, and therefore one should be cautious in extrapolating from the sample districts to the population.

SOME PATTERNS IN THE PROCESS

LOCAL VARIATION IN SERVICE DEVELOPMENT

The first point relates to the substantial variation apparent at local level in the development of service strategies as local district health authorities did not mechanistically replicate national guidelines (Ferlie, 1991).

Initially, faced with a new and unexpected situation, the first districts to experience the reality of large numbers of infected patients were forced to develop their own individual responses to the crisis. The need for additional funding meant that these developments had to be justified to the Government, and the dialogue that ensued exerted considerable influence on the development of policy at national level. The initiative then moved to the Department of Health, which translated policy into directives to districts. These were influential in both legitimating *ad hoc* structures already in existence and in initiating a structural response where districts had been slower off the mark. However, they were sufficiently broad to allow wide local variation in the structures that ensued, and the advent of earmarked government funding for HIV/AIDS freed regions and districts from the strait-jacket of the general financial difficulties being experienced during the 1980s by the NHS and allowed even greater local autonomy. Thus the periphery retained much of the initiative, and neighbouring authorities, or even particular hospitals within the same authority, could exhibit quite different responses.

There were some other sources of local variation. Some hospitals under long-term threat of closure have diversified into HIV/AIDS more readily than those whose funding was secure: teaching hospitals offer an important 'supply side' motor of service development, with clinical academics able and anxious to develop research into new diseases: the recent experience of other epidemics (Hepatitis B, TB), or an active local interest in infection control, represented ways through which the past could skew patterns of development. An example of how antecedent conditions could facilitate responses can be drawn from one of the very first hospitals to respond clinically. Not only was there a need in the local population, but the existence of an infection control tradition and facility, the formation of a prior research group around Hepatitis B, and international networks of clinical academics that could be used to access the earlier American experience all helped provide local clues in advance of the issue being constructed nationally. On the other hand, in two districts folk memories of past epidemics and perceptions of fever hospitals as places containing contagious, life-threatening diseases meant that local prejudice could hinder service development: 'There has always been a thing that the bus drivers and so on in the area have always said "get off here if you want Lassa Fever" so AIDS just added on to that, . . . right from day one . . . we have never really overcome this thing of the high contagiousness of the disease.'

Local political cultures were also important: the context was perhaps most receptive in Inner London (where social movement organisations were the best developed), but elsewhere some of the regional councils showed great nervousness in dealing with issues related to sexuality, and politicians' perception of public opinion complicated efforts to develop services for drug injectors.

In addition, where existing services had a firm ideological basis with which they operated it could be particularly difficult to effect procedural changes, particularly if many different occupational groupings were involved. Drug services were a particular instance of this problem (Cranfield *et al.*, 1991), the advent of HIV/AIDS required an ideological somersault in moving from a policy of achieving abstinence (no use of drugs) to one of harm reduction (minimising the possibility of continued drug use causing long-term damage).

Key actors varied by locality also. For instance, clinical 'product champions' emerged in all three of the high prevalence localities, but they were drawn from very different backgrounds (immunology, infectious diseases, public health) and included clinical academics as well as service clinicians. Loose top-down guidance and available funds encouraged the speedy building up of service systems around these early product champions, demonstrating the early stages of a process life cycle, which has been described in many other settings (Easton and Rothschild, 1987), and is characterised by rapid developmental change and lack of standardisation.

For all these reasons, the organisational histories of the HIV/AIDS issue soon diverged. Both virtuous and vicious circles could be seen to be developing, as champions came and went and HIV/AIDS acquired a history, label, and perception of whether or not it was a good issue to be associated with. 'Climbers' (Downs, 1967) could jump off bandwagons as fast as they clambered on. Furthermore, once a dominant coalition had formed around what was frequently seen as essentially 'windfall' money, it could prove very difficult to reallocate resources and widen the cast of actors to include specialties (such as those for women and children) which came on stream that bit later.

AGENTS OF CHANGE: THE PRODUCT CHAMPIONS

As suggested above, the 'product champion' has been found to be an important element of the innovation process in both industrial (Rothwell, 1976) and health care settings (Stocking, 1985). There is now also the beginnings of a literature on product champions in organisational process: a product champion (Burgelman and Sayles, 1986) is seen as being able to work effectively in a non-programmed environment, and also to be able to deal with a variety of groups over which there is no formal control, each of which may have different or contradictory goals, and each of which is crucial to project success. This quotation, from a doctor identified as a key clinical product champion in one of the case study districts, encapsulates this view of the role: 'somebody who wants to learn but can also see their way through the morass and see a direction, a certain vision of what needs to be achieved.'

This raises the question of diplomatic skills and of coalition building. The effective product champion (Rothwell and Zegweld, 1982) may also need considerable power and prestige in order to influence the informal politics of organisational decision-making.

The general argument was confirmed in this study: in all the districts, 'product champions' emerged to drive proposals for development and in nearly every district, a public health doctor emerged as an important figure. Indeed, HIV/AIDS, as a true epidemic, has provided stimulus for public health medicine, which has been seeking a role for itself ever since the specialty was fragmented following the 1974 reorganisation of the NHS (DHSS, 1988 – known as The Acheson Report). Apart from that common factor, there was considerable variability in who stepped forward. Some people had a particular personal interest in the issue, but often it seemed to be a question of just having been in a particular place at a particular time. By no means all product champions were doctors, but many of the most influential were key clinical consultants, though drawn from such diverse specialties in different districts as: haematology, immunology, infectious diseases, chest and respiratory medicine, genito urinary medicine and psychiatry.

The decision to come forward as an AIDS 'product champion' was not an easy one and could have far-reaching consequences, transforming the pace of work and long-term careers, for better or for worse. The glare of publicity could have negative as well as positive consequences if a perception grew of the product champion as only a 'media doctor'. As noted earlier, some innovators were of course 'climbers'. HIV/AIDS, a high-profile issue, with no organisational history behind it and money available for new development, was custom-made for those at the beginning of their careers who were hoping to make their mark early. Some of these quickly moved on to successor issues. This was only one subgroup, though, and many others have stayed firmly committed to the field. On the negative side, some people found they tended to be 'typecast' by AIDS and that this had an adverse effect on prospects for working in other areas. Self confidence and personality were perhaps factors, as AIDS services tended to attract risk takers: 'I think personality has a lot to do with it in terms of being someone who is willing to play a few new games, learn a few new tricks . . . AIDS attracted a lot of people who came in to care for AIDS and they were people who were prepared to face the new and the unknown' (clinical product champion).

Sustained energy was also important, as campaigns were launched that could drag out over many years. Sometimes a product champion could court unpopularity by asking awkward questions on committees or blowing the whistle on resource flows (as when earmarked funds were seen to be disappearing into base budgets, for example), so this was not a role for the shy and retiring.

Product champions varied in their diplomatic and coalition building skills, but putting together a wider base could be of critical importance, in particular the winning of support from the powerful acute sector specialties (surgery, medicine). There were instances of product champions failing to gain acceptance from resource allocators for their ideas for development because they themselves were relatively powerless within the organisation and they had been either not sufficiently skilled in, or dismissive of the need for, coalition-building.

The Role of Value-Laden Social Movements

Nationally and at district level, social movements and social movement organisations (SMOs) have played a central role in the development of the strategic response to HIV/AIDS. SMOs are, above all, value laden organisations concerned about life styles, often translating what has hitherto been seen as the personal into the political through tactics of consciousness-raising and group mobilisation. Members of the gay movement, from within whose ranks came many of the first cases of AIDS, were a potent influence on policy and practice at both national and local level, particularly during the early years of the epidemic. SMOs may produce a distinct organisational and ideological form (Scott, 1990): a large cultural component, an emphasis on the creation of 'free space', a preference for networks over hierarchies, the possible use of direct action, and the linkage of personal experience to drives for collective social change.

Many of the voluntary organisations that sprang up in response to HIV/AIDS had these characteristics. Most of the early initiatives outside the medical profession came from activists in the gay community, and from among people involved in 'alternative' rather than traditional approaches to medicine, which emphasised non-standard medication, and patient involvement in therapy. There was evidence of strong value systems in underpinning the development of services and some respondents would talk of the critical moment when they were 'converted' to seeing HIV/AIDS as a major issue.

Such social movements had been particularly influential in two of the districts studied. Perhaps surprisingly, these were both in provincial centres rather than Inner London where the dominance of the teaching hospital was strongest. In one case, the strength of social movements reflected a more general City-wide political culture, in the other a vigorous special team managed to form despite the less supportive regime in the City as a whole.

There is a debate about how effective SMOs are in intervening in formal decision-making processes. Staff moving in from a radical voluntary sector agency into the more bureaucratised NHS may suffer profound culture shock and find it difficult to work within the system. In particular, the more value-laden the SMO, the more it may approximate to the sectarian form of organisation (Wilson, 1967) where there is strong exclusivity or even withdrawal from the secular world.

However, Arno's (1986) case study of San Francisco suggests that such groupings can work well within more formal decision-making systems. In the UK, social movements may also have had some success in capturing the specialist HIV labour market being set up within the NHS, in effect acting as 'bureaucratic insurgents' (Zald and Berger, 1978). Staff imported from a radical voluntary sector tended to have a distinctive ideology emphasising the 'empowerment' of the consumer and the minimisation of the role of the 'expert'. Since no one was entirely sure how best to respond to HIV/AIDS new staff were often given a more or less free hand to develop new services. In terms of organisational form, this led to networks or even collectives being preferred to hierarchies, with staff encouraged to examine their own feelings and motivations as the personal was as important as the political.

On the one hand, the overt ideological stance taken by SMOs leads to intense energy, commitment and a stress on basic affirmative values. On the other hand, there may be a tendency for 'in groups' to form which may be ready to label outsiders or to scapegoat insiders in order to maintain group cohesion. In addition, organisational 'zealotry' (Downs, 1967) may result in implacable energy being devoted to promoting a narrow range of sacred policies, making it difficult to build wider coalitions. There were signs in some of our case districts that this was happening, and such exclusivity is a great enemy of sustained change, because once the political umbrella is removed, services may quickly be dismantled by those who, though left out in the cold by the 'in groups', still retain considerable power.

THE MOBILISING ROLE OF CRISIS

Dutton (1987) has argued that the processing of strategic issues will be very different in crisis and non-crisis situations. Certainly between 1983 and 1987, HIV/AIDS nationally attracted a 'crisis' label with unprecedented advertising campaigns and media coverage. The early epidemiology was taken as indicating that the UK was only four years or so behind the explosive American epidemic (in fact the pace of the epidemic grew far more slowly). The issue characteristics used by Dutton to define a crisis (importance, immediacy and uncertainty) all applied to the HIV/AIDS issue, indeed it was sometimes said that there had been nothing like it in health care since World War II.

Alongside the national AIDS crisis, particular districts were experiencing their own local crises. A 'crisis' did not emerge in every locality despite the national triggers, because in some areas the caseload was too low or there had been prior recent experience with dealing with an epidemic (such as TB), which provided an important coping mechanism.

The data collected on the organisational response to HIV/AIDS leads us to propose a three-phase model to explain organisational behaviour when confronted with an issue perceived as posing a long-term threat to the familiar assumptions and working practices on which an organisation is based. The model bears some resemblance to psychological theories about the effect on individual performance of the degree of arousal in response to a stimulus. These suggest that experiencing the same stimulus at varying degrees of intensity may produce differing levels of performance, with higher levels of arousal associated with increased energy and improved performance (Hebb, 1955), but that very high levels of arousal, leading to fear and anxiety about the possibility of making an appropriate response, may lead to paralysis rather than appropriate action (Tyhurst, 1951).

Thus in many areas there was initially a destabilising crisis of anxiety in line with the 'epidemic psychology' model (Strong, 1990). In one district an epidemiological crisis arose literally overnight as a virologist was practising using the new HTLV-3 test on stored bloods from drug users: quite unexpectedly 38% tested positive (Peutherer *et al.*, 1985): 'We went to bed on Tuesday evening believing that whatever [the district]'s AIDS problem was, it was likely to be no better and no worse than anyone else's, and we got up on Wednesday morning and found that we had this huge number of infected people.'

In another, the Control of Infection Officer had to sit down urgently with colleagues over the 1983 August Bank Holiday weekend to draw up control of infection guidelines to resolve an escalating crisis over safety:

'This caused a lot of tension and pressure because we could not get other people to take it seriously. We knew that we were going to have real patients and real problems, and people seemed to flip between not being bothered and not caring and it was something that was very minor and peripheral, to being something that was so serious that it was untouchable.'

So, in the short term, the issue was often characterised by 'incidents', waves of panic and fear, and staff refusal to work with patients. Over-anxious reactions to situations could have unintended and far-reaching consequences. For instance, in March 1985, the Public Health (Infectious Diseases) Act was amended to allow, under special and unusual circumstances, the detention of a person with AIDS on the grounds that other people were likely to be put at risk. In September 1985 the first, and to date (late 1992) only, use of those powers took place in one of our case study districts. This raised fundamental questions about civil liberties, reinvoked the memory of State regulation of Sexually Transmitted Diseases stretching back to the Victorian Contagious Diseases Act, and mobilised the Labour City Council and the well-organised local gay community around the issue. An account of a meeting, titled 'AIDS: Your Rights Under Threat', held shortly after the incident recorded that the name of the hospital concerned 'became a key word for fear and anger'.

In the medium term, as anxiety subsided to what might be seen as approaching a more 'optimal' level, the perception of a local crisis often had energising and creative effects and the pathological behaviours predicted by the crisis-as-threat model did not emerge. Instead an extraordinary outburst of enthusiasm and activity took place in the mid 1980s: ideas for new services were being generated and implemented, resources were being obtained, and qualitatively different care regimes being introduced where patients could have more control over treatment (e.g. user representation on drug trial committees). Unlike other more intractable issues in the NHS, rapid change seemed possible.

Thus, in the district that was initially rocked by controversy following the detention incident, the Director of Public Health subsequently channelled the energy generated to build bridges with the voluntary sector, and the hospital went on to develop as a much respected centre of excellence.

This was an example of using real crisis strategically to generate change, but increasingly, once the first sense of panic had subsided, an important leadership task was to orchestrate a sense of crisis so as to mobilise energy. One route which some districts used from the early days was to agitate at national policy-making level. This was easier for the high prevalence districts which had been early in using the media and developing good links into national policy-making mechanisms.

One respondent recalled a member of staff who appeared on TV with the then Minister of Health in 1983 or 1984: 'Now at that time about 14 or 15 had been diagnosed or had died with AIDS, and he was saying, "well, how many corpses do you need, do you need twenty, a hundred, two hundred, when is it enough?", you can see what is happening in the States.' Three years later, credibility was sufficiently established for key clinicians to be acknowledged as expert witnesses at government level: 'We are in a situation where we do have a public health crisis – in fact the greatest public health crisis that any of us in our professional lives have ever seen' (respondent giving evidence to Social Services Committee, 1987).

In some districts, the presentation of data helped create a sense of crisis. Although the caseload might be heavily drawn from a particular exposure category (such as haemophilia in those districts with treatment centres), the presentation of bald totals could trigger activity across a much wider spectrum of activity.

In the long term such a hectic pace could not always be sustained – the HIV/AIDS issue became intractable in its turn: 'By mid 1985 we were a publishing house, a health education house, as well as a treatment house, and we were very rapidly becoming exhausted.' It proved important, also, to try to ensure that the issue was not over hyped. As the pace of the epidemic seemed to slow in 1988 and 1989, so there was an increasing view that the AIDS crisis was more apparent than real. Ambitious extrapolations of the need for beds were vulnerable to downward revision when the predicted numbers of patients failed to materialise, leading to accusations of doctors making 'exaggerated claims' and seeing HIV/AIDS purely as 'an opportunity for the development of . . . Ward and for the better recognition of their specialty'. Furthermore, as still newer matters rose up the managerial agenda (such as White Paper reforms), the general level of arousal in the Health Service over the issue diminished. HIV/AIDS took more of a backseat, and moves were made to 'normalise' decision-making and to wind down some of the special machinery that had emerged. By 1989 a number of early innovators were withdrawing from the field, perhaps because of the attraction of the still newer issues, perhaps because of exhaustion through over-commitment, perhaps because they had been unable to win resources for their ideas, lacking the organisational power base of a clinician.

INDIVIDUAL, GROUP AND ORGANISATIONAL LEARNING

Much early learning within district health authorities was individual and experiential: clinicians learned from experience the combinations of drugs best suited to unusual infections, and technicians learned to use HIV tests by practising laboratory techniques (Bennett *et al.*, 1990). However, once HIV/AIDS was recognised as a policy issue, there was an emphasis on formal training. Staff attended lectures and seminars on clinical aspects of the syndrome and on new techniques of infection control and patient care.

However, a formal approach to learning about HIV/AIDS was sometimes insufficient to help people deal with deep-seated anxieties or feelings. There was a need for an 'unlearning' of some traditional values and attitudes if patients were to be treated with sensitivity, but AIDS is a highly charged issue and some people's perceptions were slow to change. Early initiatives, for example, attempted to calm fears of health care staff about the risk of infection, but there were still many examples of staff at all levels reacting with excessive caution. The most successful formal training programmes have been constructed to address not just the need to learn new techniques, but the more fundamental requirement to change attitudes and value systems.

Most of what people learn, however, is not imbibed through formal training but is communicated informally through casual conversation or environmental stimuli. HIV/AIDS emerged initially in low status departments such as genito urinary medicine (GUM) and drug dependency units (DDUs) and was associated with strong feelings of fear and stigma and turning the image of the issue round was an important task for some actors. Johnson (1990) suggests that symbolic change, may be seen as a manageable process, stressing the symbolic aspects to change and management, and seeing them as a relatively explicit and self-conscious task undertaken by effective change agents.

Restructuring the image was certainly achieved with some success in a number of the localities. Lobbying at national level helped secure political and financial support, and association with high status 'patrons' was also important. The photograph of the Princess of Wales opening the new ward at the Middlesex Hospital, for example, and shaking hands with the patients, went round the world and did much to change the image of the issue there. The royal laying on of hands is of course an act historically charged with special meaning.

However, generally speaking the symbolic and cultural aspects of the change process, though highly significant, took a more collective, unpredictable and hence less manageable form. The construction of new language systems and methods of visual display was an important field-driven way of attempting to frame the issue rather than the province of single 'change agents', supporting the observations of Pettigrew (1979) when he argued that ideologies go hand in hand with new organisational vocabularies in the construction of cultural norms: 'One of the key attributes of symbols in general and language systems in particular, is their potential for impelling people to action.'

Before long, a person's value system and the extent to which they were in touch with those working in the field at grass-roots level could often be inferred from their choice of words: should one refer to 'drug addicts', 'drug misusers' or 'drug injectors' for instance? As for the term 'junkies', that could only be used at a jocular level in a way that made it perfectly clear that you understood that the term was inappropriate.

The pervasive and compelling nature of the new norms that emerged was finally acknowledged by the Health Education Authority, which issued a list of 'acceptable' HIV/AIDS vocabulary: 'person with AIDS', for example, was to be preferred to 'AIDS sufferer'.

Often the office walls of HIV/AIDS staff would be covered with well-designed and frequently very explicit visual material (such as posters celebrating safe sex). This, with the plentiful supplies of leaflets and condoms, reinforced a certain set of images. 'Condom talk' has become far more socially acceptable, reflecting perhaps some of these processes.

However, structuring the environment as an aid to organisational learning is not always easy. Those seeking to educate sometimes encountered opposition to displaying information about HIV/AIDS, both overt ('we don't want your dirty pictures on our walls, thank you') and covert ('do you think they have been up long enough now?').

In every intentional learning situation, there is also the possibility for unintentional learning. The 'gravestones and icebergs' TV commercials have been criticised for unintentionally making people so frightened of AIDS that they block out the message. Some commercials about drug use have been said to reinforce stereotypes and stigmatise drug users. Mixed messages could also be a problem with formal training emphasising that HIV could not be transmitted through ordinary social contact, while at the same time anxious surgeons were to be seen 'all garbed up with helmets over their heads and radios and goodness knows what'.

In addition, while individuals, particularly if motivated, may learn relatively quickly; the diffusion of that learning to groups takes longer, and to create shared understanding at organisational level may take longer still. Indeed, group or organisational learning may never happen at all if the organisational context is not receptive.

Thus it is pertinent to ask whether AIDS has been used as a vehicle for more general organisational learning. A higher-level capacity for organisational learning has been seen by Normann (1985) as one way in which organisations can improve their abilty to manage successive strategic change processes by creating a form of organisation better able to respond to continuing environmental change. Has HIV/AIDS prompted a greater use of more minimalistic structures such as problem-solving groups (Hedberg *et al.*, 1976)? Is there a more self-conscious strategic process? Are there innovations in planning methodology away from formal long-range plans?

The answers to these questions cannot be unequivocal. Organisational development was in any case a theme in the NHS of the mid 1980s, unsurprisingly, given the range of organisational pathologies evident, such as an inability to implement formally agreed strategies for change and the lack of any strong corporate identity. A district general manager in one of our case study districts, for instance, argued that learning to cope with change was a major issue for general management:

> 'It was recognised from an early stage that one of the key management challenges was not just to implement change, but to develop an organisation's capacity to cope with change. The aim, in a sense, was to create a different kind of organisation, capable of learning, responding to and even creating change, rather than simply reacting to it.'

However, the key feature of HIV/AIDS, which distinguished it from many other change issues in the health service, was that changes in the nature of the issue tended to be rapid, unpredictable and looked likely to continue indefinitely. With little hard information available, predictions of likely numbers of patients varied, sometimes almost on a daily basis, and certainly according to which epidemiologist or clinician was talking at the time. Resources to fund HIV/AIDS were at first so slender as to force concerned doctors to use media publicity to trigger governmental action. Then suddenly, in 1989/90, the allocation was increased to such an extent that districts found it nearly impossible to arrange to spend all they were given in the time available. Even at a clinical level changes in knowledge about AIDS and how to treat it were so rapid that patients were sometimes as well informed as their doctors and the old 'doctor knows best' approach proved difficult to sustain.

> 'Most major discoveries are now not published, or they are subsequently, but they're not published in the medical journals, they're published in newspapers. That puts us at a big disadvantage . . . Whereas you can read the *BMJ* and the *New England Journal of Medicine* every week, at least know what's in it and look for things like that. You can't read all the papers every day and the magazines and the women's magazines carry all this as well. So it becomes almost impossible to maintain the feeling normally that you have, that you actually know more than the patients, when sometimes you actually don't.'

A useful analogy may be made with the requirement for continuing rather than one-off innovation in the electronics industry, where Jelinek and Schoonhoven (1990) have argued:

> The story of electronics is not of a one shot or two shot battle, but of an ongoing barrage of change that shows every sign of continuing indefinitely. Success lies not in pulling it off once, but in creating a self sustaining organisational system that will replicate technological innovation repeatedly over the long run.

There was some evidence that HIV/AIDS, coming at the same time as general management, could be used as a useful test-bed for building a new type of organisation outside the usual hierarchies. In one of our districts a general manager said:

> 'It was quite a good illustration of the way a problem can be now more effectively handled as a planning and management issue. Under general management, I had the facility without any formal sanction from the District Management Board other than "you have got a brief: AIDS", to pull together the right sort of people to carry forward that particular task, and pull in where I felt I could get the right financial help and the right service help.'

Such a self-conscious approach was, however, exceptional, and the overall verdict must be one of disappointment. While special machinery was often set up, it was rarely linked to such explicit theories of action and was vulnerable to 'normalisation' when the sense of immediate crisis faded. Although there were, and continue to be, examples within the HIV/AIDS service of innovatory and flexible methods of working, there is little evidence so far of these practices generalising to other areas of service provision and seemed to be little link over to organisational development (OD) specialists despite the potential role of the HIV field as an interesting test-bed. Had these been blue chip private organisations, would the opportunity have been taken to develop and diffuse such new forms of organisational working? In our NHS districts the host organisational culture generally proved dominant, and the opportunity for an interesting experiment in organisational learning seemed likely to be lost.

CONCLUSIONS AND A FURTHER THEME

By way of conclusion, the first point to make is that health care organisations may indeed supply good empirical material for further studies of strategic change and strategic management processes. They have perhaps been unfairly neglected in the management research literature of the 1980s which has been predominantly set in the private sector despite the long prior interest of organisational theorists in health care settings.

Although the public service orientation of health care organisations may in the future be diluted as a result of the introduction of the internal market, it has been strong enough in the past to ensure a climate favourable to research and the free flow of information. Health care organisations have been relatively permeable and transparent, for example ready to accord access to the researcher to observe at meetings. So in our current study (Pettigrew *et al.*, 1991b; Fitzgerald and Pettigrew, 1991) into the operation of the new style health authorities that have been remodelled along private sector board lines, we are able to observe board meetings in action. It has often proved difficult to get this quality of access in private sector settings, possibly because of greater concerns about confidentiality. Public sector research may then illuminate private sector issues, as well as vice versa.

The second point concerns the development of methodology. We have attempted to generate a case study methodology that is not only comparative, but pluralist, processual and historical. The skills of an ethnographer and of a historian are as important as those of a management researcher. The case studies now stretch back almost a decade, but often with more distant pre-histories (such as the response to Hepatitis B in the locality) to consider as well.

The knowledge base for such longitudinal case study work draws both on contemporary history and on the sociology of organisations. It thus has to develop a history that is interpretive as well as chronological and that can present a plurality of accounts from different perspectives, and a sociology that is empirically grounded, inductive and sensitive to the impact of time.

An interesting methodological question concerns the relationship between the perspectives of history and of organisation theory. We hope that the time has now come for a fruitful dialogue between these two branches of study. While some branches of organisation theory (such as contingency theory) are indeed ahistorical, other methodologies are far more sensitive to the importance of history in structuring organisational power relations, attitudes and assumptions. Chandler (1977), for example, presents a business history of the rise of the modern corporation as an institutional form and of management as a social grouping. The life cycle approach to the study of organisations (Kimberly, Miles *et al.*, 1980) indeed explicitly organises itself around the passage of time.

The third concluding point concerns the contribution of this study to the testing and development of substantive theory. Further evidence was supplied of substantial variability in organisational reaction, directing our attention once more to the micropolitics of the organisation. Neighbouring districts or even particular hospitals within the same authority could exhibit quite different responses.

The notion of the 'clinical product champion' as an important motor of innovation was found to be valid, and a small group of such champions were analysed within organisational process. As well as energy and personality, such champions required to have fully effective diplomatic skills and a sound organisational power base. The study also supplied instances of product champions who failed because of their powerlessness within the organisation.

The role of social movements and social movement organisations was central in two of the districts studied. Some theorists of social movements have seen them as sectarian and backward looking, unable to play an effective decision-making role in advanced societies (Touraine, 1981). We, on the other hand, found that people with an ideological commitment to, for instance, gay and lesbian rights or alternative medicine, had had some success in capturing the specialist HIV labour market being set up in the NHS, in effect acting as 'bureaucratic insurgents' from within.

We suggested a three-phase model of crisis management. In the short term there was often evidence of 'epidemic psychology', with waves of panic, fear and guilt and the frequent occurrence of 'organisational incidents'. In the medium term there was an explosion of energy and of mobilisation around the issue, but in the longer term there was a danger of burn out and of issue succession.

The symbolic and cultural aspects of the HIV/AIDS issue were indeed found to be of major importance, but they were only rarely self-consciously undertaken by change agents, but emerged in a more collective way along with a particular subculture. We would question whether 'symbols' are likely to represent tractable management material as many different symbolic systems were mobilised by the HIV/AIDS issue. Above all, perhaps, the study demonstrated the central role of values and of competing value systems in determining the organisational response. Here was not a technical or a neutral issue, but one that came loaded with a whole range of questions about attitudes, beliefs and values.

Finally, following on from this, we highlighted the informal and experiential side of much individual and small group learning. A formal approach to learning about HIV/AIDS sometimes offered little help in dealing with deep-seated anxieties or feelings. At a wider, organisational development level, the impact of educational initiatives was not always predictable, leading to unintentional messages being received along with the intentional ones.

In conclusion, can we identify a future theme that is likely to emerge in the 1990s? The obvious candidate is the question of how these districts sustain the change processes that were launched with such excitement in the mid 1980s. Now the management of crisis is giving way to the long haul. So the HIV/AIDS issue may wane as a political and managerial priority, while paradoxically continuing or even accelerating as an epidemic. A social problem need not, in other words, become a policy issue, as the American epidemic indicates. Some writers (Downs, 1967; Hogwood, 1987) have even detected an issue attention cycle, whereby public, media and political attention continually shifts to still newer issues, and old ones fade even if (perhaps especially if) unresolved.

The sustaining of momentum is a theme of general significance for organisations, but one that has particular resonance in this field. We know that creating long-term change can be a difficult task and that institutionalisation of apparently successful early innovations may be highly problematic. Goodman and Dean's (1982) study of organisations involved in major long-term change efforts, for instance, concluded: '. . . Our data painted a pessimistic picture. Change had been successfully introduced, some benefits had appeared but over time the majority of programs had become deinstitutionalised.'

The danger is that with any withdrawal of earmarked funding for HIV/AIDS, some of the early achievements could be swept aside as the districts rapidly regress to the status quo ante. It will be interesting to study these transitions, and in particular to explore whether change has been more successfully institutionalised in particular authorities.

We conclude that, although the focus may change, the response by health care organisations to the HIV/AIDS epidemic will continue to offer fascinating material for the student of organisational change processes, and the insights obtained may help to illuminate and develop organisational theory.

REFERENCES

Alford, R. (1975). *Health Care Politics*. London: University of Chicago Press.

Arno, P. (1986). The non profit sector's response to the AIDS epidemic: Community based services in San Francisco. *American Journal of Public Health,* **76**, 1325–1330.

Bennett, C., Ferlie, E. and Pettigrew, A. (1990). Developing services for HIV/AIDS: Organisational learning in DHAs. *Yearbook of Research and Development*. London: Department of Health.

Bucher, R. and Stelling, J. (1977). Characteristics of professional organisations. In R. L. Blankenship (Ed.) *Colleagues in Organisations* (pp. 121–144). London: John Wiley.

Burgelman, R. A. and Sayles, L. R. (1986). *Inside Corporate Innovation: Strategy, Structure and Managerial Skills*. London: Collier Macmillan.

Chandler, A. D. (1977). *The Visible Hand*. London: Harvard University Press.

Cranfield, S., Feinmann, C., Ferlie, E. B. and Walter, C. (1991). *The Management of Change in Post HIV Drugs Services*. Middlesex: Dept. of Psychiatry, Middlesex/UCH, School of Medicine.

DHSS (1988). *Public Health in England: The Report of the Committee of Enquiry into the Future Development of the Public Health Function* (Cmnd 289). London: HMSO.

Downs, A. (1967). *Inside Bureaucracies*. Boston: Little, Brown & Company.

Dutton, J. (1987). The processing of crisis and non crisis strategic issues. *Journal of Management Studies*, **23**, 501–517.

Easton, G. and Rothschild, R. (1987). The influence of product and production flexibility on marketing strategy. In A. M. Pettigrew (Ed.) *The Management of Strategic Change*. Oxford: Basil Blackwell.

Ferlie, E. B. (1991). The response to AIDS by British district health authorities. In P. Strong and V. Berridge (Eds) *AIDS and Contemporary History*. Cambridge: Cambridge University Press.

Ferlie, E. B. and Pettigrew, A. M. (1990). Coping with change in the NHS: A frontline district's response to AIDS. *Journal of Social Policy*, **19**, 191–220.

Fitzgerald, L. and Pettigrew, A. (1991). *Boards in Action: Some Implications for Health Authorities*. Bristol NHSTA.

Goodman, P. S. and Dean, J. W. (1982). Creating long term organisational change. In P. Goodman *et al. Change in Organisations*. London: Jossey-Bass.

Hebb, D. O. (1955). Drives and the CNS (conceptual nervous system). *Psychological Review*, **62**, 243–254.

Hedberg, B. L. T., Nystrom, P. C. and Starbuck, W. H. (1976). Camping on see-saws: Prescription for a self designing organisation. *Administrative Science Quarterly*, **21**, 41–65.

Hermann, C. F. (1963). Some consequences of crisis which limit the visibility of organisations. *Administrative Science Quarterly*, **8**, 61–82.

Hogwood, B. W. (1987). *Coping with Uncertainty*. Chichester: Research Studies Press.

Hunter, D. (1980). *Coping with Uncertainty*. Chichester: Research Studies Press.

Jelinek, M. and Schoonhoven, C. B. (1990). *Innovation Marathon*. Oxford: Basil Blackwell.

Jick, T. D. and Murray, V. V. (1982). The management of hard times: Budget cutbacks in public sector organisations. *Organisation Studies*, **3**, 141–169.

Johnson, G. (1990). Managing strategic change – the role of symbolic action. *British Journal of Management*, **1**, 183–200.

Kimberly, J., Miles, R. *et al.* (1980). *The Organisational Life Cycle*. San Francisco: Jossey-Bass.

Levine, C. H., Rubin, I. S. and Wolohojian, G. G. (1982). Managing organisational retrenchment. *Administration and Society*, **14**, 101–136.

Meyer, A. D. (1982). Adapting to environmental jolts. *Administrative Science Quarterly*, **27**, 515–537.

Mintzberg, H. (1990). *Mintzberg on Management*. New York: Free Press.

Normann, R. (1985). Developing capabilities for organisational learning. In J. M. Pennings *et al.* (Eds). *Organisational Strategy and Change*. London: Jossey-Bass.

Peters, T. and Waterman, R. H. (1982). *In Search of Excellence*. London: Harper & Row.

Pettigrew, A. M. (1979). On studying organisational cultures. *Administrative Science Quarterly*, **24**, 570–581.

Pettigrew, A. M. (1985). *The Awakening Giant*. Oxford: Basil Blackwell.

Pettigrew, A. M., Ferlie, E. B. and McKee, L. (1992). *Shaping Strategic Change*. London: Sage.

Pettigrew, A. M., McKee, L. and Ferlie, E. (1988). Understanding change in the NHS. *Public Administration*, **66**.

Pettigrew, A., Ferlie, E., FitzGerald, L. and Wensley, R. (1991). *The Leadership Role for the New Health Authorities: An Agenda for Research and Development*. Bristol: NHSTA.

Peutherer, J. F., Edmond, E., Simmonds, P., Dickson, J. D. and Bath, G. E. (1985). HTLV-iii antibody in Edinburgh drug addicts. *The Lancet*, 16 November, 1129.

Rothwell, R. (1976). Intracorporate entrepreneurs. *Management Decision*, **13**, 142–154.

Rothwell, R. and Zegweld, W. (1982). *Innovation and the Small and Medium Sized Firms*. London: Frances Pinter.

Scott, A. (1990). *Ideology and the New Social Movements*. London: Unwin Hyman.

Smith, J. (1981). Conflict without change: The case of London's health services. *Political Quarterly*, **52**, 426–440.

Starbuck, W. H., Greve, A. and Hedberg, B. L. T. (1978). Responding to crisis. *Journal of Business Administration*, **9**, 111–137.

Stocking, B. (1985). *Initiative and Inertia in the NHS*. London: Nuffield Provincial Hospitals Trust.

Strauss, A. (1978). *Negotiations*. London: Jossey-Bass.

Strong, P. (1990). Epidemic psychology: A model. *Sociology of Health and Illness*, **12**, 249–259.

Touraine, A. (1981). *The Voice and the Eye: An Analysis of Social Movements*. Cambridge: Cambridge University Press.

Tyhurst, J. S. (1951). Individual reactions to community disaster: The natural history of psychiatric phenomena. *American Journal of Psychiatry*, **107**, 764–769.

Wilson, B. R. (Ed.) (1967). *Patterns of Sectarianism*. London: Heinemann.

Wing, J. K. (1991). Vision and reality. In P. Hall and I. F. Brockington (Eds) *The Closure of Mental Hospitals*. Gaskell (Royal College of Psychiatrists).

Zald, M. and Berger, M. (1978). Social movements in organisations: Coup d'état, insurgency and mass movements. *American Journal of Sociology*, **83**, 823–861.

12

Regaining Competitiveness: A Process of Organisational Renewal

YVES DOZ, HEINZ THANHEISER

Based on research and consulting experience in large multinationals, this chapter deals with corporate renewal. As innovation increasingly determines competitive advantage, the internal modes of operations, i.e. the 'organisational capabilities', of large corporations have to change. To overcome self-generated bureaucratic sluggishness of their companies, top managers need to change their concept of structure, decision and effectiveness and engage in a process of organisational transformation. Successful processes link cognitive/intellectual and emotional 'discovery' at individual level with collective 'learning by doing' to achieve lasting 'cultural' change.

Strategic Thinking: Leadership and the Management of Change.
Edited by J. Hendry and G. Johnson with J. Newton.
Copyright © 1993 the Strategic Management Society. Published 1993 John Wiley & Sons Ltd.

THE CHALLENGE

The large companies that contend for leadership in global competition are more and more equally matched in access to resources, skills and markets (Doz and Prahalad, 1987). Information and knowledge migrate fast and the positional advantages, based on a particular configuration of resource and market deployment of a company are quickly eroded. In many industries, access to cheap labour, or to quality subcontractors, or to large, protected domestic markets alone do not confer lasting competitive advantage and are weak protection against competitors.

New products and process innovations are determining the outcome of competitive battles. Competitive advantage is seen to accrue to companies that identify unmet latent needs, and develop products to meet these needs, faster than others (Hamel and Prahalad, 1991). When one looks into the reasons why companies succeed or fail in this visible, product-based, form of competition one finds that a company's internal mode of operating drives its ability to 'invent' new markets and to subsequently exploit them. Competitive battles are won by organisational capability rather than by new products, resources or market position, *per se*.

Imaginative and effective resource deployment and successful new market creation results from the organisational capabilities of cultivating, mobilising and creatively leveraging competences and skills, and of integrating specialised inputs into the creation and exploitation of new business opportunities. Organisational capabilities are the root of competitive advantage (Doz and Prahalad, 1988).

When one considers how a number of companies that came late to global competition have overcome scale, skill, and other resource disadvantages a few patterns appear regularly.

First, these companies had ambitions well beyond the reach of their current means. These ambitions, usually, constituted a coherent long-term vision or strategic intent, which was emotionally engaging and meaningful for all employees and, therefore, worthy of their commitment and sustained efforts (Hamel and Prahalad, 1989). More important than the ambition itself was the management process used to reach it: a constant process of stretching the capabilities of the organisation and of building new capabilities over time. This required both a willingness to aim at what one cannot yet plan for, and a willingness to consider organisational learning an investment.

Second, these companies focused their resource commitments on core competences, thereby accelerating learning in areas that could be applied across many competitive arenas (Prahalad and Hamel, 1990). This allowed them to leverage their resources and to build competitive advantages that were difficult for competitors to imitate.

Third, these companies exhibited superior capabilities to bring together markets and technologies, both on their home market and internationally, and to pull together the learning arising out of participation in multiple markets (Bartlett and Ghoshal, 1989; Hamel and Prahalad, 1989).

Fourth, these companies were able to manage complex trade-offs creatively and to achieve, internationally, both a high level of responsiveness and an ability to take advantage of the co-ordination and integration opportunities offered by their multinational scope (Doz, 1986; Prahalad and Doz, 1987).

Fifth, these companies managed new product development effectively. They achieved focus in their efforts, efficient use of research and development resources and timely product development results (Doz, 1992).

Sixth, many of these companies effectively relied on alliances, partnerships and other forms of collaboration to access or to acquire competences they did not have, and to do it faster and with fewer resources than their competitors (Hamel, Doz and Prahalad, 1989; Hamel, 1990, 1991).

The development of the organisational capabilities for mobilising people and other resources and for learning cumulatively from experience is central for the successful pursuit of the various strategic development avenues outlined above. Yet, developing such organisational capabilities appears to elude many top managements.

Large companies, with few exceptions, suffer from self-generated sluggishness. This disease, often labelled bureaucracy, has the symptoms of distrust, poor communications, disenfranchised middle management, low level of employee motivation, stifling of entrepreneurial spirit, slow decision-making, a lack of collaboration across subunit boundaries, etc. The organisational capabilities of innovation, integration and learning are inhibited.

Concern with this syndrome is not new; scholars drew attention to it in the 1960s (McGregor, 1960; Bennis, 1961; Likert, 1961) and argued that at its root was a managerial mindset that had become inappropriate for the contemporary realities. The more recent, renewed focus on this big company disease is probably due to the alarming competitive decline of leading American and European corporations in several industries, particularly against Japanese competitors. Increasing numbers of chief executives are making determined efforts, some of them widely publicised in the press (e.g. GE, Xerox, Siemens), to fight the disease. The difficulties are significant.

Large companies seldom 'stand united'. They constitute but a fragile and constantly changing network of relationships between subunits and between individual managers. Collaboration across functions and across business or country boundaries is not natural, and is constantly threatened. The complexities of operations, competitive and stakeholder management are enormous, confronting top managers with multiple challenges of leadership and administration.

Over the past 50 years, there have been significant developments in the structures and administrative systems of large corporations. Most of the new approaches originated in the US and then spread into Europe. Decentralisation of formerly centralised, functionally organised companies into 'divisions' to which profit responsibility is delegated was broadly adopted in the 1960s and 1970s (Rumelt, 1974; Dyas and Thanheiser, 1976). Intended to relieve the strain on top management from the increasing product market and international diversification, the decentralised structures created new needs for co-ordination at corporate level. Various staff functions were established and developed increasingly sophisticated systems for planning, control, procurement, personnel, and other tasks. Over the decades, the staffs, often at several levels (HQ, group and division), grew in size and power. Yet companies failed to develop the capability for sharing across boundaries and collective learning.

Despite the 'modernisation' of corporate structures and systems, the mindset of managers appears to have remained remarkably similar to the Taylorist model developed at the beginning of the century. Few managers today would espouse exercising authority in as blatantly coercive ways as advocated by Taylor (to control 'dumb and lazy workmen'). But his principles of hierarchical order, clarity, specialisation, etc. – in other words, a machine-like concept of the organisation – still dominate managerial practice. The 'command and control' systems, designed to achieve compliance of an uneducated workforce, prevail in today's knowledge and skill-intensive companies. The modern bureaucracy may use subtler means for achieving compliance; none the less, its highly educated managers and knowledge workers are stifled rather than mobilised to contribute all their intelligence and energy.

Corollary to the corporate delegation to business and country subunit, and 'command and control' organisational models, strategy is seen as a top management design and choice exercise, not as the process of gaining commitment to strategic intent. Management focuses on strategy content to the detriment of strategy process, and believes that competitive advantage comes from better choices, not from the accumulation of capabilities and competencies, nor from rapid 'making sense' of new information and quick decision-making. This analytical top management approach to strategy seems increasingly unsuitable to strategic decisions in fast-changing conditions (Eisenhardt, 1990).

Focusing on the quality of the strategy process, rather than just on content, is also essential to foster organisational cohesiveness. What may be right from the standpoint of effectiveness in the choice at hand may be drastically wrong in the signals and messages the decision conveys. Managers must be able to resist the urge to 'solve the problem now' (by 'quick fixes' that relieve the anxiety inherent

TABLE 12.1 Top management's concept of organisation

'Old'	'New'
1. Concept of structure	
Clarity, order, systems	*Networks of intelligence*
● Hierarchical reporting in defined structure	● Multidimensional interactions, exchange, mobilisation and learning
● 'Command and Control' system	● 'Surrounding' problems until they are eliminated
● Functional specialisation	
● Line and staff	● Skill differentiation, flexible integration
2. Concept of decision	
Content and criteria	*Commitments to choices*
● Financial criteria	● Commitment model, teams with meaningful goals
● Analytical 'concrete' strategy	
● Specific decision tools and techniques	● Top management as 'sense-maker', process designer and facilitator
● Emphasis on planning and substantive decisions	● Emphasis on adaptation, flexibility, learning, 'real time', empowerment
● Logical choices	● Cybernetic choices
3. Concept of effectiveness	
● Problem-solving, putting matters to rest	● Process integrity, quality of resulting commitment
● Compliance with policies and procedures	● Commitment to strategic intent
● Eliminating, resolving tensions and conflicts	● Dualities and tensions as sources of progress and better decisions

to decision-making) and consider due process in how decisions are made. Procedural justice has been observed to have more impact on middle-management commitment than the content of decisions (Kim and Mauborgne, 1991).

Maintaining an agenda of ongoing issues, and treating these as 'tensions to be managed' rather than as 'problems to be solved' may also allow managers to learn to deal with dualities, with contradictory ideas and forces, and to discover new, more creative ways of reconciling these tensions (Prahalad, 1983; Evans and Doz, 1989). The contrast between the orthodox management principles and those needed to develop the strategic capabilities outlined above is summarised in TABLE 12.1.

Shedding the old mindset about how an organisation should work, and developing and institutionalising the new mindset is the major challenge facing most large companies today and, particularly, those in fast-changing knowledge and skill-intensive industries.

LIMITED RESPONSES: PROGRAMMATIC VERSUS EVOLUTIONARY CHANGE

Top management attempts at building new capabilities through culture change or corporate transformation often fall short of their expected results and end in disappointment (Beer *et al.*, 1990a). Failure is attributed both to fallacious simplifying assumptions about how change in behaviour occurs (one often-held assumption is that new beliefs lead to new behaviour) and to errors in execution such as a lack of process understanding, a lack of sustained leadership in the change process, and too frequent modification of emphasis and instruments in the course of the change process (Doz and Prahalad, 1987).

To overcome the clear difficulties of programmatic change, some observers and analysts stress the need for transformational leadership, i.e. for individuals who can inspire, manage and see the transformation process through successfully. Indeed a programmatic intervention is probably much more likely to succeed when a gifted, process-sensitive transformational leader exists. This is a rare occurrence, however, and in most situations not a controllable variable.

Evolutionary change often proceeds from small units, often on the periphery of the corporation, where experiments can be undertaken with limited risks, to potentially encompass the whole organisation (a good example is provided by Pascale's (1990) description of the role of the diversified products' division in making evolutionary change feasible at Ford). Change spreads step by step through the emulation of success, with initial success often stemming from new behaviours and approaches 'discovered' to solve concrete business problems (e.g. Beer *et al.*'s model of task alignment, 1990b). The approach puts the emphasis on changes in roles, relationships and patterns of interactions as actionable variables that cause collective change in behaviour at subunit or workgroup level. The evolutionary argument meets our own observations that individuals 'learn' new behaviours mostly by 'doing'. In that point we would subscribe to Pascale's (1990) conclusion that 'you don't think yourself into behaving differently, but you might act yourself into thinking differently'. Since we are concerned with managerial behaviour, 'doing' is primarily engaging in interaction with others; and behaviour change, therefore, can occur only in a collective context.

Yet the evolutionary approach merely transfers the transformational leadership requirement from the corporate to the subunit level: there is still a need for transformational leadership in the unit where the evolution is supposed to start. A dominant corporate culture, with all its established procedures and systems, may limit the likelihood of the process ever starting, and limit its emulation to a few subunits headed by 'deviant' leaders, if the process ever gets started.

Based on our research, and on our interventions in a number of major companies in Europe and in North America, we believe it is possible to develop a synthesis of the transformational and evolutionary approaches to successfully implement a process of organisational renewal.

Several premises, drawn from observing the limits of both the programmed and the evolutionary change processes underlie the integrated renewal processes we observed.

THREE COMPLEMENTARY DIMENSIONS

Actual lasting change in an organisation requires to address three basic and complementary subprocesses: mindset determination, strategic posture definition and power allocation (Prahalad and Doz, 1987, ch. 8).

1. *The world view, or mindset of managers* needs to be consistent with the ambition of the strategic renewal. The mindset of the managers is influenced by the cognitive maps they use, the emotional filters they have, and the data available to them. All three need to be modified in a successful strategic renewal process.

2. *Substantive strategic issues* need to be faced in the renewal process, leading to the development of consensus on a credible *strategic posture*. Strategic intent and a common strategic architecture may provide the ambition and the integrating logic, but managers still need a consensus on intermediate steps and a conviction that the competitive battle can be won. Trying to implement a culture change or a mindset change without a clear link to economic necessity and to a competitive agenda is bound to run into significant difficulties. An externally imposed performance benchmark is required in nearly all cases for successful strategic renewal to take place. Such external reference can be made real, within the organisation, only by anchoring renewal processes around key strategic issues and fostering a consensus around strategic priorities.

3. Managers act in an *organisational* context (Bower, 1970). This context provides explicit and implicit rules of the game that structure and regulate relationships and interactions in the organisation and, therefore, how major decisions are made (Crozier, 1964). Trying to achieve strategic renewal without making the organisational context evolve is bound to fail. In fact, one of the major fallacies of programmatic change is its ignorance of the impact of the specific organisational context within which managers operate. The organisational context is the single most important determinant of managerial behaviour in an organisation. It has to support the new strategic direction.

We have observed programmatic change processes fail because they focused only on out-of-context, broad mindset changes with a conceptual and intellectual content, but little else. Beer and his colleagues make a similar observation about the processes they researched (Beer *et al.*, 1990b). Conversely, evolutionary change may peter out for want of a clear strategic intent and a mindset change. The evolution is perceived by managers as a series of piecemeal adjustments over time in the rules of the game within the organisation, each addressing one strategic issue or another, but growing increasingly disjointed and making consistency in strategy and organisational context difficult to maintain. All three sub-processes need to be effected by the change processes.

Not all entry points and sequences are equally feasible, however (Doz and Prahalad, 1981a, b). Mindset changes are required for a new strategic consensus to emerge and for changes in the rules of the game to become legitimate. Thus, although the three processes are closely intertwined, we have observed successful renewal processes to start with mindset changes about the competitive and market environment, followed by an emergent consensus on strategic priorities, followed by the evolution of the rules of the game. The formalisation of new rules, for instance procedures for budgeting, measurement, and assessment, takes place last, registering and stabilising the results of the change process (Doz and Prahalad, 1981a, b).

LEARNING BY DOING

One of the most frequent fallacies about organisational change is a belief that new thinking will lead to new behaviour more or less automatically. Top management may feel strongly about getting its messages (on vision, values, leadership style, etc.) understood. Thus top management starts communicating these messages through speeches or one-way broadcasts or, more participatively, through seminars with two-way discussion. Yet, this top-down approach typically achieves very little in terms of behaviour change. In a rather extreme example of this, one of us was recently invited by a very large German organisation to assist in 'hammering the message into the heads' of all managers. It was quite difficult to convince the senior managers concerned that this would hardly be a constructive first step.

Similarly, and as any teacher is painfully aware, the impact of intellectual insights is short-lived: unless applied and reinforced by experience, the memory of concepts fades quickly. The half life of unused conceptual learning is measured in weeks, not in months. This applies to problem-solving and analytical concepts; for behavioural prescriptions, the situation is even worse. As we all know from personal experience, being told to behave differently is much less effective than discovering for oneself a new way.

Effective change, therefore, can take place only through a process of personal discovery. This process can be structured, but it involves a personal journey, not merely receiving new information and new concepts. The discovery is not just cognitive, but also emotional and relational. Not just discovering new frames of reference, but more importantly discarding old ones – an act of unlearning – requires an emotional dimension to the process (Lewin, 1951). Relational discovery involves experiencing and testing new forms of relationship. In that sense, learning by doing is not just an individual experience, but a collective one, in particular as managerial action primarily involves behaviour in relationships.

MIDDLE-OUT

In the same way as substantive messages cannot be merely 'broadcast' by the top management, the renewal process itself cannot proceed in a mere top-down cascade alone. The key to regaining competitiveness is often more intense lateral communication and team work, a stronger identity to a community of middle and senior managers, collectively responsible for the future of the enterprise. A top-down process contributes to perpetuate vertical communication patterns and hierarchical attitudes that stifle the process of regaining competitiveness. Similarly to technological innovation, which may be best served by a process in which middle managers play the key leading roles (Nonaka, 1988), organisational renewal benefits from the shared expectations, collectively held change agenda, and peer pressures that middle managers can bring. We have also observed that the most conservative levels in an organisation are often those right below top management. A middle-out process can deliver a powerful mandate for change to these seniormost conservative levels, one that cannot be ignored. Middle management leadership also yields credibility to operators and shop-floor personnel: the commitment of middle management makes the change real. It is not just another top management initiative.

Top management, however, must not only be willing to unleash and orchestrate a change process it cannot fully control, but also to be seen as willing to question its own role. First, senior management must be playing a game led by middle managers, or even by workers and operators. In General Electric's 'work out' process, for example, recommendations that come out of the 'town meetings' (workshops of managers and employees responsible for a particular set of tasks or processes at an individual location) once approved by the local management are not to be overturned or censored by higher levels of management. This, in itself, bears witness to the logic of empowerment that is part of General Electric's renewal process. Second, top management must be willing to let certain issues become discussable when, in the previous working of the organisation they were not (Argyris, 1985). Top management must be willing to let the 'theory-in-use' of the organisation be discovered, debated and explicated. This may be the single strongest commitment needed on top management's part for the process to succeed.

CONSISTENCY AND CONTINUITY OF CONCEPTS AND FRAMEWORK

In recent years we have witnessed a tremendous inflation of 'new wisdom' in management. Total quality, total customer satisfaction, customer chains, time-based competitiveness, cycle time reduction, process integrity, lean manufacturing, product development rugby, empowerment, etc. have become the new slogans. In addition, the old truths remain valid: we need delegation, participation, innovation, permanent improvement, initiative and drive, entrepreneurship, and so forth. An abundance of good things.

While each of these prescriptions often has value in and of itself for most companies, the risk is that a company launches into one after the other, only to achieve none really fully. The bureaucratic disease brakes the momentum of change and efforts peter out. In this process, cynicism grows about whatever is the flavour of the month, as well as scepticism about top management's commitment, for any significant length of time, to any approach and to any priority.

A renewal process can be successful only if the management sticks to priorities, frameworks and concepts for long enough for the relationships, behaviours and attention priorities consistent with these concepts, frameworks and priorities to take root within the organisation. It is essential that a simple unifying theme, anchored in the articulated strategic intent be chosen, adhered to with consistency, and given an expanding concrete meaning over time as the renewal process advances. Otherwise, managers at the operating level, where it takes a lot of time to get real change results, will adopt a wait-and-see attitude: 'soon they [top management] will drop this one and go after something else, so why bother too much . . .'.

In summary, our research leads us to suggest that the debate of programmatic versus evolutionary change is somewhat spurious and creates a false dichotomy. What matters is not so much whether the change process is started at the top or at the bottom – most successful change processes incorporate programmatic and evolutionary elements – but whether the enabling conditions for a potentially successful renewal process are met: a top management understanding and willingness to work in conjunction on three complementary processes:

- a reframing in mindsets, the fostering of a new strategic consensus and a redefinition of the 'rules of the game' embedded in the organisational context
- awareness of the importance of 'learning by doing' and of a solution–discovery approach
- acceptance of the pivotal role of middle managers as change leaders in the process and willingness to address the 'theory in use' of the organisation.

The top management commitment to a set of priorities, frameworks and concepts has to be consistently adhered to over time, throughout the process.

THE TRANSFORMATION PROCESS

The transformation process itself can achieve real behavioural change in using methods drawing both on a programmatic and an evolutionary change process.

Our research (for research method, see Appendix) suggests that the key unfreezing step in the process is the creation of one (or a series of) 'temporary system(s)' that differ(s) from the existing day-to-day functioning of the organisation. Whether workshops, task teams, or other arrangements, these temporary systems create new setting and new networks between managers that allow an alteration of organisational norms, interactions, and power arrangements.

Temporary systems can be task-oriented teams, addressing a particular strategic issue and its organisational causes, as well as workshops for groups of managers. In both cases, it is important to balance 'hands-on' relevance with the need to take some distance from the existing day-to-day functioning of the organisation. A temporary system built around a workshop format must not be seen as a 'training' event by participants, an ever-present danger when human resources and management development specialists are entrusted with the design and delivery process (Beer *et al.*, 1990b). A task-oriented team, on the other hand, must receive sufficient conceptual and informational input, and be sufficiently challenged to take a different innovative perspective, rather than fall back on the well known and well proven.

In our action research, we have found a combination of both approaches to be most effective: discovery workshops followed by task teams. The discovery workshop has an intellectual, an emotional and a relational thread. The intellectual thread provides the basis for a rational 'buy-in' of the need for renewal and of the concepts underlying renewal. Concepts and examples of best practice are used to analyse and reconceptualise one's own competitive situation and organisational capabilities. Contrary to the approach of most strategy consultants, the process does not rely on prepackaged, startling data and analysis, but on a change of perspective induced by the participants themselves using the concepts provided to reinterpret their own situation. The discovery is achieved by the participants, not provided to them, it draws on issues brought by them, and on facts known to them, not on brilliant outsiders' analysis nor on the massive provision of new data. The discovery process is cumulative and additive, taking the results from previous working sessions and reworking them in light of new conceptual insight. The workshop faculty provides the concepts, with relevant external illustrations – for example, drawn from competitors – in a stimulating and challenging fashion, but lets the participants bring and process information from their own company.

The emotional thread is required for the temporary system to challenge the day-to-day functioning of the organisation. Unlearning is required, and this is an emotionally painful process. The change in mindset triggered by the intellectual thread is also likely to evoke anger, frustration, embarrassment, and possibly a feeling of incompetence, all very strong emotions. The process design must allow these emotions to be accepted, given time to be felt, made legitimate, and resolved. A successful transformation workshop is an emotional roller-coster for the participants, with periods of frustration, anger, and despair alternating with periods of elation and progress.

The relational thread is equally fundamental. The true benefits of the temporary system come from the shared experience between participants of a new type of relationship, and power distribution. A taste of empowerment, win–win relationships and synergistic collective action is provided in the renewal process itself. The workshop is not a series of individual experiences, but primarily a collective one.

Drawing on these three threads, the discovery workshops lead to specific task-teams and to short-term action commitments, both being ways to ensure a link between the workshop process and actual change. Typically, the workshops lead participants to a heightened awareness of the limits and dysfunctions of their day-to-day context and to a greater ability to decode the functioning of their organisation, allowing them to unearth the theory in use. It also allows some distancing from the day-to-day context, making it more easily discussable. Issues of measurement and rewards, and the games played around these often become discussable, in a workshop context, when they are taboo in day-to-day in-context relationships.

When workshops are tightly linked to subsequent task-team processes, individual managers and employees practice new behaviours in temporary organisational settings. New roles and relationships are experienced that allow new attitudes and skills to be developed and tested. Training and personal development become part of the change process, rather than disjointed and often frustrating off-line training activities with little relevance to on-line, in-context operational management.

Task-teams provide the relay channelling the energy generated by the workshops into reforming the network of relationships, and the elements of organisational context that shape that network. Thus, while the task teams typically address substantive business issues (such as how to penetrate new markets or better leverage existing core competencies) their output is not only, or not even so much, substantive advice, as it is also a diagnosis of elements of organisational context and suggestions for their reform.

Task-teams may then legitimately move their focus from substantive strategic or operational issues to the underlying organisational processes and capabilities. Process analysis is one of the key tools that task-teams can use. Analysis of the systems that regulate relationships within the organisation is another potential tool to diagnose the capabilities of the organisation and to identify leverage points to remove blockages and to develop new capabilities. The architecture of management systems used to manage information, to manage managers, and to handle conflicts and tensions can then be redrawn to encourage and facilitate the development of required organisational capabilities rather than stifle and hamper such development (Doz and Prahalad, 1981a, b).

CONCLUSION

In summary, task-teams and project work create linkages, over time, between strategic issues, individual competence, and organisational context. They yield both individual experiences of personal development and growing collective dissatisfaction with the organisational context at the root of the bureaucratic disease. Growing expectations of change put increasing pressure on the 'rules of the game' of the old organisational context. This will lead top management to reconsider and, eventually, reform the management systems that constitute the organisational context.

Formal changes to key management systems, such as those used for measurement and reward, appraisal and promotion, and for resource allocation, are often made quite late in the process. Such changes stabilise and institutionalise the results from the renewal process, and provide the basis for permanently embedding the new capabilities in the organisation.

Regarding the end point of transformational processes, the results of our research are, as yet, inconclusive. Competitive success and improved financial performance are the final outcomes sought in renewal processes. However, in large complex corporations, the causality of success and failure is rarely clear-cut. An internal measure for whether a lasting cultural transformation has been achieved is the extent to which the new functioning of the organisation is becoming an experienced reality for more and more, and eventually all, of its members. Since renewal aims at increasing the ability of organisational learning, the most appropriate perspective for top management may be that transformation is a never-ending process. The journey becomes the goal.

A schematic summary of the renewal process is given in FIGURE 12.1.

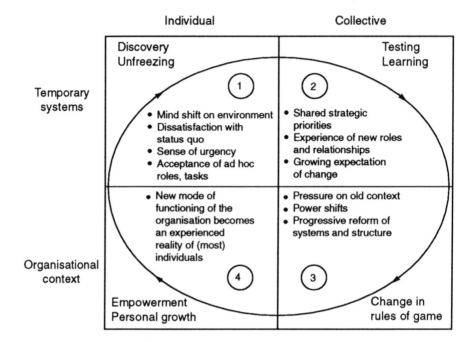

FIGURE 12.1   A map of the renewal process

APPENDIX

THE RESEARCH METHOD

The general argument developed in this chapter draws on the results of a two-phase, long-term research project. In the first phase, data on 16 strategic redirection programmes in the context of major multinational companies were obtained (through extensive interview and process observation fieldwork) by Yves Doz and C. K. Prahalad. Many of these 16 examples were researched through longitudinal process research, over the 1975–85 period. Comparative analyses of these change processes, and a conceptual framework interpreting the analysis were published in 1981 and 1987 (Doz and Prahalad, 1981a, b; Doz and Prahalad, 1987).

In the second phase of the research, the authors of this chapter, and others working with them were involved in assisting companies, in an action-research mode, conceiving and managing strategic renewal processes. In most cases, the involvement of the authors with individual companies lasted several years, which allowed a rich understanding of the management of strategic transformation processes to emerge and evolve.

ACKNOWLEDGEMENTS

Acknowledgement is due to Michael Brimm, of INSEAD, who helped to make explicit many of the arguments presented here, and to C. K. Prahalad, University of Michigan, who pioneered and led many of the corporate renewal efforts that form part of our experience.

REFERENCES

Argyris, C. (1985). *Strategy, Change and Defensive Routines*. Marshfield, MA: Pitman.

Bartlett, C. and Ghoshal, S. (1989). *Managing Across Borders*. Cambridge, MA: HBS Press.

Beer, M., Eisenstat, R. A. and Spector, B. (1990a). Why change programs don't produce change. *Harvard Business Review*, **68**, 158–166.

Beer, M., Eisenstat, R. A. and Spector, B. (1990b). *The Critical Path to Corporate Renewal*. Cambridge, MA: HBS Press.

Bennis, W. (Ed.) (1961). *Planning of Change*. New York: Holt, Rinehart & Winston.

Bower, J. (1970). *Managing the Resource Allocation Process*. Boston, MA: Harvard University Press.

Crozier, M. (1964). *The Bureaucratic Phenomenon*. Chicago, IL: Chicago University Press.

Doz, Y. (1986). *Strategic Management in Multinational Companies*. Oxford: Pergamon Press.

Doz, Y. (1992). New product development effectiveness: A triadic comparison in the information technology industry. In T. Nishiguchi (Ed.) *Managing Product Development*. New York: Oxford University Press.

Doz, Y. L. and Prahalad, C. K. (1987). A process model of strategic redirection in large complex firms: The case of multinational corporations. In A. Pettigrew (Ed.) *The Management of Strategic Change*. Oxford: Basil Blackwell.

Doz, Y. L. and Prahalad, C. K. (1988). Quality of management: An emerging source of global competitive advantage? In N. Hood and J. E. Vahlne (Eds) *Strategies in Global Competition*. London: Croom Helm.

Doz, Y. L. and Prahalad, C. K. (1981a). An approach to strategic control in multinational companies. *Sloan Management Review*, **22**, 5–13.

Doz, Y. L. and Prahalad, C. K. (1981b). Headquarter influence and strategic control in multinational companies. *Sloan Management Review*, **23**, 15–29.

Dyas, G. and Thanheiser, H. (1976). *The Emerging European Enterprise*. London: Macmillan.

Eisenhardt, K. M. (1990). Speed and strategic choice: How managers accelerate decision making. *California Management Review*, **32**, 39–54.

Evans, P. and Doz, Y. (1989). The dualistic organization. In P. Evans, Y. Doz and A. Laurent (Eds) *Human Resource Management in International Firms*. London: The Macmillan Press.

Hamel, G. (1990). Competitive collaboration: Learning, power and dependence in international strategic alliances. The University of Michigan, PhD dissertation.

Hamel, G. (1991). Competition for competence and inter-partner learning within international strategic alliances. *Strategic Management Journal*, Summer Special Issue: Global Strategy, **12**, 83–103.

Hamel, G. and Prahalad, C. K. (1989). Strategic intent. *Harvard Business Review*, May–June, 63–76.

Hamel, G. and Prahalad, C. K. (1991). Corporate imagination and expeditionary marketing. *Harvard Business Review*, July–August, 81–92.

Hamel, G., Doz, Y. and Prahalad, C. K. (1989). Collaborate with your competitors and win. *Harvard Business Review*, **67**, 133–139.

Kim, W. C. and Mauborgne, R. A. (1991). Implementing global strategies: The role of procedural justice. *Strategic Management Journal*, Special Issue: Global Strategy, **12**, 125–143.

Lewin, K. (1951). *Field Theory in Social Sciences*. New York: Harper & Row.

Likert, R. (1961). *New Patterns of Management*. New York: McGraw-Hill.

McGregor, D. (1960). *The Human Side of Enterprise*. New York: McGraw-Hill.

Nonaka, I. (1988). Toward middle-up-down management: Accelerating information creation. *Sloan Management Review*, **29**, 9–18.

Pascale, R. T. (1990). *Managing on the Edge*. New York: Simon & Schuster.

Prahalad, C. K. (1983). Developing strategic capability for top management. *Human Resource Management*, **22**, 237–254.

Prahalad, C. K. and Doz, Y. (1987). *The Multinational Mission: Balancing Local Demands and Global Vision*. New York: The Free Press.

Prahalad, C. K. and Hamel, G. (1990). The core competence of the corporation. *Harvard Business Review*, May–June, 79–91.

Rumelt, R. P. (1974). *Strategy, Structure, and Economic Performance*. Boston, MA: Division of Research, Graduate School of Business Administration, Harvard University.

13

Implementing Strategy: Two Revisionist Perspectives

TONY ECCLES

SPEED OF CHANGE

It is widely claimed that strategic change takes a long time. Hinings and Greenwood (1988) ask 'How long does a strategic re-orientation take? Child and Smith (1987) and Pettigrew (1985, [1987]) take a view of decades rather than years.' In other words, the strategic reorientation of a large organisation apparently takes longer to implement than both world wars combined, plus half of the years in between them. Given that 'decades' means 20 years at the least, it is surprising that Hitler – who came to power in 1933 – was able to transform the strategy of a country and its organisations and start World War II in only six years. Perhaps there was more task-oriented impetus than one has previously supposed behind Goering's saying 'When I hear anyone talk of culture, I reach for my revolver'.

However, if one is talking of a complete sequence, perhaps it does take a long time for the new circumstance to be fully accepted, particularly if the previous régime has been successful and no extraneous force appears to cast doubt on its continued relevance. It can take a fair time for comprehension in such circumstances. But that is a long way from claiming that you cannot make effective

Strategic Thinking: Leadership and the Management of Change.
Edited by J. Hendry and G. Johnson with J. Newton.
Copyright © 1993 the Strategic Management Society. Published 1993 John Wiley & Sons Ltd.

changes in a much shorter time. Indeed, there is often no choice but to change quickly; the organisation may be faced with the prospect of 'adapt or collapse'.

So why do we downplay the evidence from company doctors and acquisition specialists who expect, and sometimes achieve, rapid implementation of change in the organisation which they take over? Strategists also urge the managers of companies to act quickly and decisively, seemingly sanguine about the effects and unswayed by concerns that a diffident approach might be better received.

Merger and acquisition studies do not suggest that incoming owners should tread carefully and remain gently sensitive to the previous culture for years. Far from it; the usual recommendation is that the new owners should make their mode of running their acquisition immediately and decisively obvious, so that there is no doubt about their intent, nor is there much opportunity for confusion, rumour and disorder to fester. In acquisitions, the application of external power, a rapid alteration of the context in which the acquired organisation is to operate, plus the evanescence of previous assumptions, all combine to create a situation in which the staff of the acquired company expect change and, by so doing, make the implementation of major change more feasible. Turnaround studies also support the view that rapid change is not only feasible but, in many circumstances, desirable and, in severe cases, critical to the organisation's very survival. As one experienced acquirer has put it, 'Three months after we arrive, there must be significant changes – after that, newness is a wasting asset' (Alexander, Chief UK Operating Officer, Hanson plc, 1990).

Assiduous corporate acquirers do seem to know a thing or two. It is not normal for companies acquired by the likes of Hanson or BTR to collapse in disorder – let alone collapse in profits. Perhaps outsiders don't spot the bodies in the hedgerows, but what we can usually observe in such companies is a transformation of returns on the assets acquired and an enhancement in profits that is not solely due to accounting ingenuities.

Yet to read and listen to some analysts, you can gain the feeling that the delicacy of multiple, interdependent problems in complex organisations would be enough to put anybody off trying ever to change anything. The detrimental possibilities of major change are abhorred as being likely to savage the sensitive organism that forms the essence of the present organisation. One occasionally feels that if some of those who write on organisational change had been in charge of American policy in 1941, the USA would still be trying to work out how to respond to Pearl Harbour.

Naturally there are circumstances when a major change takes time. The size of an organisation may militate against speed. Yet some delays turn out, on inspection, to have been quite unnecessary, having arisen from managerial disagreements, lack of understanding of what was involved, absence of commitment to provide sensible resources, or from plain managerial incomprehension or torpor. The organisation may be ossified for reasons other than size and so change will take longer than when it is seen to be of low or acceptable risk, within the firm's capabilities and necessary or even vital.

Organisational perceptions of time may be at the root of the belief that implementation of a major change is a lengthy process. Energetic people often want implementation to occur promptly after taking the decision to do something. They become discouraged if time passes without obvious progress and resent the fact that the completion of most managerial initiatives often takes longer than one wishes. In our attempts to use rapid innovation as a competitive weapon we have become impatient and we expect results quickly. Consequently, the time it takes to implement a strategy may well be seen as excessive by those involved, even if the actual timescale is relatively short.

Top managers tend to ascribe such delays as being either due to bungle, truculence and incompetence at lower levels, or else due to the innate slowness of implementing change. In fact, their perceptions may be quite unreliable. Having decided to make changes, announced them and then moved on to other issues, they may have overlooked the work required to see that people have been briefed and equipped properly for the task of making the changes in an effective manner. Indeed, the very fact of their interest having moved on may well have contributed to the waning pace of the strategic change. The new rationale may not even be understood, let alone accepted. No longer driven on by the top executives, the signal to staff is that commitment has declined and, perhaps, that the staff's own efforts should switch to newer priorities. Managerial persistence – a hallmark of sustained organisational purpose – has drooped.

Furthermore, strategic situations are not dormant, but are full of the residues, the backwash, the adjustment of previous strategic changes and so it is not difficult to see the organisation as taking a long time to damp down these oscillations. Sensitive observers may be more aware of these residual signals than managers who have long moved on to their next prospective drama. The sensitivity does not indicate that the major impact of a given change has to straddle decades, but merely that its dying oscillations and memories may linger.

Any conflict between strategists and behavioural scientists could well result not so much from a misunderstanding, but from a difference in goals. The strategist may be content with an organisation that has changed its habits and that is now performing better, so long as insurrection is not breaking out and deflecting the organisation from its objectives. It may be that the strategists are a touch more cavalier about the consequences of strategic change on the inhabitants of an organisation, whilst the human behaviour people are more sensitive about the human nuances that can affect the onset of new habits. The behavioural scientist might, in contrast, feel unhappy if the people in the organisation are reporting cognitive dissonance, personal alienation and other indications of angst – which the strategist is prepared to shrug off as being merely the temporary phenomena of adjustment and, perhaps, as being an inevitable cost that is to be offset by the new advantages.

The issue then becomes that of deciding in what circumstances rapid change is feasible. It can be argued that there are eight distinguishable conditions that can meet that test:

1. organisational crisis
2. irresistible external pressure, be it from new owners, bidders, competitors, capital markets, legislation, etc. (which may create an organisational crisis)
3. the spin-off or buy-out from an organisation (which, like a takeover, can also arouse crisis-like conditions)
4. entry into a new market/setting up a novel kind of operation in the company
5. the introduction of a power-wielding new top team – or even just a new CEO
6. an entrepreneurial organisation with power concentrated into the hands of a decisive individual or small coterie
7. an appropriate shift in the organisation's structure and its effort/reward motivators
8. a persuasive new vision that causes people to rearrange their perspectives and their behaviour.

Now it can be argued, as with transformations resulting from merger and acquisition activities, that the rapid resulting changes come generally from the use of power and are coerced transformations. But if, nevertheless, they are transformations, then it can no longer be generally claimed that rapid change is impossible – only that it occurs in certain forceful circumstances and might not be self-induced in the absence of externally applied pressure. Power and urgent necessity feature large in the determinants of the pace at which change can be affected. Suffice it to say that the factors that will determine the pace and extent of strategic change are contingent upon the particular circumstances. But the idea that strategic change inevitably takes many years to accomplish is demonstrably false.

THE STRATEGIC CHANGE PROCESS

The second oddity is the widespread claim that strategy formulation and strategy implementation are aspects of one process and are frequently concurrent, if not indistinguishable. Yet there are times when strategy formulation and planning manifestly are *not* concurrent with strategy implementation. The following six circumstances exemplify situations in which it would be imprudent to synthesise strategy formulation with strategy implementation and when the two elements are all but certain to be separable parts of the strategy process.

1. *Unagreed bid for listed public company* Unless the bidding company wishes to see the market price of its target company's shares rise against it, plus the early warning that would be given to a rival bidder, the formulation of the plan to acquire must be kept secret. The circle of the informed must be restricted to increase the chance that a leak will not happen. Whilst planning can take place discreetly in order to put together a plan for the post-acquisition period and perhaps to put a team of people and some existing resources on standby pending the takeover, no implementation in the acquired firm can occur prior to the acquisition. Even if you were a wholly benign acquirer, it would be silly not to formulate some prior thoughts about the way that you intend to win the hearts and minds of the key employees, customers and suppliers in the event of your taking over the firm.

2. *Retrenchment in highly unionised firm* Again, the formulation of plans to downsize an organised workforce is likely to remain confidential for a while. Of course, a good management will want to take its staff into its confidence as early as practicable; but that may not be at least until some thought has been given to the various options, costs, contingencies, timescales, public reactions and customer responses. To begin to implement an unnegotiated, unagreed manpower reduction would be to invite resistance, confusion and counter-productive diversions so as to put at risk the estimated benefits of the retrenchment action.

3. *Adverse change in a low-trust situation* Unionisation is not a necessary condition for resistance to occur and in any low-trust situation the scope for unhelpful reaction is latent, particularly if the low trust has already led staff to set up their own mechanisms for countering or neutralising unwelcome management initiatives. Throwing open an unstructured discussion to all staff without at least some skeletal parameters emanating from management, does not look like a device calculated to breed trust, respect, efficiency or progress.

4. *Confusion-inducing speculation* Even if trust is high, uneasiness can spread rapidly and staff imagination will ensure that gripping, perhaps lurid, speculations will arise. Staff will put pressure on management by asking them to deny particular rumours, a well-known device to force management's hand before it has worked out the implications of its own assertions, denials and promises, which it may have been jostled into giving before its plans and options have been properly refined. An organisation can become exhausted quite quickly by speculative rumour. Productivity and customer care rarely rise in such circumstances.

5. *Entry into a joint venture* It would be a poor negotiator who entered into a negotiation without some prior thought and agreement about the goals of the negotiation, the terms that were desired and the scope of the commitment that might ensue. Given that there might be more than one possible joint-venture partner and that most joint ventures are likely to have some impact on the competitive state of the industry, it would be surprising if the early, formative stages of the joint venture foray were not to be characterised by discreet, far from open, investigation of the options and desired conditions. Given the disturbing implications for employees, it would be logical for the early discussions to be held within a small confidential group and even the early

negotiations between the two parties might be concealed from those lower down in the two organisations for reasons mentioned above in circumstances 2, 3 and 4.

6. *Major investment commitment* A major investment (or a divestment/closure) may commercially be sensitive, of concern to national or local populaces and their politicians, need approval by regulators, have manpower connotations, be share-price sensitive, of interest to one's competitors or affect one's own management by virtue of the proposed investment pre-empting company resources or revealing unwelcome corporate priorities. The chance of just making the investment, simply doing it, of making implementation concurrent with formulation is very small – and none too sensible since it would denote that no prior thought had been given to the project.

Other examples may arise in which the integration of strategy formulation and strategy implementation would be impracticable, imprudent, counter-productive or downright senseless – at least in a Western business culture.

How did we get addicted to this more recent view that formulation and implementation are so interwoven? It appears to have been an overreaction to the grandiose planning vogues of the 1970s, which inferred that you could plan a future that you could control. After the first OPEC oil shock a more modest view of strategy evolution came forward that incorporated the influential paradigms of incremental and emergent strategy. Unfortunately, the insights offered by incrementalism and emergence elbowed aside the old planning paradigm and led to an excessive reliance on these newer delineations of strategic process to explain the evolution of strategy in organisations. Each of them mounted a telling challenge to the pretensions of the 'plan the future' advocates, but their authors did not claim that incrementalist and emergent processes were the only ways by which strategy was developed and actioned.

James Brian Quinn's (1980) book, *Strategies for Change: Logical Incrementalism*, persuasively argued that the strategic process frequently included a number of individually minor steps that could add up to a strategic sequence. He argued that the process of incrementalism was a logical system for testing out strategic changes at low cost and in manageable elements.

Academic analysts latched on to the merits of 'logical incrementalism', not just because it was observable that incremental actions by managers did sometimes lead to a change in an organisation's strategy and also helped to explain the rather erratic path of strategy development in many organisations. Analysts pointed out that an evolutionary view of strategy, such as incrementalism (and emergent strategy, too), was consistent with a strategy model containing feedback loops to encourage strategic adaptation as circumstances changed and organisational experiences were interpreted. But then good, traditional, planned-change models also include those feedback loops.

Incrementalism also had the apparent merit of tailoring strategy more smoothly to circumstance than could be achieved by less frequent but individually more dramatic strategic changes – the underlying assumption being that when increments occurred they were apposite, as opposed to being a sequence of random changes. Incrementalism also seemed to lower overall risk for the corporation, since any increment was, almost by definition, small compared to any major strategic upheaval.

The problem is that there are circumstances where incrementalism cannot work or cannot work well. Not all increments can be reinterpreted after they have occurred as being part of a smooth overall plan. Some will be in a direction unhelpful to the organisation. Others will be insufficient to make a real difference. Heightened international competition seems likely to create a continued increase in the size of the average threshold at which a bet could have a significant effect. Stakes cannot be diminished when making some kinds of strategic move. One cannot dive 40 feet into a swimming pool by diving the first ten feet and then stopping to review the situation.

Nor is risk necessarily reduced. One definition of an increment must be that it can be free-standing, a project complete on its own, for if it cannot have those qualities, if it is inevitably just part of a longer sequence of strategic action, proceeding increment by increment would have little more chance of providing management with a respite to reconsider its longer-term actions than would occur within a traditional, preplanned intervention that had some feedback devices to modify the plan as it unfolded.

Henry Mintzberg (Mintzberg and Waters, 1985) also developed his theme of 'emergent' strategy in which a strategic change arises not from a striking decision at an incisive moment, but from the evolution of a new strategy as a result of a series of actions. Mintzberg is persuasive in arguing that emergence is often the way by which an organisation evolves its strategy (though this can mean planning for action rather than the action that defines strategic change for our purposes). Certainly there are examples of innovations in strategic habits, products and policies that have arisen rather than been decided consciously.

Emergence can also enable experimentation to take place at lower levels of risk than would occur when betting on the success of the whole sequence from the start. That, however, does not necessarily lower the overall risk, for reasons already discussed. If an emergent set of steps takes too long, gives too many counter-opportunities to competitors, or simply fritters away benefits because each emergent step is below the threshold of effectiveness, then emergence is not a viable strategic route. You are not likely to get into space launching effectively by starting to make firework rockets for Halloween.

The probability that emergent or incremental strategies are the dominant forms of strategy development is not high, unless one approaches tautology by pointing out that any strategy that fails to arrive complete and resplendent with every element prespecified is, by definition emergent or incrementalist – in which case all strategies are emergent/incrementalist and the case is proven.

But Mintzberg is too sophisticated to suggest such and, indeed, infers more the opposite. Mintzberg (1988, p. 16) has described eight types of strategies ranging from highly deliberate to rather emergent. TABLE 13.1 shows seven types of strategy; the eighth, imposed strategy, has not been included because an externally imposed strategy is not the organisation's own.

Mintzberg's diagnosis recognises that deliberate strategies are widespread. Without precise definitions for the inhabitants of each category and an idea of the relative population sizes of the seven categories, one cannot be sure but, unless consensus organisations are markedly more numerous than the others, the indication from

TABLE 13.1 Mintzberg's strategies (see Mintzberg, 1988)

Strategy type	Deliberate or emergent
Planned	Highly deliberate
Entrepreneurial	Relatively deliberate, but can emerge too
Ideological	Rather deliberate
Umbrella	Partly deliberate, partly emergent (deliberately emergent)
Process	Partly deliberate, partly emergent and deliberately emergent
Disconnected	Can be deliberate for those who make them
Consensus	Rather emergent

Mintzberg is that deliberate strategies are more prevalent than emergent ones. This should make us wary of abandoning the older notion of strategy as being formulated, planned and then implemented.

That does not mean that a deliberate, knowing, preconsidered strategy cannot be incremental. A deliberate strategy to create a new retailing concept in one unit of a chain of stores could provide feedback to prove, disprove or modify the original concept. But the formulation of that strategy has preceded its implementation. Formulation and implementation in such an instance are no more concurrent than they would be if the new strategy had been planned and the feedback loop from the experience of the initial experiments sensibly interposed into the plan.

The spectrum of possible relationships between formulation and implementation is illustrated in FIGURE 13.1. There is no known support for the extremes where formulation and implementation would either have no connection or else be integrated inseparably. The traditional view of the strategy process has been that the two phases of formulation and implementation are sequential, perhaps abutting contiguously. The emergent and incrementalist views have been that the two phases are concurrent, even synonymous to the degree that it is deemed pointless even to try to separate them. As Hamermesh (1986, p. 41) puts it, 'the processes of strategy development and implementation are both continuous and symbiotic'. Yet in the circumstances specified earlier, links are continuous only once they have been established after formulation of the strategy.

Our argument is that, under the polarising influence of those decrying the traditional planning model, we have all but evacuated the middle ground. The gap in the middle is an illusion. We have merely forgotten how populated it is. This error has led to a number of decidedly odd definitions of strategy implementation

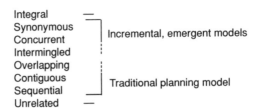

FIGURE 13.1   Relationship: Formulation/implementation

in some texts on strategy implementation – notably the confusing of planning with action.

For example, Hrebiniak and Joyce (1986, p. 9) state that: 'The two basic activities in implementing strategy are planning and organisational design.' They are not. Those are intermediate stages between formulating (developing and deciding) a strategy and the action that is implementation.

Again, in Stonich (1982, p. xvii), it is argued that the 'essential difference' between strategy formulation and strategy implementation is that 'strategy formulation is deciding *where* your company is today and *where* your company should be tomorrow', whilst 'strategy implementation is deciding *how* to get your company from where it is today to where it should be tomorrow'.

Once again, this ignores the crucial act of implementing the plan that has been decided. Implementation does not mean operationalising a strategy of, say, expanding into Europe by the act of agreeing that the way to do it would be to buy a European company. Implementation of that chosen strategy is actually buying the European company and expanding into Europe. Deciding how to get a company somewhere is a necessary prelude, but getting it there is the implementation of the plan. These misconceptions produce what one might call the stunted model of strategy implementation, one that omits the vital stage of action.

The distinction between the definitions of implementation that have been criticised above and actual implementation is easy to illustrate. For example, were we to accept the views of such writers on implementing strategy, it would be a poor lookout for the travel trade. People would formulate their strategy by deciding to go on holiday. Implementation would evidently consist of planning and designing the proposed vacation. Actually going on holiday would presumably be of little account – perhaps even unnecessary – and would be, it seems, a mere operating routine.

What these authors have been focusing on are intermediate stages between formulating (creating and deciding) and the action that is implementation. It is an odd misconception, since there seems little room for dubiety about the meaning of implementation. Implementation is action. It is not planning to act; nor thinking about acting; nor clearing the organisational decks for action; nor persuading others to back your proposed plan; nor even just deciding what action should occur and how it should take place. It is the action itself, whatever it is and however it is occurring, with all its attendant elements of error, feedback, adjustment, and frustration. Or, as Miller and Friesen (1980) put it 'all of their turmoil, expense and confusion'.

Of course it can be agreed that the very process of planning as a necessary prelude to action may create changes, particularly in the attitude and behaviour of those involved in the planning process (De Geus, 1988). But that still doesn't turn planning into implementation; at best planning is an early part of the implementation process. Planning is better defined as a precondition of implementation, an intermediate stage. Miles and Snow (1984) captured the essence of this intermediate stage when they wrote about 'fit' as being 'a process as well as a stage – a dynamic search that seeks to align the organisation with its environment and to arrange resources internally in support of that alignment. In practical terms the basic alignment mechanism is strategy, and the internal arrangements are organisational structure and management processes'.

It is these 'internal arrangements' that the previously quoted writers are discussing when they profess to be addressing the implementation of strategy. Yet is is evident that, by addressing the planning and organising stages, they are habitually confusing the prelude with the event. They seem to confuse laying the table with having a dinner party. Choosing and agreeing the menu and deciding how to cook the food is not, of itself, going to produce cooked food. In contrast, the contention here is that action is an inescapable part of the strategic change process and that strategy implementation habitually follows the initial stages of formulation.

FIGURE 13.2 illustrates stages in the evolution and implementation of a purposeful strategic change in which the formulation of the proposed strategy is linked with both the planning of its inferences and the selling of the strategy as groups of relevant people endorse it, modify it, and assemble the resources needed for implementation to occur. There is feedback at every stage and the stages can shift

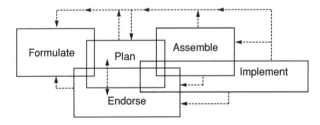

FIGURE 13.2   1991 Eccles model

temporally, depending on the context, scope and type of strategic change being undertaken. Not every strategic change will take this shape, but what is being rejected is the fatalistic notion that the five elements are just mixed together as though no pattern, form, sequence or orderliness was present in the process of strategic change.

The propositions of this chapter are: (1) that strategic change can take place quickly, particularly when those at the top of the organisation have significant power, and (2) that planned, sequential strategic change is more common than has been recently credited.

REFERENCES

Alexander, T. (1990). *Financial Times*, 23 August.

Child, J. and Smith, C. (1987). The context and process of organization transformation: Cadbury Ltd in its sector. *Journal of Management Studies*, **24**, 565–594.

De Geus, A. P. (1988). Planning as learning. *Harvard Business Review*, March–April, 70–74.

Hamermesh, R. G. (1986). *Making Strategy Work: How Senior Managers Produce Results*. New York: John Wiley.

Hinings, C. R. and Greenwood, R. (1988). *The Dynamics of Strategic Change*. Oxford: Basil Blackwell.

Hrebiniak, L. G. and Joyce, W. F. (1984). *Implementing Strategy*. New York: Macmillan Publishing Co.

Miles, R. E. and Snow, C. C. (1984). Fashion, fit and the hall of fame. *California Management Review*, **11**, Spring, 10–28.

Miller, D. and Friesen, P. H. (1980). Momentum and revolution in organisational adaptation. *Academy of Management Journal*, **23**, 591–614.

Mintzberg, H. (1988). Opening up the definition of strategy. In J. B. Quinn, H. Mintzberg and R. M. James (Eds) *The Strategy Process*. London: Prentice-Hall.

Mintzberg, H. and Waters, J. A. (1985). Of Strategies Deliberate and Emergent. *Strategic Management Journal*, **6**, 257–272.

Pettigrew, A. (1985). *The Awakening Giant*. Oxford: Basil Blackwell.

Pettigrew, A. (1987). Context and action in the transformation of the firm. *Journal of Management Studies*, **24**, 649–670.

Quinn, J. B. (1980). *Strategies for Change: Logical Incrementalism*. Homewood, IL: Irwin.

Stonich, P. J. (Ed.) (1982). *Implementing Strategy*. Cambridge, MA: Ballinger.

Conclusion

14

Dilemmas of Strategic Learning Loops

CHARLES M. HAMPDEN-TURNER

My conviction, shared by most contributors to this book, is that strategy is about learning quickly and that learning occurs through cybernetic ·loops and circular processes. All systems of this kind tend to have negative feedback with the power to constrain, correct and 'fine tune' the process. As such, learning loops are replete with *dilemmas*, for example with 'more' followed by 'less', 'error' followed by 'correction', 'disturbance' followed by 'stabilization', in what Gregory Bateson (1975) termed the ecology of mind.

Two well-known disputes among strategic experts illustrate the existence of dilemmas. In the first, Henry Mintzberg takes exception to the traditional business policy approach taught by Kenneth Andrews at the Harvard Business School. Andrews (1980) had explained that strategies were *designed* at the corporation's apex by top management and later implemented (or not) by those further down. Mintzberg (1991) argued that on the contrary, strategies frequently *emerged* from various parts of the organization, especially those interacting with customers in the field and were later picked by top management (or overlooked).

This dispute is a variant of the top-down – bottom-up conflict and tends to enlist political sympathies for or against the authority of Harvard and its MBAs. Is strategic thinking to be reserved for an élite? Is it the role of the great mass of employees to implement what their seniors have merely thought of? Apart from such

Strategic Thinking: Leadership and the Management of Change.
Edited by J. Hendry and G. Johnson with J. Newton.
Copyright © 1993 the Strategic Management Society. Published 1993 John Wiley & Sons Ltd.

ideological excitements is the fact that all or most of the contributors to this book are themselves entrepreneurs of a kind who sell their expertise in strategy and need to differentiate themselves from competitors. Hence 'not designed strategy, but emergent strategy' is at one and the same time a sincere conviction *and* a competitive stance *vis à vis* other experts.

There is another important aspect to such critiques of the status quo. Mintzberg (1991) is saying that on the whole emergent strategies have been relatively neglected compared to strategies designed at the top. He is not denying that strategies are often designed and that this has contributed to the success of many companies. He is saying that to look for viable strategies only at the top of the organization is to miss much and neglect most of the organization's potential.

I must confess that I am personally on Mintzberg's side politically, ideologically and as a diagnostician of corporate imbalances, but it is important not to get carried away in our adversarial enthusiasms. It is more helpful, perhaps, to corporations to see designed versus emergent strategies, less as a debate or social case than a *dilemma within strategic learning loop* (see FIGURE 14.1).

Once we put both design and emergence within a loop the significance of both terms changes because the learning loop does not *start* at any one point, except, of course, when the corporation itself started (usually a long time ago). As far as day-to-day reality is concerned there never was a corporation in which at least some strategies had not already emerged to prove their value, and there

FIGURE 14.1   Dilemma within strategic learning loop

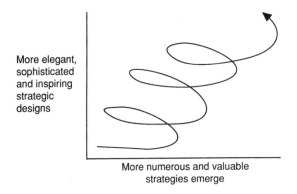

More elegant, sophisticated and inspiring strategic designs

More numerous and valuable strategies emerge

FIGURE 14.2   A virtuous helix

never was a top management that did not pay selective attention to certain of these past achievements, thereby adding its own influence to the overall design.

In other words top managers *design with* extant strategic initiatives, while employees at the grass roots *emerge with* those types of initiatives that have found favour with their superiors in the recent past. There is no inherent reason why better and more numerous initiatives should not emerge, which top managers weave into ever more sophisticated, elegant and inspiring designs. The more employees see their own initiatives and emergent strategies embedded within an overall strategic design the more genuine is their experience of participation. The questions 'Will this strategy be implemented by my subordinates?' 'Can I get them to "own" it?' 'How can I motivate them to do what I want?' do not really arise because they have *already done*, at least in parts, what is being recommended. The strategy is designed from their achievements. The result resembles a virtuous circle or, better, a 'virtuous helix', as shown in FIGURE 14.2.

WE HAVE MET THE ENEMY

One reason the cybernetic model of learning is not as salient as it might be is that we academics have been trying to persuade our customers that strategies start with ideas and concepts supplied by universities. It follows that top managers start with 'pure ideas' floating in the academic ether and design original strategies that they (subordinates) must then carry out. This division of labour is insulting. We think they have nothing better to do with their lives than fulfil and vindicate our thoughts. No wonder the national rates of economic development are inversely related to the number of business schools!

We are forever trying to create Athena, who sprang fully armed from the head of Zeus. The elements of any strategic synthesis must emerge from the organization itself rather than the academy. As they used to say in the 1960s, 'We have met the enemy and he is us . . .'. The hope that strategic thinking is part of the hypothetico-deductive method is in *our* imagined self-interest so that we may more nearly resemble the faculties of more exact disciplines. In fact, knowledge is accumulated inductively from the field to the board room, in any corporation where strategies are emergent.

Unfortunately for us, this is less academically respectable and the learning site, where knowledge accumulates, is the company and not the college, and this knowledge may not be of universal applicability.

STRATEGIC INTENT VERSUS STRATEGIC FIT

A second dilemma that has sharply emerged in the strategy literature is that between *strategic fit* and *strategic intent*. This time the challenge comes from Hamel and Prahalad and is well described in this volume by Kees Van Der Heijden in Chapter 6. The indictment of the status quo is that there has been too much attention paid and too much focus upon, existing niches, analyses of portfolios, existing products, channels and customers, financial targets and in general too many attempts to fit into an objectively describable environment. What is needed is a search for new rules, developing portfolios of core competencies, forming new markets, products and relationships, accepting strategic challenges, and in general shaping the environment according to the subjectivity of our strategic intent. It is argued that the more turbulent and uncertain the business environment becomes, the more likely is this latter pro-active approach to achieve success.

Once again, we should not confuse the need for academic consultants to compete and dispute, with the larger reality of learning systems that require corporations to have powerful strategic intentions *and* fit the requirements of their markets and customers.

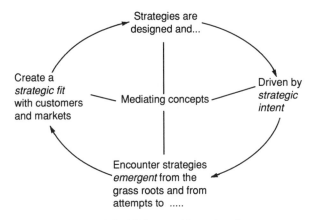

FIGURE 14.3 Elaborated learning loop

We can join this dilemma to the previous one by creating a loop with four elements, as shown in FIGURE 14.3.

We can, of course, think up subtle, and not so subtle, epithets to apply to the advocates of strategic fit, but is this the best use of our time? That most of us make a living out of distinctive strategy is a fact, but it is not necessarily a fact about our corporate customers. They have to let strategies emerge from the best fits achieved with customers and form their designs and intentions from these. We are once again arguing about where a circular phenomenon is believed to 'start'. That it starts nowhere is the beginning of wisdom, as is the realization that we now have four places to intervene or facilitate, not just one place.

In the middle of the loop above are mediating concepts, and these can be very important in suggesting the reconciliation of dilemmas. Often these are metaphors, for example, Mintzberg's (1991) concepts of 'crafting strategy' with one's hands on the 'clay' of industrial experience, beautifully captures the finger-tip shaping of something emerging from the rotations of the potter's wheel. You both design *and* respect what is forming in front of you. You have an intention but the final fit of hands to clay is full of chance and serendipity.

MEDIATING CONCEPTS

Many of the papers in this collection introduced important mediating ideas. I especially appreciated the idea of strategic conversation within management teams and the notion of rent as the surplus product of interactions, both advanced by Van Der Heidjen in Chapter 6. Dutton and Penner, in Chapter 4, use the concept of identity to mediate contradictory demands. One's identity, whether as a person or an organization, typically mediates between continuity and change. In what respects does 'staying the same' in certain important respects entail 'necessary change'? An identity makes us recognizably the same beings through the course of a life or organizational cycle. You cannot get an issue like homeless persons crowding your facility upon the strategic agenda unless the organization feels that it has some responsibility towards these persons. Thomas Lenz argues in Chapter 7 that mediation varies according to urgency and the perceived competence of those in place. Orchestration by leaders is the rule in situations of sufficient competence and low urgency; executive action when competence is sufficient and urgency high; orderly transition from one leader to another when competence is insufficient and urgency low; and shock treatment when competence is insufficient and urgency high. All these four modes could be used to alter the relative balance between the four learning elements in Figure 14.3.

Levenhagen, Porac and Thomas in Chapter 3 see the mediating forms as transactions between the mental models of major participants, driven by their norms and values. These clash through rhetoric and become more or less congruent. By stressing market formations these authors see markets as malleable outcomes of mutual interaction rather than the impersonal mechanism of allocation preferred by many economists. As Robert Reich (1987) has put it 'markets are us'. Lastly, the authors 'recant linearity' and suggest a systems model that is circular.

Colin Eden argues in Chapter 5 that the values held by important groups and principals can be mapped cognitively and that 'goal maps' can be 'merged' and that goals cluster as employees are organized into 'support systems for group decisions'. Strategic visions and mission statements are important ingredients in reconciling goals, while scenarios create alternative futures from seemingly contradictory outcomes. Instead of arguing about who is right, the company prepares plans robust enough to survive different contingencies.

In Chapter 1 Maznevski, Rush and White suggest mediation by consensual mapping of meaningful strategic visions. Maps of 'organizational cause' identify what various groups see as the main drivers. I am reminded here of Gregory Bateson's (1975) thesis that 'causes' are arcs abstracted from circles. Some would say of FIGURE 14.3 that strategic design causes intent and emergent initiatives, others that emergent strategies cause strategic fit and later designs. Yet such 'causes' combine in circular forms.

Hellgren and Melin in Chapter 2 see strategic change as growing out of incompatibilities, particularly incompatibility between the leader's strategic way-of-thinking, the organizational culture and the surrounding industrial wisdom. The greater the discrepancies and tensions the more abrupt will the attempted changes be.

Richard Whittington looks in Chapter 8 at the influence of strong family cultures in mediating and, in some cases, suppressing conflicts. Because families have tight affective bonds, people within them may be able to disagree while remaining in communication. Learning together strategically may be a question of staying together long term and having values beyond money. However this chapter retains a peculiarly Anglo-Saxon aversion to 'paternalism'. Must a family ideal inevitably infantilize? How do the Japanese excel in this respect? Why does Germany have so many excellent companies that refuse to grow beyond their human scale? All Whittington's leaders were Jews. Could they know something that we don't?

I am particularly grateful to Crossan, Lane and Hildebrand who stress in Chapter 9 the Icarus Paradox, that a company brilliantly successful in one respect only will soon become pathological. This is precisely what we would expect from learning circles such as the one in FIGURE 14.3. If you obsess on any one element and see it as 'the cause', all other dynamics will elude you and you crash. Another Greek myth told of Oedipus (or swollen foot) the grandson of Labdakus (lame) and the son of Laius (left sided). All three *limped*, as one does when one value in a circle grows and grows in relative salience. Greek tragedy was about re-establishing harmony, or as the Japanese call it, *wa*. The authors call this 'integration'. It is the reconciliation of contentious versus groupthink orientations, and replaces impoverished with complex schema. Integration is a combination of freedom *with* social responsiveness, another reconciled dilemma. Crucial is the role of belief. 'You can see what you believe in.' 'What you cannot see is what you cannot believe.' Certain belief systems make mediation and integration possible. Others seize upon polarities.

Ewan Ferlie and Chris Bennett described in Chapter 10 changes of strategy in the National Health Service in response to the AIDS crisis. Here the mediating functions were the ongoing historical processes of the unit concerned, carried forward by 'clinical product champions' and the view of crisis as opportunity to reorganize the elements needing to be learned in order to meet the crisis. Finally, the authors borrow from Gerry Johnson (1990) the role of symbolization in mediating crises or dilemmas, from the Greek symbol 'to throw together', a symbol (see especially the work of C. G. Jung; edited by Campbell, 1971) stands for the reconciliation of opposites.

The above contributors are clearly influenced by the work of Andrew Pettigrew who, with Richard Whipp, contributes a chapter on historical process as emphasized in *The Awakening Giant* (Pettigrew, 1985). In Chapter 12 Whipp and Pettigrew stress that the strategic leader must both understand the shifting competitive forces *and* mobilize the corporation's resources to deal with these. The strategy itself must be modifiable through use, thereby representing a feedback loop. Indeed competition and strategy of leadership are of doubtful validity, so context sensitive must it be. Three styles of mediation are emphasized: (1) transactional leadership, as exchange of rewards for compliance; (2) representational leadership, where different positions in the learning process are the synthesis of resources and competencies; and (3) transformational leadership, which transforms the meaning of the organization and its strategy. The central characteristic of successfully leading change is the quality of connectedness.

Doz and Thanheiser in Chapter 11 introduce yet additional forms of vital mediation and associate this with regaining competitiveness through organizational renewal. The first essential is to push your ambitions and 'strategic intent' beyond current means and accomplishments and then struggle to attain this (Hamel and Prahalad, 1989) building new capabilities where necessary. The point is to reconcile the ideal with the real; ambitious intentions with enhanced achievements. The second essential is to define core competencies and make these the foci of your available resources. You respond to customers in the area of your chief strengths. The third characteristic of effective strategies was the reconciliation of the company's own technologies with market opportunities. Remaining mediations include a catch-all category, 'complex trade-offs managed creatively', well-timed product development and the use of partners and alliances to supply what the company itself lacked.

An important supplement to first thinking strategically and then implementing your thoughts, according to these contributors, is acting first and then adjusting your thinking. They call this the evolutionary aspect of strategic learning, where the fit with the environment comes about through chance but is then recognized as valuable on reflection. In a final chart, 'discovering and un-freezing' is balanced against 'changes in the rules of the game', the individual is balanced with the collective, and temporary systems with the more enduring context of the organization. The view is cybernetic.

Lastly, in Chapter 13, Tony Eccles employs the term 'symbiosis' for the vital capacity for strategy to work in integral, synonymous, concurrent, intermingled and overlapping ways. The traditional view of formulation followed by implementation at a far later time is questioned. Action is itself a part of the strategy, planning overlaps assembly and implementation through circular iterations. Such processes are continuous. Strategy can shift as one configuration and changes can, in certain instances, lead to rapid transformations.

Overall, the majority of contributions in this book see strategies and leaders as engaged in the mediation and reconciliation of contrasting values and principles. This is variously achieved by:

- strategic conversations
- creating a corporate identity
- mediating between change and continuity
- orchestrating values
- acting urgently to restore balances
- shock treatments
- transactions among mental models
- creating congruence among models
- forming as well as responding to markets
- creating convergent goal-maps
- creating alternative scenarios
- consensual mapping of strategic visions
- growth stimulated by incompatibilities
- cultures reminiscent of the family
- recognizing paradox
- integrations of viewpoints
- belief systems that see more
- ongoing historical processes
- symbolization of contrasting values
- strategic thoughts modifiable through use
- transactional, representational, transformational leadership
- connectedness
- strategic intentions reconciled with achievements

- customer needs reconciled with core competencies
- company technologies reconciled with markets
- preformulation reconciled with evolution
- symbiosis of overlapping strategic elements
- circular, cybernetic, self-reinforcing loops.

TWELVE FACES OF STRATEGY

It is clear, then, that the theme of this book concerns itself chiefly with how strategic elements achieve coherence. And this brings me to my own conception, which borrows from much the same pool of experts and positions as previous chapters. We may begin by considering ten major positions from the literature as follows:

1. Strategy as artful design and master plan (Kenneth Andrews, 1980; Keniche Ohmae, 1983).
2. Strategy as competitive positioning (Michael Porter, 1990).
3. Strategy as the rational development of core competencies (Bruce Scott and George Lodge, 1985; Max D. Hopper, 1992; Gary Hamel and C. K. Prahalad, 1989).
4. Strategic intent with deviance-correcting feedback loops (W. Edwards Deming, 1982; C. K. Prahalad and Yves Doz, 1987).
5. Strategic opportunism and the release of human potential (Daniel J. Isenberg, 1984, 1987; Tom Peters, 1987).
6. Emergent strategy: how employees participate in policy (Henry Mintzberg and James Quinn, 1991; Ikujiro Nonaka, 1988).
7. Strategic adaptation: co-operating with customers (Igor Ansoff, 1984).
8. Evolving strategy by logical increments (James Brian Quinn, 1978).
9. The strategy of amplifying customer-induced deviance (Magorah Maruyama, 1982).
10. Strategy as the achievement of 'total quality' and ever escalating bench-marks (Frederick Taylor, 1941; Joseph Juran, 1974).

Putting these positions together we get a circle of strategic learning (FIGURE 14.4), in which opposite elements represent contrasting principles. But if strategic learning constitutes a circle, if there are tensions between strategic principles on opposite sides of this circle, for example between 'designed' and 'emergent' strategies, and between deviances corrected to serve the strategy and amplified to serve the customer, then the question arises, how can these five pairs of propositions upon the circle be reconciled with one another? How especially can we reconcile the principles at the far ends of the five axes? That is:

Principles: 1–6 designed strategy versus emergent strategy
2–7 competitive positioning versus adaptive co-operation
3–8 rational competence versus evolutionary increments
4–9 deviance correction versus deviance amplification
5–10 opportunities/potentials versus standards/rewards

The answer lies in two further principles:

11. Strategy as the corporate cultures formed by the fine-tuning of dilemmas.

and

12. Strategy as a virtuous circle of time-accelerated organizational learning.

My view of culture as embraced in principle 11 includes the integrations, symbols, families, maps, conversations, orchestrations, congruences and symbioses urged by the contributors to this book. It also entails continuous processes of accelerated, cybernetic learning.

These integrations and learnings often include new creative syntheses and understandings. Let us go through axes 1–6, 2–7, 3–8, 4–9, and 5–10 to see how these might work.

AXIS 1–6–RECONCILING DESIGNED WITH EMERGENT STRATEGY

We have already seen that you can design strategies out of the successful strategic moves that have already emerged. Strategizing does not have to precede successful achievements, it can pick them up and fashion policy after they have occurred. You 'craft' from the 'clay' of industrial achievements. Instead of strategizing with ideas that may or may not be appropriate to your corporate culture, you strategize with what you have witnessed the culture accomplish.

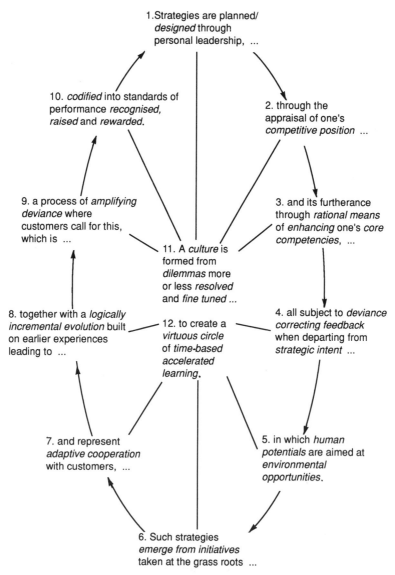

FIGURE 14.4   Twelve faces of strategy

You will not have to 'sell' your strategy to Mary, Dick and Tom, or obsess as to whether they 'own' it, because they will have achieved several of its principle elements in the first place. The strategy will be a part recognition of what they have done.

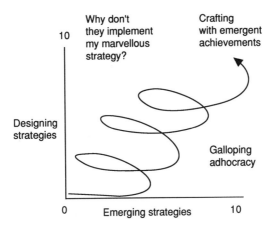

FIGURE 14.5   Emergence and design

We can create a 'space' for strategic steering by bending axis 1–6 at a right angle (see FIGURE 14.5). At 10/1 is 'why don't they implement my marvellous strategy?' The idea of designed strategy has been over-emphasized. Unbelievably, people have not been born simply to vindicate your vision! At 1/10, galloping adhocracy, the emergence of initiatives is so rife that the corporation's strategic nervous centre is breaking down. But consider the 'virtuous circle' or helical path from leading 0 to 10/10. You watch for what emerges, weave its finest elements into a strategy, and offer it to your organization only to see more initiatives emerge both within your strategy and beyond it, so you design once more with the elements you prefer. This, as I see it, is the nub of Henry Mintzberg's case.

AXIS 2–7-RECONCILING COMPETITIVE POSITIONING WITH ADAPTIVE CO-OPERATION WITH CUSTOMERS AND PARTNERS

Michael Porter's (1990) advocacy of competitive positioning suggests a dilemma. This dilemma revolves around the crucial issue of what is the competitive unit? This can be as small as the individual or top management team, or as large as a cluster including the corporation, its customers, partners, regulators, standard setters, educational and research institutions and industry associations. The

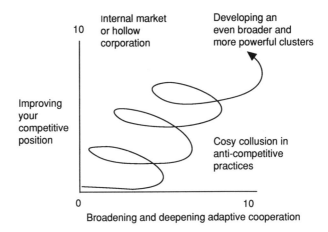

FIGURE 14.6   Co-operative competing

cluster is another of Porter's (1990) concepts. The question has to be answered: with whom do we co-operate closely so as to compete more successfully and more widely? Some suggested allies, regulators and standard setters are often considered enemies and the source of gross interference. But this is not necessarily so. Whole markets for the better care of the handicapped, for pollution control equipment, for electronically monitored machine safety can arise from regulation or from voluntary standards. To have your executives on an EC standard-setting committee is a great advantage. Germans chair over 50% of these!

At the other extreme some corporations are not even a competitive unit in themselves but a 'game' contest or internal market for individuals to advance themselves competitively. In the hollow corporation, the senior management team plus shareholders are the competitive unit. Manufacturing takes place in whichever country has the lower wage rates and here they compete with each other. The dilemma can be drawn as in FIGURE 14.6.

Co-operating can also be taken to the extreme of cosy collusion which evades competing and fixes prices for an easier life. What the helical pattern moving from bottom left to top right demands is an endless search for new members to add strength to your cluster, so that this network of alliances can outflank and outperform competitors. You add or subtract from allies and help develop these, so that your network or chain combines or adds most value.

Axis 3–8-Reconciling the Rational Development of Core Competencies and Technologies with Building Incrementally on the Customer's Strategy

Perhaps this book has under-emphasized the role of sheer reason and technological advance. In the pursuit of profit maximization, many companies lose their sense of technological progress and core competence, as something worth sacrificing short-term profits for. Yet the Japanese have shown us that you can get so far ahead in consumer electronics, fax machine photovoltaic cells, make relatively slim profits and use volume learning to force down the price and you are no longer worth competing against! American corporations simply back out. In the airline industry CRSs (Computerized Reservation Systems) and yield management systems, which calculate how full the plane will probably be and raise or lower prices accordingly, have crushed Eastern, People Express, Frontier, TWA, Pan Am and so on. Never underestimate technological weapons or the need to 'stick to your knitting' and develop your core competencies. The flexible manufacturing pioneered by Taichi Ohno (1978) at Toyota sweeps all before it. But there is also another point of view, often diametrically different, that of major customers, partners etc. An effective strategy is to build incrementally on *their* logics, and their views of the world. If you take microchips, these are brilliant and complex little brains in their own right, but they are also means by which Volvo builds a safer car, Philips plays its interactive compact discs or Bosch calculates when the bearings on machines are wearing down. In order to sell microchips it is your *customer*'s whole system solution and logics you need to know, not just the better chip. The dilemma is illustrated in FIGURE 14.7.

A brilliant technological breakthrough will take you through start-up to a brief stardom as the leading edge supplier, but come maturity you start to falter as customers' purposes rise in salience. Even so, the attempt to be 'all things to all people' can dilute your competence and fatally divert you. The resolution is to make a future date or rendezvous between your own developmental logic and that of your key customers so that by, say, 1997 you aim to contribute significantly to Volvo's launch of the World's Safest Car, which sells on sealing itself when hitting water, smothers engine fires and has a theft-proof ignition which reads your thumb print. The ideal is to co-evolve with your partner like two symbiotic organisms and be a 'rational empiricist' employing 'calculated evolution'.

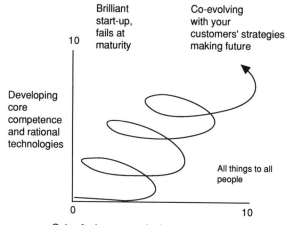

FIGURE 14.7   Rational empiricism

AXIS 4–9–RECONCILING DEVIANCE REDUCING FEEDBACK WITH DEVIANCE AMPLIFYING FEEDBACK

The corporation that homes in on its target like a guided missile is a very popular Western metaphor. Peter Senge's (1991) *The Fifth Discipline* is a deserving best seller. The corporation measures its degree of deviance from its strategic intent (see the work of Hamel and Prahalad, 1989) and relentlessly tracks down and eliminates the gap.

Acccording to this view, making mistakes can be a quicker way for the learning organization to learn. Using the 'steady, fire, aim' process of Cadbury Schweppes the time taken to get it *totally* right on the first go is saved. In human and social interactions getting it right initially is often impossible. Your customer is like your girl or boyfriend, you try something and discover what she or he likes. But despite its relative novelty and alleged internationalism, deviance reduction remains stubbornly Western in its biases. Whoever said that the original strategic intent was the correct one?

Magorah Maruyama (1982) has pointed out that the Japanese prefer deviation amplifying feedback loops. The customer prefers something else beside your strategic intentions and you go with that. Thus Richard Pascale (1984) has shown the successful launch of

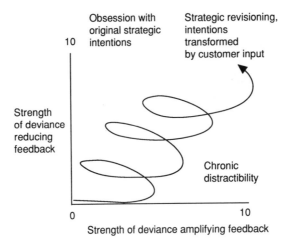

FIGURE 14.8 Amplifying and correcting

Honda motor scooters in the USA, occurred through an error. The launch of the more powerful machine collapsed in technological problems and a curious crowd of Americans gathering around the Super-cub; used only for transporting executives, occasioned a total abandonment of the original strategy in favour of following up this curiosity. The dilemma is illustrated in FIGURE 14.8.

It is possible to monitor every 'error' without asking if, from the customers' viewpoint, it might not be superior to what you wished to accomplish. Deviance reduction can become obsessive. Similarly you cannot change your strategy every time a customer calls. You will become chronically distracted. The aim is to revision periodically and let your customers' viewpoints transform your strategic intentions so that you see additional reasons and dimensions in the work you do. How many computer companies have learned from their hackers about the value of a feature that was designed for quite other purposes? The ideal is dialogue where the other's view 'reframes' your own in radical reinterpretations.

AXIS 5–10–RECONCILING THE CAPACITY OF EMPLOYEES TO LEARN FROM STANDARDS WITH THE CAPACITY OF STANDARDS AND PROCEDURES TO LEARN FROM EMPLOYEES/CUSTOMERS

The setting of strict time standards and the careful specification of needed hand motions dates from the work of Frederick Winslow

Taylor, but lives on under many guises, management by objectives (MBO), bench-marking and total quality management (TQM). In all such cases, management lays down some standards to be reached. Employees are induced to pledge themselves or agree to reach these desirable objectives and are subsequently evaluated on their approximation to this ideal. The 'good employee', who may receive pay for performance, with incentives or a bonus for exceeding targets is defined as one who comes up to set standards or surpasses them. Why complain? The problem, as with all our axes, is not what is seen, but what is *not* seen, because we concentrated so hard on one horn of the dilemma.

There is a totally opposed way of looking at the issue. Is the standard worthy either of the employee's potential, or of customers' changing needs and what actually *happens* when a live, breathing employee, face to face with an evaluator is compared to the standard? Chris Argyris and Donald Schon (1978) have pointed out that it is the evaluator who usually blinks, employing a 'defensive routine' so as not to upset the employee. The comparison of performance with standard is routinely fudged. It *has* to be, if the standard is either out of date or inappropriate. The dilemma is illustrated in FIGURE 14.9.

At top left we have the well-known methods of standard setting, including the routine of job description and the evaluation of job

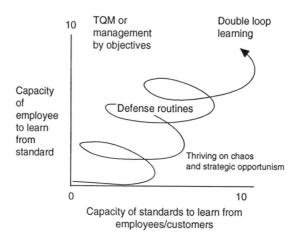

FIGURE 14.9   Who evaluates the evaluations?

holders in the light of that description. At bottom right we see that 'transcending' standards as Tom Peters (1987) has urged and the leaping at targets of opportunity as advocated by Daniel Isenberg (1987) is not a panacea either. You may lose all enduring estimates of quality. There is also the danger of fudging it all somewhere in the middle, i.e. compromizing with a 'defensive routine' when faced with a potentially vulnerable subordinate.

The only answer, argue Argyris and Schon (1978), is a system of 'learning how to learn', what Gregory Bateson (1975) called 'meta-learning' and Argyris has also termed 'double loop learning', where by turns, standards are first made worthy of people's potentials and customers' needs and then employees are evaluated against those standards, before upgrading the standards yet again.

CONCLUSION

In all the cases we have reviewed above, the reconciliation is a virtuous circle or helix, by which both horns of the previous dilemma are included and developed. But the concept in the top right-hand corner of our five dual-axis charts is somehow more than the axes that comprise it. There has been a conceptual leap, from learning against standards to learning about how to learn, from deviance reduction and/or amplification to periodic revisioning, from rationality colliding with empiricism, to co-evolution and a rendezvous of strategies. To confront a dilemma is an invitation to create something new, to leap a level beyond so as to integrate the earlier dichotomy. This 'beyond' is the 'identity' of Dutton and Penner (Chapter 4), or the 'integration' of Crossan, Lane and Hildebrand (Chapter 9), and is the end point of most of the formulations and proposals contained in this book. As we move from the static and academic world of strategic prescription and organizational dogma to the practical and dynamic world of circumstance, paradox and dilemma, the chapters in this volume bring together a range of mediating symbols, maps and conversations. With their help we can begin to think beyond the dilemmas, to relate to the circumstances, and to engage in strategy as learning.

REFERENCES

Andrews, K. (1980). *The Concept of Corporate Strategy*. Homewood, IL: Richard D. Irwin.

Ansoff, I. (1984). *Implanting Strategic Management*. London: Prentice Hall.

Argyris, C. and Schon, D. A. (1978). *Organizational Learning: A Theory of Action Perspective*. Reading: Addison Wesley.

Bateson, G. (1975). *Steps to an Ecology of Mind*. New York: Ballentime.

Campbell, J. (Ed.) (1971). *The Portable Jung*. New York: Viking.

Deming, E. W. (1982). *Quality, Production and Competitive Position*. Cambridge: MIT Press.

Hamel, G. and Prahalad, C. K. (1989). Strategic intent. *Harvard Business Review*, May–June, 63–77.

Hopper, M. D. (1992). *Rattling Sabre: New Ways to Compete on Information*. Boston: Harvard Business Review.

Isenberg, D. J. (1984). How senior managers think. *Harvard Business Review*, **62**, 80–90.

Isenberg, D. J. (1987). The tactics of strategic opportunism. *Harvard Business Review*, **65**, 92–97.

Johnson, G. (1990). Managing strategic change–The role of symbolic action. *British Journal of Management*, **1**, 183–200.

Juran, J., *et al.* (1974). *Quality Control Handbook*. New York, McGraw-Hill.

Maruyama, M. (1982). The second cybernetics: Deviation amplifying mutual causal processes. *American Scientist*, **51**, 64–79.

Mintzberg, H. and Quinn, J. B. (Eds) (1991). *The Strategy Process: Concepts, Contexts, Cases*. London: Prentice Hall International.

Nonaka, I. (1988). Toward middle-up-down management: Accelerating information content. *Sloan Management Review*, **29**, 9–18.

Ohmae, K. (1983). *The Mind of the Strategist*. Harmondsworth: Penguin.

Ohno, T. (1978). *Toyota Production System*. Cambridge MA: Productivity Press.

Pascale, R. (1984). Prospectus on strategy: The real story behind Honda's success. *California Management Review*, **XXVI**, 47–72.

Peters, T. (1987). *Thriving on Chaos*. London: Macmillan.

Pettigrew, A. (1985). *The Awakening Giant*. New York: Basil Blackwell.

Porter, M. (1990). *The Competitive Advantage of Nations*. New York: Free Press.

Prahalad, C. K. and Doz, Y. L. (1987). *The Multinational Mission: Balancing Local Demands and Global Vision*. New York: Free Press.

Quinn, J. B. (1978). Logical incrementalism. *Sloan Management Review*, **20**, 7–21.

Reich, R. B. (1987). *Tales of a New America*. New York: Vintage Books.

Scott, B. R. and Lodge, G. C. (1985). *American Competitiveness*. Boston: Harvard Business School Press.

Senge, P. M. (1991). *The Fifth Discipline*. New York: Harper & Row.

Taylor, F. W. (1941). *The Principles of Scientific Management*. New York: Harper & Row.

Index